D1557815

OXFORD ENGLISH MONOGRAPHS

General Editors

Lordship and Literature

*John Gower and the Politics
of the Great Household*

ELLIOT KENDALL

CLARENDON PRESS · OXFORD

OXFORD
UNIVERSITY PRESS

Great Clarendon Street, Oxford OX2 6DP

Oxford University Press is a department of the University of Oxford.
It furthers the University's objective of excellence in research, scholarship,
and education by publishing worldwide in

Oxford New York

Auckland Cape Town Dar es Salaam Hong Kong Karachi
Kuala Lumpur Madrid Melbourne Mexico City Nairobi
New Delhi Shanghai Taipei Toronto

With offices in

Argentina Austria Brazil Chile Czech Republic France Greece
Guatemala Hungary Italy Japan Poland Portugal Singapore
South Korea Switzerland Thailand Turkey Ukraine Vietnam

Oxford is a registered trade mark of Oxford University Press
in the UK and in certain other countries

Published in the United States
by Oxford University Press Inc., New York

British Library Cataloguing in Publication Data
Data available

Library of Congress Cataloging in Publication Data
Data available

Typeset by SPI Publisher Services, Pondicherry, India
Printed in Great Britain
on acid-free paper by
Biddles Ltd, King's Lynn, Norfolk

ISBN 978–0–19–954264–2

1 3 5 7 9 10 8 6 4 2

For Phyllis Molesworth

Acknowledgements

Like a piece of medieval politics, this book has come about through untold exchanges of support and good counsel. After a number of years of resolute 'misrecognition', I am aware how heavily the balance of these exchanges tells against me. Foremost among those who have encouraged and guided me in this project is Paul Strohm, who supervised the thesis from which the book has emerged. I am indebted to his rare and inspirational intellect. Mere thanks seem equally slight in acknowledging the influence, friendship, and love of learning of Roger Nicholson, without whose example in early days I would surely not be doing what I am doing. I have been very fortunate in my colleagues at the University of Exeter and, before that, at UCL. In London, Ardis Butterfield and Henry Woudhuysen backed my writing and improved it considerably as a result. Together with Susan Irvine and Richard North they were much-valued, warm-hearted colleagues. It has been a huge pleasure to work at Exeter, and in relation to my research, thanks go especially to Eddie Jones, Andrew McRae, Pascale Aebischer, Karen Edwards, Nick McDowell, Anthony Musson, Nicholas Orme, Philip Schwyzer, and Yolanda Plumley.

Other teachers and colleagues have helped my thinking knowingly and unknowingly. The examiners of my thesis, Sally Mapstone and James Simpson, offered very important insights, and I would also like to thank Oxford University Press's anonymous readers for their thorough, scholarly responses and astute recommendations. I remain grateful to Val Flint, Michael Graves, Michael Neill, and Philip Rousseau for showing me how to think about history when I was an undergraduate. More recently, I have benefited from the enthusiasm, scholarship, and generosity of many researchers, including Helen Cooper, Rita Copeland, John Ganim, Simon Gaunt, Douglas Gray, Ralph Hanna, Nicola McDonald, Laurie Maguire, Miri Rubin, Stephanie Trigg, David Wallace, John Watts, and Bob Yeager.

Institutional support has come from the University of Exeter and UCL, and from the University of Oxford, where I wrote my thesis. The British Council and the Association of Commonwealth Universities provided invaluable patronage, and Wolfson College, Oxford, subsequently appointed me to a research fellowship. The Board of Trustees of Auckland

Grammar School and Worcester College, Oxford, also granted funding. I would like to acknowledge the assistance of the staff at the Bodleian Library, Oxford, and the British Library in London. At Oxford University Press, my cause has been efficiently and vigorously maintained by Jacqueline Baker, Andrew McNeillie, and Tom Perridge. A substantial amount of chapter 3 has been published as an article in *Medium Ævum*, 76 (2007) and I am grateful to the journal for permission to republish this work.

Friends have given joy, help, and new perspectives, not all of them addressed to Gower's poetry or manorial custom: Mark Flugge, Jessie Shattuck Flugge, Ned Fletcher, Natalie Walker, Anthony Bale, Tim Phillips, Lara McClure, Kirstie Blair, Matthew Creasy, Isabel Davis, Claire Harman, Alex Gillespie, Fraser and Sarah Stephen-Smith, Andrew Cameron, Tom Rutledge, Annabel Whibley, Rachel and John Wevill, Tim and Hannah Wise, William and Anna Gordon, Howard Gilbert, Camille, Joe, and Geetha Mazarelo, Clare Loughlin-Chow. David and Sheelagh Turner have given me a beloved northern home, sustaining conversation, and a great deal of happiness, and Katie Turner and Damon, Michael, and Ruby Watts have further enriched this mix. My parents, Bernard and Diane, have seen me through with love and unconditional support, and I am deeply grateful. Crucially also, the friendship and good advice of my siblings, Emma, Simon, and Hadley, and my brother-in-law, Ian Cartmill, have been a constant background. No one has been more important than Marion Turner. Her energy, intelligence, kindness, and humour exceed all thanks.

This book is dedicated to my grandmother, with my love.

Contents

List of Abbreviations

Arch. Cant.	*Archæologia Cantiana*
Annales	Walsingham, *Annales Ricardi Secundi*
BIHR	*Bulletin of the Institute of Historical Research*
CA	*Confessio Amantis* (Gower, *Complete Works*, ii–iii)
CCR	*Calendar of Close Rolls*
CIPM	*Calendar of Inquisitions Post Mortem*
CP	Cokayne, *The Complete Peerage*
CPR	*Calendar of Patent Rolls*
Cronica	*Cronica tripertita* (Gower, *Complete Works*, iv); tr. Stockton in Gower, *Major Latin Works*, 289–326
CT	*The Canterbury Tales* (Chaucer, *Riverside Chaucer*)
Cupide	*The Boke of Cupide* (Clanvowe, *Works*)
DL	Duchy of Lancaster
EETS	Early English Text Society
EconHR	*Economic History Review*
EHR	*English Historical Review*
ELH	*ELH: English Literary History*
ES	extra series
Favent	Favent, *Historia*
Feudal Aids	*Inquisitions and Assessments Relating to Feudal Aids*
Fœdera	Rymer, *Fœdera, Conventiones, Literæ*
HMSO	Her/His Majesty's Stationery Office
JEGP	*Journal of English and Germanic Philology*
JMRS	*Journal of Medieval and Renaissance Studies*
KB	*Select Cases in the Court of King's Bench*
LGW	*The Legend of Good Women* (Chaucer, *Riverside Chaucer*)
Macaulay	Gower, *Complete Works*, ed. G. C. Macaulay (editorial material)
MED	*Middle English Dictionary*
Mirour	*Mirour de l'Omme* (Gower, *Complete Works*, i); tr. Wilson in Gower, *Mirour de l'Omme*
NS	new series
OS	original series
PF	*The Parliament of Fowls* (Chaucer, *Riverside Chaucer*)
PROME	Given-Wilson et al. (eds), *The Parliament Rolls of Medieval England*

Rot. parl.	*Rotuli parliamentorum*
RR	Lorris, Guillaume de, and Jean de Meun, *Le Roman de la Rose*; tr. Dahlberg in de Lorris and de Meun, *Romance of the Rose*
SAC	*Studies in the Age of Chaucer*
SATF	Société des anciens textes français
SC	Special Collections
SR	*The Statutes of the Realm*
TEAMS	Consortium for the Teaching of the Middle Ages
TRHS	*Transactions of the Royal Historical Society*
Vox	*Vox clamantis* (Gower, *Complete Works*, iv); tr. Stockton in Gower, *Major Latin Works*, 47–288
WC	*The Westminster Chronicle*

Introduction

Politics was never far from the aristocratic affinity in late medieval England. Lordship and the social networks it negotiated explain the courses of power in medieval society in ways that more formal institutions cannot. Furthermore, the workings of these institutions, including royal councils, the central courts, parliament, and the church, cannot themselves be fully understood without an account of aristocratic networks. These networks' unofficial *but structured* influence throughout society is increasingly being recognized.[1] This book discusses power as the product of exchanges. It develops an extensively economic view of the aristocratic affinity, framed in terms of household-based exchange, since lordship was practised through household structures, intangible and tangible. I am interested especially in the ways that literary (and not-so-literary) texts imagine the great household (aristocratic and royal), its networks, and their politics; the ways that texts activate and reconfigure ideas and assumptions that shaped society and the life of various groups.

My main focus for this exploration, *Confessio Amantis*, is a vast, subtle poem about the personal and the political written in English by John Gower, a landowner, probably in the late 1380s. The aristocratic household and affinity are, I am convinced, the key to the politics of the *Confessio*. The poem's version of aristocratic politics, in turn, enhances our understanding both of discourses that governed political action in the late fourteenth century, and of (even) less easily specified imaginaries and principles that supplied individuals with what Pierre Bourdieu calls a 'habitus', a system of unexamined dispositions whereby internalized social structures inform the 'regulated improvisations' of practice.[2]

---

[1] See e.g. Simon Walker, *The Lancastrian Affinity 1361–1399* (Oxford, 1990); Christine Carpenter, *Locality and Polity: A Study of Warwickshire Landed Society, 1401–1499* (Cambridge, 1992), esp. 3–4, 281–8; and 'Gentry and Community in Medieval England', *Journal of British Studies*, 33 (1994), 340–80; John Watts, *Henry VI and the Politics of Kingship* (Cambridge, 1996).

[2] Pierre Bourdieu, *Outline of a Theory of Practice*, tr. Richard Nice (Cambridge, 1977), 72–3, 78–95.

In what measure a particular act or representation was generated by the 'second nature' of the habitus or by more deliberate conformity to socially accepted discourses may be impossible to say. It is evident, however, that the social conditions and language of the landed household very significantly informed both deep assumptions and self-conscious expressions in the period, and the *Confessio* exemplifies this.

Recently, discussion of public life in medieval England has been shifted to include areas that have traditionally been viewed, and often sidelined, as private interests, especially the life of aristocratic social networks. Studies of landed society from the perspective of local groups rather than central government have led this change, along with some important work that has concentrated on the crucial role of unofficial structures at the centre as well.[3] Since the valency of 'private' power was recognized, under the stimulus of K. B. McFarlane's interpretation of politics, a more 'public' approach to it has furthered understanding of its structures.[4] This has meant considering landed groups not just as lords and followers pursuing personal objectives, but as politicians disposed to serve certain interests and aware of political responsibilities. This study is an attempt to interpret the *Confessio* anew in the light of this historiography and to extend our understanding of aristocratic structures and habitus by examining a poetic reinforcement of them.

The *Confessio* itself presents politics as something that cannot be contained in explicit norms and theorized forms, and the poem appropriately mixes theory with exemplary narrative that *embodies* politics.[5] By attempting

[3] For studies of the 'localities', see Walker, *Lancastrian Affinity*; Carpenter, *Locality and Polity*; Michael J. Bennett, *Community, Class and Careerism: Cheshire and Lancashire Society in the Age of Sir Gawain and the Green Knight* (Cambridge, 1983); Nigel Saul, *Knights and Esquires: The Gloucestershire Gentry in the Fourteenth Century* (Oxford, 1981); S. J. Payling, *Political Society in Lancastrian England: The Greater Gentry of Nottinghamshire* (Oxford, 1991). For networks and the royal centre, see Gerald Harriss, 'Political Society and the Growth of Government in Late Medieval England', *Past and Present*, 138 (1993), 28–57; and 'The Dimensions of Politics', in R. H. Britnell and A. J. Pollard (eds), *The McFarlane Legacy: Studies in Late Medieval Politics and Society* (Stroud, Glos., 1995), 1–20; Chris Given-Wilson, *The Royal Household and the King's Affinity: Service, Politics and Finance in England 1360–1413* (New Haven, Conn., 1986); Watts, *Henry VI*.

[4] See K. B. McFarlane, *The Nobility of Later Medieval England* (Oxford, 1973); '"Bastard Feudalism"', *BIHR* 20 (1943–5), 161–80; and 'Parliament and "Bastard Feudalism"', *TRHS* 4th ser. 26 (1944), 53–79. Both articles are repr. in McFarlane, *England in the Fifteenth Century: Collected Essays* (London, 1981). See also Edward Powell, 'After "After McFarlane": The Poverty of Patronage and the Case for Constitutional History', in Clayton et al. (eds), *Trade, Devotion and Governance: Papers in Later Medieval History* (Stroud, Glos., 1994), 1–16, cited in Watts, *Henry VI*, 4.

[5] Cf. Bourdieu's remarks on the habitus as 'a practical sense which reactivates the sense objectified in institutions' and 'enables the institution to attain full realization' by (revisionary

to describe the poem's politics I will inevitably be misrepresenting the way in which they are communicated, diminishing the poem's subtlety. Many of Gower's more prepossessing political statements—such as the Prologue's apocalyptic complaint or book 7's account of 'policie'—disappear from view over the course of the *Confessio*.[6] The language of household-based relations, on the other hand, permeates every level of the text, grounding political concerns in the very fabric of the poem; in the good lordship of Venus, the retaining and affinity roles of personified vices, the rhythms of the hall and the secrecy of the chamber, and the exemplary onus of myriad narrated gifts, gestures, and ripostes conditioned by household structures.

Some of the poem's immanent political force has been discussed without much critical attention being paid to the great household. As James Simpson observes, the poem's lover is determined to turn his back on the world of politics and, abetted by his confessor, persistently flattens and fragments history and is heedless of narratives' political meanings. Yet politics is not so easily dismissed: 'Both because the psyche itself turns out to be a political arena, ruled by the tyrant prince Cupid, and because the predatory brutalities of sexual desire have explicitly political conse-quences, political reflection often resurfaces in this text.'[7] The relationship between amatory (or ethical) and political themes in the *Confessio* has attracted a lot of scholarly attention.[8] 'Political reflection' in its own right has been considered from many angles, above all focused on kingship,[9] but also illuminating the poem in relation to a generalized non-chivalric

and transformative) 'incorporation' in practice: Pierre Bourdieu, *The Logic of Practice*, tr. Richard Nice (Cambridge, 1990), 57. See also James Simpson's discussion of Gower's practical, Aristotelian approach to politics, in *Sciences and the Self in Medieval Poetry: Alan of Lille's Anticlaudianus and John Gower's Confessio Amantis* (Cambridge, 1995), 134–271.

[6] For cautionary comment along these lines, see Paul Strohm, 'Form and Social Statement in *Confessio Amantis* and *The Canterbury Tales*', *SAC* 1 (1979), 17–40, 26–9.

[7] James Simpson, *Reform and Cultural Revolution*, Oxford English Literary History, 2 (Oxford, 2002), 220.

[8] See e.g. Simpson, *Sciences and the Self*, 211–17; and *Reform and Cultural Revolution*, 121–48, 219–23; A. J. Minnis, 'John Gower, *Sapiens* in Ethics and Politics', *Medium Ævum*, 49 (1980), 207–29; Kurt Olsson, 'Natural Law and John Gower's *Confessio Amantis*', *Medievalia et Humanistica*, NS 11 (1982), 229–61; Elizabeth Porter, 'Gower's Ethical Microcosm and Political Macrocosm', in A. J. Minnis (ed.), *Gower's Confessio Amantis: Responses and Reassessments* (Cambridge, 1983).

[9] George R. Coffman, 'John Gower in his Most Significant Role', in *Elizabethan Studies and Other Essays in Honor of George F. Reynolds* (Boulder, Colo., 1945), 52–61; Russell A. Peck, *Kingship and Common Profit in Gower's Confessio Amantis* (Carbondale, Ill., 1978); and 'The Politics and Psychology of Governance in Gower: Ideas of Kingship and Real Kings', in Siân Echard (ed.), *A Companion to Gower* (Cambridge, 2004), 215–38; Judith Ferster, *Fictions of Advice: The Literature and Politics of Counsel in Late Medieval England* (Philadelphia, 1996), 108–36.

interest,[10] the church,[11] and structures of gender.[12] The developments in the historiography of aristocratic and household-based politics have yet to make their mark on readings of Gower's poetry however. More importantly, these developments seem to me acutely underexploited for literary interpretation in general. Royal courts, the church, and cities continue to be available to critical energies in ways yet seldom extended to the great household.[13]

A broadly economic view of the social networks and other structures of the great household offers new insight into the politics of *Confessio Amantis*. The language and exchanges of the great household make political meaning of the *Confessio's* explicitly amatory and personal penitential material, introducing questions of aristocratic 'economics'—lordship, service, and political support—into discussions of sin and desire. At a theorized level, Gower objectifies princely politics in book 7 with the help of Aristotelian economics—the science of the household. Adapting the Aristotelianism of the political theorists Brunetto Latini (*c*.1220–94) and Giles of Rome (*c*.1247–1316), Gower places economics in the midst of a tripartite *divisio* of interdependent practical philosophies from which 'politics' emerges.[14] Aristotelian economics governs a king's family and 'al

---

[10] Anne Middleton, 'The Idea of Public Poetry in the Reign of Richard II', *Speculum*, 53 (1978), 94–114; R. F. Yeager, '*Pax Poetica*: On the Pacifism of Chaucer and Gower', *SAC* 9 (1987), 97–121; Winthrop Wetherbee, 'Classical and Boethian Tradition in the *Confessio Amantis*', in Echard (ed.), *Companion*, 181–96.

[11] Larry Scanlon, *Narrative, Authority, and Power: The Medieval Exemplum and the Chaucerian Tradition* (Cambridge, 1994); Winthrop Wetherbee, 'Constance and the World in Chaucer and Gower', in R. F. Yeager (ed.), *John Gower: Recent Readings* (Kalamazoo, Mich., 1989), 65–93; María Bullón-Fernández, *Fathers and Daughters in Gower's Confessio Amantis: Authority, Family, State, and Writing* (Cambridge, 2000), 86–100.

[12] Larry Scanlon, 'The Riddle of Incest: John Gower and the Problem of Medieval Sexuality', in R. F. Yeager (ed.), *Re-Visioning Gower* (Asheville, NC, 1998), 93–127; Diane Watt, *Amoral Gower: Language, Sex, and Politics* (Minneapolis, 2003); Isabel Davis, *Writing Masculinity in the Later Middle Ages* (Cambridge, 2007), 76–107.

[13] Recent literary studies that evince a new regard for the landed household's political economics, its discursive complexity, or its local profiles include Ad Putter, 'Gifts and Commodities in *Sir Amadace*', *Review of English Studies*, NS 51 (2000), 371–94; Arlyn Diamond, '*Sir Degrevant*: What Lovers Want', in Nicola McDonald (ed.), *Pulp Fictions of Medieval England: Essays in Popular Romance* (Manchester, 2004), 82–101; Kellie Robertson, 'Corporeal Style: Representing the Gentry Household', *The Laborer's Two Bodies: Literary and Legal Productions in Britain, 1350–1500* (New York, 2006), 119–52 (focusing on the Paston letters); D. Vance Smith, *Arts of Possession: The Middle English Household Imaginary* (Minneapolis, 2003); Lynn Staley, *Languages of Power in the Age of Richard II* (University Park, Pa. 2005). See also Elliot Kendall, 'The Great Household in the City: The *Shipman's Tale*', in Ardis Butterfield (ed.), *Chaucer and the City* (Cambridge, 2006), 145–61.

[14] See Simpson, *Sciences and the Self*, 211–27; Rita Copeland, *Rhetoric, Hermeneutics, and Translation in the Middle Ages: Academic Traditions and Vernacular Texts* (Cambridge, 1991), 207–12 (207 for *divisio* as textual ordering and Aristotelian categorization).

the companie | Which in his houshold schal abyde' (*CA* 7. 1674–5) as well
as the 'astat' (with senses of both financial estate and social standing) that
supports the household. In fact, the household infiltrates the other wings
of practical philosophy as well, since ethics is concerned with the ruler's
food, drink, clothing, and daily routine, and 'policie' encompasses more
and less intimate household functions under headings including chastity,
largesse, counsel and flattery, and war. I agree with those who argue that we
can take our cue from book 7's *divisio* of practical philosophy to discern
the primacy of politics in the *Confessio*, but I make the household—and
economics in an expanded, public sense—my focus throughout.[15] The
household economy does not so much lead on to politics; it *is* politics.

Beyond theorizations, all of the *Confessio*'s many and various generic
strands, including exemplum narrative, penitential instruction, and
courtly love, embellish its politics. The material culture and politicized
exchanges of the great household feature in scores of tales told by
confessor Genius, and frequently occupy the literal level of allegorical
and metaphorical language in the tale collection's frame narrative.
Household language signals activity by the poem's political imaginary
where the matter in hand may seem unrelated. The poem is also about
subjectivity, sexuality, religious doctrine, and poetic authority, to name a
handful of themes, while the flourishing of English poetry in the late
fourteenth century and Gower's own writings in three languages
(French and Latin as well as English) also provide meaningful contexts
in which to make sense of the *Confessio*. This study, however, is interested in how deeply a particularly aristocratic politics runs in this poem,
and in the poem's place in a wider environment of representations,
dispositions, and activity belonging to this politics.

The larger objective, therefore, is to add to the understanding of
political life and the discourses that structured it in late medieval
England, especially by situating in that sphere a reactivation and reworking of aristocratic dispositions that is marked by high literary
ambition and discursive complexity. As the historiography of royal
and aristocratic networks and political culture continues to advance
the understanding of medieval politics, the *Confessio* seems to me very
well suited to illustrate how unofficial politics took their place at the
centre of influential, collective views of public life. Discussions of the

[15] Simpson argues that the whole poem amounts to a discussion of politics through
(sexual) ethics and economics: *Sciences and the Self,* 220–3; cf. Simpson, *Reform and
Cultural Revolution*, 145, 219–23. Cf. Copeland, *Rhetoric*, 212: Gower's tales belong to
'a *divisio* of ethics that leads from private to public virtue'.

relationships between texts and history have enhanced the means by which literary (that is, culturally ornamental or discursively challenging) practice and representations can be contextualized in a historical moment without being reduced by over-simple biographical or topical decodings. Texts are complex, their meanings shaped by discourses with their own histories, evidence for which must be sought in other texts. Just as texts combine genres or types of expression, audiences are also complex, and their habitus, their accretions of ideas, and their expectations (or confusion) about a text's kind and function frame their reception of it.[16] I am interested alike, therefore, in parliamentary and poetic, annalistic and administrative texts. This study prioritizes the *Confessio* in part to make sense of it as an intervention in existing ideas, but also in an instrumental sense as a point of access to the wider textual and political environments I have mentioned.[17] In this second capacity, Gower's conceptually and technically rich poem is not finally privileged over other texts, including, in this case, a petition to parliament about livery badges, a short poem about a cuckoo and a nightingale, Chaucer's dream poetry, chronicle accounts of politics in the 1380s, and the painted 'text' of the Wilton Diptych.[18]

The twin exercise of excavating and historically situating the *Confessio's* politics requires an interpretative model capable of analysing textual, material, and social elements in equivalent terms. I conscript Bourdieu's economic theory of practice to this end. After discussing the

---

[16] On the relationship between texts and history, the pressures and combinations of genres, and how audiences' experiences of other utterances may influence the reception of a text, see J. G. A. Pocock, 'Texts as Events: Reflections on the History of Political Thought', in Kevin Sharpe and Steven N. Zwicker (eds), *Politics of Discourse: The Literature and History of Seventeenth-Century England* (Berkeley, Calif., 1987), 21–34; Pierre Macherey, *A Theory of Literary Production*, tr. Geoffrey Wall (London, 1978), esp. 39–50, 66–84, 90–101; Fredric Jameson, *The Political Unconscious: Narrative as a Socially Symbolic Act* (Ithaca, NY, 1981), 17–150; Paul Strohm, *Hochon's Arrow: The Social Imagination of Fourteenth-Century Texts* (Princeton, 1992), 3–9. See also M. M. Bakhtin, *The Dialogic Imagination: Four Essays*, ed. Michael Holquist, tr. Caryl Emerson and Michael Holquist (Austin, Tex., 1981), 66–7, 324–31 on 'heteroglossia'. The semantic histories of words such as 'law', 'maintenance', and 'livery' present case studies of heteroglossia salient for this book.

[17] The formulation 'textual environment' is Paul Strohm's (*Hochon's Arrow*, 66 and n. 7). Strohm associates it with J. G. A. Pocock's conception of discourses as linguistic matrices 'within which texts as events occur' but which texts 'also modify' ('Texts as Events', 28, 29).

[18] Cf. Strohm's advocacy of a 'belated Copernican... revolution in our thinking about textuality, in which a Ptolemaic view of the favored text as the stable center of an ordered system gives way to an acknowledgement of the text as just one component of a less prioritized array' (*Hochon's Arrow*, 8).

basic character and social importance of the landed household in the late Middle Ages, chapter 1 describes models of exchange which offer a means of specifying 'rules' and tensions at work in the *Confessio* and the political world of late fourteenth-century England.[19] Chapter 2 considers contexts of various scope for viewing the politics of the great household and the *Confessio*, from late medieval history of uncentralized and centralizing power to a particular aristocratic assault on the king's household in 1388. The discussion traces a network of other landowners associated with Gower, which hints at a primary public likely to respond to transformations of their own class dispositions in the poem. The remaining chapters extend exchange models and the consideration of late medieval history into discussion focused on the meanings of Gower's poem. Chapters 3 and 4 address the frame narrative. Chapter 3 argues that the great household provides the imaginative geography for the confession's treatment of deadly sins and allegorized ethics. Chapter 4 puts forward a political reading of Amans's self-representation and personal drama, discussing the aristocratic imaginary within the frame narrative's rendering of courtly love conventions and laicization of influential penitential schemes of thought and practice. The next three chapters take as themes the most politically important kinds of exchange organized by the great household, and these themes are principally examined in relation to narratives told by Genius. Chapter 5 is devoted to aristocratic marriage and examining the patterns of the exchange of women built up by Genius's tales. Chapters 6 and 7 deal with a politics of uncentralized dispute resolution, exploring Gower's poetry in the light of recent discussions about aristocratic local interests and attitudes to justice and the law. The exploration draws particular attention to convergences between parliamentary complaint about disorderly retinues and Gower's ethically differentiating (naturalizing and denaturalizing) representation of exchanges of violence. Finally, chapter 8 narrows in specifically on the theorization of kingship in the *Confessio*'s seventh book. This chapter examines contradictions produced when the poem seeks to secure a flexible, uncentralized politics by means of a sovereign rule: unacknowledged tensions result from the attempt to state as an explicit rule dispositions that are elsewhere in the poem played out and symbolically reinforced by narrative and imagery (including positive tales of kings deposed). Together, these chapters are

---

[19] On the equivocal range of the word 'rule', between pattern and prescription, see Bourdieu, *Theory of Practice*, 27.

designed not to give an exhaustive account of *Confessio Amantis*, nor even of *all* of its political dimensions, but to elucidate the great household and its networks as the dominant social structures in the poem's political imaginary and as powerful structures in the society in which the poem was produced. To understand political life at the time that Gower was writing as fully as we can, our enterprise must make new room for gentry, magnate, and royal households.

1

The Great Household and
an Economics of Power

At the end of the prologue to *Confessio Amantis* is a shorthand version of a perfect world. In the now longed-for golden age, the harper Arion once reconciled 'the comun with the lord, | And lord with the comun also' (*CA*, prol. 1066–7). This hardly amounts to a detailed social programme. Yet the idealizing image of unified hierarchy, with its combination of commitment and generality, would have been less opaque in the fourteenth century than it is in the twenty-first. Whether they shared the prologue's political hopes or not, late medieval audiences would almost inevitably have understood this image to refer to a social world structured by the great household.

The lord and commons image is a reflection of dispositions at the heart of Gower's poem and an example of imaginative structures that went deep and wide in late medieval society, generated by and supporting aristocratic dominance. The great household supported an immense range of relationships, activities, behaviours, and representations in the period. Service in a great household was desirable and employed a substantial portion of the population.[1] The great household produced the ruling classes in the sense that lay education for children of the landed elite meant tutelage as a member of another family's establishment. Not school but household provided their introduction to aristocratic life.[2] Royal government in late fourteenth-century England was still household-based in basic ways even if this fact is occluded when we talk about the 'state' in the Middle Ages. Although, for instance, the

---

[1] Kate Mertes, *The English Noble Household 1250–1600* (Oxford, 1988), 52–74; Chris Given-Wilson, *The English Nobility in the Late Middle Ages: The Fourteenth-Century Political Community* (London, 1987), 87–98.

[2] Nicholas Orme, 'The Education of the Courtier', in V. J. Scattergood and J. W. Sherborne (eds), *English Court Culture in the Later Middle Ages* (London, 1983), 63–85; and *From Childhood to Chivalry: The Education of the English Kings and Aristocracy 1066–1530* (London, 1984), esp. 16–65.

exchequer had emerged as an institution essentially separate from the household under the Norman kings, the Plantagenet wardrobe (a household office) still managed huge amounts of treasure and accounted directly for considerable proportions of crown expenditure.[3]

Social significance is mirrored (and was reinforced) by discursive prevalence. The great household imaginary can be recognized in texts of many kinds, from court rolls to romances to religious poetry and visionary writings. Inquests, for example, defined household-based forms of association and their conduct in powerful terms of right, wrong, truth, falsehood, justice, and the common good;[4] the barest plot summary of a romance tends to betray the centrality of the great household to the narrative;[5] and visionaries and exegetes expressed religious ideas in the language of aristocratic politics, such as Julian of Norwich's imagery of divine good lordship, and the opening allegory in *Cleanness* of the badly dressed guest to be 'Hurled to þe halle dore' and banished from the great house.[6] The great household's social and political pre-eminence and its influence on medieval habits of thinking and categorization are very neatly reflected by the game of chess. A prestigious game played in hall and chamber (often for money), chess symbolized the strategic and military stuff of political life according to a household framework. In Western Europe, a pawn was a 'pedes'

[3] See John Watts, 'Looking for the State in Later Medieval England', in Peter Coss and Maurice Keen (eds), *Heraldry, Pageantry and Social Display in Medieval England* (Woodbridge, Suff., 2002), 243–67. On royal households and government in England see also Given-Wilson, *Royal Household*; T. F. Tout, *Chapters in the Administrative History of Mediaeval England: The Wardrobe, the Chamber and the Small Seals* (Manchester, 1920–33); and *The Place of the Reign of Edward II in English History*, 2nd edn (Manchester, 1936); Michael Prestwich, *Plantagenet England 1225–1360* (Oxford, 2005), 55–61 (discussing Tout's theory of rivalry between household and state departments at 61); Judith A. Green, *The Government of England under Henry I* (Cambridge, 1986), 38–50.

[4] e.g. *KB* v. 90–1; vi. 103–4; vii. 21–2, 83–8. Paul Strohm discusses one of these cases, that of 'the Yorkshire maintainers', in terms of non-aristocratic imitation of aristocratic practice (*Hochon's Arrow*, 180–2).

[5] See Stephen Knight, 'The Social Function of the Middle English Romances', in David Aers (ed.), *Medieval Literature: Criticism, Ideology and History* (Brighton, 1986), 99–122; Helen Cooper, *The English Romance in Time: Transforming Motifs from Geoffrey of Monmouth to the Death of Shakespeare* (Oxford, 2004), 50–7, 221–9, 324–31.

[6] Julian of Norwich, *A Book of Showings to the Anchoress Julian of Norwich*, ed. Edmund Colledge and James Walsh (Toronto, 1978), esp. 502–3, 513–54. See Alexandra Barratt, 'Julian of Norwich and the Holy Spirit, "our good lord" ', *Mystics Quarterly*, 28 (2002), 78–84; and 'Lordship, Service, and Worship in Julian of Norwich', in E. A. Jones (ed.), *The Medieval Mystical Tradition in England: Exeter Symposium VII* (Cambridge, 2004), 177–88. *Cleanness*, in *The Poems of the Pearl Manuscript: Pearl, Cleanness, Patience, Sir Gawain and the Green Knight*, ed. Malcolm Andrew and Ronald Waldron, 5th edn (Exeter, 2007), ll. 17–176 (quote at l. 44).

or footman, figures associated with counsel (a bishop, earl, 'senex', or fool) replaced the Arabic *al-fil* (elephant) piece, and a collection of chess pieces was known as a 'familia' or 'mesnie', meaning the household group or retinue.[7] This collective noun is a cultural reflex; the chess *mesnie* attests that the great household was a deeply naturalized category for political thinking in the later Middle Ages.

THE LATE MEDIEVAL GREAT HOUSEHOLD

The great household is best regarded as an expansive category. Historians often recognize landholding that grants lordship over others as distinguishing a varied but coherent elite in the Middle Ages. This landed group or aristocracy encompassed the lay nobility, gentry, and higher clergy, all of whom enjoyed the private jurisdiction and other customary privileges of manorial lordship as means to organize social relationships and extract from subordinates rents, services, and other dues.[8] My use of the phrase 'aristocratic household' thus conceals a great diversity of establishments, including minor gentry households based on single, relatively small manors and supporting perhaps ten or fewer servants, as well as baronial and episcopal households coordinating hundreds of persons across vast estates and various regions. Nonetheless, as studies of such establishments have shown, they were collectively distinguished by some important institutional forms (including the hall as a 'public' site for manor court and feast), and by shared cultural horizons (especially involving lordship, hospitality, and status in the countryside).[9] Royal households often ask to be considered

[7] Richard Eales, 'The Game of Chess: An Aspect of Medieval Knightly Culture', in Christopher Harper-Bill and Ruth Harvey (eds), *The Ideals and Practice of Medieval Knighthood* (Woodbridge, Suff., 1986), 12–34; Malcolm Vale, *The Princely Court: Medieval Courts and Culture in North-West Europe 1270–1380* (Oxford, 2001), 170–6.

[8] See e.g. Christopher Dyer, *Making a Living in the Middle Ages: The People of Britain 850–1520* (London, 2003), 8; Harriss, 'Dimensions of Politics', 1–7; Carpenter, *Locality and Polity*, 73–7, 244; Mark Bailey (ed.), *The English Manor c.1200–c.1500* (Manchester, 2002), 2–3.

[9] Mertes, *Noble Household*, 14–15, 17–51, 185–6; C. M. Woolgar, *The Great Household in Late Medieval England* (New Haven, Conn., 1999), 8–29, 47–50, 83–110; Given-Wilson, *English Nobility*, 87–93; Felicity Heal, 'Reciprocity and Exchange in the Late Medieval Household', in Barbara A. Hanawalt and David Wallace (eds), *Bodies and Disciplines: Intersections of Literature and History in Fifteenth-Century England* (Minneapolis, 1996), 179–98; Christopher Dyer, *Standards of Living in the Later Middle Ages: Social Change in England c.1200–1520*, rev. edn (Cambridge, 1998), 58–85.

as part of the same spectrum for these reasons. *Confessio Amantis* tacitly marginalizes clerical great households, as I will argue later in this study, but their affinity with lay households (by family connections and modes of power) demands that they be included in a general historical model of the great household for the late fourteenth century.

The great household produced a class habitus that in turn informed a broadly shared style of life for the landed elites of late fourteenth-century England.[10] The gradations within the aristocratic category as here defined can seem vertiginous, but drawing hard divisions anywhere above the lesser gentry invariably proves unsatisfactory when considering society at the level of provincial communities or the manor. Of course, we also obscure overlaps and affinities (in commercial enterprise and cultural self-fashioning) by distinguishing a group of manorial gentry 'aristocracy' from other free landholders or from merchants and professionals without a significant landed interest but nonetheless wealthy and involved in government.[11] Yet a focus on land and patrimony remains valuable. Land held in heredity (alongside the estates of the higher clergy) gave 'a stake, formal or informal or both, in the governance of the body politic'.[12] It also shaped the style of life that comprised an aristocratic group identity. Marx says that 'the lord of an entailed estate... belongs to the land', that '*it* inherits *him*'.[13] He qualifies his own proposition, but in this form it vividly evokes the relationship between patrimonial land and aristocratic status. In the first place, land was still the root of aristocratic power in the fourteenth century, and it was valued not just for present profit but for the power and standing of successors. Strong scholarly opinions identify the care and family transmission of the patrimony as the defining interest of the late medieval aristocracy.[14] This interest directed the efforts and capital of

[10] For the conceptual framework behind this and the following paragraphs, see Bourdieu, *Theory of Practice*, esp. 17–22, 77–86, 180–3.
[11] Sylvia L. Thrupp, *The Merchant Class of Medieval London* (Chicago, 1948), 125, 130–90, 259–69; Caroline M. Barron, *London in the Later Middle Ages: Government and People 1200–1500* (Oxford, 2004), 152–3, 224, 248–50; Pamela Nightingale, 'Knights and Merchants: Trade, Politics and the Gentry in Late Medieval England', *Past and Present*, 169 (2000), 36–62; Dyer, *Making a Living*, esp. 136–7, 218–27, 343–6; Dyer, *Standards of Living*, 46, 77–83, 193, 205–8; Saul, *Knights and Esquires*, 249–51.
[12] Carpenter, *Locality and Polity*, 244.
[13] Karl Marx, *Economic and Philosophic Manuscripts of 1844*, ed. Dirk J. Struik, tr. Martin Milligan (London, 1970), 100 (emphasis added), quoted in Bourdieu, *Logic of Practice*, 57–8.
[14] Carpenter, *Locality and Polity* 75–7, 244–62, 284; Given-Wilson, *English Nobility*, 127–46, 163–6; cf. Harriss, 'Dimensions of Politics', 3–7; Robert Bartlett, *The Making of Europe: Conquest, Colonization and Cultural Change 950–1350* (London, 1993), 50,

those group members who acted to avoid outsider status into similar strategies, including alliance by marriage. The aristocracy treated inherited lands differently from newly acquired holdings as a rule. Inherited lands were much less readily sold, divided, or bequeathed away from the main line of inheritance.[15]

A patrimony and the habitus it informed also made other conversions of capital thinkable and 'natural' for an aristocrat. Many variables, including dress, buildings, charity and pious monuments, warfare, social connections, and office-holding, helped to make social status, which is determined by habitus-regulated self-fashioning and, ultimately, by others' perceptions. Stephen O'Connor clearly illustrates the complexities of the generation of status by analysing the decisions taken by two landowning London contemporaries of Gower.[16] The different paths taken by these merchants (who were both mercers) show that land alone was not sufficient to produce gentry status, either by modifying an individual's aspirations or by determining others' perceptions. John Pyel returned to his ancestral village to pursue aristocratic status in a provincial community—a strategy which included renovating a church and labelling it with the Pyel arms—and took advantage of the neighbourhood of the Northamptonshire manors of his close associate, the duke of Lancaster. On the other hand, Pyel's fellow mercer, Adam Frannceys, cultivated links with aristocrats but retained a clear 'London orientation' and does not seem to have used his land to break with his merchant status.[17] Landholding was not simply destiny. It did not automatically inculcate an aristocratic habitus. Nonetheless, land and the lordship it provided—control over labour and coercive force—were necessary to aristocratic status. Especially in the case of inherited land, they gave access to and expectation of other signs of status, and legitimated an individual's possession of these signs. The absence of land and lordship could negate such signs or reinscribe them as stigma of conceit and presumption (as in the case of a Yorkshire 'retinue' who

quoting Georges Duby, 'Lineage, Nobility and Knighthood', in *The Chivalrous Society*, tr. Cynthia Postan (London, 1977), 59–80, 75 for 'a narrowing and a tightening of the family around the male line' in aristocratic society by the later Middle Ages.

[15] Given-Wilson, *English Nobility*, 162–6; and below, n. 23; cf. Bourdieu, *Theory of Practice*, 182.
[16] Stephen O'Connor, 'Adam Frannceys and John Pyel: Perceptions of Status among Merchants in Fourteenth-Century London', in Clayton et al. (eds), *Trade, Devotion and Governance*, 17–35.
[17] O'Connor, 'Adam Frannceys and John Pyel', 25.

distributed livery and maintained each other's disputes apparently without aristocratic leadership).[18]

The make-up of the great household, like aristocratic status, also resists fixed definitions. It included the lord, the lord's immediate family, and domestic servants, but also many who were much less permanently or regularly in attendance where the lord was. These might include retainers owing military service or legal or administrative advice. There were permanent members who enjoyed neither a family nor service relationship (but could identify with aspects of both), such as boys attached to the household for their education. The personnel actually gathered, working, and living around a lord could look very different depending upon whether the household was attending to business at a far-flung manor, travelling on a war footing in foreign parts, or celebrating a feast such as Christmas, Easter, or Pentecost, when any core membership would be swollen by 'occasional' members as well as guests. The less distinct ties of the household leach into the spheres of informal retinue, affinity, and neighbourhood.[19]

Diverse membership reflects diverse business, and the importance of great households as an infrastructure for politics in the Middle Ages is difficult to overestimate. I began this study by mentioning work that has situated aristocratic social networks in the thick of late medieval public life in England. From this work, lordship emerges as a pervasive political relationship, even a 'constitutional' one; and the operation of lordship depended on the great household.[20] To appreciate the great household's significance we need to recognize both that it was more public than domestic terms now suggest and that this stems from the significantly personal or 'private' quality of medieval politics. The aristocratic habitus was strongly oriented towards family status, but aristocratic family status was bound up with public matters, public loyalties, and a localized or

---

[18] Strohm, *Hochon's Arrow*, 180–2. For other approaches to social class and status, see S. H. Rigby, *English Society in the Later Middle Ages: Class, Status and Gender* (Basingstoke, 1995), 182–95; Saul, *Knights and Esquires*, 6–29; Carpenter, *Locality and Polity*, 35–95; Paul Strohm, *Social Chaucer* (Cambridge, Mass., 1989), 2–10.

[19] On the membership of aristocratic households and affinities, see Mertes, *Noble Household*, 52–62; Woolgar, *Great Household*, 15–16, 21–5, 53–6; Walker, *Lancastrian Affinity*, 8–12. For comments on the wide contemporary ambit of the term *familia*, see J. M. W. Bean, *From Lord to Patron: Lordship in Late Medieval England* (Manchester, 1989), 18. Christine Carpenter discusses the kinds of social tie that might be considered to condition aristocratic politics in 'Gentry and Community', 360–74.

[20] See above, 2 n. 3. For the value of thinking constitutionally about royal and aristocratic politics in this period, and for lordship as 'a private and public agency for the satisfaction of shared interests', see Watts, *Henry VI*, 1–12, 81–101 (quote at 92).

wider stake in the body politic. Family, land, and lordship were more vital to status than secular office was. Power came from lands, treasure, and courts personally possessed by lay lords, and the lord's household employed officials and secretariats and could summon armed men.[21] Politics turned, as ever, on personal contact and relationships, including bonds of kinship recognized or forged by marriage. Christine Carpenter has gone so far as to remark:

So persuasive is the evidence of the primacy of the personal connection [behind the formal record] that one is tempted to reduce all formal relationships in this period—including leases, dealings with public officers, debt and credit—to the level of the personal network. It would be unwise to assume that nothing was ever done for routine or institutional reasons but unnecessary to deny the deep personal exigencies that must lie behind the protection of things as fundamental to these people as family and property.[22]

These prevailing personal connections were sustained by the instruments or hospitality of the great household. The household provided both financial structure and social context for political ties and endeavours.

Just as landed estate and family interest structured the aristocratic class habitus, so they tended to structure these endeavours. Marriage—a household bond—not only shifted wealth and cemented political alliances but served the more basic function of the production of heirs (see below, 132–7). Magnate and gentry families generally preferred to intermarry, linking great households and (especially where an heiress was involved) redistributing lands amongst them. Even the new popularity of the legal devices of entail, jointure, and enfeoffment to use, which gave landholders some control over the descent of their properties, reflects a continued sense of connection between family and patrimony in the fourteenth century. Studies have shown that, by prohibiting beneficiaries from permanently alienating land and by landholders' overwhelming tendency to use them according to principles of non-partible inheritance in the male line (ducking anticipated wardships or female co-inheritance), these devices reinforced rather than destabilized patrimonial integrity and the links between land and family.[23]

---

[21] See Robert Bartlett, *England under the Norman and Angevin Kings 1075–1225* (Oxford, 2000), 121–2. Cf. Carpenter, *Locality and Polity*, 244–5, 283–5.

[22] Carpenter, 'Gentry and community', 369; citing Carpenter, *Locality and Polity*, 244–62, 284–5.

[23] See McFarlane, *Nobility*, 61–82, 268–78; Given-Wilson, *English Nobility*, 138–53; S. J. Payling, 'The Economics of Marriage in Late Medieval England: The Marriage of Heiresses', *EconHR* 54 (2001), 413–29. Payling discusses the com-

The household was about more than keeping power in the family. It was also the key to using that power. Lords enjoyed extra-domestic authority and benefits through their estate administrations and non-manorial jurisdictions (in private county and hundred franchises), but the household was the heart and nerve centre of the aristocratic life. The estate administration run by stewards, bailiffs, and reeves was tied to the great household by retinue and administrative channels.[24] A free tenant on a manor remote from a lord's main residence or where the demesne (land allocated to the lord's exclusive use) had been leased to a farmer might have little experience of the great household. Estates were run for the lord's benefit, however, and much was channelled through the household. Whether farm-filtered or direct, the bulk of proceeds owed to the lord from rents, sales, market tolls, fines, or other non-regular dues would come to the household by way of the receiver general. Depending on the household's size, further clerks might handle these revenues, and household clerks wrote the documents which controlled the most important estate business and granted lands.[25] Estate administrations had become separated from the household in the largest lordships by the late fourteenth century, but even then overall governance would be in the hands of a formal council which included senior household officers such as the treasurer and steward.[26] Once in receipt of estate revenues in money and kind, the household converted this capital into food, drink, liveries, money fees, and other largesse to sustain ties useful to protect political interests or to further particular objectives. Building and furnishing expenses for parish churches, high-status halls, chambers, and parks ultimately supported these aims as well and belong to the same economy.[27] Manorial capital, in other words, was eventually made into political capital.

mon late medieval strategy of marrying an heiress to a high-status younger son to preserve the identity of a patrimony that might otherwise, on marriage to an heir, be swallowed up by a larger patrimony (417–18, 424–6).

[24] Bailey (ed.), *English Manor*, esp. 97–104; Mertes, *Noble Household*, 130–1.

[25] M. T. Clanchy, *From Memory to Written Record: England 1066–1307*, 2nd edn (Oxford, 1993), 56, 92–6; cf. Bailey (ed.), *English Manor*, 104–6, 175.

[26] Given-Wilson, *Nobility*, 98–103; Mertes, *Noble Household*, 126–31.

[27] In ordinary years, most great households spent most of their revenue on food, drink, and livery, while building projects could account for very high exceptional expenditure (Dyer, *Standards of Living*, 55, 78–83). On the political role of architecture in fashioning aristocratic identities, see Matthew Johnson, *Behind the Castle Gate: From Medieval to Renaissance* (London, 2002).

By these conversions the household accounted for more than land and was able to structure social networks wider than kinship, particularly through service and office-holding, retaining, and hospitality. Seigneurial politics had always depended on the household's display of power to strengthen the persona of the lord and mobilize social capital. The household's formal role in lordship, however, expanded and intensified in the fourteenth century because the household-based associational forms of so-called 'bastard feudalism'—especially retaining by livery, rights of food and drink in the household (bouche of court), and money fee—were growing while tenurial 'feudal' forms declined.[28] This transition contributed to a growth in the size of aristocratic households and probably meant that more of the gentry became members of retinues. Even strictly tenurial bonds of lordship, of course, created a tie between households and belonged to the household, both because aristocratic land was imbued with family meaning, and because land was ultimately controlled (and alienated) by household officers and seals. Tenurial lordship, furthermore, was commemorated by homage or other ceremonies which typically took place in the lord's hall (as manorial court).[29] Lordship over men, either by land or by annuities and liveries paid out directly by the chamber or wardrobe, was the product of household exchange.[30] Marriage and more ephemeral household exchanges also reinforced lordship and energized the aristocratic social networks that were so central to late medieval politics. These are starting points to model aristocratic politics economically.

[28] The literature debating 'bastard feudalism', its origins and effects is extensive. See e.g. McFarlane, '"Bastard Feudalism"'; G. L. Harriss, introduction, in K. B. McFarlane, *England in the Fifteenth Century: Collected Essays* (London, 1981), pp. ix–xxvii; Scott L. Waugh, 'Tenure to Contract: Lordship and Clientage in Thirteenth-Century England', *EHR* 101 (1986), 811–39; Bean, *From Lord to Patron*; Walker, *Lancastrian Affinity*, 1–7, 235–61; the 'Bastard Feudalism Revised' debate among P. R. Coss, David Crouch, and D. A. Carpenter in *Past and Present*, 125 (1989), 27–64; 131 (1991), 165–203; cf. D. A. Carpenter, 'The Second Century of English Feudalism', *Past and Present*, 168 (2000), 30–71. I tend to agree with the perspective of Harriss, Waugh, Walker, and others who assess 'bastard feudalism' as fundamentally conservative of 'the pattern of lord/client relations that had been worked out over the two previous centuries' (Waugh, 'Tenure to Contract', 839).

[29] For an earlier period, see Susan Reynolds, *Fiefs and Vassals: The Medieval Evidence Reinterpreted* (Oxford, 1994), 370–2 (and 18–20, 28–31 for homage); Carpenter, 'English Feudalism', 67–9.

[30] For early practices of livery, see Frédérique Lachaud, 'Liveries of Robes in England *c.*1200–*c.*1330', *EHR* 111 (1996), 279–98; Bean, *From Lord to Patron*, 143–6.

MODELS OF LORDSHIP

A consistent, coherent model of practices and representations of practices allows us to identify convergences in discourse and disposition between texts of various kinds and between texts and social practice. The model acts as a conversion mechanism to render calculable particular relationships between apparently disparate discursive elements—literary, legislative, theoretical, historiographical. A model devised in accord with Bourdieu's 'general theory of the economics of practice' has the particular advantage of exposing practices' political contours which texts and performances augment, misrecognize, and euphemize. The model will do this because the economics of practice presupposes that exchanges produce power in the form of surpluses and deficits of material and symbolic capital.[31] Such an approach not only distills a more or less coherent politics from the many discursive modes of *Confessio Amantis*; it also helps to situate the poem's politics in a contemporary textual environment and, implicitly, in the political world in which these texts intervened.

Within a general economic model of practice, I differentiate two modes of exchange very salient for an analysis of late fourteenth-century politics and political discourse. Taking a lead, and borrowing terms, from the work of Felicity Heal, I call these modes aristocratic 'reciprocalism' and, secondly, 'magnificence'.[32] As modes of 'gift' exchange that are not *explicitly* economic, both reciprocalism and magnificence are opposed to a third, commercial mode of exchange. Reciprocalism seems to me to model discourses and dispositions that dominate aristocratic views of politics in the period and are ambitiously recombined in *Confessio Amantis*. Competing (commercial and magnificent) discourses variously challenge aristocratic reciprocalism's twin fundamental tenets, that power properly follows ostensibly free (gift) exchanges, which

---

[31] Bourdieu, *Theory of Practice*, esp. 1–15, 171–97 (quote at 177). See also Marcel Mauss, *The Gift: The Form and Reason for Exchange in Archaic Societies*, tr. W. D. Halls (London, 1990). For similarly conceived economic approaches to late medieval culture, see Putter, 'Gifts and Commodities' (reading the romance *Sir Amadace* as a forceful statement of an aristocratic interest in giving); Andrew Galloway, 'The Making of a Social Ethic in Late-Medieval England: From *Gratitudo* to "Kyndenesse"', *Journal of the History of Ideas*, 55 (1994), 365–83 (discussing the intellectual history of 'gratitude' in the context of gift economies and social cohesion).

[32] Heal, 'Reciprocity and Exchange'. See also her *Hospitality in Early Modern England* (Oxford, 1990).

cement ties within and between great households, and that these exchanges themselves are shaped by contours of obligation and social status established by prior similar exchanges. Any exchange, in other words, that is not beholden to a past, to accumulated social capital, potentially subverts reciprocalism.

Reciprocalism and its competitors fit into influential accounts of medieval political society which map conflict and accommodations between centralizing interests on the one hand and local, uncentralized, or 'centrifugal' interests on the other. Such accounts tell a story of the centralizing interests of the crown and the uncentralized ones of the magnates and gentry, but they also find similar tensions between powerful nobles and lesser landowners. I try to avoid terms like 'decentralizing' and 'devolved' to eschew implications that centralized power either was the norm in the Middle Ages or should be considered more satisfactory from our point of view, with other power structures invariably representing degradation from a centralized starting point or 'highest form'. 'Local' and ideas of local aristocratic networks have a strong place in current discussions of late medieval society and politics and I often have recourse to them.[33] Associations of 'local-ness' with separateness and being definitively outside the centre must be avoided however.[34] Cogent ideas about access to the centre and responsibilities binding centre and locality are very important to medieval interests and discourses resistant to centralized authority. The emphasis is often on the centre's duty to support established patterns of status and interaction within localities.[35]

[33] See e.g. Gerald Harriss, *Shaping the Nation: England 1360–1461* (Oxford, 2005), 187–206; Carpenter, 'Gentry and Community', noting 'the importance of highly localized groups' (353) in gentry society, and 'the crucial issue of the effectiveness of the link between center and locality' (363); and studies of aristocratic society in localities cited above, 2 n. 3.

[34] Cf. Ralph Hanna's case for viewing fourteenth-century London in the light of 'interpenetrative Court and City relations', aristocratic communities 'fully interpenetrative with their locales', and far-reaching regional traffic along administrative networks: *London Literature, 1300–1380* (Cambridge, 2005), esp. 123–9, quotes at 124, 125.

[35] Harriss, 'Political Society', esp. 32–9; Simon Walker, 'Yorkshire Justices of the Peace, 1389–1413', *EHR* 108 (1993), 281–311, esp. 310–11; and *Lancastrian Affinity*, 252–61 (Walker is fully cognizant of the regional magnate, as well as royal government, in the role of centre); Given-Wilson, *Royal Household*, 245–51; Watts, *Henry VI*, 91–101; Hanna, *London Literature*, 130–2. Cf. Watts's thoughts on sensitivity to public opinions on the part of the centre within 'an extensive, perhaps universal, political class' in later medieval England: 'The Pressure of the Public on Later Medieval Politics', in Linda Clark and Christine Carpenter (eds), *Political Culture in Late Medieval Britain* (Woodbridge, Suff., 2004), 159–80, esp. 173–80 (quote at 174).

Non-commercial household exchange was idealized under the concept of largesse. Non-commercial exchange is ostensibly free according to 'the sincere fiction of a disinterested exchange' while actually operating on the misrecognition (*méconnaissance*) of the economic quality of all exchanges.[36] The fundamental profit, or by-product, of non-commercial exchange is obligation itself; for such exchanges and their deferred, inexact counter-exchanges tend to sustain indebtedness and prompt further exchanges.[37] As Genius remarks in the *Confessio*:

> With yifte a man mai frendes make,
> Bot who that takth or gret or smal,
> He takth a charge forth withal,
> And stant noght fre til it be quit.
>
> (5. 7726–9)

For the reciprocalist, that 'charge' ideally passes back and forth, morphing and developing so that it is never 'quit', and continues to bind people (and households) together. The social, symbolic capital thus accumulated by non-commercial forms of exchange in lordship is equivalent to the medieval concept of 'worship'. The landowner who converts different forms of capital according to the expectations of certain members of society gains from those persons and groups 'a capital of obligations and debts which will be repaid in the form of homage, respect, loyalty, and, when the opportunity arises, work and services'.[38] The symbolic approximation of this capital is worship. Lords accrued worship when they used their authority and landed power to protect social inferiors, advance followers, and otherwise satisfy interests of the gentry especially. The more widely lordship succeeded in taking account of multiple (gentry) groups and interests, the less likely it was to be undermined by competing lordships.[39]

Hospitality upheld the worship of the aristocratic host and his guests through lavish but hierarchically modulated expenditure. The Westminster chronicler, recording a baronial wedding ceremony in the household of the bride's father, the earl of Arundel, in 1384, conventionally and paradoxically imagines largesse at once absolutely open and hierarchically structured. For the duration of the festivities, 'omnibus

[36] Bourdieu, *Theory of Practice*, 5–6, 171 (quote at 171).
[37] Mauss, *The Gift*, 3, 13–14; Bourdieu, *Theory of Practice*, 6–7, 177–83.
[38] Bourdieu, *Theory of Practice*, 195.
[39] Cf. Carpenter's discussion of land as the basis of power in late medieval England in *Locality and Polity*, esp. 244–5, 283–5; Heal, 'Reciprocity and Exchange', 180; Watts on royal lordship and the localities: *Henry VI*, 91–101.

intrare volentibus sive exire libere patebat introitus et egressus' (all who wished to enter or leave were free to come and go; *WC* 88), while the earl personally honoured the entire ('tota') royal household and 'secundum statum cujuslibet eorum unumquemque remuneravit' (gave each of them a present according to his rank; *WC* 88). The celebrations and the mass of guests that at first seem nebulous are then brought into focus and given structure by the chronicler's selection of a prestigious group of guests and the duke's hierarchically informed hospitality. This passage further represents the function of hospitality and household ceremony as a setting or point of realization for other acts of gift exchange that reinscribe social networks. As sites where groups from different households met and expectations of exchange were publicly tested, occasions of hospitality could be explosive as well as constructive. When Henry Percy, earl of Northumberland, refused hospitality to his kinsman John of Gaunt, duke of Lancaster, in June 1381, the consequence was a damaging quarrel centred on Gaunt's charging Percy before the king with *disnaturesse* (or *unkindenesse*), disloyalty to a kinsman. Gaunt, fleeing before reports of the great rising in the south, was warned away by Percy's messengers evidently because, with news uncertain in the north, the earl could not be sure of the duke's standing with the king in the face of the commons' violence and accusations of treason. The resulting dispute saw armed retinues in the streets during the Westminster parliament that November, attracted sensational comment from chroniclers, led to the imprisonment of the messengers, Sir John Hothum and Thomas Motherby, and had continued political impact in the former allies' ongoing hostility over the rest of the decade.[40] Most pertinent here is the consideration that the quarrel grew out of the great household's expression of (or failure to express) aristocratic loyalty, where loyalty means obligations to give and to receive, or, more precisely, the inexact accounting of deep histories of mutual exchange. As ideal or dishonour, hospitality presented epitomes of lordship.

Challenges to reciprocalist politics included exchanges belonging to the category of the commercial—those exchanges which are explicitly

---

[40] *The Anonimalle Chronicle, 1333–1381*, ed. V. H. Galbraith (1927; Manchester, 1970), 152–6; *WC* 20, 406–8; S. K. Walker, 'Letters to the Dukes of Lancaster in 1381 and 1399', *EHR* 106 (1991), 68–79; Anthony Goodman, *John of Gaunt: The Exercise of Princely Power in Fourteenth-Century Europe* (Harlow, Essex, 1992), 81–2, 89–91. Walker argues that Gaunt 'sought systematically to exclude Northumberland from Marcher office between July 1381 and April 1384' because of their quarrel ('Letters', 74). Gaunt's charge of *disnaturesse* features in Galloway, 'Making of a Social Ethic', 374–6.

economic, exactly completed by a counter-exchange of calculated value, producing no residual obligation.[41] (In practice, commercial exchange tends to be hedged about by less calculable exchange that does carry such obligation, but this should be analysed according to non-commercial modes.) In fact, great households were significantly commercial operations. Their self-presentation, however, privileged non-commercial modes for the highest profile social activity, for exchanges that decisively converted resources (however accumulated) into political capital. It made sense to sell grain on the open market or purchase spices and textiles according to price or quality; it was quite a different matter to alienate an estate, marry a daughter, or provide a feast without discriminating between recipients by manifold, unstated calculations of (disguised) political capital.[42]

Competing with reciprocalism within its own territory, meanwhile, were 'magnificent' habits of household-based 'free' exchange that more aggressively voided assumptions about mutual obligation, essentially by disabling counter-exchange. The *Confessio* normally valorizes reciprocalist household exchange and does so chiefly by denigrating magnificence. Since they were non-commercial, both modes could be idealized as largesse.

The exchanges of the reciprocalist household produce benefits for givers and recipients, and are expected to do so. They are nonetheless directed at establishing hierarchical relations. The powerful are expected to give the most. A lord was required to expend considerable amounts of time, materials, and symbolic capital on 'good lordship' in order to sustain a capital of worship.[43] Those with the most, however, are also expected to receive the most. Genius's epigrammatic assessment that 'What man hath hors men yive him hors' (5. 7719) distils one side of aristocratic reciprocalism's asymmetrical principle whereby exchange is expected to reflect a recipient's wealth, worship, and connections. Worship enhanced by good lordship attracted further individuals seeking lordship, bringing more material and social capital to the lord and making 'capital go to capital' (just as Genius aphorizes).[44] Immediately noticeable

---

[41] Cf. Bourdieu, *Theory of Practice*, 5–7, 171–83.

[42] Mertes, *Noble Household*, 75–122, 131–8; Dyer, *Standards of Living*, 27–108; Nightingale, 'Knights and Merchants'. See C. M. Woolgar (ed.), *Household Accounts from Medieval England* (Oxford, 1992–3) for published examples of diet (daily or weekly), wardrobe, and cash, corn and stock accounts.

[43] Cf. Bourdieu, *Theory of Practice*, 180.

[44] Ibid. 181.

in the figure of political stability that I cited from Gower's prologue at the beginning of this chapter is the chiasmus of *comun* and *lord*, *lord* and *comun*, and its implication of reciprocity between classes. Arion's music addresses not only the lord's grievances against social inferiors but their own grievances against the lord. In accord with aristocratic reciprocalism, however, the *Confessio's* particular version of the politics of mutual obligation is not so simple or symmetrical as the chiasmus avows. My discussion of the poem aims to amplify its political complexities.

Reciprocalist exchanges (or reinvested capital) earned a lord worship most securely by conferring benefits on appropriate, expected recipients.[45] Reciprocalist lordship thus exploits the bond-forming potential of non-commercial exchanges, building up obligations and privileged relationships which are conduits for future exchanges. These therefore tend to occur within and between household-based groups where persons are already linked by networks of previous exchanges. In Genius's portrait of Parsimony, a household officer who never earns credit of worship and 'thonk' (5. 4684), and acknowledges no networks of kinship, neighbourhood, or service beyond his lord, we see a negative image of the ideal exchange practice of reciprocalist lordship (below, 69–73). This ideal is clearly one of the great household oriented outwards and giving lavishly, but it is equally important to reciprocalism that exchanges follow established (or at least immediately recognizable) social contours so that they can reinforce stable, hierarchically structured networks.[46]

Magnificence produces quite different expectations of exchange, even if it appears to be simply an intensification of reciprocalist lordship. The magnificent lord still seeks to generate worship and indeed obedience through conspicuous consumption and exchange, but does so unencumbered by the expectations, that is, the unstated calculations, of potential recipients and counter-givers.[47] Magnificence thus enjoys more flexibility than reciprocalism and resembles commercial exchange

---

[45] Heal emphasizes that 'to be effective [gifts and hospitality] needed to be congruent with the expectations of both donors and recipients' ('Reciprocity and Exchange', 189).

[46] Carpenter proposes network theory as a model for the study of local politics in 'Gentry and Community'. Networks do not, of course, presuppose a particular model of exchange.

[47] For Heal's discussion of magnificence in similar terms, see 'Reciprocity and Exchange', 193–4. 'Magnificence' can otherwise be used to refer more generally to the deployment of household resources, in opposition to the 'providence' which marshals those resources in the first place. See e.g. David Starkey, 'The Age of the Household: Politics, Society and the Arts *c*.1350–*c*.1550', in Stephen Medcalf (ed.), *The Context of English Literature: The Later Middle Ages* (London, 1981), 254–6.

in this regard. The magnificent lord is not constrained by sedimented structures of obligation and worship in selecting recipients. By the same token, exchanges may fall to those sharpest to present themselves. Yet magnificence is not really a marketplace of social capital, for the lord's giving disdains calculation and in fact *intends* no benefit to its recipients. Such benefits as do accrue are incidental; they are noise or exhaust in the system. Commercial exchange closes obligation by an exact answer. Magnificence *pre-empts* obligation not by completing exchanges (commercially), but by radical unilateralism. It threatens to short-circuit exchange processes since it refuses to be obliged. It implies the absence of any external worship or counter-gift capable of obliging the giver, producing a general strategy of contempt.[48] My formulation of magnificence is informed by Louise Fradenburg's theory of 'the totalized discourse of the sovereign', although I agree with Lee Patterson that texts and actions produced within this discourse inevitably subvert it in some measure, allowing other claims or viewpoints room.[49] Magnificence is not interested in enduring ties and networks of mutual obligation and each exchange is entered for the present interests of only one party. Spectacles of majesty such as crown-wearings, certain statements of theocratic kingship, Richard II's blank charters of prospective treason, and the introduction of suddenly powerful 'new men' (such as Robert de Vere and Simon Burley) into unwelcoming local communities all belong under the heading of magnificence.[50]

Magnificence strives to be unanswerable. It is latent in unusually sophisticated cultural phenomena in so far as these countenance no rival or reply. The *Confessio* abounds with mythically sophisticated and exotic culture proffered in (almost) unanswerable exchanges. Minos's 'strange and merveilous' labyrinth (*CA* 5. 5272–5304), Gurmond's

[48] On the abstention of superiors from reply, and the resultant strategy of contempt, see Bourdieu, *Theory of Practice*, 12–14; cf. Mauss, *The Gift*, 39–40.

[49] Louise Fradenburg, 'The Manciple's Servant Tongue: Politics and Poetry in *The Canterbury Tales*', *ELH* 52 (1985), 85–118, esp. 88–9; Lee Patterson, 'Court Politics and the Invention of Literature: The Case of Sir John Clanvowe', in David Aers (ed.), *Culture and History 1350–1600: Essays on English Communities, Identities and Writing* (New York, 1992), 29 and n. 113. I would stress the value of reading the sovereign or the magnificent lord as a possible rather than the essential aristocratic discourse.

[50] Bartlett, *England under the Norman and Angevin Kings*, 127–9; Ernst H. Kantorowicz, *The King's Two Bodies: A Study in Mediaeval Political Theology* (Princeton, 1957), 42–86, (and for the sacral crown) 336–40; Joseph Canning, *A History of Medieval Political Thought 300–1450* (London, 1996), 17–25, 131–4, 142–4, 162–7; Caroline M. Barron, 'The Tyranny of Richard II', *BIHR* 41 (1968), 1–18, 10–14; Nigel Saul, *Richard II* (New Haven, Conn., 1997), 24–7, 163–4; and below, 49–57.

bejewelled skull-cup (1. 2527–45 and below, 169–71), Siculus's brazen bull (7. 3310–23 and below, 257), and Antiochus's riddle (8. 402–17) all amplify the connection between cultural elaboration and magnificent politics. These artefacts are iconic examples of unanswerable culture, designed to baffle or overwhelm recipients, to exclude them from informed participation in exchange and thereby to prevent them from creating sequences of obligation. Minos's maze, for example, is a perversion of the great household's architecture and its varied patterns of access, which normally spell out social hierarchy and relative claims on the lord's attention.[51] One of Ricardian literature's most vivid studies of magnificence in this symbolic register is the first part of Chaucer's 'Squire's Tale'. Chaucer offers a fantasy of unilateral, centralized royal power, which is presented through the gift by the tale's courteous knight of an exotic brass horse and confirmed as a central theme by the narrator's preoccupation with the court's reactions to the horse. The horse promises the miracle of the ruler's being everywhere at will with sole control (*CT* 5. 313–34). This high culture is about power (as is the knight's magical sword) and surveillance. It is unburdened by discourse of justice or the common good. Like a theocratic ruler, Genghis Khan stands to gain an unconstrainable source of power, but the knight's gifts come with none of the moral limiting factors intrinsic to divine grace (factors which can be conflated with the expectations of a political community).[52] Moreover, the benefactor knight's secret tutoring and the court's overextended and finally obstructed curiosity intimate that Genghis Khan's subjects (however mighty) are to be excluded from his new mode of power. The courteous, exotic knight manages to create with his wondrous gifts an insulated, isolating relationship with the king—a kind of political community of two ('"bitwix us two"'; 5. 317, cf. 333). The sword and mirror, 'ful roially yfet [taken] ... | And born anon into the heighe tour' (5. 174–6), and the mysterious horse, with its powers specially known by the prince, distance him from the ruled. It is hard to say how the Squire might judge Genghis Khan or his court (last seen yawning and inert; 5. 354–61) were he to complete his tale; but all

---

[51] See Johnson, *Behind the Castle Gate*, 67–84. Commenting on the spatial ordering of buildings taken to be socially calibrated, not magnificent, Johnson suggestively states, 'Such an ordering meant that the visitor to a castle, of perhaps a certain social rank and gender and possessing the appropriate cultural knowledge, would not necessarily see the castle as random or *labyrinth-like* at all' (69, emphasis added).

[52] For theocratic authority as 'limited but not controlled', see Canning, *Medieval Political Thought*, 25.

of the truncated tale is about an exclusive great household, and the Squire may be embarking on an incest narrative, which would confirm the household's insularity.[53] In any case, both parts of the tale that we have seem dedicated to setting up Genghis Khan's court as a site of magnificence. (The tercelet in the second part is both lover and flatterer, so, like the courteous visitor of the first part, can be glossed as an encroacher of royal power.)

Whatever would have become of Genghis Khan's court in a completed 'Squire's Tale', magnificence in *Confessio Amantis* is routinely a sign of corrupt household economies. In this, Gower's poem aligns itself with a public whose politics are uncentralized and (asymmetrically) reciprocal, and offers to correct those who have less respect for aristocratic hierarchies and communities. The poem entered a matrix of reciprocalist language by which historical power structures operated and were defended. It is worth observing at this stage that events and actions on one hand and discourse on the other are different but complex and interacting quantities. Political principles are not hardwired; reciprocalist language was neither automatically summoned by appropriate conditions nor always employed soundly and predictably. The 'common profit', 'community of the realm', and the king's 'good' partners in rule meant different things to different agents under different circumstances. 'Alien' status is an opprobrious element of reciprocalist discourse, but it could be used to make rather than mark outsiders and a foreigner who obliged reciprocalist interests might not attract it at all. The French noble Simon de Montfort harnessed xenophobic sentiment when in power. Accusations that he patronized 'grant nombre des aliens' at Richard II's court contributed to the provincial Simon Burley's downfall.[54] These examples demonstrate the power as well as the adaptability of discourse. Political language is not merely ornament to the 'real' business of individual motives and actions. Discourse works at different levels to shape politics. It helps to inculcate dispositions that draw individuals' own motives (or their understanding of their strongest interest) towards a 'regular situation'.[55] It also serves the interest to conform when individuals are more self-conscious about fitting into a regular situation. At this level, discourse is crucial in determining the

---

[53] *CT* 5. 651–69. Cf. *CT* 2. 77–80 (the Man of Law's censure of the '"wikke ensample of Canacee"'). For incest as magnificent exchange, see below, 163–5.

[54] J. R. Maddicott, *Simon de Montfort* (Cambridge, 1994), 127–8, 145–6, 230–6; *WC* 274.

[55] Bourdieu, *Theory of Practice*, 17–22, 77–8 (quote at 22).

scope and success of political actions regardless of the genuineness with which it is deployed. Reciprocalist, magnificent, and other political stances are important from this viewpoint not because they are sincerely or conveniently adopted, but because they delimit the range of available, publicly justifiable actions.[56]

Structures of reciprocalism and magnificence, and the great household imaginary in general, were powerful contestants for both the socially 'natural' and the socially 'contracted' regulation of politics in late fourteenth-century England. The next chapter views fourteenth-century lordship and government according to this model and examines particular interventions in and appropriations of the contest besides *Confessio Amantis*. I also consider the economic conditions (of local networks and large-scale changes) that helped to generate reciprocalist and, in different ways, magnificent political practice.

[56] Watts argues for this view in *Henry VI*, 3–9. He signals a basic debt to J. G. A. Pocock, 'Languages and their Implications: The Transformation of the Study of Political Thought', in *Politics, Language and Time: Essays on Political Thought and History* (London, 1972), 3–41; and to Quentin Skinner, 'The Principles and Practice of Opposition: The Case of Bolingbroke versus Walpole', in Neil McKendrick (ed.), *Historical Perspectives: Studies in English Thought and Society in Honour of J. H. Plumb* (London, 1974), 93–128; and 'Some Problems in the Analysis of Political Thought and Action', in James Tully (ed.), *Meaning and Context: Quentin Skinner and his Critics* (Cambridge, 1988), 97–118, esp. 108–11.

2

The Political Economy in
the Late Fourteenth Century

RECIPROCAL LORDSHIP AND CENTRALIZATION

England in the late Middle Ages was a prodigiously centralized polity.
The king was not merely the realm's mightiest lord. As Robert Bartlett
observes of an earlier period:

Kingship provided a foundation of claims that were inherently wider
and...capable of greater expansion than those of any non-royal lord:...all
adult males took an oath of allegiance to him; he could not be sued; some
offences fell only under his jurisdiction; and he was hedged about with the
distinctive symbolism of regality [including anointing and coronation].[1]

Offices of state—the exchequer, chancery and the major law courts—
enjoyed remarkable competencies, their ambits and industry evinced by
colossal record-keeping. Increasing dependence on records was alone
enough to anchor the fiscal and administrative departments in one place
and by the 1340s, with the court of king's bench also settling at
Westminster, greater London had become a strong focal point or
'capital' for political society.[2] Most fourteenth-century parliaments
met there, and the Plantagenets' various decorative agendas for Westminster abbey signalled 'England's priority in developing symbolic
notions of the centralized state'.[3]

Yet the king was not a sovereign prince in majesty in any simple
sense; nor could he blanket out aristocratic society with a comprehensive professional bureaucracy. Looking for organs of 'state' to trace the
'evolution' of government deflects us from medieval government's

---

[1] Bartlett, *England under the Norman and Angevin Kings*, 122.
[2] A. L. Brown, *The Governance of Late Medieval England 1272–1461* (Stanford,
Calif., 1989), 43, 57–9; Harriss, 'Political Society', 34.
[3] Paul Binski, *Westminster Abbey and the Plantagenets: Kingship and the Representation
of Power 1200–1400* (New Haven, Conn., 1995), 5.

inevitable reliance on household-based power (royal and aristocratic). By inspecting the Middle Ages under assumptions of royal dominance or using Tudor institutions as our template, we risk repeating the misjudgement of historians whom Michael Clanchy dubs ' "King's Friends" '.[4]

Following the work of K. B. McFarlane and, more recently, Christine Carpenter, Simon Walker, and others, there is now extensive and expanding research into the local power structures that the late medieval English aristocracy developed by long processes of household exchange. Standard accounts of politics in the period now take this milieu into account, along with its effects on the centre.[5] Writers who discuss the centre are now increasingly careful to account for it as a zone thickly connected to (other) localities and influenced by informal politics.[6] This work has shown that aristocratic networks tended to resist intrusion, that is, alteration without respect for landholding patterns, histories of exchanges, and the community hierarchies these had established. Politics, in other words, usually worked when they conformed to reciprocalist principles. Magnificent elements of authority could reinforce power if concentrated in time and space or backed by extraordinary resources, but such authority generally needed to be ballasted by reciprocalist rule. The aristocracy had an overriding interest in the protection of their landholding, inheritance, and power structures. Central authority was generally welcome if it served these interests (as individual landowners perceived them at a given time) but provoked resistance when it impinged on them, by bringing in tow central agents, for example, who could not readily be subordinated to local power.[7]

Local or regional society could alter dramatically and suddenly at the advent, for example, of a marriage, reversion or grant which redistributed lands, forged new ties and introduced a great household into local politics with new prominence. The success of this alteration would ride on factors such as the relative standing of the houses involved and the existence (or lack) of previous ties between them (or with rivals for the

---

[4] M. T. Clanchy, 'Law, Government, and Society in Medieval England', *History*, 59 (1974), 73–8, 77.

[5] Harriss, *Shaping the Nation*, 187–206; Given-Wilson, *English Nobility*, 160–79; Harriss, 'Political Society'; and studies cited above, 2 n. 3. For comment on this trend, see Powell, 'After "After McFarlane" '; Carpenter, 'Gentry and Community'.

[6] Excellent examples of this care include Watts, *Henry VI*; and Helen Castor, *The King, the Crown, and the Duchy of Lancaster: Public Authority and Private Power 1399–1461* (Oxford, 2000).

[7] See studies cited above, 19 n. 35.

exchange). Object lessons are provided by the Greys' careful entry into Bedfordshire and Buckinghamshire landed society during the fourteenth century and the less successful relocations of several powerful men who enjoyed the favour of Richard II (including John Holland in the south-west and Robert de Vere and Simon Burley in the south-east).[8]

In the late Middle Ages, political society and its local power structures expanded to include an increasingly politically active gentry class. Over the course of the thirteenth century and into the fourteenth, the prevailing idea of 'the community of the realm' which should assist the king in government came to be filled up not just with barons and the most powerful tenants-in-chief but with gentry as well, not to mention urban elites of wealthy merchants and legal professionals.[9] Indeed, socially very diverse and extensive groups could lay claim to membership of the 'community of the realm' in the fourteenth century, sometimes in explosive style (as in the revolt of 1381) and generally thanks to an expansion of literacy, and economic and governmental changes.[10] Against these pressures (and partly by accommodating them), the aristocracy sustained its exceptional political influence and a perception of its own near-identity with the *communitas regni*. If, as Gower indicates of a parable, the *Confessio* uses 'oure englissh' (prol. 23) to reach the widest possible domestic audience (6. 980–5), this would seem to represent a wary rather than an encouraging response to emergent senses of the 'commons', 'commune', or 'community' more extensive than those that the poem's elite public would welcome. In so far as the poem speaks to the lower orders, it reinforces elite interests and mainly recommends quiescence. The *Confessio* was consistently produced as a huge luxury book and Gower most particularly imagines his audience as the king and 'jangling' court (prol. 24–92*) and 'my lordis alle' (8. 3129).[11] Although the poem's readership

---

[8] Given-Wilson, *English Nobility*, 48–53, 162; Saul, *Richard II*, 163–4, 243–4; Chris Given-Wilson, 'Richard II and his Grandfather's Will', *EHR* 93 (1978), 320–37.

[9] In the fifteenth century, these types of the influential would be joined by gentlemen bureaucrats: Harriss, 'Political Society', 33–4.

[10] Watts, 'Pressure of the Public'.

[11] For the production of *Confessio* manuscripts, see A. I. Doyle and M. B. Parkes, 'The Production of Copies of the *Canterbury Tales* and the *Confessio Amantis* in the Early Fifteenth Century', in M. B. Parkes and Andrew G. Watson (eds), *Medieval Scribes, Manuscripts and Libraries: Essays Presented to N. R. Ker* (London, 1978), esp. 163–7, 177, 194–200; Derek Pearsall, 'The Manuscripts and Illustrations of Gower's Works', in Echard (ed.), *Companion*, 73–97. On scribal consistency marking deference to Gower as 'a respected monument', see Jeremy J. Smith, 'Linguistic Features of Some Fifteenth-Century Middle English Manuscripts', in Derek Pearsall (ed.), *Manuscripts and Readers in Fifteenth-Century England:*

seems to have been rather wider than such address pretends, Gower does not promote a new popular activism.[12]

The composition and enhanced role of parliament reflected the political influence gained by the gentry as consenters to tax (and therefore to the policies which required it) and reinforced this influence through increased contact with the centre. Furthermore, the royal government allowed the gentry a heightened role in local government and justice administration akin to that they had intermittently demanded during the thirteenth century. The general eyres, originally 'regular, country-wide visitations by royal judges with specific powers and duties', first fractured into single-purpose commissions under Edward I and then these gave ground, especially in the fourteenth century, to commissions of the peace staffed significantly by local men of substance.[13]

The Literary Implications of Manuscript Study (Cambridge, 1983), 112. Asterisked references follow distinctions between recensions as printed in Macaulay.

[12] On the *Confessio*'s address and possible audiences, see Kathryn Kerby-Fulton and Steven Justice, 'Scribe D and the Marketing of Ricardian Literature', Kathryn Kerby-Fulton and Maidie Hilmo (eds), *The Medieval Professional Reader at Work: Evidence from Manuscripts of Chaucer, Langland, Kempe, and Gower* (Victoria, BC, 2001), 217–37; Middleton, 'Public Poetry'; Peter Nicholson, 'The Dedications of Gower's *Confessio Amantis*', *Mediaevalia*, 10 (1988, for 1984), 159–80; Lynn Staley, 'Gower, Richard II, Henry of Derby, and the Business of Making Culture', *Speculum*, 75 (2000), 68–96; Watt, *Amoral Gower*, 2–4. Kate Harris surveys the early (predominantly aristocratic) ownership of *Confessio* MSS in 'Ownership and Readership: Studies in the Provenance of the Manuscripts of Gower's *Confessio Amantis*', D.Phil. thesis, University of York, 1993, esp. 119–56. For the *Confessio*'s use in fifteenth-century anthologies, including a major compilation by a gentry household of Derbyshire, see A. S. G. Edwards, 'Selection and Subversion in Gower's *Confessio Amantis*', in Yeager (ed.), *Re-Visioning Gower*; *The Findern Manuscript: Cambridge University Library MS Ff.I.6*, introd. Richard Beadle and A. E. B. Owen (London, 1977); R. H. Robbins, 'The Findern Anthology', *PMLA* 69 (1954), 610–42. For the remit of the 'comun vois', 'communis vox', and 'vox plebis' in Gower's poetry, cf. Watts, 'Pressure of the Public', 170 and n. 51.

[13] Bartlett, *England under the Norman and Angevin Kings*, 191; Anthony Musson and W. M. Ormrod, *The Evolution of English Justice: Law, Politics and Society in the Fourteenth Century* (Basingstoke, 1999), 42–74; Prestwich, *Plantagenet England*, 515–22; G. L. Harriss, *King, Parliament, and Public Finance in Medieval England to 1369* (Oxford, 1975), 98–127; and 'Political Society'; R. G. Davies and J. H. Denton (eds), *The English Parliament in the Middle Ages* (Manchester, 1981), 1–87; J. R. Maddicott, 'Edward I and the Lessons of Baronial Reform: Local Government, 1258–80', in P. R. Coss and S. D. Lloyd (eds), *Thirteenth Century England I* (Woodbridge, Suff., 1986), 23–5; Anthony Verduyn, 'The Commons and the Early Justices of the Peace under Edward III', in Peter Fleming, Anthony Gross, and J. R. Lander (eds), *Regionalism and Revision: The Crown and its Provinces in England 1200–1650* (London, 1998), 87–106. These discussions argue for diverse views of centralization and aristocratic interests. For further consideration, see below, 175–82, 215–17.

Reciprocalist discourse had undiminished currency when Gower wrote and continued to be reminted to support (and sometimes urgently to shore up) the position of household networks in society. Accounts of late medieval government often characterize the period as one in which uncentralized power was re-emergent. Broadly speaking, the Angevin regimes expanded central authority. The jurisdictions of royal justices increased and *curiales* or 'court men' at times achieved an unusually high profile in shire government. Henry III was also seen to be attempting such expansion of crown influence as well as narrowing access to government at the centre.[14] While succeeding Plantagenets did not abandon all efforts to push royally administered justice into the localities, the late Middle Ages is still sometimes seen as an ebbing or perverting of an Angevin achievement, even 'a major and permanent capitulation by central government', before the house of Tudor restored the power of the 'emasculated' crown.[15]

This picture is qualified by studies that bring the great household, its non-commercial economy, and informal politics into focus, and by the political imagination of texts like *Confessio Amantis*. These unsettle assumptions about the efficacy of centralized over decentred power or about the separation of centre and periphery. The relationship between landed society and the royal centre (or locally intrusive magnate authority) was neither simple nor polarized at any time in the Middle Ages. The crown never enjoyed a monopoly on judicial authority and legitimate force. Multiple jurisdictions overlaid each other in a given territory, with customary courts (including franchised hundred and borough jurisdictions as well as honour and manor courts) persisting alongside the expanding common law in a judicial 'palimpsest'. In marcher and palatinate areas, local lords enjoyed extraordinary independence. Even with customary law much eroded in the country at large, the unfree, villein population remained without access to the common law in

---

[14] D. A. Carpenter, 'King, Magnates, and Society: The Personal Rule of King Henry III, 1234–1258', *Speculum*, 60 (1985), 39–70; cf. Michael T. Clanchy, 'Did Henry III Have a Policy?' *History*, 53 (1968), 207–19; and *England and its Rulers 1066–1272*, 2nd edn (Glasgow, 1998), 222–40. See also D. A. Carpenter, 'The Decline of the Curial Sheriff in England, 1194–1258', *EHR* 91 (1976), 1–32.

[15] J. R. Lander, *The Limitations of English Monarchy in the Later Middle Ages* (Toronto, 1989), 30, quoted in Harriss, 'Political Society', 29, 30. See also other work discussed by Harriss: Richard W. Kaeuper, *War, Justice and Public Order: England and France in the Later Middle Ages* (Oxford, 1988); P. R. Coss, 'Bastard Feudalism Revised' and 'Debate: Bastard Feudalism Revised'. Harriss also considers exceptions to 'consensus on the failure of late medieval English government' (30).

Gower's time.[16] For their part, landholders were generally neither able nor seeking to cut themselves off from royal authority (just as the Angevins never eliminated household-based power in the political system). The late fourteenth-century peace commission, for example, suited reciprocalist interests by giving local gentry new authority in combination with royal justices and lawyers from the central courts.[17]

Again, it pays to bear in mind the typically 'public private' quality of medieval political authority. Magnificent or 'commercial' politics inhere not in bringing central authority to the localities but in doing so without accommodation of local aristocratic interests.[18] Equally, letting notions of the 'state' obscure the importance of the royal household as in many ways the true centre of the realm's government can distort our sense of centralization. In particular, geographical fixity is an uncertain measure of centralization. The two can coincide, but need to be distinguished. Thus, chancery's settling in Westminster, as the result of huge growth in its business, was a symptom of administrative centralization, yet the same change simultaneously pulled in a different direction. Embedded, chancery no longer routinely kept the company of the royal court outside London. It was thereby slightly displaced from the royal centre even as access to it was made more predictable.[19] Compare the staffing of the common bench, increasingly in demand at Westminster, by a cadre of lay professionals rather than ministers from other branches of government: this may have diluted the royal 'personality' of this court even as it built up state-like barriers to reciprocalist expectations of justice through the problem of officialness itself (see below, 210–21).[20] Unlike St Stephen's chapel in the 'privy palace', the great hall at Westminster (which accommodated the courts of common pleas and king's bench, the chancery, and, in adjoining rooms, the exchequer) seems to have been sparely decorated. Even after Richard II came to add statues of kings and other devices of royal and dynastic symbolism, visually the hall probably chiefly communicated routine and efficiency.[21]

[16] Musson and Ormrod, *Evolution of English Justice*, 8–9 (offering 'palimpsest' at 8); Bailey (ed.), *English Manor*, 167–84.

[17] Harriss, *Shaping the Nation*, 50–2; cf. Musson and Ormrod, *Evolution of English Justice*, 68–74; Walker, 'Yorkshire Justices'; and *Lancastrian Affinity*, 242–7; Christine Carpenter, 'Law, Justice and Landowners in Late Medieval England', *Law and History Review*, 1 (1983), 205–37, 216–18.

[18] For 'public private' cf. Bartlett, *England under the Norman and Angevin Kings*, 121–2.

[19] Clanchy, *Memory to Written Record*, 58–67, 164–6.

[20] Musson and Ormrod, *Evolution of English Justice*, 28–36; Paul Brand, *The Making of the Common Law* (London, 1992), 1–20, 57–75.

[21] Watts, 'Looking for the State', 248–50. Note his speculation that the green wall behind the common bench (as well as various green paraphernalia of government) may

Itinerancy in this context can amount to a disruptive, magnificent assertion of central authority. So, the removal of chancery and other offices northwards with the king during Edward III's old age or during Richard II's impatience first with conciliar supervision in 1387 and then with London in 1392 represents a reminder of where (on the crown's terms) the centre of power really lies.[22] Other users of chancery and common bench must have preferred a less magnificent view of the provision of the institutions' core business of the common law.

At the centre, the expansion and consolidation of the king's advisory great councils in the form of 'parliament' is part of a longer history of expectations that men of a certain status will be preferred as the king's proper advisers.[23] These expectations lie at the hub of a discourse which imagines 'great men' speaking for the 'community of the realm' to ensure that royal rule is not arbitrary. The discourse is reciprocalist, and often conceives outsiders or 'new men' as the symptom of improperly directed royal power. John Watts describes the 'portmanteau image' of the treacherous new-man counsellor, its appearance, 'often with remarkable completeness, in a host of texts' and its availability at 'all social levels'.[24] The 'new man' stigma most easily attached to those who, if not quite raised 'from the dust' as Orderic Vitalis fancies of Henry I's servants, were parachuted into political society from beyond existing networks or

---

represent 'vestiges of a symbolic programme quite unrelated to the projection of an essentially royal kind of authority' (250). For a floorplan of the palace buildings, from H. M. Colvin (ed.), *The History of the King's Works* (London, 1963–82), iii, see Harriss, *Shaping the Nation*, 49; and for the hall's remodelling under Richard II, see Eleanor Scheifele, 'Richard II and the Visual Arts', in Anthony Goodman and James L. Gillespie (eds), *Richard II: The Art of Kingship* (Oxford, 1999), 260–2.

[22] Michael J. Bennett, 'Richard II and the Wider Realm', in Goodman and Gillespie (eds), *Richard II: The Art of Kingship*, 192–4.

[23] J. C. Holt, 'The Prehistory of Parliament', in Davies and Denton (eds), *English Parliament*; Michael Prestwich, 'Parliament and the Community of the Realm in Fourteenth-Century England', in Art Cosgrove and J. I. McGuire (eds), *Parliament and Community* (Belfast, 1983), 5–24; D. A. Carpenter, 'The Beginnings of Parliament', in *The Reign of Henry III* (London, 1996), 381–408; McFarlane, 'Parliament and "Bastard Feudalism" ', 65–70; H. G. Richardson, 'The Commons and Medieval Politics', *TRHS* 4th ser. 28 (1946), 21–45; K. L. Wood-Legh, 'Sheriffs, Lawyers, and Belted Knights in the Parliaments of Edward III', *EHR* 46 (1931), 372–88; and 'The Knights' Attendance in the Parliaments of Edward III', *EHR* 47 (1932), 398–413.

[24] Watts, 'Pressure of the Public', 168–9. Watts is interested in this 'framing metaphor' as a sign of the spread of political consciousness and agency throughout society, but this does not exclude, I think, my interest in the ways that such tropes were used (also) to serve certain landed interests.

acceptable templates of land and status.[25] Thomas Walsingham attacks Richard II's Cheshire retainers in these terms and Froissart depicts the Lords Appellant and others sneering dangerously at their enemy Robert de Vere (earl of Oxford and newly duke of Ireland) as a 'povre homme' risen in the world. Defended by his lord ('son seigneur l'adveue'), the parvenu duke's career has distended reciprocalist exchange patterns, which spells ruin for the country.[26] The magnificence of both Edward II and Richard II in endowing new nobles out of proportion to their previous positions in landed society proved disastrous. Almost all of the new peers granted titles by Edward III's father and grandson (fourteen of sixteen, including de Vere) fell within five years of their creation. Edward III himself created no fewer than six new earls at one go in 1337 to replenish a comital order much depleted by violence, but Edward managed to appoint friends and supporters who were acceptable to political society at large and he was also able, with resourcefulness, some scrimping and some promises, to provide for them without sowing divisions (or none, at least, that would get the better of him).[27]

GOWER'S KENTISH GROUP AND THE COUP OF 1388

The efficacy of reciprocalist language at the time Gower wrote the *Confessio* is grimly demonstrated by the assault on Richard II's government and household in the so-called Merciless Parliament of February 1388. The coup grew out of tensions that had already strained to breaking point in 1386 and it was led by five magnates. The king's uncle the duke of Gloucester and the earls of Arundel and Warwick appealed major royal supporters of treason and were joined before the appeal proceeded in parliament by the earls of Nottingham and Derby (the king's cousin).[28]

[25] Orderic Vitalis, *The Ecclesiastical History of Orderic Vitalis*, ed. and tr. Marjorie Chibnall (Oxford, 1969–80), vi. 16, quoted in David Carpenter, *The Struggle for Mastery: Britain 1066–1284* (London, 2003), 157.

[26] Jean Froissart, *Œuvres de Froissart: Chroniques*, ed. Baron Kervyn de Lettenhove (Brussels, 1867–77), xii. 235–6; *Annales*, 208, tr. in Chris Given-Wilson (ed. and tr.), *Chronicles of the Revolution, 1397–1400: The Reign of Richard II* (Manchester, 1993), 73–4; cf. *WC* 82, 354 for retainers 'lifted up' (*elati*) by noble favour.

[27] Given-Wilson, *English Nobility*, 29–54. Walsingham gives a 'new man' critique of some of Richard's creations in *Annales*, 222–4, tr. Given-Wilson in *Chronicles of the Revolution*, 74–5.

[28] For these events and their background, see Saul, *Richard II*, 148–204; Harriss, *Shaping the Nation*, 451–68.

A reciprocalist discourse of outsiders and (wronged) great men was the lifeblood of the Appellants' confrontation with the court. The parliamentary texts of the Appellants may not share all of Froissart's registers—they do not liken de Vere to an otter in a pond who devours ('deveure') rewards[29]—but across appeal, *Chroniques*, and *Confessio* the view of a distorted political economy is shared; the obligational grammar is the same.

Gower himself was connected with a group of gentry and barons which the court alienated to its cost before the 1388 assembly at Westminster. Gower's ties to this group and its solidarities at odds with men favoured by the king indicate a background for the winter crisis of 1387–8 fuller than that provided by the interests of the five Appellants alone. These ties and solidarities also suggest a kind of core or complicit 'public' for *Confessio Amantis*; a comfortable audience whose resistance to magnificence the poem is equipped to consolidate.[30] Traceable connections within this group speak of gradually building ties threaded by neighbourhood, kinship, and business and political dealings. The group's members appear, in other words, to be vintage aristocratic reciprocalists.

I focus on this group as a site of reciprocalist interests and dispositions despite the fact that Gower also had some links to figures very prominent in the crisis of 1387–8. Henry, earl of Derby, appears initially to have been a joint-dedicatee of the *Confessio* (subordinate to Richard II) and became its sole dedicatee on the poem's revision in the 1390s.[31] More than a decade after the Merciless Parliament, Gower seems to have had a presentation copy of *Vox clamantis* and other of his Latin poems put together for Thomas Arundel when he was Henry IV's archbishop of Canterbury. Arundel, brother of the earl, had opened the Merciless Parliament as chancellor, was an influential politician at odds with the king and his household throughout the 1380s and 1390s, and

---

[29] Froissart, *Chroniques*, xii. 235.

[30] For the concept of a 'public' as an audience implied or projected by a text (but not historically verifiable), see Anne Middleton, 'The Audience and Public of *Piers Plowman*', in David Lawton (ed.), *Middle English Alliterative Poetry and its Literary Background: Seven Essays* (Cambridge, 1982), 101–4; cf. Macherey, *Theory of Literary Production*, 73, 78–80, 90–101.

[31] On the *Confessio*'s dedications and possible motivations for their alteration, see Macaulay, ii, pp. xxi–xxvi; Nicholson, 'Dedications'; George B. Stow, 'Richard II in John Gower's *Confessio Amantis*: Some Historical Perspectives', *Mediaevalia*, 16 (1993), 3–31; John H. Fisher, *John Gower: Moral Philosopher and Friend of Chaucer* (London, 1965), 117–19; Sylvia Federico, *New Troy: Fantasies of Empire in the Late Middle Ages* (Minneapolis, 2003), 114–17; Kerby-Fulton and Justice, 'Scribe D', 220.

was immensely important as a patron and later censor of writing.[32] Another major supporter of the Appellants, John, the third Baron Cobham, can be associated with Gower long before 1388. From the perspective of Gower's associations in the 1380s, Derby and Arundel appear to be nodes less integrated in a certain reciprocalist network than less illustrious figures. Cobham features here primarily as a leading figure in a network concentrated away from Westminster, not, for instance, as a member of the continual council that regulated the royal household and clashed with the king during the year from November 1386.[33] Nevertheless, Cobham's example demonstrates that it is spurious to try finally to divide 'local' and 'central' impetuses in aristocratic politics. It seems equally true to say that Cobham's role at the centre in the 1380s drove his part in the crisis of 1387–8 and that his role at the centre was driven by his local landed interests. Cobham was an especially strong link between Westminster (council, parliament, and sometimes court) and a local aristocratic milieu in which Gower was closely involved.

I invoke biographical information here not in order to suggest that Gower enjoyed full control of the meanings of his poem or that he designed the *Confessio* as a statement of his own aristocratic status. Rather, Gower's landholding and aristocratic social connections indicate his own access to interests and dispositions, or 'schemes of perception', that would inform the social imagination, and thus the politics, of his writing. This information also, as I have said, illustrates a wider group and potential audience who would be disposed to recognize the textualized politics of the great household and to make reciprocalist meaning of the *Confessio*. Gower was an acquisitive landowner—however small-scale—who may have joined the landed classes by way of a legal career.[34] He dealt with influential persons, and his residence in Southwark at

---

[32] The manuscript is Oxford, All Souls' College MS 98. See Macaulay, iv, pp. lvii, lx–lxii. For Thomas Arundel's career and literary importance, see Margaret Aston, *Thomas Arundel: A Study of Church Life in the Reign of Richard II* (Oxford, 1967); Nicholas Watson, 'Censorship and Cultural Change in Late-Medieval England: Vernacular Theology, the Oxford Translation Debate, and Arundel's Constitutions of 1409', *Speculum*, 70 (1995), 822–64; Kathryn Kerby-Fulton, *Books under Suspicion: Censorship and Tolerance of Revelatory Writing in Late Medieval England* (Notre Dame, Ind., 2006), calling the impact of Arundel's Constitutions 'relatively minimal' (contra Watson; 397).

[33] For this council, see *WC* 166–74; Saul, *Richard II*, 161–72.

[34] For Gower's possible legal connection, see Fisher, *John Gower*, 55–8. For the legal profession as one of the major avenues to landed status during the demographic crisis of the late fourteenth century and beyond, see S. J. Payling, 'Social Mobility, Demographic Change, and Landed Society in Late Medieval England', *EconHR* 45 (1992), 51–73, 65–70.

St Mary Overy priory (where he may have lived for the best part of his literary career) placed him in the path of aristocratic commerce to London, from the south-east and further afield, for business in Westminster or the city.[35] Gentry and magnate inns or town houses were numerous in Gower's Southwark neighbourhood, with a kind of aristocratic 'enclave' running eastwards from the priory along Tooley Street and the palace and precinct of the bishops of Winchester sprawling massive to the west.[36] Several town houses belonging to or leased by powerful aristocrats also lay just across the river, and the second Sir Arnold Savage, one of the busiest landed communicants between Kent and the centre, rented for his city residence (in 1391–2 at least) an inn near London Bridge and a stone's throw from St Mary's.[37]

Documents generated by Gower's land transactions point to his belonging to a Kent-based group of landowners which encompassed some of the county's longest-established knightly families and most politically active individuals, and his will suggests that he sustained some of these links into his old age. Gower's sometime neighbour Savage was also an executor to his will.[38] Several documents of the 1380s, meanwhile, describe Gower as 'esquier de Kent' and his property dealings place him in a circle which includes the likes of Savage, the Cobhams of Cooling and Sterborough, Sir Thomas de Brockhull, William de Septvans, and Sir Nicholas de Louvein.[39]

---

[35] For Gower's manors and land transactions in Kent and East Anglia, see Fisher, *John Gower*, 47–54, 64; *CCR: Richard II, 1381–1385*, 211, 214, 619. For Gower and St Mary's see Fisher, 54–63. For a history of the priory and Southwark's juncture with the south-east, see Martha Carlin, *Medieval Southwark* (London, 1996), 67–75, 191–6. For aristocratic connectedness to, and life in, London, see Caroline M. Barron, 'Centres of Conspicuous Consumption: The Aristocratic Town House in London 1200–1550', *London Journal*, 20 (1995), 1–16; and *London in the Later Middle Ages*, 76–81; Hanna, *London Literature*, 123–9.

[36] Carlin, *Medieval Southwark*, 30–5, 44–51 (quote at 51).

[37] Barron, 'Centres of Conspicuous Consumption', 2, fig. 1; 8 and n. 40; cf. Marjorie B. Honeybourne, 'A Sketch Map of London in the Time of the Peasant Revolt, 1381', in Ruth Bird, *The Turbulent London of Richard II* (London, 1949), at 156; London, Guildhall, Calendar of Bridgemasters' Account Rolls, Roll 11 (m 1.2), quoted in Fisher, *John Gower*, 341 n. 1. Fisher (*John Gower*, 66) interprets this account as a record of Savage's ownership of the inn, although, as a receipt 'for 14s. 8d., received of increase of rent', it seems rather to indicate his tenant status as the one who 'now holds' the inn.

[38] Gower's will has been printed by Henry J. Todd in *Illustrations of the Lives and Writings of Gower and Chaucer* (London, 1810), 87–90; and tr. Macaulay (iv, pp. xvii–xviii).

[39] *CCR: Richard II, 1381–1385*, 211, 214, 619. Brockhull dealt with Gower in two separate land deals (Fisher, *John Gower*, 53 and n. 56; 54 and n. 58). See below for the other individuals named here and their connections to Gower through the Septvans inheritance (nn. 41–2).

The coincidence of names on a list need not signal a lasting relationship of course. Yet documents for which we might imagine a commercial, impermanent context can actually speak of a much more established social setting. This is especially true of evidence of land transactions, in which access to the vendor in the first place and the ability to secure title after an agreement could depend on extensive networks. I have already quoted Christine Carpenter's remarks on 'the primacy of the personal connection' behind records of formal relationship, and the dispersal of the Septvans inheritance to which Gower was party in the 1360s well illustrates her point.[40] More saga than transaction, Gower's purchase of Aldington Septvans links him to various powerful Kentish names. John, Lord Cobham, headed an inquiry in 1366 into several Septvans alienations (including the Aldington moiety) and was one of the purchasers when Gower sold Aldington Septvans together with Kentwell seven years later.[41] Much later still, Cobham would be glowingly recommended in Gower's *Cronica tripertita* (1400), celebrated as a beacon of virtue amongst corruption and a 'verus amicus' of the realm (*Cronica*, 2. 213–15). Few attract equivalent praise in the poem, although it is difficult to say how much this is due to respect and affection on Gower's part and how much to the ancient, eremitic, and exiled baron's suitability as a foil in the maligning of King Richard. Cobham's relative, Reginald second Baron Cobham of Sterborough, probably counted Aldington Cobham in his inheritance when Gower owned the other moiety of Aldington (and in 1369 he also inherited the town house later known as Cobham's Inn very close to St Mary Overy and in its fee).[42] Most directly, Gower was involved with Nicholas de Louvein as partner in the pursuit of the Septvans inheritance. The two evidently shared custody of the young heir with one Richard Hurst during 1365 and 1366.[43]

The tight-knit group to which these men belonged included several extremely powerful landholders, was at the heart of local politics, and was

[40] Carpenter, 'Gentry and Community', 369; and above, 15.

[41] For the proceedings surrounding William de Septvans's proof of age and alienation of his lands, see *CIPM* xi. 468, and xii. 75–9; *PROME* ii. 291–3, which Fisher sets out in an appendix (*John Gower*, 313–18) and discusses (51–4). For Cobham's purchase of 1373, see Fisher, *John Gower*, 53 and n. 56.

[42] John's and Reginald's grandfathers were half-brothers; see Teresa May, 'The Cobham Family in the Administration of England, 1200–1400', *Arch. Cant.* 82 (1967), 1–31, at 2–3. Reginald's father shared Aldington with the elder Sir William de Septvans; and both moieties were being rented by another Cobham (Henry) in 1346. Reginald held an Aldington manor in 1403. See *Feudal Aids*, iii. 40; *CIPM* xviii. 253. For Cobham's Inn, see Carlin, *Medieval Southwark*, 45; *CIPM* xviii. 254.

[43] *CIPM* xii. 76–7.

never likely to welcome the courtiers who crashed into its political society in the mid-1380s. Local reciprocalist interests such as this group's are written all over the coup of 1388, legible in the texts it generated. Savage and John, Lord Cobham, were two of Kent's largest landholders and both were prominent far beyond the region.[44] Cobham was connected by marriage to the Courtenay earls of Devon and the de Bohun family.[45] He fought in the French wars, and had a long record of diplomatic and administrative service to national government under both Edward III and his grandson.[46] Before his time on the continual council, Cobham was appointed above the young king's tutor Sir Simon Burley to act as the king's personal governor in 1379.[47] Savage was retained by Richard II and became a chamber knight by 1392–3 (but was no longer listed as such by 1395–6). In the early years of Henry IV's reign, he was a steward of the prince of Wales, twice speaker of the commons, and a council member.[48] Savage was, in fact, a vigorous critic of the royal household as speaker and seems even, in 1401, to have called for the abolition of all livery badges (including the king's and his son's).[49]

[44] For the Kentish landholdings of Cobham's father, in 1346, see *Feudal Aids*, iii. 22, 41, 42, 49, 51. For the Sterborough Cobham lands in 1403, see *CIPM* xviii. 250–4. On the limitations of a county focus for this kind of discussion, which I have not very well avoided, see Carpenter, 'Gentry and Community', 340–55; cf. Bennett, *Community, Class and Careerism*, 5–52; and (on a lord's 'country' and county) Given-Wilson, *English Nobility*, 160–1, 172–5.

[45] His wife, Margaret, was the eldest daughter of Hugh de Courtenay, the tenth earl, and Margaret de Bohun, sister to the last earl of Hereford and grand-daughter of Edward I. Other members of Gower's Kentish circle were allied to major noble households by marriage as well. The younger Reginald, Lord Cobham of Sterborough's first wife was daughter of the earl of Stafford, and Reginald's mother was Joan, daughter of Thomas, Lord Berkeley. De Louvein married the earl of Oxford's daughter, Margaret. See May, 'Cobham family', at 2–3; *CP* iv. 298.

[46] For Cobham's military career, his embassies with France, Flanders, and Rome, and his places on major royal commissions, see *Fœdera*, iii/2. 126–7, 136; iii/3. 25, 36, 37, 41, 48–9, 76, 90, 97, 121, 160, 162–3, 184; iii/4. 77; *CPR: Richard II, 1381–1385*, 138 (Mar. 1382); *WC* 24 and n. 3; J. G. Waller, 'The Lords of Cobham, their Monuments, and the Church', *Arch. Cant.* 11 (1877), 49–112, 73–9; *CP* iii. 344.

[47] Anthony Tuck, *Richard II and the English Nobility* (London, 1973), 44.

[48] For Savage's career and connections (his father was attached to the Black Prince and his mother was Richard II's nurse), see J. S. Roskell, 'Sir Arnald Savage of Bobbing: Speaker for the Commons in 1401 and 1404', *Arch. Cant.* 70 (1956), 68–83; Bruce Webster, 'The Community of Kent in the Reign of Richard II', *Arch. Cant.* 100 (1984), 217–29, 225; Given-Wilson, *Royal Household*, 166, 189.

[49] The rolls of parliament for 1404 record Savage's denial of ever making such a request (*PROME* iii. 523); but for the likelihood that he did call for prohibition (whether or not on his own initiative) see Given-Wilson, *Royal Household*, 240. For Savage's parliamentary activity in 1401 and 1404, see Roskell, 'Sir Arnald Savage', 76–8, 80. For the livery debate in general, and gentry objection to livery badges, see below, 188–93.

Their activities on the national scene did not separate these two notables from local politics. On the contrary, there is every sign that Cobham and Savage were tightly bound to goings on south-east of London and to the other Kentish gentry associated with Gower. Apart from its various links to Gower, the group is criss-crossed by connections through marriage, land, and local office. In its political activity and its history of bond-forming it displays the hallmarks of reciprocalism. The Cobhams, Brockhulls, Savages of Bobbing, and Septvanses were four of the most established families in the area.[50] Their Ricardian scions were very prominent on local commissions of the peace, of array, and of specialist inquiry, and were frequently elected as knights of the shire.[51] They cooperated not only in political and administrative duties but in marriage alliances;[52] and it is also worth recalling the way in which the Aldington fees circulated in this gentry circle. The Cobhams of Sterborough and the Septvanses shared the dual manor of Aldington in the fourteenth century, and Sir Thomas de Brockhull joined John, Lord Cobham, in the coalition that bought Aldington Septvans from Gower in 1373, before both moieties of the manor ended up in the Brockhull family.[53] Gower himself had venerable ties to the Cobhams if he was in fact related to Sir Robert Gower, for in 1334 the first Baron Reginald had stood security for Sir Robert when his lord of Athol went over to the Scots.[54]

---

[50] Roskell, 'Sir Arnald Savage', 68; Rosamund Allen, 'Cobham, John, Third Baron Cobham of Cobham (*c.*1320–1408)', *Oxford Dictionary of National Biography* (Oxford, 2004), online edn, www.oxforddnb.com/view/article/5744. Cobham, Brockhull, and Septvans are among the 25 names which Webster finds in the records of feudal aids for both 1346 and 1412 ('Community of Kent', 220).

[51] The third Baron Cobham served on every Kentish commission of the peace in Richard's reign until 1397, and crops up on a variety of local commissions of arbitration, works (a bridge over the Medway seems singularly troublesome), defence, and other administration (e.g. *CPR: Richard II, 1381–1385*, 136, 201, 308, 506, 519, 525, 598; *1385–1389*, 80, 90, 103, 167, 223, 416). Sir Arnold Savage went to three Ricardian parliaments for Kent (1390–1), is named on numerous local commissions, and was twice sheriff. Sir Thomas de Brockhull was appointed sheriff before Savage (1383), was five times knight of the shire (1382–97), and four times justice of the peace in the 1380s. See Webster, 'Community of Kent', 222–3 and n. 28, 225–6; May, 'Cobham Family', 7–10; Allen, 'Cobham, John'; Roskell, 'Sir Arnald Savage', 71–5.

[52] May, 'Cobham Family', at 2–3; Fisher, *John Gower*, 66. The mother of the baronial line of Cooling Cobhams was Joan Septvans, daughter and co-heir of Sir Robert, and the Savages and Cobhams were affined when Sir Arnold's daughter, Eleanor, became Reginald, Lord Cobham of Sterborough's second wife.

[53] *Feudal Aids*, iii. 40; Fisher, *John Gower*, 53–4.

[54] Fisher, *John Gower*, 38–46.

If this group's equilibrium depended on sedimented, reciprocalist exchanges, then the intrusion into local landed society of newcomers from court in the 1380s was calculated to provoke resentment. Such resentment would prove a touchpaper for the explosion of 1388. Anthony Tuck has noted the prominence of Kentish anger among the 1388 commons' hostility towards Simon Burley, and John, Lord Cobham, was a key supporter of the Lords Appellant. The continual council on which he sat had been charged with inquiry into royal expenses and revenues, including all Richard's estate alienations to date.[55]

Several of King Richard's friends abruptly entered Kentish landed community and affairs in the 1380s. The courtier-justice Sir Robert Belknap acquired some fourteen manors in the county in quick time, and four manors came to Sir Nicholas Brembre, the merchant capitalist and former mayor of London whose intimacy with Richard would prove fatal in 1388.[56] Most disruptive of all was Sir Simon Burley. The second son of a minor Herefordshire landowner, Burley rose to power at court and eventually attained land to support his position by very controversial means when he secured the rich Leybourne inheritance in Kent (an estate made over to the endowment of several religious houses by Edward III).[57] He immediately thrust to local administrative and jurisdictional pre-eminence from his new proprietorial base. After becoming constable of Dover and warden of the Cinque Ports in 1384, he was regularly appointed justice of the peace and commissioner of

[55] Tuck, *Richard II and the English Nobility*, 76, 125–6. Cf. Favent, 21. See also Anthony Goodman, *The Loyal Conspiracy: The Lords Appellant under Richard II* (London, 1971), 35–41, on the regional make-up of support for the Appellants; and *WC* 166–74 and Saul, *Richard II*, 161–6 for the continual council and its domestic remit (which it exceeded).

[56] Webster, 'Community of Kent', 221. For Brembre's rise to royal favour, see Bird, *Turbulent London*, 2–7, 90–1. Justice Belknap would be among the judges who provided the king with ammunition against parliament and the continual council in 1387.

[57] John L. Leland, 'Burley, Sir Simon (1336?–1388)', *Oxford Dictionary of National Biography* (Oxford, 2004), online edn, May 2006, www.oxforddnb.com/view/article/4036. For the Leybourne inheritance, see Given-Wilson, 'Richard II and his Grandfather's Will', esp. 327–32. For the theory that the Kentish estates were to be part of a package for Burley along with the comital title of Huntingdon, see also Tuck, *Richard II and the English Nobility*, 75–6; and J. N. Palmer, 'The Parliament of 1385 and the Constitutional Crisis of 1386', *Speculum*, 46 (1971), 477–90, 490. Cf. Henry Knighton, *Knighton's Chronicle 1337–1396*, ed. and tr. G. H. Martin (Oxford, 1995), 336–8. Saul conjectures that parliament failed to confirm the promotion partly because it 'offended against the commons' deeply held and firmly traditional conception of honour', which held a title to be 'above all a reflection of a man's inherited standing' (*Richard II*, 117). The continual council unsuccessfully put pressure on Burley to surrender the Leybourne manors.

array, and, in June 1386, was named sole member of the previously nine-strong county quorum.[58] Burley and the others had no inherited claim to such prominence in Kentish affairs. Their intrusion seems to have sharpened in Cobham and other local men of substance an awareness of their own local prerogatives. Noting Burley's absence among attestors to Cobham family charters, Nigel Saul surmises that the local reaction to Burley and his 'high-handed' administration was 'to close ranks against him and make him a virtual outcast in his adopted county'.[59] When the duke of Gloucester and his allies seized control in 1388, Burley was to find himself tragically short of friends.

Political practice by text in 1388

The appeal and impeachments of 1388 are performative texts of one of the most significant crises of English politics in the fourteenth century. They also share a textual environment with *Confessio Amantis* courtesy of reciprocalist discourse. The 1388 texts naturalize aristocratic reciprocalism and attack Richard's court as magnificent, collecting and cloaking particular histories and motivations under an ideology that is coherent (more or less) and enabling (gruesomely). The appeal and impeachments succeed by reproducing the operative contemporary opposition between asymmetric reciprocalism and magnificence in a powerfully focused way (much more directly instrumental and danger-ous than Gower's poetry). They demonstrate the potential of this discourse in a particular context in the 1380s.

The appeal seeks to couch its rebellious energies in an authoritative language, to resort to a historically inviolable (and largely implicit) model of responsible, reciprocalist governance. Its short preamble, designed to establish the 'facts' of the process by which the appeal came before parliament, strenuously attempts to associate the Appellants' radical and innovative attack on the centre with the ordinary interests of 'the king and kingdom', repeating that phrase (*le roi et soun roialme*) eleven times in the version in the parliament roll.[60] (The Appellants had reason to over-egg

---

[58] *CPR: Richard II, 1381–1385*, 348, 590; *1385–1389*, 81, 253; Saul, *Richard II*, 115–17, 163–4; Webster, 'Community of Kent', 221.

[59] Saul, *Richard II*, 164 and n. 52.

[60] *PROME* iii. 229. Versions of the appeal are also printed in *WC* 236–68; Knighton, *Knighton's Chronicle*, 452–96. The preamble uses 'le roi et soun roialme' in three volleys of three when designating appeal procedure. One of these volleys is one short in the Westminster chronicle.

their legitimacy because appeal in parliament for treasonous accroachment was unprecedented procedure.[61]) Similarly, the texts assume a natural and static hierarchy of commons, lords, and king. 'Common profit' stems from the flow of power up and down through each tier of this hierarchy. The commons' interests are represented by the nobles and the king is set at the apex, secured by the counsels of his nobles.[62] The general accusation of the appeal is that the accused have been accroaching (*accrochantz*) to themselves royal power. The accroachment charge allowed judicial proceedings to assume that a reciprocalist royal *intention* remained intact (but suppressed). Accroachment preserves the idea of the king's representativeness as *doxa* (in Bourdieu's sense of that which is taken for granted and beyond question), while alleging that the exchanges of his household have been misdirected by unrepresentative counsel.[63] In the appeal, the treason in accroachment lies in excluding from royal authority its natural informants (here the nobility representing the commons).[64] In article after article, the exoneration of Richard for direct acts of his will accepts that those with access to the king have substantive influence on royal power, so that, by extension, legitimate counsellors have a full role to play in government. Furthermore, the appeal prescribes the king's obligations to his subjects by oath. The coronation oath is cited in several clauses, and the second article's inference that subjects representing the common interest of the kingdom (that is, the Lords Appellant) can bind the king to make a new oath is remarkable.[65] The appeal enshrines a mutual, as opposed to

[61] For the novelty and arbitrariness of the Appellants' procedure, authorized by parliament's unspecified 'ancient custom' and 'law and usage' (*ley et cours du parlement; PROME* iii. 236), see Alan Rogers, 'Parliamentary Appeals of Treason in the Reign of Richard II', *American Journal of Legal History*, 8 (1964), 95–124, 95–117; J. G. Bellamy, *The Law of Treason in England in the Later Middle Ages* (Cambridge, 1970), 95–6 (on treason and accroachment); Saul, *Richard II*, 191–3.

[62] Gower's image of rulers borne up by advisers (so that 'the pouer | Of hem that ben the worldes guides | With good consail on alle sides' should be 'kept upriht'; *CA*, prol. 144–7) is of the same mould.

[63] Cf. Watts, *Henry VI*, 18. For the law of accroachment in the period, see Bellamy, *Law of Treason*, 62–74, 95–8. For *doxa*, see Bourdieu, *Theory of Practice*, 164–71.

[64] The deflection of blame from king to accroachers demands some severe textual contortions. So Neville, de Vere, and company 'ont fait le roy mander' (made the king order) his council to fix shire elections, 'firent le roy comander' (caused the king to order) levies for de Vere against the senior Appellants (cf. art. 39), and even caused Richard to inform ('notifier') *themselves* that they were appealed of treason. See arts. 36–8 (*PROME* iii. 235). On counsellors' 'stirring and moving' and its later valency, see Watts, *Henry VI*, 61–3.

[65] *PROME* iii. 230. The implicit (reserved) claim was made good when Richard renewed his coronation oath at the end of the parliament (*WC* 294, 342). The king had already been obliged to swear his personal oath to the Appellants during the events preceding the Merciless Parliament (*WC* 228).

unilateral or 'high', concept of treason, based on reciprocal *trouthe* rather than the prince's uncontestable claim to obedience.[66]

The subjects to whom the king owes a duty are imagined in two tiers—the nobility and 'the people' or commons. The commons need access to the king to receive justice, while the nobility (the social specification of 'bones counseillers') require access both to receive justice and to give their 'good will' and advice (art. 3, *PROME* iii. 230). Generally speaking, the articles of impeachment, presented by the commons (or by the Appellants and the commons according to the Westminster chronicler's text[67]), pay more attention to the role of the commons than does the appeal presented by the lords alone, but they never confuse the ranking of the tiers. Article 10, for example, protests that the chamber knights 'ought to have informed the good lords and peers of the kingdom' (*PROME* iii. 242) of the appellees' treasons, assuming a clear hierarchy of responsibility for the good of the kingdom.

The 1388 texts enlist and ennoble reciprocalism principally through a strong antithesis. They present opponents' behaviour as magnificent and ubiquitously anathematize magnificence as antithetical to common profit, causing the 'undoing of the king and his kingdom'.[68] The accroachers' abuses are essentially arbitrary, so that the appellees are rewarded 'saunz...desert de eux' (without desert in themselves; *PROME* iii. 230). The abuses are, in particular, unmoderated by claims of history and local conditions (and are consequently excessive and exclusive). In several articles, the abrogation of history, place, or rank seems to determine or intensify the scandal and treason of an act. Thus, King Richard's demand for parliamentary indemnity for his friends is 'contrary to the ancient ordinances and liberties of parliament' (art. 16, *PROME* iii. 232; cf. arts. 24, 36). Negotiations with Charles VI acquire added calumny because conducted with no regard for rank or origin, partly through 'persons of lowly condition (*petit estat*), as well aliens as denizens'.[69]

The accroachers' control of patronage simultaneously dislodges the king from his apex role and, by causing him to give within the appellees' 'affinite', makes him an exclusive private patron (arts. 6–7, *PROME* iii. 230). The impeachment of Burley asserts that he threw away

---

[66] For these opposing concepts of treason, and the development of the 'high' form in the late fourteenth century, see Richard Firth Green, *A Crisis of Truth: Literature and Law in Ricardian England* (Philadelphia, 1999), 206–21; and below, 229–30.

[67] *PROME* iii. 241; *WC* 268.

[68] Cf. art. 6 and impeachment art. 13 (*PROME* iii. 230, 242).

[69] Arts. 28–9 (*PROME* iii. 234).

resources on Bohemians and other 'aliens'. Most of the 'aliens' in question presumably had a claim to belonging at court through Queen Anne, but being Bohemian (or associated with Bohemians) made them vulnerable to representation as outside acceptable, established structures of exchange. In a conjunction which acquires particular resonance with Gower's description of the magnificent court of Love and its 'newe guise of Beawme' (*CA* 8. 2470), otherness from normative (order-giving) social structures implies excess. By gifts to the 'abundance (*grant pleinte*) of aliens', the king is 'greatly impoverished (*grantement enpoverez*)' and the people 'utterly oppressed' (impeachment art. 7; *PROME* iii. 242). Outside the hierarchy that makes up the realm, the Bohemians block and divert its proper conduits for resources.[70]

The exclusiveness of sovereign power under the influence of the accroachers is presented in the extremely suspect language of 'covin' and private association. The appellees work 'par lour faulx covein' (by their false covin; arts. 3, 4, *PROME* iii. 230; cf. art. 19) and conspire that their advice should be followed 'so privily (*si privement*) that none should know of it until it had been done' (art. 28, *PROME* iii. 234). Those who cooperate with them, such as royal justices and clerk, lawyer and poet Thomas Usk, are 'de lour covyne' (of their covin; art. 26, *PROME* iii. 234).[71] The appellees' refusal of the expectations of established political networks (those who should 'know of it') sees them placed outside transparent, safe socialization altogether; it makes their political relations and operations threateningly impenetrable. The opacity of covin contributes to an impression that the appellees' political association is conjured up and shameful, not evolved from a respectable sedimentary history of exchanges. This idea of the covin's treasons as ruptures of novelty in history's continuum is intensified by the texts' preoccupation with the past as an unvariegated and inviolable arbiter of the present. Richard's alleged grant of suzerainty to de Vere with the ducal title of Ireland, for example, is held to defy a formidably complete and unified past in which Ireland has been 'from time immemorial' subject to the kings of England (art. 11, *PROME* iii. 231; cf. art. 5). The

---

[70] For grievances against the extravagance of Richard's household which came to a head under Appellant rule, see Given-Wilson, *Royal Household*, 110–38.

[71] For Usk and politics in the 1380s, see Paul Strohm, 'Politics and Poetics: Usk and Chaucer in the 1380s', in Lee Patterson (ed.), *Literary Practice and Social Change in Britain, 1380–1530* (Berkeley, Calif., 1990), 83–112; Marion Turner, *Chaucerian Conflict: Languages of Antagonism in Late Fourteenth-Century London* (Oxford, 2007), 93–126; and 'Conflict', in Paul Strohm (ed.), *Middle English*, Oxford Twenty-First Century Approaches to Literature, 1 (Oxford, 2007), 263–6.

article's formulaic account of history and political geography has no brief for the fragmentary conquerings of Henry II and others.

A totalizing imperative pre-empts the imagination of counter-exchanges that answer the covin. It corroborates the covin's magnificent separation from the past with an intention to deny reciprocal interaction (and the possibility of political leverage against it) in the future. The accroachers, and the corrupted king, seek to nullify the meaning or existence of any outside the covin. The appellees' 'faulx coveine' 'bars' the good effects of the lords' counsel—their legitimate political signification (art. 3, *PROME* iii. 230). A general clause preceding three more on the parliament of 1386 claims that enemies of the appellees 'dared not speak' (*n'oserent parler*) of their tribulations 'for fear of death' (*PROME* iii. 231), and the next clause (art. 15) imagines the extirpation of the extra-covin:

Et sur ceo les ditz traitours et mesfesours veantz ceste bone et honurable oppinioun de parlement, et pur desturber celle bone purpos par lour faulx counsail, firent qe nostre seignour le roi commanda a meire de Loundres de faire sudeinement lever un graunt poar de gentz de Loundres, d'occire et mettre au mort touz les ditz seignours et communs, hors pris ceux qe furrunt de lour coveine.[72]

And thereupon the said traitors and misfesors, seeing this good and honourable opinion of parliament, and to disrupt this good purpose by their false counsel, caused our lord the king to order the mayor of London to arrange to be suddenly levied a great power of the people of London to kill and put to death all the said lords and commons except those who were of their covin.

The totalizing force of the plan described is both temporal and spatial. It is as a flashpoint of annihilation (of both 'oppinioun' and persons) epicentred on the covin—taking hold 'sudeinement' in order 'd'occire et mettre au mort'. It confronts not selected targets but seeks to negate all ('touz') that is not the covin. The appeal's totalization of the appellees' activity also encompasses a kind of instrumentality—a forespeaking (in Fradenburg's term) of individuals' contributions that excludes being and signification without the destruction of person.[73] The Londoners and their mayor occupy this position in article 15, as far as they feature at all.

---

[72] *PROME* iii. 231. Proving that magnificence can be differently valued, art. 17 endorses a totalizing strategy in the Appellant cause: 'that no person should counsel the king nor influence him in any way contrary to the said ordinance and statute [enabling the continual council]; and if anyone should do so, on the first occasion he would lose all his goods and chattels; and on the second offence, he would suffer the penalty of life and limb' (*PROME* iii. 232). The previous article blames the accroachers for a parallel exclusion of (parliamentary) counsel.

[73] See Fradenburg, 'Manciple's Servant Tongue', 88–9.

By construing their only permitted relationship to the royal will as purely instrumental, the appeal submerges all those who are not particular enemies of the appellees in the totalizing discourse of covin, whereby they can have no worth except as forespoken signifiers of the (accroached) royal will and power.[74] Particular enemies are already nullified as objects of hate (art. 1, *PROME* iii. 230) and violence.

The appeal and impeachments of 1388 fit the Appellants' enemies into a force-enabling reciprocalist framework. However novel or alienating the royalists' exchanges actually were (and the story of Burley in Kent attests that these categories were not mere fictions), the ability to describe them in terms of magnificence against a reciprocalist political-ethical context was the king's opponents' essential political leverage. Discussions akin to K. B. McFarlane's, which dismisses the Appellants' 'few and half-hearted constitutional professions' as at best a reaction to Richard's resort to the judges in 1387, and as reflecting principles scarcely 'even skin-deep', diminish the political principles and discursive structures upon which the Appellants relied, sincerely or otherwise. McFarlane sidelines political language that other historians would now argue was crucial in determining the scope and success of the Appellants' actions.[75]

In the February parliament, reciprocalism justified a lethal escalation of opposition to the royal centre. The fuse that burned down to the parliamentary trials had been lit by Richard's famous questions to the judges, which elicited what one historian has called 'the most remarkable statement of the royal prerogative ever made in England in the Middle Ages'.[76] Strenuously focused on the king's will as the initiator of parliamentary exchanges and on the continual council as a statutory derogation of the king's regality, the questions and answers set out the most magnificent construction of kingship that the common law could furnish. The ensuing crisis nonetheless proved the continued ability of great householders to

---

[74] Later articles are primarily concerned with such instrumentality or forespeaking. Arts. 19 and 33 describe oaths or 'obligaciouns' that are comprehensive and unilateral, imposing no duty on the king. Those sworn must surrender their being to a blank, almost undelimited royal will ('a vivere et morrer', to live and die with the king; *PROME* iii. 235). For the Londoners' oath of allegiance of October 1387 (art. 33), see *Calendar of Letter-Books Preserved among the Archives of the Corporation of the City of London at the Guildhall: Letter-Book H*, ed. Reginald R. Sharpe (London, 1907), 314–15; and Bird, *Turbulent London*, 92 and n. 3.

[75] K. B. McFarlane, *Lancastrian Kings and Lollard Knights* (Oxford, 1972), 28; cf. Saul, *Richard II*, 181–2 and see above, 26–7 and n. 56.

[76] Saul, *Richard II*, 174. For the questions to the judges and the episode's impact, see *WC* 196–202; Knighton, *Knighton's Chronicle*, 392–8; S. B. Chrimes, 'Richard II's Questions to the Judges, 1387', *Law Quarterly Review*, 72 (1956), 365–90; Saul, *Richard II*, 173–5.

challenge and curtail the power of the centre. The rebellious lords may even have deposed the king for a matter of days when they were closed up in the Tower with him at the very end of December.[77] The parliamentary trials produced their most developed expression of opposition. The council commissioned in November 1386 had been working to control expenditure in the royal household, and the trial texts similarly seek to make exchanges of power (in the form of gifts and words, land and counsel) conform to historically sedimented hierarchical patterns. Exchanges are illegitimated because unprecedented; illicit gifts are represented as traumatically lacking either a past (de Vere's new rights in Ireland) or recognized kinds of recipient (patronage of Bohemians and 'alien' courtiers). So Richard's opponents sought to recontain all manner of royal exchanges within a reciprocalist ideology.

ROYAL MAGNIFICENCE

For his part, Richard II was only scratching the surface of magnificent gestures and representations of his regality when he provoked the reciprocalist aggression of 1388. Over the following decade he would go much further in exploiting magnificent discourses of kingship, which invariably stressed power over obligation in the role of the monarch. Not since Henry III's theatre of piety and daily grand spectacles of almsgiving had an English king cultivated a persona so out of reach of all his subjects.[78] Much earlier, Angevin predecessors (with the partial exception of Richard I) had centralized power without, it seems, embracing theocratic or Roman law ideas of sovereign or princely authority. Adopting the sociological language of Max Weber, Michael Clanchy has described how the late twelfth-century expansion and professionalization of royal justice challenged seigneurial franchises bureaucratically, by 'routinizing' and depersonalizing, not (directly) mystifying, the crown's authority.[79] Later, Edward I's lawyers invoked

---

[77] See Saul, *Richard II*, 188–90.
[78] See Nicholas Vincent, *The Holy Blood: King Henry III and the Westminster Blood Relic* (Cambridge, 2001), 7–19, 185, 191–6. Binski, *Westminster Abbey*, esp. 44, 50–4, 84–6; D. A. Carpenter, 'An Unknown Obituary of King Henry III from the Year 1263', and 'The Burial of King Henry III, the Regalia and Royal Ideology', in *Reign of Henry III*, 255, 438; Carpenter, *Struggle for Mastery*, 338–9, 453–4.
[79] Clanchy, *Memory to Written Record*, esp. 66–8, citing Max Weber, *The Theory of Social and Economic Organization*, ed. and tr. A. M. Henderson and Talcott Parsons (London, 1947), esp. 363–73.

civilian authorities to place the royal prerogative beyond the law, but historians note that the king was careful not to provoke great men by forcing such claims (for example by arbitrary exploitation of feudal incidents). Richard II's mature kingship was 'unusually combative and divisive', more interested than Edward's in turning the theory of majesty into practice without concessions.[80] Ricardian rule, especially in the 1390s, now looks more like Tudor absolutism than Plantagenet monarchy. In Saul's view, Richard's kingship appears less dislocated than this comparison suggests when seen in a continental context of assertive and self-consciously mighty courts in the late fourteenth century.[81] Yet Richard (despite efforts in the north-west midlands) did not secure, or could not in crisis mobilize, a power-base adequate to his brand of magnificence, which was far more aggressive than Henry III's but just as brittle when it came to a trial of strength.[82]

Whatever heights royal magnificence was to reach in the 1390s, the tensions of the 1380s show that in those years it already had a place in the Ricardian conception of kingship. The 1388 appeal's sense that the crown has let slip its bond to the great men of the kingdom is inverted by the questions to the judges and by other royal designations of power. Anthony Tuck has argued that Richard's management of the nobility in 1385, in particular, evinced a view of titled nobles as embodiments of the king's majesty (to echo Lee Patterson) rather than landed lords in their own right.[83] When the earl of Buckingham became the duke of Gloucester in 1385, for instance, his new rank was supported by an annuity assigned upon the customs not the conventional and more permanent grant of lands. Tuck contends that such totally novel means of conferment 'seemed to undermine the relationship between

[80] Carpenter, *Struggle for Mastery*, 152–8, 233–42, 258–61, 473, 478; Maddicott, 'Edward I and Local Government'; quotation from Castor, *The King, the Crown, and the Duchy of Lancaster*, 17.

[81] Carpenter, *Locality and Polity*, 637–8; Caroline M. Barron, 'The Deposition of Richard II', in John Taylor and Wendy Childs (eds), *Politics and Crisis in Fourteenth-Century England* (Gloucester, 1990), 145; and 'Tyranny'; Nigel Saul, 'The Kingship of Richard II', in Goodman and Gillespie (eds), *Richard II: The Art of Kingship*, 37–41.

[82] Given-Wilson, *Royal Household*, 222–6; Bennett, *Community, Class and Careerism*; R. R. Davies, 'Richard II and the Principality of Chester 1397–9', in F. R. H. Du Boulay and Caroline M. Barron (eds), *The Reign of Richard II: Essays in Honour of May McKisack* (London, 1971), 256–79.

[83] Tuck, *Richard II and the English Nobility*, 84–5; Patterson, 'Court Politics', 17. I would like to thank Marion Turner for alerting me to the discussions and primary material considered in this paragraph.

land and status which had become so firmly established in Edward III's reign'.[84] Suggestively, Tuck juxtaposes this fiscal strategy with an image of nobility as royal adornment that received several iterations in 1385. Royal charters for Richard's new creations in that year (including Gloucester's dukedom) imagine nobles as shedding light (back) onto or from the crown and, in the earl of Suffolk's charter, as 'gems' and 'precious stones' that 'glitter' (*micare*) and 'shimmer' (*coruscare*) on the crown.[85] The symbolism is thus most elaborate in the charter that 'raised from low estate' a merchant's son, as the charge would run in the commons' impeachment of Suffolk in October 1386 (*PROME* iii. 217). The imagery construes nobles as signs of royal authority, to 'honour our diadem' (*PROME* iii. 207), and accords with a policy of decoupling nobility from territorial power. It casts a glare over reciprocalist notions of land going to land and status going to status. Unlike Gloucester, Richard's favoured officers received generous landed endowment, but this patronage expressed the king's power to give rather than the recipient's obligative aristocratic status. Richard discusses dukes and earls as the king's jewels rather than tenants-in-chief.

Expressions and policy of magnificence were to grow after the restrictions occasioned by the continual council (1386–7) and Appellant rule (1388–9), and the short-lived assertiveness capped by the questions to the judges in between. Taking cues from his father's, the Black Prince's Aquitainian court, and from other continental courts, especially those of the Valois and of Queen Anne's family in Bohemia, Richard's kingship produced some extraordinary flourishes in household material culture, iconography, decorum, and legislation.[86] The exaltation of the crown reached new and precarious heights from 1397 in particular. Two pieces of art made for Richard during this period or slightly earlier are arresting images of the king exalted, that is, tending towards a status beyond obligation by inferiors. Both present an image of the youthful crowned

---

[84] Tuck, *Richard II and the English Nobility*, 84. Tuck also discusses the ennoblement without tenurial support of John Beauchamp of Holt (84–5).

[85] *PROME* iii. 205–7 (quotes at 207); cf. Tuck, *Richard II and the English Nobility*, 84. For Suffolk's career, see Saul, *Richard II*, 117–20.

[86] Saul, *Richard II*, 342–58; cf. Gervase Mathew, *The Court of Richard II* (London, 1968), 1–11, 21–52. See also Scheifele, 'Visual Arts'; Binski, *Westminster Abbey*, 194–5, 202–4 (for Bohemian influence in painting and illumination); Kay Staniland, 'Extravagance or Regal Necessity? The Clothing of Richard II', Marian Campbell, '"White Harts and Coronets": The Jewellery and Plate of Richard II', and Lisa Monnas, 'Fit for a King: Figured Silks Shown in the Wilton Diptych', in Gordon et al. (eds), *The Regal Image of Richard II and the Wilton Diptych* (London, 1997), 85–114, 165–77.

king decisively separated from the ordinary order of things. A large portrait of Richard enthroned with orb and sceptre, apparently commissioned for Westminster, shows the king frontally, full-square and impassive, an earthly imitation of Christ in judgement. The *imitatio Christi* evokes a theocratic conception of the prince as vicar of Christ and *semideus*. Paul Binski is struck by the uncompromising quality of the 'distant state likeness, confronting the viewer and stressing the distance between image and spectator by a manifest display of rank'. He notes the isolation (that is, the non-exchanging quality) of the enthroned figure, which 'lends to the image a decidedly autocratic aspect, the trappings and stance of power displayed, but not conferred'.[87]

Richard cuts a much less imposing and more communicative figure on the interior panels of the celebrated Wilton Diptych, but the overall statement of regality is more remarkable. Critics contest particular symbolic meanings, but that the panels express some dense and sublime notion of kingship is not in dispute. Supported in a kind of adoration tableau in the left-hand panel by the royal saints Edmund and Edward the Confessor, and St John the Baptist, Richard is also receiving a blessing and, it seems, a banner from the infant Christ, who is poised in the arms of his mother and surrounded by a company of garlanded angels in the right-hand panel. The red-cross banner, topped with an orb enclosing an island, may represent the Virgin's entrusting of the British Isles to Richard.[88] Whether Richard is here being granted a particular *imperium* or not, the heavenly exchange appears specially privileged and intimate, most strikingly because the attendant angels boldly display Richard's own white hart badge (along with the broomcod collar of Charles VI of France) while the king boasts the same livery. The angels rest their hands and animated looks on each other and the Virgin, and their visible association with Richard draws him into this intimate circle. The badges and gestures curiously domesticate the heavenly host, but the exquisitely feathered angels are so ethereal (and the gold-rich diptych so splendid) that the more abiding effect is to elevate gift presentation (and petition if the angels are read as Richard's

---

[87] Binski, *Westminster Abbey*, 204 (see 203–4 for the portrait and its artistic and political contexts).

[88] For this interpretation, see Nigel Morgan, 'The Signification of the Banner in the Wilton Diptych', in Gordon et al. (eds), *Regal Image*, 179–88; Anthony Goodman, introduction, in Goodman and Gillespie (eds), *Richard II: The Art of Kingship*, 10–12; Scheifele, 'Visual Arts', 267–8. For alternative readings of the Diptych and its banner, see the articles by Dillian Gordon and Maurice Keen in *Regal Image*, 19–26, 189–96; Bennett, 'Wider Realm', 203 and n. 66 (conjecturing Ireland on the standard's boss).

sponsors). It is as though the diptych has shifted Richard's household exchange into a transcendent realm. The scene asks how any member of mortal society could be adequate partner to a king who belongs to an exchange situation at once so apparently natural yet so dizzying.

The king could dramatize the iconography of the Westminster portrait and the Wilton Diptych by actual 'crown-wearings'. These were ceremonial spectacles occasioned by feast days or other celebrations; they ritualized kingship and, as William of Malmesbury once wrote, displayed 'the glory of the king as he went about exalted by his bejewelled diadem'.[89] The *Eulogium* continuator may be describing such ceremony when noting that Richard II would sit enthroned in state from dinner until vespers 'nulli loquens sed singulos aspiciens' (talking to no one but watching everyone), during which time none might cross his gaze without gestures of deference.[90] Here the magnificent relationship with viewers implicit in the Westminster and Wilton paintings is played out. The constraining of their bodies by those present signifies an abasement of self, a signalling of impotence to initiate or require any exchange from the crowned prince. It recognizes the sovereign's belonging to an other and transcendent sphere. The totalizing effect of the king's unengageable gaze, blank to the particular worth of any individual, is also especially marked in the *Continuatio eulogii* account and the Westminster portrait. Indeed, the whole world symbolized by the orb in the portrait is (already) in the king's grasp and beneath his gaze.[91]

Further theory and symbolism of Ricardian magnificence supported the image of the king crowned in majesty. New, grandiose, and more deferential forms of address were encouraged. Saul has shown that 'Your highness' ('vestrae celsitudinis'), 'your royal majesty' ('vostre roiale mageste'), and 'prince' superseded 'my lord' in parliamentary petitions and letters in the 1390s, signalling the same sovereign and theocratic

---

[89] William of Malmesbury, *Vita Wulfstani*, ed. R. R. Darlington, Camden Soc. 3rd ser. 40 (London, 1928), 2. 12 (34), quoted in Bartlett, *England under the Norman and Angevin Kings*, 128. For a treatise on the regalia by William Sudbury, a monk of Westminster, answering a question from the king near the time he was asking the judges about his prerogative, see Sudbury, *De primis regalibus ornamentis regni Angliae*, in Richard of Cirencester, *Speculum historiale de gestis regum Angliae*, ed. J. E. B. Mayor, Rolls Ser. (London, 1863–9), ii. 26–39; and Patricia J. Eberle, 'Richard II and the Literary Arts', in Goodman and Gillespie (eds), *Richard II: The Art of Kingship*, 239–40.

[90] *Eulogium historiarum sive temporis*, ed. Frank Scott Haydon, Rolls Ser. (London, 1858–63), iii. 378, tr. Given-Wilson in *Chronicles of the Revolution*, 68.

[91] On the totalizing impetus of the idea of the sovereign, see Fradenburg, 'Manciple's Servant Tongue', and below, 245–59.

quality bodied forth in the Westminster portrait.[92] Richard revitalized the cult of Edward the Confessor which had been central to Henry III's princely piety but had languished under the three Edwards since. In 1395, Richard was emblematically 'wed' to the saint when the royal arms were impaled with the Confessor's (as visible in the heraldry on the exterior of the Wilton Diptych). Richard also sought to advertise divine sanction for his kingship by the specially precious chrism of St Thomas of Canterbury, which may have been intended in rivalry to the heavenly oil of Clovis's baptism that anointed French kings.[93] Crusading and millenarian prophecies (at least one of these associated with the holy oil of St Thomas) seem to have informed grand designs. Diplomacy was in train in 1397 to have Richard elected Holy Roman Emperor in place of his brother-in-law, the emperor-elect Wenceslas. Richard was at least envisaged acting in 1397 as 'entier emperour de son roialme d'Engleterre' (*PROME* iii. 343/Jan. 1397 mem. 2), and Walsingham remarks that Richard's lavish new peerage creations in the same year earned the epithet 'duketti' 'in derision' (*derisorie*), suggesting that they were the (self-aggrandizing) toys or ciphers of a petty tyrant.[94]

The means by which Richard promoted a majestic and thereby quasi-divine, theocratic idea of his rule (including forms of address and ceremonial protocols) were influenced by writings of civil law. Giles of Rome's *De regimine principum* has been nominated as a particular influence and Richard and his advisers found civilian ideas of the subject's unilateral duty of obedience and of the prince as supreme lawgiver appealing.[95] These ideas provided the essence of the chancellor's speech when, in an

[92] Nigel Saul, 'Richard II and the Vocabulary of Kingship', *EHR* 110 (1995), 854–77; cf. 'nostre tresexcellent tresredoute tressoverain et tresgracious seigneur le Roi' on a blank charter from the citizens of Essex, echoing the parliamentary petitions of 1391: Barron, 'Tyranny', appendix, 18; *PROME* iii. 290.

[93] *Annales*, 223, 297–300; Shelagh Mitchell, 'Richard II: Kingship and the Cult of Saints', in Gordon et al. (eds), *Regal Image*, 115–24; Binski, *Westminster Abbey*, 199–200; Saul, 'Kingship of Richard II', 41–3; T. A. Sandquist, 'The Holy Oil of St Thomas of Canterbury', in T. A. Sandquist and M. R. Powicke (eds), *Essays in Medieval History Presented to Bertie Wilkinson* (Toronto, 1969), 330–44; John W. McKenna, 'How God Became an Englishman', in Delloyd J. Guth and John W. McKenna (eds), *Tudor Rule and Revolution: Essays for G. R. Elton* (Cambridge, 1982), 27–8.

[94] Sandquist, 'Holy Oil', 331–2, 337–9; Bennett, 'Wider Realm', 197, 202; *Annales*, 199 (the imperial title), and 223, tr. Given-Wilson in *Chronicles of the Revolution*, 74 (the 'duketti'); cf. Given-Wilson, *English Nobility*, 52.

[95] Richard H. Jones, *The Royal Policy of Richard II: Absolutism in the Later Middle Ages* (Oxford, 1968), 144, 154–63; Saul, *Richard II*, 385–8; cf. Saul, 'Kingship of Richard II', 44–7; and Nigel E. Saul, 'Richard II's Ideas of Kingship', in Gordon et al. (eds), *Regal Image*, 30 on a tract attributed to John Thorpe, treasurer of Ireland. For introductory discussions of civilian (and canonistic) ideas of majesty and its qualification, see Canning, *Medieval*

already menacing atmosphere in London, he confirmed the tone for the compliant parliament of September 1397, in which the government moved ruthlessly against the king's enemies of 1387–8.[96] Taking as his text 'There shall be one king for all' (Ezekiel 37: 22), Bishop Stafford dwelt on the patriarchal power and prerogatives of the monarch, the subject's obligation to be 'obedient to the king and his laws' and the need to restore the king's 'liberty and power' if it had been in any way diminished.[97] Unlike, for example, the coronation oath, this speech holds duty to belong wholly to those beneath the king in the social order. Where his subjects are utterly obliged to the king, there is no guarantee of benefits from the king except his own will and personal ethic, idealized as 'roiale benignite' (*PROME* iii. 347). Famously, at his deposition, Richard was accused of having ruled by 'the impulse of his will' (*arbitrium voluntatis*) over the laws of the realm, 'frequently' declaring 'that his laws were in his mouth, or sometimes in his breast: and that he alone could alter and create the laws of his realm' (*PROME* iii. 419).[98]

Civilian ideas of princely rule nourished a disposition that is legible in Richard's questions to the judges of 1387 and found its apotheosis in measures that sought to legislate the totalized obedience and nil dissent which Bishop Stafford had propounded as the guarantee of the king's peace. Parliament re-enacted the provision of the Statute of Westminster against *scandalum magnatum* (or slander against the great) in 1378 and again in 1388, and extended its protection to superior royal officials.[99] Marion Turner locates this legislation within a wider, 'obsessive redefining of what constituted treason' that was part of Richard's resistance to dissenting voices across his reign.[100] The government rendered the burden of treason one-sided in the king's favour.[101] As early as 1396, Richard was deploying his infamous blank charters by which subjects offered themselves up, as traitors, to total and

---

Political Thought, 133–4, 162–7; Antony Black, *Political Thought in Europe 1250–1450* (Cambridge, 1992), 136–46. Black (1–13) gives a helpful introduction to medieval kinds or 'languages' of political thinking.

[96] For this parliament, see e.g. *PROME* iii. 347–85; Given-Wilson, ed. and tr., *Chronicles of the Revolution*, 54–74; Saul, *Richard II*, 375–81, 388.

[97] *PROME* iii. 347/Sep. 1397 mem. 13. For fainter variations on the obedience theme in chancellors' speeches of Oct. 1383 and Jan. 1395, see *PROME* iii. 150 (mem. 10), 329 (mem. 5).

[98] Given-Wilson, ed. and tr., *Chronicles of the Revolution*, 168–9, 177–8.

[99] *SR* ii. 9, 59; Green, *Crisis of Truth*, 244.

[100] Turner, *Chaucerian Conflict*, 8–11 (quote at 10).

[101] Green, *Crisis of Truth*, 222.

unilateral exchanges with their sovereign king.[102] In the January parliament of 1397, a petition calling for reform of the king's household saw its presenter, Thomas Haxey, a clerk and a proctor for the abbot of Selby (Yorkshire), adjudged a traitor after the king declared that those who 'presume any ordinance or governance of the king's person, or his household', greatly offend 'against his regality and his royal majesty' (*PROME* iii. 339).[103] The snuffing out of Haxey's complaint was apparently the occasion of a totalizing rule against dissent, which, in Turner's phrase, effectively 'made disagreeing with [Richard] an offence punishable by death'.[104] Haxey was retrospectively condemned, that is, under a lords pronouncement that any person who 'moved or stirred' (*moverit vel excitaverit*) the commons or anyone else to propose reform touching the king's 'person, or our rule, or our regality' should be judged a traitor (*Rot. parl.* iii. 408). Haxey was pardoned promptly, but the days of conciliar control of the king's household were evidently long gone. The parliament had witnessed a stark, authoritarian statement that obedience was the tone required by Richard's kingship and, with the attack on former Appellants later that year, there was more to come.

Magnificence was so pronounced only late in Richard's reign, after the *Confessio* had been composed and, indeed, revised in the early 1390s. Magnificent royal politics, and active opposition to it, were part of the political and discursive environment in which the *Confessio* was first produced. The king's fully developed regal personality, however, makes such a context still more significant for the later reception of the poem (especially alongside other of Gower's productions including the fiercely anti-Ricardian *Cronica tripertita*). Details and events of Richard's reign should, in any case, indicate dispositions and discursive intersections rather than a topical 'decoding' for the resolutely non-topical *Confessio*,[105] although they can contribute to conjecture about Gower's revision of his work and its dedicatory passages. (This removes King Richard from the poem's address and, to my mind, aims to damp the outermost frame's play between courtly

---

[102] Barron, 'Tyranny', 10–14 and appendix, 18.

[103] Haxey's petition focuses on patronage to curial bishops and their households, and may represent the interests of royal clerks who saw royal resources being channelled away from their careers. For the petition and events surrounding it, see *PROME*, 'Introduction January 1397', iii. 338–9 and 341, appendix Jan. 1397, item 1 (*Rot. parl.* iii. 407–8); A. K. McHardy, 'Haxey's Case, 1397: The Petition and its Presenter Reconsidered', in James L. Gillespie (ed.), *The Age of Richard II* (Stroud, Glos., 1997), 93–114 (which ascribes further matters in the parliament roll to Haxey's case against Richard's household).

[104] Turner, *Chaucerian Conflict*, 11.

[105] See Anne Middleton's remarks on topicality in 'Public Poetry', 95.

artfulness and 'bookish' seriousness more clearly to favour the latter and an earnest, responsible politics.[106]) Certainly, the *Confessio* shares interests with the 1387–8 opponents of magnificence in Richard's government. In Gower's case, these interests may have been chafed by localized pressures since subsumed in the generalized voices of his poetry, but larger historical forces also, and more compellingly, make sense of the *Confessio*.

ECONOMIC CRISIS

A wide, deep context for the poem's asymmetrical reciprocalism is provided by the economic and social changes of a period after 1348–50. Solidarity with asymmetric reciprocalism positions the *Confessio* in opposition to magnificence on one hand and also to the economic liberation of disadvantaged groups. The landed elites struggled to hold back this liberation in the late fourteenth century, but long-term economic trends eventually allowed wage earners and tenants to make lasting headway against the elites' resistance, especially once grain prices began to fall after 1375 and popular frustrations had exploded in the great rebellion of 1381. From this perspective, the *Confessio*'s reciprocalism is a literary refortification against forces which threaten chronically to weaken lordship, particularly by breaking down great household economies into more flexible, commercial, and temporary, and less physically enmeshed arrangements, in which tenants and labourers enjoy new freedom and economic leverage.

Christopher Dyer crystallizes the ways in which the momentum of the economy after 1350 'worked against the interests of the aristocracy'.[107] Late fourteenth-century England's population failed to recover from the

---

[106] On revisions to the *Confessio*, see Macaulay, ii, pp. xxi–xxviii, cxxvii–cxxxviii; M. B. Parkes, 'Patterns of Scribal Activity and Revisions of the Text in Early Copies of Works by John Gower', in Richard Beadle and A. J. Piper (eds), *New Science Out of Old Books: Studies in Manuscripts and Early Printed Books in Honour of A. I. Doyle* (Aldershot, Hants, 1995); and three articles by Peter Nicholson, challenging linear and factional narratives of revision: 'Gower's Revisions in the *Confessio Amantis*', *Chaucer Review*, 19 (1984–5), 123–43; 'Poet and Scribe in the Manuscripts of Gower's *Confessio Amantis*', in Derek Pearsall (ed.), *Manuscripts and Texts: Editorial Problems in Later Middle English Literature* (Cambridge, 1987); 'Dedications'. See also Stow, 'Richard II in John Gower's *Confessio Amantis*'; Fisher, *John Gower*, 88–91, 117–20, 311–12; Federico, *New Troy*, 114–17; Dhira B. Mahoney, 'Gower's Two Prologues to *Confessio Amantis*', in Yeager (ed.), *Re-Visioning Gower*.

[107] Dyer, *Making a Living*, 268. The following paragraphs are heavily indebted to Dyer's interpretation of the period in *Making a Living*, esp. 265–97, 330–62.

catastrophe of 1348–50 (largely, perhaps, because the Black Death came after a period of overpopulation and decline and was followed by a series of plagues in 1361–2, 1369, and 1375). Change was not uniform, but, in general terms, persistently low population depressed rents as demand for tenancies remained depleted, and it eventually pulled down the price of grain once good harvests returned. Meanwhile, low population buoyed up the costs of labour and the prices of manufactured goods (which reflected these costs). None of these changes favoured the landed classes.

'Those accustomed to suffer want', however, got used to a new prosperity according to the chronicler of Rochester priory.[108] Peasants could negotiate easier tenancy terms, with labour services commuted to money rents for example, and servile tenants had a good chance of ridding themselves of that status if they found their way to a new manor. The labour shortage inhibited acquisitive peasants as well as lords, but allowed wage earners to hold out for improved pay and more flexible conditions (including arrangements by the day or by the task).

The landed elites reacted to this new climate of opportunity with attempts to entrench old asymmetric structures, though the ground continued to move underneath them. The labour law issued and re-issued in 1349, 1351, and 1388 represents, in part, an attempt summarily to restore the pre-pestilence employment environment.[109] The sumptuary law of 1363 pretends to repair hierarchy by explicating a highly stratified visual code of social rank, having decried 'the outrageous and excessive apparel of divers people, against their estate and degree' (*SR* i. 380). Poll taxes in 1377, 1379, and 1381 were designed to catch the new (relative) prosperity of wage earners, which had not been forestalled by the earlier labour laws and escaped the lay subsidy (assessed on moveable goods). At the level of the manor, many lords attempted to hang onto their privileges by exerting them more strenuously. The increase in manorial court revenues after the Black Death was, as Dyer observes, 'a remarkable development as the number of tenants had fallen drastically' (285). Amercements for neglect of property or services, or for evasion of customary dues such as marriage fines

---

[108] *Historia Roffensis*, in Rosemary Horrox (ed. and tr.), *The Black Death* (Manchester, 1994), 73, quoted in Dyer, *Making a Living*, 274.

[109] *SR* i. 307–9, 311–12; ii. 56–8. For fuller contextualizations of the Statute of Labourers, see Larry Poos, 'The Social Context of Statute of Labourers Enforcement', *Law and History Review*, 1 (1983), 27–52; Chris Given-Wilson, 'Service, Serfdom and English Labour Legislation, 1350–1500', in Anne Curry and Elizabeth Matthew (eds), *Concepts and Patterns of Service in the Later Middle Ages* (Woodbridge, Suff., 2000), 21–37; Strohm, *Hochon's Arrow*, 57–65.

or entry fines (payable on the transfer or inheritance of landholdings) were rigorously pursued.

Conditions favouring society's lower orders persisted and deepened, however, and the aristocracy's reactionary efforts lost force during the 1370s and were gravely shaken by their subordinates' backlash in the great rising of 1381. Lords clutched at familiar privileges tightly enough to frustrate and provoke those who recognized prospects for advancement or they made concessions to tenants in less volatile negotiations. Whether they relaxed their grip carefully or had it prised apart by manorial court boycotts and acts of violence, however, lords' hold over peasants and workers generally weakened in the final decades of the fourteenth century. In the 1380s, good harvests returned and grain prices fell, wages continued to rise, and the memory of revolt secured 'a new balance' in which all parties realized that the lords' inferiors 'had improved their bargaining power'.[110]

Adapting to this situation, the aristocracy attenuated great household structures which supported a reciprocalist economy. Labour services were commuted into simple money rents and other manorial obligations were conflated with rents, abandoned, or reduced. Lords sometimes converted customary tenure (subjecting tenants to the custom of the manor) into short-term leasehold. Commutation of labour services often accompanied the leasing of demesne land, which according to Dyer was 'the really decisive and universal change [in the manorial economy] through much of lowland England' in the late fourteenth century.[111] Powerful lords also cut back on large-scale hospitality and reduced the number of manor houses on active duty for their itinerations.[112] All of these consolidation measures contributed to the great household's receding as a physical and interventionary presence in the English countryside.

Adjustments in management and tenancy designed to conserve lords' wealth often disrupted the great household's structures of reciprocalist exchange, which were means to refresh indefinitely renewable

[110] Dyer, *Making a Living*, 293. For the politics of the 1381 rising, see R. B. Dobson (ed. and tr.), *The Peasants' Revolt of 1381*, 2nd edn (London, 1983); R. H. Hilton and T. H. Aston (eds), *The English Rising of 1381* (Cambridge, 1984); Rodney Hilton, *Bond Men Made Free: Medieval Peasant Movements and the English Rising of 1381*, 2nd edn (London, 2003); Strohm, *Hochon's Arrow*, 33–56; Steven Justice, *Writing and Rebellion: England in 1381* (Berkeley, Calif., 1994); Herbert Eiden, 'Joint Action against "Bad" Lordship: The Peasants' Revolt in Essex and Norfolk', *History*, 83 (1998), 5–30.

[111] Dyer, *Making a Living*, 295.

[112] Dyer, *Standards of Living*, 98–101.

asymmetrical ties between tenant and lord. Leased demesne meant less contact with the lord's officials and the lord who ceased visiting a manor entirely would no longer preside there at tenant feasts. Where cash rents collected regularly replaced fines or reliefs attached to major stages or events in a tenant's life (and often paid in kind) there was also less scope to symbolize the lord–tenant tie as one of *unresolved* obligation. The spectrum of exchanges should not be polarized: labour services, for example, were negotiated as commercial arrangements (exactly quantified in explicit exchange for landholding). Nonetheless, a hereditary tenant who owed a customary heriot (death duty) of the 'best beast' experienced (or misrecognized) the manorial economic disguised by customary valuation and timing and as part of a long narrative of lordship in a way that a tenant paying a fixed rent on a nine-year lease with no additional obligations did not.

Profound economic pressures on the landed household in Gower's day must be reckoned with, albeit changes were not as drastic as the calamity of the Black Death might lead us to expect. Hereditary peasant tenure and certain customary dues (often in the form of money fines) were widespread in the 1390s. The great household also, as I have mentioned, continued to govern estate infrastructure where it lost its more active lordship role. Newcomers to landed society were more likely to come from professional elites than the peasantry—from careers with access to burgeoning sources of wealth outside agriculture—and such landholders would still expect to wait at least a generation before their family profited from the exchanges (especially of marriage) that redistributed large quantities of land.[113] Yet change was pervasive and was diminishing the great household as the nerve centre of far-flung estates and a dominant presence in the lives of its tenants. Aristocratic endeavours to restrain change demonstrate how alarming it could seem to the landed elites (as well as partly explaining its delayed and uneven progress after the Black Death). The *Confessio's* reciprocalism is in this light a symptom of ongoing aristocratic reaction against economic liberation and of anxiety that the great household was now in retreat and social hierarchy critically compromised—an anxiety that may have been all the more acute in Gower's case if he had achieved landed status from careerist beginnings.

The economic liberation of poorer groups in society produced voices that were trenchant in invoking liberation but are, in Fredric Jameson's

---

[113] Payling, 'Social Mobility', 53, 65–70; Saul, *Knights and Esquires*, 229–32.

terms, 'for the most part stifled and reduced to silence [or] marginalized' in Gower's text.[114] These voices threatened aristocratic reciprocalism more radically than elite magnificence did. The rebels' demands presented at Smithfield in 1381, for instance, apparently envisaged that 'no lord should have lordship in future, but it should be divided among all men'.[115] The rebels seem to have been calling for a society in which village and town communities formed the tier of government immediately below the king. The *Confessio* represents rather different political potential in 'the poeple'. Gower enlists the 'comun vois, which mai noght lie' (prol. 124; cf. 7. 2329–33) to authorize the *Confessio*, or its basic critique of a divided world at least, just as *vox plebis* is imagined behind the complaint of *Vox clamantis*.[116] The commons also have radical and positive political agency in some of Genius's stories, notably when communities abandon foolish King Roboam and overthrow the treacherous kings Perseus and Tarquin (*CA* 2. 1840–51, 7. 4097–4129, 7. 5115–23). Such voice and action, however, are allowed almost no opportunity to speak of liberation from aristocratic hegemony. For constructive effect, it seems, the raw truth of the 'comun vois' needs to be taken on and used by learned poetry or elite leadership. Without such direction, it sweeps despotic mortals to the status of deities in pagan times (5. 835–42, 981–1000), and Genius expresses no optimism about the future of the communities who end legitimate dynasties in the cases of Roboam and Perseus (whereas the aristocracy-led deposition of Tarquin produces 'betre governance'; 7. 5123).[117] Popular unrest is primarily a barometer of dominant groups' performance in the poem, and it authorizes restored hierarchical unity, not novel, liberating political structures. 'Comun clamour' implicitly seeks a return to political placidity. In an ideal order, the 'comun poeple stant menable' (7. 2762) under well-administered law, an amenable and pliant populace.[118]

---

[114] Jameson, *Political Unconscious*, 85.

[115] *Anonimalle Chronicle*, ed. Galbraith, tr. in Dobson (ed. and tr.), *Peasants' Revolt*, 164, quoted in Dyer, *Making a Living*, 290.

[116] e.g. *Vox*, at 2. 1 (1); 6.15; cf. *Cronica*, 3. 326–35 (the people jubilantly praise God for raising up Henry IV and help to authorize his kingship by election). See Watts, 'Pressure of the Public', 170–1 and n. 51; Middleton, 'Public Poetry'.

[117] Cf. the split between Henry IV's mercy and the 'Publica vox' calling for justice against his opponents in *Cronica*, 3. 382–99 (quote at l. 395).

[118] Cf. the sense of 'menable' where nature, in spite of reason, makes humans 'menable / To love' (*CA* 3. 390–1). Consider also Galloway's reading of the tale of Adrian and Bardus (*CA* 5. 4937–5162) as one that 'emphasizes the inevitability, the "naturalness", of social differences', particularly through the peasant Bardus, who is both superstitious and 'resigned to lordly ingratitude': 'Making of a Social Ethic', 378.

Apparently admirable commons in the tale of Apollonius of Tyre are largely impotent foils to the protagonist's good lordship, whether bewailing his disappearance at Tyre or raising a statue in gratitude for his gift of wheat at Tarsus (8. 472–95, 559–70). This means of marginalizing the political agency of the commons or non-elite groups dovetails with the large portions of the *Confessio* that do not represent the commons at all.

The voice of the commons never expressly challenges the structure of society led by landed power. It is not the voice of the free, ununified, bestial commons of the first book of *Vox clamantis*.[119] While the (sparse) energy of the commons could conceivably be taken into the liberative language and dispositions of some audiences, to an aristocratic public or equivalent dispositions it would speak only of unity secured by asymmetric reciprocity, and thus far would pose no threat. In terms of Bourdieu's taxonomy of correspondences between 'the objective order and the subjective principles of organization', the landed household's primacy in the social world belongs to the unspoken field of *doxa* in the *Confessio*.[120] Competing household modes jostle within the 'field of opinion', which is divided between 'orthodoxy' (here reciprocalism) and 'heterodoxy' (principally magnificence). No popular or subordinate interest—even considering a glimpse of golden age capital all 'set to the comune' (5. 5)—more than momentarily succeeds in 'pushing back the limits of *doxa*' to bring the basic dominance of aristocratic and royal power into the field of the discussed and disputable.[121] Certainly, entering an arena of competition (the field of opinion) means that *reciprocalist* lordship cannot appear entirely natural (as *doxa* does), and heterodox magnificence raises the spectre of the self-maiming and self-destruction of landed power. But *external*, sub-elite challenges to the great household's authority—so vigorously represented in the *Vox*, in the aftermath of the 1381 revolt—are closed away again by the *Confessio* in the zone of the undiscussed and undisputed.[122]

The corresponding preponderance of magnificence within the *Confessio*'s zone of the heterodox might be explained as an internalization of subordinates' antagonistic voices within a hegemonic debate. Aristocratic

[119] For the threatening, subversive voice of the people in the *Vox*, see Justice, *Writing and Rebellion*, 207–16.

[120] Bourdieu, *Theory of Practice*, 164–71 (quote at 164).

[121] Ibid. 169.

[122] For Gower's marginalization of the church as a rival to lay temporal authority, see below, 101–14.

reciprocalism was being challenged from opposite social positions in the 1380s. Within discourse of the great household, however, liberated socially inferior voices are difficult openly to confront (as the beast-rebels of 1381 in *Vox clamantis* attest). A text like the *Confessio*, with a primarily aristocratic and elite public, may be strongly disposed to strategies that marginalize voices and dispositions of liberated subordinates while focusing anxiety about the great household's basic position on the less alien, apparently more tractable antagonist, elite magnificence—an isotope of the same economic structure that produces the text's own orthodoxy.

Furthermore, the logic of the reciprocalist critique of magnificence folds the liberated lower orders' challenge to hierarchy into elite magnificence itself. As I aim to show in the context of gentry opposition to livery badges (below, 188–93), magnates were blamed for (magnificently) failing to distinguish lesser aristocracy as natural, privileged beneficiaries of their exchanges. Giving that was irresponsible of hierarchical continuities, guided by expedience, and thus open to the opportunistic, would surely abet 'new men' and dangerously independent and commercially minded individuals of all levels of society. When he decries retainers 'nimis elati' (overmuch lifted up, *WC* 82) by magnate badges, the Westminster chronicler is appealing to the nobles as both cause and potential correctors of the situation. If the lower orders are silenced and denied an active part in 'mending' the social order at the same time as the magnates are made responsible, then we begin to appreciate how aristocratic and royal magnificence can be invoked as reciprocalism's most urgent problem, defying reciprocalism on its own ground and also representing and permitting deeper threats.

Throughout the Middle Ages texts of many kinds understand the great household to be basic to the good order of society. A dialogue between forms of reciprocalism and magnificence is recurrent in these texts. When *Confessio Amantis* was composed and first consumed, however, this dialogue took the particular impression of the poem's own historical situation. Magnate magnificence threatened to cast the gentry adrift in an unfamiliar sea of competition and lower groups' pressure for greater freedom from the ties of lordship (that is, the great household's exchange complex) eroded the gentry's economic privilege and sense of prestige. Signs of royal magnificence meanwhile provoked aristocratic resentment. Major economic changes and court policy were acute factors behind reciprocalist statements about the great household in the 1380s and 1390s. That all of these forces contributed to the class dispositions and politics of the *Confessio* is indicated by the household-based discourses that the poem shares with contemporary texts, regardless of how consciously or specifically Gower comprehended the economic and political changes taking place in his world. Gower's poem offers us a lens on a landed habitus in the late fourteenth century. To explore the poem in this way will uncover the lordship economics that it disparages, promotes, or takes for granted in service, hospitality, marriage, dispute resolution, and kingship. It is as well to begin with occasions when Gower uses language of the great household in the most particular and unexpected ways.

3

Service Allegory: The Great Household in Genius's Confession

Gower's major English poem is framed as a confession between a lover and Genius, Venus's priest. When Genius talks about sin he talks about aristocratic power as well. Woven through Genius's and Amans's confessional language is a lexical strand rooted in a social imagination of the great household and its asymmetric reciprocalism. As the confessor enumerates individual vices, for instance, he describes several as 'withholde' by superior vices. So Detraction has 'withholde' *Malebouche* (*CA* 2. 389); Hate, False Seeming (3. 964–5); Avarice, *Covoitise* (5. 1994); and Rapine, Extortion (5. 5510–11). In the penitential categorization of sins, these phrases simply indicate a close association of types of vice or the graded subdivision of a sin heading.[1] But, at the literal level of the allegory, there is also a specifically political sense in play.[2] 'Withhold' appeared as a word meaning 'retain' in indentures of retinue when these began to be written in English in the fifteenth century, the phrase 'beleft and witholden' approximating the French 'demorez et retenuz' of earlier indentures.[3] Thus, we can understand that *Malebouche* has been 'retained' by Detraction. The 'withholding' usage for retaining imagery

[1] For the conventional taxonomy of the deadly sins in medieval theology and penitential manuals, see Morton W. Bloomfield, *The Seven Deadly Sins: An Introduction to the History of a Religious Concept, with Special Reference to Medieval English Literature* (East Lansing, Mich., 1952), 70–89, 193–4.

[2] On the importance and complexity of the ' "literal" ' in allegory, see Maureen Quilligan, *The Language of Allegory: Defining the Genre* (Ithaca, NY, 1979), 27–9, 64–79, cited by Simon Gaunt in 'Bel Acueil and the improper allegory of the *Romance of the Rose*', *New Medieval Literatures*, 2 (1998), 65–93, 69 n. 10. On the language of service and lordship in medieval allegory, see Patterson, 'Court Politics'; Barratt, 'Julian of Norwich and the Holy Spirit'; and 'Lordship, Service, and Worship'; and the studies cited below, 99 n. 1.

[3] See Bean, *From Lord to Patron*, 33 n. 1. For examples from John of Gaunt's retinue, see Eleanor C. Lodge and Robert Somerville (eds), *John of Gaunt's Register, 1379–1383*, Camden Soc. 3rd ser. 56–7 (London, 1937), pt 1, nos. 23–7, 45, 48, 54; and appendix 3, 'Unpublished Indentures of Retinue with John of Gaunt, Duke of Lancaster', in Walker, *Lancastrian Affinity*, 292–303.

was already conventional in English literary texts before indentures of
retinue were composed in English. It was a highly economical trope in
the courtly love diction of love as service and, alongside Gower, Chaucer
and Sir John Clanvowe supply other instances of it in Ricardian dream
poetry. In the prologue of Chaucer's *Legend of Good Women* (first
composed 1386–8), the narrator protests that he knows nought of
courtly faction of 'lef or flour' but is 'witholde yit with never nother'
(*LGW*, G 70, 76; cf. F 192). Clanvowe's *Boke of Cupide* (*c.*1387–91)
ends with the nightingale's song resounding in the dreamer's head:
'"Terme of lyve, love hath withholde me"'.[4] As Lee Patterson has
observed, the first part of this phrase as well as the term '"withholde"'
echoes the language of indentures of retinue, and the song, indeed,
crystallizes the terms of service which have saturated the nightingale's
speech throughout the poem. She is an indentured retainer to love.[5]
That Gower likewise uses the word to refer to a spectrum of practice
which *includes* indentured retaining is evinced by an instance which
seems to refer to a written contract explicitly, whereby 'fals Semblant | Is
toward [Hate] of covenant | Withholde' (*CA* 3. 963–5).[6] 'Withhold' by
itself need not signify a relationship defined by indenture. Retaining, it
must be remembered, could be effected by annuity or fee, or by giving
livery, without being codified in an indenture.[7] What is important at
this point is that when 'withhold' is used to define personal relations it
bears the sense of retaining, of a relationship between a lord and an
inferior that is formalized by some means (fee, livery, indenture, or a
combination thereof) originating in the lord's household.

The language of the retinue and the affinity in the *Confessio*'s allegory
of vices goes well beyond the term 'withhold'. Indeed, it not only
ornaments but structures the poem's scheme of vices. The taxonomical

---

[4] *Cupide*, l. 289.

[5] Patterson, 'Court Politics', 10. For the precise resonance of the nightingale's refrain,
see e.g. the Lancastrian lifetime indentures printed by Simon Walker. Under such an
instrument, Sir Gerard Usflete 'est demorez et retenuz envers le dit duc pur paes et pur
guerre a terme de sa vie' (is attached and retained to the said duke for peace and for war
for the term of his life; Walker, *Lancastrian Affinity*, 295). For Amans's service relationship with Venus, and possible connections between Clanvowe's and Gower's dream
visions, see below, 100–1, 109–18, 124 n. 55. For the nightingale's refrain in a non-
metaphorical context, see *CA* 3. 2411, where Alexander 'hath . . . terme of lif withholde'
his pirate prisoner. Chaucer uses 'withholde' to describe a literal retaining relationship in
his pilgrim parson's disdain 'to been withholde' with a London guild (*CT* 1. 511).

[6] Cf. the 'terme of lif' example of Alexander and the pirate cited in n. 5 (*CA* 3. 2411).

[7] Bean, for one, warns against equating retaining with indentured retaining: see *From
Lord to Patron*, 10–39 (esp. 10–11, 20–2).

vicious allegory of Gower's *Mirour de l'Omme* anticipates its English successor, but is not so heavily invested in a household service imaginary. The main allegorical framework of the French poem is of the family rather than the wider *familia*: the daughters of Sin, brides in political marriages to the World, are introduced along with their daughters, the vices (*Mirour*, ll. 781–9888), and are countered by God's daughters (the seven virtues) and their daughters (ll. 10033–18372). There are some brief elaborations of great household metaphorical society, for example in the five retainers of Covetousness ('cynk servans de retenue'; l. 6314), forerunners of Avarice's household in the *Confessio*, and in the aristocratic upbringing of Patience's fourth daughter, Concord, 'Dedeinz les chambers dame Pes' (in lady Peace's chambers; l. 13816). Later, in the *Confessio*, however, the household imagination of vices reaches a different magnitude.

This imagination can be traced in its particulars: in Gower's use of 'withhold' and other language related to the retaining spectrum. Once or twice, the proximate use of 'withhold' confirms a retaining context for such language. Thus, a vice can be 'of covine and of felawschipe ... withholde', as 'Unkindeschipe' is by Avarice (*CA* 5. 4888–9).[8] Elsewhere, the relation of being 'withhold' is further defined by household office. 'Skarsnesse,' or Parsimony, is expressly said to be 'withholde' (*CA* 5. 4673) as Avarice's chamberlain. Other vices are located in a retinue by the attribution of office alone. Fool Haste and Somnolence are also chamberlains (3. 1096, 4. 2705); Negligence is Sloth's 'Secretaire' (4. 888); and False Seeming serves as Envy's secret 'Messagier' who is 'Of prive conseil' (2. 1917). Further vices are simply designated as a 'servaunt' of another or ascribed an unspecified 'office' in a vicious household.[9] Occasionally, one vice is said to be 'of conseil' to another. 'Counsel' designates a less formal relationship than 'servant' or 'office', and a much less defined function than specific office titles. At the same time, however, it suggests a greater degree of intimacy and, in an aristocratic context, a relationship typically defined within household and retinue.[10]

---

[8] Cf. 2. 1895, where 'covine' and 'houshold' are used together.

[9] e.g. gloss at 1. 1344, 1. 1884–5, 3. 25–7.

[10] Cf. *SR* ii. 113 for a livery statute which accommodates legal advisers as 'counsellors' in receipt of livery. At *CA* 7. 3882–7 (Solomon's counsellors), Gower implies that counsel functions through retinue and perhaps even that counsel and retinue are conterminous notions. Counsel and household office are linked in the roles of False Witness and Perjury (5. 2861–2).

Another ill-defined term associating several vices with retaining or analogous relationships is 'compaignie'. In a livery ordinance of 1390, 'compaignie' refers to some household-based relationship of subordination and domination, although it may betoken a bond less formal than retaining (albeit related to it) and is probably best thought of in terms of affinity rather than retinue.[11] Gower certainly connects the term to the household at times, for Detraction is 'fostred with Envie | Of houshold and of compaignie' (2. 437–8), and 'Surquiderie,' or Presumption, 'stant with Pride of compaignie' in 'the thridde office' of the sin's court (1. 1877–8, 1884).

Genius's descriptions of the chief sins and vices, then, are shot through with the great household's language of personal relations. But I have also made the larger claim that this language has a systematic, structural aspect. Affinities of vices complement Gower's *divisio* or structuring system of deadly sins until it subsides in the poem's final books. Books 1–4 imagine a five- or sixfold division of each major sin comprising metaphorical affinities, before book 5 (over twice the length of any other 'sin' book) features an explosion of subordinate vices and ushers in a newly elaborated metaphorical retinue structure.[12] Moreover, the household imaginary populates the poem's courtly love allegory as well as these systems of sin allegory and vicious service. Danger, the lady's allegorical servant and a figure fixated on by Amans, allows the lover's narrative to emblematize reciprocalist hope with surprising resonance, and I shall turn to the lover's relationship with Venus in the next chapter. First, however, I shall examine the unhappier side of service metaphors in the house of Avarice.

THE MAGNIFICENT HOUSEHOLD OF AVARICE

The *Confessio*'s politics of obligation are clear in the magnificence of book 5's sprawling household group of vices. The branches of the book's leading sin are all eleven individually figured over the course of the book as

[11] *SR* ii. 75. On this ordinance and the livery debate in which it participated, see below, 188–93, 215–21, 247–8. The ordinance's collocation 'compaignie et retenu' may be intended to distinguish badges and *compaignie* as a mode of household association weaker than retinue, but it often simply looks like legalistic pleonasm.

[12] Not every vice is clearly figured as a retainer or servant in the early books of the poem, but later personifications imply that the retaining system has been in place throughout. See *CA* 2. 1875; cf. 1. 1245 ('serve may [Disobedience] noght for pride'), but see also 1. 1884 (implying Disobedience's service) and gloss at 1. 1344 (giving Disobedience servants of his own).

servants of a noble household. The lord of the household is Dame Avarice, 'Which is of gold the Capiteine' (5. 1972), and her servants are related to her in those multifarious ways which have informed recent characterizations of the late medieval lordly affinity—as a 'sea of varying relationships' with a common focus in service and loyalty to a lord, or as concentric, overlapping circles of association centred on a lord.[13] The vices do not fit into a simple linear hierarchy. Rapine, for example, is 'In the lignage of Avarice' (5. 5505) and seems to have his own household or retinue. Embracing some complexity of this kind, Gower constructs out of the vices of Avarice a basically coherent edifice of retaining and affinity relationships. The model of lordship projected is wholly magnificent, and the unworthiness and seeming precariousness of Avarice's household sustain an intensive, implicit argument for reciprocalist lordship.

Perhaps the sharpest evocation of the magnificence of Avarice's household and its disruption of social order comes in the allegorical vignette of Parsimony, who is retained as keeper or wardrober to (the now male) Avarice. The portrayal describes the inward-working antithesis of an ideal household economy, which opens a divide between the noble household and the local community:

> Blinde Avarice of his lignage
> For conseil and for cousinage,
> To be withholde ayein largesse,
> Hath on, whos name is seid Skarsnesse,
> The which is kepere of his hous,
> And is so thurghout averous,
> That he no good let out of honde;
> Thogh god himself it wolde fonde,
> Of yifte scholde he nothing have;
> . . . .
> And thus Skarsnesse in every place
> Be reson mai no thonk porchace,
> And natheles in his degree
> Above alle othre most prive
> With Avarice stant he this.
> . . . .
> He takth, he kepth, he halt, he bint,
> That lihtere is to fle the flint
> Than gete of him in hard or neisshe

[13] G. A. Holmes, *The Estates of the Higher Nobility in Fourteenth-Century England* (Cambridge, 1957), 79; Harriss, introduction, p. xi.

Only the value of a reysshe
Of good in helpinge of an other,
Noght thogh it were his oghne brother.
For in the cas of yifte and lone
Stant every man for him al one,
Him thenkth of his unkindeschipe
That him nedeth no felaschipe:
Be so the bagge and he acorden,
Him reccheth noght what men recorden
Of him, or it be evel or good.
For al his trust is on his good,
So that al one he falleth ofte,
Whan he best weneth stonde alofte

(5. 4671–706)

The keeper of the wardrobe was the great household's chief financial
officer. Accountable for the lord's treasure, he was ultimately responsible
for the materials which sustained the vast system of exchanges, commercial and non-commercial, that were organized within the *hospicium*,
the 'practical domestic structure' of the household (as opposed to its
identity as social network). On the giving side of the tally, these
exchanges included various non-commercial forms such as liveries,
charity, and hospitality—from the provisioning of the resident retinue
to the reception of guests and feast-giving.[14] Hospitality and gift-giving
anticipated and prepared the channels along which other benefits of
lordship—office, fee, maintenance, marriage—should course. At a ru-
dimentary level, therefore, the keeper managed the valves controlling
the circulation of social energy in the household's community. In this
context, Parsimony's portrait is a study in first principles of reciprocalist
lordship. From its contrary, a reader can deduce normative largesse to be
giving to suitors 'Be reson' to 'thonk porchace'. Good lordship, that is,
generates worship by apparently generous exchanges.[15]

The portrait makes much of Parsimony's intimate relationship with
the lord Avarice. He is thrice-privileged in this regard, by kin or 'lignage'
(as a cousin of the lord), by political function (as counsellor), and by

---

[14] Heal, 'Reciprocity and Exchange', 179–88; Woolgar, *Great Household*, 17–18,
111–35. Woolgar notes that households might contain another department also
called the wardrobe but distinct from the general financial department and responsible
for luxury items such as spices and cloth (*Great Household*, 17). For the keeper in the
royal household during the fourteenth century, see Given-Wilson, *Royal Household*,
9–10, 95–110.

[15] Cf. Mauss, *The Gift*, 3; Bourdieu, *Theory of Practice*, 5–6.

domestic office (as 'kepere of his hous' and one of his chief officers). The
family tie may be inflected with Parsimony's corrupt practice by a
French pun in 'cousinage', linking kinship and sharp dealing.[16] The
(magnificent) endogenous service and commercial lordship which Parsimony represents does not so much decapitate the entire body politic
(in the way that purely negligent lordship does) as amputate it from the
neck down. Where it does not destabilize relations with all servants,
magnificence's one-sidedness turns household exchange inwards, narrowing its range to core household relations that can most directly
represent the power of the lord. Avarice's lordship, through Parsimony,
makes household relations exclusively and narrowly private, disrupting
the proper informal networks of quasi-private, quasi-public exchange
that lend the noble household a potent agency in and between both
spheres. By his 'unkindeschipe', Parsimony cuts off relations that are
assumed to have a natural place in household politics. His position as
'Above all othre most prive | With Avarice' makes him blind to the
informal claims of 'felaschipe'. Withdrawing to the reductively private,
he adopts a blankly public perspective to that without, so that when he
administers patronage, 'Stant every man for him al one'. In the context
of developing legal bureaucracy in the period, this impartiality aligns
Parsimony with literate law, formal process, and objective rather than
ethical 'truth'.[17]

It is not simply niggardliness of giving that is at issue here. The
problem is not only that every man is 'al one' in his lucklessness, but
that before Parsimony every man is 'al one' *per se*. The antidote is not an
indiscriminate giving that mirrors or reverses his indiscriminate keeping. Good lordship, the portrait argues, is not about blind charity and
unorganized giving, but about exchange that works within the informal,
but ordered and enduring structures of personal networks and affinities.
The relationships that we can see Parsimony deny and disrupt are not
impartial commercial or 'market' relationships, but relationships that
are positively discriminatory. The ideal negative image of his undiscriminating stewardship is an asymmetric hospitality and giving which
privileges and sustains bonds created by the 'felaschipe' or loyalty of kin
(5. 4696), neighbourhood, or service.

[16] For the contemporary range of meaning of *cosyn*, see Ruth M. Fisher, ' "Cosyn" and
"Cosynage": Complicated Punning in Chaucer's "Shipman's Tale"?', *Notes and Queries*,
12 (1965), 168–70; P. B. Taylor, 'Chaucer's *Cosyn to the Dede*', *Speculum*, 57 (1982),
315–27, 321, 324 and n. 21.
[17] See Green, *Crisis of Truth*, esp. 121–64; and below, 182–7.

The hospitable ideal is non-commercial and underpinned by gift reciprocity promising the symbolic profit of worship in return for good lordship. Materialist Parsimony is oblivious to the system's ruling principle and benefits. He places no value on worship or reputation ('Him reccheth noght what men recorden | Of him'). Instead, he values material wealth alone, however it is attained. Gower thus sets up a dichotomy between, on the one hand, natural human feeling—the opposite of 'unkindeschipe'—and social capital (worship), and, on the other, overtly economic elements. Good lordship is aligned wholly with the first part of this dichotomy and by implication removed from the second. At the same time, Parsimony's overt economics, contemptuous of 'gift' obligation, is seen blindly to produce social instability, proving a veritable invitation to ruin (5. 4705–6).

After illustrating parsimony with a single tale (of Babio and Croceus), Genius moves on to embellish the vice of *Ingratitudo* (gloss at 5. 4888) or 'Unkindeschipe' (which is somewhat broader than ingratitude).[18] The confessor's moralizing is very generalized, but the poem's household imagination still (fitfully) inflects the portrait. Like Parsimony, *Unkindeschipe* seems to be an agent of lordship. He receives service and owes unspecified 'thonk' (5. 4900–1).[19] There is a suggestion of a calculative estate economy in the exaggerated image 'He gruccheth forto yive o grein, | Wher he hath take a berne full' (5. 4906–7). Even here, however, a discretionary not commercial economic norm may be implied, and the portrait generally works to normalize informal obligation and imprecise, perhaps deferred, reciprocation. Like Parsimony, as well, *Unkindeschipe* is ignorant of the force of established social ties, including those of service and kin (he 'thenkth he scholde noght ben holde | Unto the moder which him bar'; 5. 4890–1). Obscuring these bonds once again are exclusively private, horizontal, and internalizing ties, for *Unkindeschipe* is retained 'Of covine and of felaschipe | With Avarice' (5. 4888–9).

The metaphorical portraits of Parsimony and *Unkindeschipe* combine to offer a critique of truncated lordship. Such lordship refuses an ideal of secure, unequal relationships and non-commercial exchange tending towards the deferred and gestural, in gift, 'lone', and 'thonk'. Non-commercial exchange camouflages or defers real benefits, but, in doing

---

[18] For a literary-sociological discursive history of these terms, see Galloway, 'Making of a Social Ethic', discussing Gower at 376–8.

[19] For Gower's earlier amalgam of highly generalized allegory and socially diverse specification of *Ingratitude* and various types of 'l'omme ingrat', see *Mirour*, ll. 6589–6732, esp. 6607–12, 6625–36; Galloway, 'Making of a Social Ethic', 376.

so, avoids completing transactions and the sequences of obligation they initiate.[20] By organizing such exchange asymmetrically, reciprocalist lordship reinforces hierarchical social bonds and the influence of the lord. Avarice's wardrober's strangulation of largesse and his blindness to obligation implicitly normalizes the reciprocalist household economy.

THE HOUSEHOLD OF THE INTERIOR: AMANS ASSIMILATES GENIUS'S DOMESTIC DISCOURSE

As sinew for the skeleton of Genius's confession, the priest's service and household language is systematic, but it has relatively little to do with his amatory explication of the vices. Yet the language of service does at times seep into the flesh of self-narrative in the lover's confession. Here it (more obviously) takes on the aspect of household metaphor conventional in medieval love lyric and elaborated in the *Roman de la Rose*. The confession itself is the product of a service relationship between Amans and Venus, and it educates the lover in reciprocalist household values.

During the confession, Genius's household language colonizes Amans's speech about his own interiority and his cause in love. The confessor provides some instant cues from his household taxonomy of vices. He asks 'if thou art of [Hypocrisy's] compaignie' (1. 1586), for example, and Amans later imagines himself a liveried retainer of Procrastination, 'clad of his suite' and allowed to 'stonde upon his rowe' at public occasions (4. 26–7). Amans's most significant allegorical contribution to the poem's political imaginary, however, comes with an account of his interiority as court faction-fighting and, especially, its extension to the figure of Danger.

True to his allegorical mode, Genius represents Fool Haste in book 3 as the chamberlain of *Contek* and then sketches a scenario of factional in-fighting between Fool Haste and an opponent virtue:

> Contek, so as the bokes sein,
> Folhast hath to his Chamberlein,
> Be whos conseil al unavised
> Is Pacience most despised
>
> (3. 1095–8)

---

[20] Bourdieu, *Theory of Practice*, 5–7.

Genius's representation of the competition between foolish haste and
patience as the victory of an incompetent household officer exploiting
his position of intimacy with his lord to pursue a factional rivalry
apparently prepares Amans to figure his own internal strife in like terms:

> Min herte is wonderly begon
> With conseil, whereof witt is on,
> Which hath resoun in compaignie;
> Ayein the whiche stant partie
> Will, which hath hope of his acord,
> And thus thei bringen up descord.
> Witt and resoun conseilen ofte
> That I myn herte scholde softe,
> And that I scholde will remue
> And put him out of retenue,
> Or elles holde him under fote:
> For as thei sein, if that he mote
> His oghne rewle have upon honde,
> Ther schal no witt ben understonde

(3. 1157–70)

The two factions, or psychological tendencies (the one intellectual, the
other emotional), vying for influence over Amans are presented as
miniature retinues. Reason is retained by Wit, and Hope stands in a
similar relation to Will. Both parties contest the larger issue of service to
Amans. Gower's household metaphor is again sophisticated enough that
interplay between its two semantic domains—the social and the psychological—does more than set up a static dichotomy of will and
reason. Amans ponders not just alternative parties seeking his favour,
but alternative political strategies recommended by counsellors Wit and
Reason. Where the household governance of Genius's personified vices
tends to result in entrenched states of division, here the prospect of
firmly ordered unity is offered. Will could be expelled from Amans's
retinue, but he could also be controlled by being held 'under fote' within
the retinue.

  This complication of the household metaphor seems an extremely
suggestive imprint of late fourteenth-century anxiety about the slippage
of fixed ideals of hierarchy. Wit and Reason's caution against allowing
Will 'His oghne rewle' could be strengthened by the example of Sloth's
apparent retaining of the negligent servant Sleep, whom 'Venus out of
compaignie | Hath put awey'. Sloth, it seems, now shelters Sleep from

the just demands of his former mistress (4. 3259–61). In both cases, Gower's text is informed by the kind of unease which contemporary economic liberation of the disadvantaged made acute and which, as I have said, motivated aristocratic complaint about lesser persons opportunistically outmanœuvring their betters. The Will passage is about psychological balance, but a social concern for an exhaustive system of subordination and domination is also present. Psychological complexity (whereby Will represents affective forces that cannot simply be erased or permanently repressed) parallels a reciprocalist assumption that lordship should stabilize disorderly social elements rather than exclude and forfeit responsibility for them.

CHAMBERLAIN DANGER

The substance of Amans's climactic petition to the powers of love at the end of the poem is the expulsion from retinue of his lady's chief servant:

> So that Danger, which stant of retenue
> With my ladi, his place mai remue.

(8. 2285–6)

Danger and the lover's contest forms a key strand of the poem's frame narrative and within it Gower creates a new Danger who embodies ideas of household politics and service valorized by the *Confessio* and central to contemporary political contests about the proper distribution of power.[21] Danger finds his main source in the wild villein Dangier in the *Roman de la Rose*. In both the *Rose* and the *Confessio*, the Dangier figure seems allegorically to represent the same kind of impediment to the lover's cause, especially, that is, opposition intrinsic to the object of desire, such as the lady's unfavourable feelings or disapproval.[22]

---

[21] For the main phases of the contest with Danger, see 1. 2439–45, 3. 1516–87, 5. 6597–6652.

[22] See C. S. Lewis, *The Allegory of Love: A Study in Medieval Tradition* (Oxford, 1936), 123–4, 364–6; Charles Muscatine, 'The Emergence of Psychological Allegory in Old French Romance', *PMLA* 68 (1953), 1160–82, 1162–3, 1181; W. R. J. Barron, 'Luf-Daungere', in F. Whitehead, A. H. Diverres, and F. E. Sutcliffe (eds), *Medieval Miscellany Presented to Eugène Vinaver* (Manchester, 1965), 1–18, 7. For interpretations of Dangier which encompass resistances extrinsic to the lady, but which, in any case, apply as readily to Gower's allegory as the *Rose*'s, see John V. Fleming, *The Roman de la Rose: A Study in Allegory and Iconography* (Princeton, 1969), 189; Charles Dahlberg, 'First Person and Personification in the *Roman de la Rose*: Amant and Dangier', *Mediaevalia*, 3 (1977), 37–58, 42.

Yet Gower's Danger is a changed man, a civilized and powerful noble servant. Gower makes Danger a chamberlain. The transformation of Dangier's literal attributes confirms the importance of the aristocratic household in the *Confessio*'s social imagination and develops the poem's conservative politics of service and household organization against the lover's brand of courtliness.[23] A glance at Danger's literary past confirms the strength of Gower's refashioning of the figure into a supreme chamber servant. Setting Gower's chamberer in the context of parliamentary and chronicle attacks on similar historical figures illuminates the imaginative territory in which Danger towers at the centre of the idealized aristocratic household.

Danger is never titled 'chamberlain' and Amans's two major accounts of him differ in tone and describe him performing rather different chamber duties. Gower's allegory, it seems, was not prompted by any especially focused notion of a chamber servant 'character'.[24] Without wishing finally to isolate Danger's literal profile from the allegory's fullest range of meanings, however, I notice that Danger's service strongly evokes the intimate and unspecialized work of chamberers in contemporary great households. He is called 'consailer' (counsellor and perhaps the more official councillor) and 'wardein'. He watches over the lady in both passages and he appears to be in charge of her seal. Danger might seem to enjoy higher status as counsellor in book 3 than the dauntless guard he becomes in book 5, but a medieval audience would likely have been put in mind of the same kind of servant on each occasion. Aristocratic households in the fourteenth century usually had only a few chamber servants, who could find themselves performing diverse roles, from bedmaking to sensitive embassies or 'simple companionship'.[25] *Camerari/a, –us*—'chamberer' or 'chamberlain'—was more a locator than a job title in the great household and the lord's proximity and trust, rather than a particular set of tasks, were the essence

---

[23] Socio-historically interested ways of reading courtly love poetry have been notably advanced by critics of the troubadours. See e.g. Sarah Kay, *Subjectivity in Troubadour Poetry* (Cambridge, 1990), 40–9, 111–31; Simon Gaunt, *Gender and Genre in Medieval French Literature* (Cambridge, 1995), 1–21, 122–79; and other studies cited below, 99 n. 1.

[24] Contrasting the *Confessio*'s allegory to personifications in the *Roman de la Rose*, J. A. Burrow argues that even Danger lacks substance and 'can be no more than a sustained trope *in the everyday world* of the lover's narrative': 'The Portrayal of Amans in *Confessio Amantis*', in Minnis (ed.), *Responses and Reassessments*, 7 (emphasis added).

[25] Mertes, *Noble Household*, 42.

of the role. It would not have been unusual, it seems, to find the same chamberer acting variously as chamber supervisor, adviser, guard, and access controller.[26]

I am interested here in Danger's associations with this context. I say relatively little about the poem's treatment of love and sexual relations in this chapter, but Gower's innovative celebration of Danger carries propositions about private as well as public aspects of the household and these are mutually reinforcing. Danger helps readers to imagine steady service and female sexual reserve alike, both conducive to continuity in a household. I want, however, to hold onto the recognition that the literal level of Danger's allegory engages language clearly outside the sphere of sexual love. I am interested to see how Gower's love poetry makes use or takes the impress of a contemporary language of politics so that, in this case, Danger becomes a representational site that privileges wider, reciprocalist household relations—'slow-burn', non-expedient, and status-sensitive—as well as 'honeste' married love.[27]

Amans initially describes Danger as a chief servant and 'consailer' (3. 1538) to the lady. Depicted as the filter to all attempted personal exchanges with the lady, Danger occupies one of the most important roles available to a late medieval chamberer:

> For I was nevere yit so slyh,
> To come in eny place nyh
> Wher as sche was be nyht or day,
> That Danger ne was redy ay,
> With whom for speche ne for mede
> Yit mihte I nevere of love spede;
> . . . .
> For ay the more I to him bowe,
> The lasse he wol my tale alowe.

[26] Mertes, *Noble Household*, 42–6; cf. 21–5 for areas in which chamberers might intersect the office of steward, treasurer, or clerk of the household. Gower uses 'chamberlein' in this general, place-marking sense of unspecialized attendance, as well as in a more restrictive sense as a title of office. For place-marking, see *CA* 5. 3672–4 (Jason's attendants), 6. 2098, 7. 4990–3 (Arruns's chamberlain), 8. 800 (Athenagoras's); cf. 4. 1193. Contrast Elda's remote service as 'kinges Chamberlein' in the tale of Constance (2. 718–26); cf. 7. 3949.

[27] For discussion of 'honeste' love in the confession, see J. A. W. Bennett, 'Gower's "Honeste Love"', in John Lawlor (ed.), *Patterns of Love and Courtesy: Essays in Memory of C. S. Lewis* (London, 1966), 107–21; Minnis, '*Sapiens* in Ethics and Politics'; Olsson, 'Natural Law'; all repr. in Peter Nicholson (ed.), *Gower's Confessio Amantis: A Critical Anthology* (Cambridge, 1991); Peter Nicholson, *Love and Ethics in Gower's Confessio Amantis* (Ann Arbor, Mich., 2005).

He hath mi ladi so englued,
Sche wol noght that he be remued;
For evere he hangeth on hire Seil,
And is so prive of conseil,
That evere whanne I have oght bede,
I finde Danger in hire stede
And myn ansuere of him I have

(3. 1539–59)

Constantly frustrating Amans, Danger controls all access to the object of
desire. He is 'mi ladi consailer' (3. 1538), with a deft pun on *concelen*
(conceal). He sustains the lover-courtier's desire by withholding, which
is suggestive in both erotic and political contexts.[28] He controls exchange like a chamberer. Examining the role of the king's chamberlain
allows us to focus on a level of chamber service fully informing this
passage and important in all great households, albeit less intensively
supplied in smaller establishments and elusive in household records. In
the royal household in the fourteenth century, the chamberlain—the
term usually designates the under-chamberlain or chamberlain of the
household technically deputizing for the master-chamberlain or chamberlain of England—held a position vital in determining the character
of the king's lordship.[29] After a revival beginning under Edward I, the
under-chamberlainship was important not simply because it involved
overall supervision of the chamber's treasure and jewels. The chamberlain also supervised both written and personal access to the king. In this
capacity, he stood in the king's 'stede' and assumed responsibility for
governing the conduits of the personal royal exchange nexus, controlling the flow of patronage, justice, and counsel about the king's person.
Petitions for the personal attention of the king usually required the
endorsement of the chamberlain. He was routinely included among the
chief government and household officials appointed to assist the triers of
petitions assigned in each parliament, and during Westminster parliaments the committee trying domestic petitions was to conduct its
business 'in the chamberlain's room, near the Painted Chamber'.[30]
A statute of 1390 recognizes the chamberlain as a key filter of royal

[28] For a Lacanian reading of kingship in terms of prohibition and the fashioning of
desire, see Paul Strohm, *Theory and the Premodern Text* (Minneapolis, 2000), 193–200.
[29] The superior title had become hereditary by the fourteenth century. See Given-
Wilson, *Royal Household*, 8–9; cf. *PROME* iii. 16.
[30] *PROME* iii. 204 (1385 Oct., mem. 7); see also e.g. ii. 226, 268, 299, 321; iii. 4, 99,
337, 523; iv. 63. For the commons' and other uses of the Painted Chamber, see Watts,
'Looking for the State', 248 n. 14.

justice. Responding to complaints about the easy circulation and abuse of royal pardons for very serious crimes, the statute decrees that petitions to the king seeking pardon for treason or certain violent crimes cannot be warranted by the privy seal without the endorsement or signature of the chamberlain or under-chamberlain.[31] As Chris Given-Wilson states, however, 'it was above all the physical presence of the chamberlain, as the man who actually attended personally on the king and either allowed men to pass through into the royal presence, or turned them away, which suitors to the king had to overcome'.[32] Given-Wilson cites cases in the 1370s when the earl of Pembroke and (momentarily) even Alice Perrers found that the path to royal justice stopped at the chamberlain.[33] Just as Pembroke and Perrers had to approach the king through his chamberlain, so Danger's intervention 'in hire stede' is the structural flaw in Amans's pursuit of the privilege of intimacy with his lady.

I do not mean to claim that Danger is identifiable as a royal under-chamberlain, only to enlist under-chamberlains for a heightened impression of the intermediary duties shared by chamberers in less visible great households and by Danger. Observations about the typically unspecialized quality of chamber service should be remembered here. The servant who performed the 'filtering' role in an aristocratic household would probably not have enjoyed any *special* 'chamberlain' title. Where specialization was found in the chamber, the senior affiliate might have been called secretary, wardrober, or even clerk of the chamber or treasurer. Access control may have fallen variously to this officer, to any chamberer (a chamberlain in the basic sense), or, outside the chamber, to the steward.[34] Danger's disciplinary skills and chancorial responsibilities (implied by the lady's 'Seil') might even cast him as a steward, but his intimacy with the lady and his duties in the chamber in book 5 make that household department the more suggestive context.

When he is confessed on the vices of stealth and theft in book 5, Amans represents Danger as 'a wardein redi ay' (5. 6614) who guards the chamber against forced or covert intrusions:

---

[31] *SR* ii. 68–9; cf. *PROME* iii. 268. See also *PROME* iii. 444 (1399 Oct., mem. 3; a commons petition for reliable delegated treatment of petitions to the king, answered with the designation of the chamberlain and council).

[32] Given-Wilson, *Royal Household*, 72.

[33] Ibid. 72–3; cf. *PROME* iii. 12–13.

[34] Mertes, *Noble Household*, 22–4, 44–6.

For that Serpent which nevere slepte
The flees of gold so wel ne kepte
In Colchos, as the tale is told,
That mi ladi a thousendfold
Nys betre yemed and bewaked,
Wher sche be clothed or be naked.
To kepe hir bodi nyht and day,
Sche hath a wardein redi ay,
Which is so wonderful a wyht,
That him ne mai no mannes myht
With swerd ne with no wepne daunte,
Ne with no sleihte of charme enchaunte,
Wherof he mihte be mad tame,
And Danger is his rihte name;
Which under lock and under keie,
That noman mai it stele aweie,
Hath al the Tresor underfonge
That unto love mai belonge.
The leste lokinge of hire yhe
Mai noght be stole, if he it syhe;
·   ·   ·   ·   ·   ·   ·   ·   ·   ·   ·   ·

And that me grieveth wonder sore,
For this proverbe is evere newe,
That stronge lokes maken trewe
Of hem that wolden stele and pyke

                                        (5. 6607–33)

Despite Amans's language of wonder and magic, the description of
Danger's function 'To kepe hir bodi' is appropriate to any ordinary
chamberlain in a noble household. Chamberlains were responsible for
the lord's laundry, washing, sanitary arrangements, and dressing, and
were ideally to be in close attendance on the lord 'nyht and day'.[35]

The metaphor of the lady's (bodily) 'Tresor' and Danger's custody of
it, meanwhile, suggests an office which took various titles in the fourteenth-century great household and was more or less narrowly defined

---

[35] Starkey, 'Age of the Household', 250–1; Woolgar, *Great Household*, 42, 167,
170, 172. The latter relies on John Russell's fifteenth-century *Boke of Nurture*,
in Frederick J. Furnivall (ed.), *Manners and Meals in Olden Time*, EETS, os 32
(London, 1868), 176–83. At one point, this treatise notes that a chamberlain should
be in sufficiently close attendance that he should 'haue þe bason for chambur &
also þe vrnalle | redy at alle howres when he wille clepe or calle' (*Manners and
Meals*, 182).

depending upon household size and the lord's needs. This role might have fallen to a chamberlain, or to a designated wardrober, to the head servant of the chamber or perhaps to a receiver who accounted for traffic of the lord's treasure out of the chamber. The 'Tresor' metaphor's emphasis on the retention of commodities also resembles the royal household's office of porter of the chamber as it was set out for a serjeant porter in a household ordinance of Edward II:

Item vn sergeant porter, qi gardera la porte par la ou le roi gist, issint qe nulle y entre fors ceux qi le deuent faire de droit; ne qil suffre qe nulle ne port hors de la court pain, vin, ne seruois, viande, littre, ne busche, ne nul autres chosez, fors ceux qi deiuent faire; ne rien ne soit emportez saunz certeins liuereez et autres chosez qi deiuent estre porte de droit.[36]

And a serjeant porter, who shall keep the door where the king lies, so that none enter but those who ought to of right; and will neither suffer that anyone carry out of the court bread, wine, ale, victuals, bedding, or firewood, or any other things, except those which they ought. Nor should anything be carried out except certain liveries and other things which ought to be taken of right.

The serjeant porter is to protect the structure of household exchange. He oversees material things and keeps them within the chamber where a chamberlain (also) controls the access of counsel and suit from without. The chamber porter guards against internal dissipation or haemorrhaging by exchange unauthorized by the household, by the illicit practice of those who can otherwise claim legitimate attendance about the lord.

Wild hedger to civil chamberlain

As chamber servant, Gower's Danger has come a long way. He is implanted in the heart of civilized, aristocratic society even though his black and bristly ancestor in the *Roman de la Rose* hales from the literary family of the wild man. Guillaume de Lorris's and Jean de Meun's Dangier is irreducibly ambivalent. He offers a valid critique of values which the *Rose's* lover assumes to be normative, but his social status and physical appearance mean that he cannot inhabit an alternative aristocratic ideal. Wild critics of civil society can inject reformative energy into a narrative, but success is typically accompanied by the critic's own transformation and absorption by reformed society, and this never happens to Dangier.[37] He certainly serves

[36] Quoted in Tout, *Reign of Edward II*, 266. The full ordinance (6 Dec. 1318) is printed by Tout (244–81).

[37] For the conventional attributes of the wild man, their incorporation in the *Rose*, and the function of wild critic, see Richard Bernheimer, *Wild Men in the Middle Ages:*

aristocratic interests, for by resisting the reproductively unsecured love of Deduit's garden, as Sarah Kay points out, he opposes 'the greatest possible threat to a social hierarchy dependent on the strict regulation of reproduction and inheritance'.[38] Dangier is aligned with the kind of long-sighted conservative principles which his counterpart in the *Confessio* will also defend, and de Meun provocatively links him with Renouart, the Saracen of the Guillaume d'Orange episode *Aliscans* who is despised by Louis Martel's decadent, etiolated court but properly understood by heroic, 'redeemed', and *eiron*-type characters.[39] Amant's fear of Dangier resembles stunted readings of savage 'helpers' by incompetent observers such as Louis and invites readers to side with progressive attitudes akin to that of Guillaume d'Orange himself (or Calogrenant, who overcomes his apprehension to listen to the gigantic bullherd's advice in Chrétien de Troyes's *Yvain*[40]).

Even the warmly appreciated savage critic, however, remains other and on the 'extreme fringes of society'.[41] The late medieval savage-civil dialectic inscribes the aristocratic (at the centre of the civil) as a quantity in relation to which the function of the savage fringe is definitional or corrective, but always external. The savage critic may alter but will not replace the cultured centre, and is (re)integrated in the civil in reforming it. Thus, successful social critics in Chrétien's *Perceval*, *Le Chevalier au Cygne*, and the Middle English *Sir Percyvell of Gales* progress towards exemplary chivalric destinies having emerged from the wilderness to shock courts in decline. Renouart himself learns to control his native force, eventually relinquishes his artless club in favour of a knight's weapon, and ultimately gains a deluxe kit of Christian chivalry— knighthood and spurs, a horse, equestrian martial skills, a noble wife, a 'country', retainers, and baptism.[42] Crucially, Renouart's chivalry

A Study in Art, Sentiment, and Demonology (Cambridge, Mass., 1952), 1–29; John Block Friedman, *The Monstrous Races in Medieval Art and Thought* (1981; Syracuse, NY, 2000), 26–33, 163–77.

[38] Sarah Kay, *The Romance of the Rose* (London, 1995), 109.

[39] For the sympathetic and often unobtrusive *eiron* types in comedy and their romance counterparts, see Northrop Frye, *Anatomy of Criticism: Four Essays* (Princeton, 1957), 40, 172, 195–6.

[40] Dangier's direct antecedent, the bullherd of *Yvain*, is also a savage helper figure, but, more mediator than critic, his engagement with aristocratic culture is significantly less conflictual and dialectic than that of Dangier and Renouart. See Jacques Le Goff, *The Medieval Imagination*, tr. Arthur Goldhammer (Chicago, 1988), 57, 117–21.

[41] Le Goff, *Medieval Imagination*, 56.

[42] *Aliscans (Rédaction A)*, ed. Claude Régnier (Paris, 1990), ll. 7894–7994, 8086–8154; cf. *Aliscans*, ed. E. Wienbeck, W. Hartnacke, and P. Rasch (Halle, 1903), ll. 8470–8. On the club or tree branch as the non-cultural weapon of the savage, see Friedman, *Monstrous Races*,

is never secure, but Dangier cannot match his trappings of aristocratic society in the first place and is early and proleptically consigned to the *Rose*'s losing side.[43] The poem is covert and hesitant, that is, about its own critique of courtliness.

Nonetheless, Dangier's representation is modulated and he makes some arrested movements towards the aristocratic centre. Having started as a hedger, 'Dangiers li vilains' is later discovered captaining a company of thirty guard. He never clearly avoids social difference in an aristocratic setting however. As captain 'portier' (porter), he is a bruiser of relatively low rank in Jalousie's household and is liable to be beaten as an underling by his mistress (*RR*, ll. 7664–8). He continues to be referred to as 'vilains' and described with the lexicon of savagery in the second part of the *Rose* and has in fact become more wild in manner than de Lorris's Dangier, who had the measured intelligence of Chrétien's bullherd.[44] As Renouart's career demonstrates, the repulsion between aristocratic and wild is very powerful, and wildness prevails for Amant's toughest opponent in the *Rose*. His aristocratic acculturation is achieved by *Confessio Amantis*.

Gower's Danger shares the critical function of 'Dangiers li vilains', but he is no wild man. His corrective to Amans's perspective relies on the same oblique mobilization of an allegory's literal level that operates in the *Rose*. Yet Danger's social literal attributes are completely reconfigured and retain no obvious trace of his wild heritage. The aristocratic is polarized in the poem across Amans and Danger's rivalry, and Danger reflects not only a repudiation of Amans's *fin'amor* but a separate version of the aristocratic. This version is informed primarily by an imaginary of service and hierarchy in the great household.

The shift in Danger's social status between the savage servant of the *Rose* and the *Confessio*'s chamberer is immediately apparent. Gower's Danger is described almost exclusively by his proximate and cooperative relationship with the lady herself (not symbolic mediations of her as in the *Rose*). Household associations add prestige to this impression of intimacy. The

---

32–4. For Renouart's faltering transition from club to sword, see e.g. *Aliscans*, ed. Régnier, ll. 4738–4823, 5096–5101, 6964–93; cf. ll. 7110–14.

[43] *RR*, ll. 3502–4; cf. ll. 10591–602. *Rose* translations are based on Guillaume de Lorris and Jean de Meun, *The Romance of the Rose*, tr. Charles Dahlberg, 3rd edn (Princeton, 1971).

[44] See Dahlberg, 'First Person and Personification', 45–7, for a view of Dangier as essentially civil (beyond Amant's perspective). Cf. Jacqueline de Weever, 'Dangier, the Saracen-Guardian of the *Roman de la Rose*', *Mediaevalia*, 21 (1996–7), 27–45, 32–4.

lord's chamber was the most exclusive space of the great household and members of its staff were those in closest contact with the lord's person.[45] The post of under-chamberlain in the royal household was usually filled by a personal friend of the king. By the time of Edward II's 1318 household ordinance, the under-chamberlain was counted among the three most senior household officers (alongside the steward and the keeper). The post was held by men of high and often noble rank from the time of Edward III onwards.[46] The receiver, who kept 'under lock and under keie' the king's personal hoard of money, jewels, and plate, tended likewise to be an intimate of the king. He could, under the chamberlain, have responsibility for vast sums of money and Richard II's lay receivers were esquires and knights of the chamber. A number, including Simon Burley (also chamberlain) and John Beauchamp (later Richard's steward), were men of rising prestige.[47]

Danger the chamberer has quite cast off his socially inferior literary past. Gower jettisons obnoxious and ambivalent qualities available in the *Rose* (including wildness) or else isolates them within Amans's perspective. Where Dangier is ambiguously wild, Danger is inconspicuously civil. Only analogy with the dragon of Colchis (*CA* 5. 6607–9) invokes any sense of the exotic and liminal around Danger, and his visual and behavioural representation is actually consistently faint. Amans says nothing about his features or clothing and the fact that his enemy notices no physical or cultural otherness is the strongest signal that Danger possesses the sameness of the civil.

At the same time, Gower distils in Danger a character of implacable duty which is his major convergence with Dangier's literal attributes in the

---

[45] For vivid evidence of the associations of status, intimacy, and trust which could cluster around the chamberlain, we have the *Ancrene Wisse*'s allegorical imagination of Love as God's 'chamberleng, his conseiler, his spuse': *Ancrene Wisse*, ed. Bella Millett, EETS, os 325–6 (Oxford, 2005–7), i. 154 (7. 356–7). Consider also Chaucer's Arcite's advantage in securing service with 'a chamberleyn | The which that dwellynge was with Emelye' (*CT* 1. 1418–19) as a page of her chamber (1. 1426–7). For Arcite/Philostrate's duplicitous yet meteoric career in chamber service at Theseus's court (which comes to have more to do with intimacy with the duke than with Emily), see *CT* 1. 1426–48, 1497–8, 1540–71; and Richard Firth Green, 'Arcite at Court', *English Language Notes*, 18 (1981), 251–7.

[46] For the development of the chamber between the reigns of Edward I and Richard II, see Tout, *Chapters*, ii. 314–60; iv. 227–348; Given-Wilson, *Royal Household*, 10–11, 206.

[47] For Richard II's receivers, see Tout, *Chapters*, vi. 56–7. See also Given-Wilson, *Royal Household*, 85–92. On chamber responsibilities for treasure in non-royal households, see Mertes, *Noble Household*, 44–6.

Rose. Danger has neither Dangier's violence and drowsy negligence nor his explicit courtesy. His behaviour is recounted only through Amans's memory and in the continuous present, so that he acquires a paradigmatic quality and seems to be impervious to personal confrontation. Remote and impenetrable, he may have borrowed only one element of de Lorris's Dangier's character which it is tempting to describe as officiousness. De Lorris ironizes his lover's eager combativeness by puncturing it with official unconcern (' "Adès aime, mais que tu soies | Loing de mes roses toutes-voies" ', 'Love forever, as long as you are always far from my roses'; *RR*, ll. 3199–3200), which anticipates Amans's relationship with Danger in the *Confessio* ('Of merci nevere a point I hadde'; *CA* 3. 1561). Otherwise, the two Dangiers are scarcely recognizable as cousins and, in terms of social profile, Gower's Danger seems akin to the lovers in both poems. Neglecting the wild, the literal level of Gower's allegory adopts an insulated (but not complacent) vantage point on the aristocratic, uninterested in socially inferior otherness. Danger occasions cultural shock neither for Amans nor for the reader. Yet Gower's chamberer proves to be an even more formidable opponent than de Lorris and de Meun's hedger-cum-porter. Dangier suffers setbacks and is finally routed with the rest of Jalousie's garrison, but Danger remains 'evere … in o place' (8. 2264). In the *Confessio*, the guardian figure is fully integrated into aristocratic normalcy, but not absorbed into the lover's values. The *trewe* servant Danger mounts a challenge to Amans's view of courtliness from the inside.

How (not) to bring down a chamberlain

Gower's Amans, like de Lorris's Amant, represents a *fin'amor* ethos of sophisticated leisure and hyper-refinement encapsulated by knightly devotion to a lady. The (magnificent) contours of exclusivity and irresponsibility in such courtliness are not limited to personal devotion and the sovereign authority symbolized by the lady. As Kay's reading based on the threat to a prospective and hierarchical aristocratic economics indicates, Dangier represents a corrective to Amant's courtly values in the *Rose*. The difference in the *Confessio* is that Danger's resistance is mounted from within shared social space and that it is persistently privileged by the poem. To valorize Danger, the poem turns to its own purposes Amans's invective and exploits reluctant admiration in Amans's 'wardein' account (5. 6597–6652) and Supplication.

Amans's defamation of Danger as a chamberlain belongs to the same textual matrix as commons' reciprocalist complaints against actual royal chamberlains of the late fourteenth century. As Amans would have it, Danger monopolizes the attention of his lady and rebuffs worthy suitors such as himself. Danger, according to Amans, has too exclusive and too comprehensive a relationship with the lady. The criticism of Danger as 'so prive of conseil' will echo in the description of Parsimony as 'most prive | With Avarice' (5. 4686–7), and the lover's vituperation generally alleges a narrow, inward-looking service relation detrimental to good lordship. With the lady shut away, the chamberlain Danger represents to Amans the blank face of unresponsive lordship. The lover's attitude towards Danger thus has considerable affinity with the climate of resentment that could thicken around contemporary royal chamberlains. The intimacy of the chamberlain's relationship with the king placed him in a crucible heated by every would-be adviser's and suitor's expectations of exchange with the monarch. If consultation, largesse, or justice were unavailable, the primary interface of such exchange could easily be suspected of diverting its course or clogging it at source and soaking up its benefits himself.

Several under-chamberlains of the late fourteenth century fell foul of contemporary expectations about their conduct in office. Parliamentary attacks against them qua chamberlains invoke stubborn reciprocalist criteria of outwardness and inclusiveness in the office; that the chamberlain, in other words, should represent lordship responsible to the political community beyond the chamber, and not just to the king. The Merciless Parliament attacked around fifty members of the royal household, but Simon Burley, who had been the king's chamberlain for the entire reign to date, was one of the parliament's special targets.[48] The 1388 articles of impeachment accuse him as part of the inner circle of accroachers who have, to borrow Amans's phrase, 'so englued' the king that 'entierement eux lui firent de tout a eux doner soun amour, et ferme foy et credence, et haier ses foialx seignours et liges, par queux il deust avoir este de droit plus governe' (they caused him entirely to give them his love and firm faith and belief, and to hate his faithful lords and subjects by whom he ought of right rather to have been governed; *PROME* iii. 241; cf. iii. 230). This text and Amans's accusation against Danger equally blame a servant for exploiting his position of intimacy to dam up his superior's good will and cut it off from others. Article 7 of the impeachment makes Burley's chamberlainship in particular responsible for a brand of magnificent lordship in the king's household (*hostelle*) that manages to be at once profligate with household exchange

---

[48] On the proceedings of the Merciless Parliament in general, see above, 35 n. 28.

(dispensing 'great gifts of the revenues and commodities of the king-dom') and exclusive of an entire community of worship. For the gifts' recipients are outsiders—'aliens, beamers [Bohemians] et autres'—iden-tified by their not belonging to any assumed class of proper recipients.[49] Burley was tried and executed in 1388 as a too *prive* chamberlain.

Men who were chamberlains before and after Burley were brought down by the same kind of resentment. In the 'Good Parliament' of 1376, William, Lord Latimer, under-chamberlain to Edward III, was accused alongside the merchant and moneylender Richard Lyons of various malpractices such as selling licences to merchants to circumvent the staple and the brokerage of royal debts for his own profit.[50] The impeachment introduces the 'malx faitz' with its sine qua non of royal intimacy: it describes Latimer as 'chamberleyn, et du prive conseil... nostre seignur le roi' (chamberlain and of the privy council of our lord the king; *PROME* ii. 324). At the end of Richard II's reign, William Scrope (made earl of Wiltshire in 1397) became detested for the concentration of power and royal gifts in his hands. Executed at Bristol in July 1399, he was one of the few courtiers to meet with death in the face of Bolingbroke's 'transition' policy of lenience. Scrope had been under-chamberlain 1393–8 (when he became treasurer of England) and late in this period he truly did soak up royal beneficence. In the first parliament of Henry IV's reign, the recently executed Scrope was remembered in a petition for the restoration of Thomas, earl of Warwick. The petition draws a familiar, hard division between royal advisers driven by 'soleyne covetise et singuler profit' (filthy covetise and singular profit) and working 'par covyne', on the one hand, and wronged lords prevented from working in the common interest on the other.[51] Scrope is the only one of the evil counsellors to be identified by office (as well as noble title).[52] It seems that no late fourteenth-century accus-ation of covin around the king was complete without his chamberlain.

[49] *PROME* iii. 242; cf. iii. 247 (1388 Feb., mem. 4): the chancellor, steward, and chamberlain (now Peter Courtenay) are appointed to enforce the exile of any Bohemians not retained by the queen with Appellant approval.

[50] For this parliament, see George Holmes, *The Good Parliament* (Oxford, 1975). For the proceedings of Latimer's impeachment, see *PROME* ii. 324–7.

[51] *PROME* iii. 436 (1399 Oct., mem. 8). The dichotomy is unusual in this case for its inclusion in the evil covin of the (deposed) king himself.

[52] The inference to be drawn is, of course, that whatever offices or commissions the others held were effects, rather than structural components, of their unmerited privilege as nobles and counsellors—none held a major office in Richard's household at the end of the reign. Scrope had himself been treasurer more recently than chamberlain, although he held the latter office at the time of the events the petition describes.

Danger is not Burley. The ill-fated historical chamberlains attest the extent to which discourses of proper power could be concentrated around the position of chamberlain. Representations of Burley and Danger invoke the same political ideals (and I have already argued for reciprocalist discourse as a motor for the *Confessio* and the 1388 impeachments alike; see above, 43–9). Danger, however, realizes the chamberlain's potential as a focus for political discourse by his exemplarity, in the opposite fashion to Burley. Free of the circumstances of actual political life, Danger fulfils those idealized expectations of household service which were used to prosecute Richard's tutor. Amans thinks of his enemy Danger as having the same kind of extraordinary and exclusory influence attributed to Latimer and Burley, but Gower does not back him up.

Amans's rhetoric compromises his attack and enables a sceptical reading of it, first, by revealing his own interestedness and unreliability and, secondly, by implicitly idealizing Danger. Unlike the commons of 1376 and 1388, therefore, Amans is unable to expel a chamberlain from office or to 'manace' him 'to be ded' (*CA* 3. 1525, 1533). The parliamentary attacks claim an exhaustive perspective identifying with and legitimated by the common good or the 'profit du roi et du roialme' (*PROME* iii. 229). Amans conspicuously fails to legitimize his representation of Danger by generalizing in this way.[53] The Danger portraits have none of the detached authority of Genius's Parsimony portrait (5. 4671–709), for example, and offer no equivalent for the commons' postures of responsible, constructive devotion to the common good which stand foil to their censures of *prive* chamberlains. Where social hierarchy naturalizes privilege in the commons texts (so that 'great men' are assumed to have priority in sharing the king's pursuit of the common good), Amans's primary justification for access to the lady seems to be personal aspiration (encoded in the discourse of courtly love). The reciprocalist discourse which informs the commons texts and the *Confessio* is thoroughly hostile to desire that runs free of entrenched, hierarchical social structures, and it fits best with Danger's behaviour not Amans's grievance.

[53] The ironizing of Amans's critique in turn threatens to unmask the parliamentary attacks. In revealing the polemical strategy of the lover's conventional account of the chamberlain, the *Confessio* analogously destabilizes parliamentary implementations of the same discourse. In the *Rose*, Amant's perspective, serving Amor's order, is not consistently undermined and it contends strongly with Dangier's point of view and a parodic reading of itself.

Amans's attack is first of all compromised by his ingenuous disclosure of his own motives to his confessor. In introducing the 'consailer', Amans's language *about himself* has been violent, extreme, and obsessive:

> And him wolde I long time er this,
> And yit I wolde and evere schal,
> Slen and destruie in special.
> The gold of nyne kinges londes
> Ne scholde him save fro myn hondes,
> In my pouer if that he were
>
> (3. 1518–23)

This outburst associates Amans rather than Danger with lethal violence and (in the insufficient surfeit of gold) with a trope appropriate to the exotic, marvellous zone of the wild. Later, Amans is confessing to the vice of thievery in intent or 'be mi will' (5. 6563) when he describes Danger as a 'wardein'. Amans confesses deception and dishonesty repeatedly in terms of theft, stealth, and the inauspicious phrase 'stele and pyke' (5. 6633, cf. 5. 6681). The phrase takes on a decidedly unsavoury nuance when, contemplating the possibility of Danger's exile, Amans revives insomniac fantasies from vigils spent watching his lady's window from his own lodgings. He imagines invading her room by necromancy 'So that I mihte under the palle | Som thing of love pyke and stele' (5. 6680–1). But Danger remains in office and thus deserves credit for prohibiting sinister voyeuristic and potentially violent tendencies. While insisting on the distinction between act and intent, Amans himself seems to recognize that his premonitions of violation have an uncomfortable affinity with several tales of rape told by Genius shortly before (those of Theseus, Tereus, and Neptune and Cornix).

These premonitions, furthermore, are not anomalies in Amans's portrayal. (In so far as Danger is interpreted allegorically as a quality of the lady's own personality and volition, of course, the potential of rape is always inherent in Amans's desire for his utter and violent removal.) The fantasies extend more innocuous-seeming surveys of the lover's ineffectual designs and unsolicited attentions into a shadowy hinterland of antisocial behaviour. Such behaviour taints the full spectrum of Amans's conduct as emotionally and socially suspect. The guest whose emotions depend wholly on the presence of his lady and swing schizophrenically between passionate woe and explosive, dancing expression ('Me thenkth that for the time I mihte | Riht sterte thurgh the hole wall'; 6. 184–5), and the reader who feeds his desire and hope on romances (6. 875–98), is the same master who, seeming to 'rave' (3. 91), will vent his frustration on hapless servants when hope subsides and desire remains. The comically helpless wooer, who stands tongue-tied and 'assoted' (4. 680–702), and deflects advances into incessant awkward chamber play and courtly recreation before retiring at last for a sleepless night (4. 1168–97, 2771–2839), is the same obsessive watcher who will spend such waking time fantasizing about black magic and secret rape, and the same brooding lover whose frustration feeds on itself in language of hate and murder. The portrayal of Amans in the *Confessio* argues that expressions of *fin'amor* both encourage and camouflage obsessive and antisocial habits of mind.[54]

Accordingly, Amans's critique of Danger's service rebounds to expose the lover's own hypocrisy. The fragmentation and materialization of the lady's body and gestures into itemized glances and other 'Tresor... | That unto love mai belonge', for example, recalls from the same book the punctilious, hoarding magnificence of *Unkindeschipe* who will not part with 'o grein' of his provisions (5. 4906). Yet the atomizing description of Danger's guardianship reveals an obvious trace of the observer's obsessive imagination. His intervention by representation assumes a distinctly voyeuristic and fetishistic quality as Amans pictures Danger guarding his naked lady or locking up the disembodied 'lokinge of hire yhe'.

Amans, not Danger, is associated with divisiveness. Danger is first attacked by Amans shortly after Genius has invoked the model of the obstinate chamberlain in Fool Haste (3. 1095–9), who is as successful in excluding Patience from meaningful audience with *Contek* as Danger is in thwarting Amans. Danger's service is not, however, based on the internalizing, non-representative intimacy of household groups such as *Contek*'s and those of other allegorized vices in the poem. The intimacy between Fool Haste and his master is linked to the injury of the common good (and not just to the injury of a lover's singular and selfish interest), reproducing the strategy of the commons' attacks on chamberlains. Thus, Danger and Fool Haste are not striking as parallels but as contrasts to each other. In his representation of Danger, Amans performs the very divisiveness that Gower sees as characteristic of coterie politics. Selfishly motivated and lacking a rhetoric of common profit, Amans plays the role of a zealous courtier opponent to Danger:

[54] Readers of the *Confessio*, however, are not usually inclined to censure Amans. J. A. Burrow e.g. prefers to applaud the way in which Gower evokes sympathy for 'the felt experience of *senilis amor*', and he finds nothing stronger than 'folly' in Amans's 'unseasonable' desire ('Portrayal of Amans', 15). See also Nicholson, *Love and Ethics*, 99–100.

If that I mihte finde a sleyhte,
To leie al myn astat in weyhte,
I wolde him fro the Court dissevere,
So that he come ayeinward nevere.

(3. 1571–4)

Despite, or perhaps because of, Amans's insistence that 'betwen Danger and me | Is evere werre til he dye' (3. 1564–5), Danger's mood of imperturbable vigilance works against any impression that he is embroiled in factional contests. Unlike chamberlain Fool Haste, or Latimer, Burley, or Scrope, Danger is not associated with any covin. Amans can make no charge that Danger's counsel is 'al unavised' (3. 1097), a destructive influence on the lady's household or rooted in a concern for his own singular profit. Furthermore, Genius's warning against impatience in response to Amans's complaint (3. 1613–58) makes the contrast between Danger and Fool Haste acute, for it casts 'folhastif' (3. 1635) Amans himself in the latter role. The success of the commons' rhetoric in 1376 and 1388 was in taking possession of a language of public righteousness while encumbering opponents with notions of treachery and covin. Amans seems only *self*-righteous against an immovable foe.

The 'trewe' chamberlain

Amans's unreliable perspective facilitates a reading of Danger quite at odds with his intentions. Indeed, estimations of Danger's infallibility and integrity only gain in persuasiveness coming from the mouth of his 'mortiel enemy'.[55] Amans portrays a chamberer whose obligation to his mistress epitomizes reciprocalist service, and he inadvertently attributes to this service a stabilizing social influence which evokes the poem's widest political ideal. Danger's integrity (as well as his select status) distinguishes him from the unprincipled descendants of the troubadours' *lauzengiers*, the rivals to the lover who can serve as scapegoats for shameful court behaviour (in which the lover almost automatically participates by defaming them).[56]

[55] Even before the Supplication, Amans manages to state and restate his inability to win over, circumvent, or defeat Danger something like twenty times. Again, the allegorical level of meaning, according to which Danger represents the Lady's personal virtue and sexual integrity, can steer interpretation. For Amans might be thought proud of, as well as frustrated by, his lady's high standards and chastity.

[56] On *lauzengiers* as 'the scapegoats of [courtly love lyric] . . . and the dumping ground of many of its contradictions', see Sarah Kay, 'The Contradictions of Courtly Love and the

Take, for instance, Amans's frustrated assertion that Danger 'For evere...hangeth on [the lady's] Seil' (3. 1555). This sounds like the parliamentary accusations against royal chamberlains, but there is a pun here which reveals Amans's skewed perspective and Danger's true qualities. The primary meaning of 'Seil' is that of the lady's official seal, implying that Danger is in constant attendance on his lady or authorizes her writs and fully embodies her official persona.[57] Amans clearly resents this, but intimacy was expected of actual chamberlains and did not invariably prompt criticism. The royal chamberlain's duties to endorse petitions and to supervise access to the royal person imply activity close about the king. The chamberlain might be dispatched for lengthy spells on major military and diplomatic missions (such as Richard II's marriage negotiations), but he was most probably expected to return from such business to attendance on the king and not to his own estates.[58] The other possible meanings of *seil* suggest that Danger does not use to his own ends the authority in which he is permitted to participate, but dutifully subordinates himself to it. The noun could refer to an occasion or point in time, and carried the further sense of happiness, good fortune, or prosperity, so that Danger is associated not just with the instrument of his office but with a responsiveness to circumstances and needs, and with the continued integrity of the lady's lordship.[59] In this light, Amans's complaint about the pernicious, unrelenting influence of his lady's chief counsellor sharpens into a representation of an ideal service relationship embodying the poem's key values of *trouthe*, unity, and responsible household relations.

The quasi-metonymical relationship between Danger and the lady that is suggested at this point in Amans's complaint defines the thrust of the complaint overall. Danger ('my lady's "concealer"') frustrates

Origins of Courtly Poetry: The Evidence of the *Lauzengiers'*, *Journal of Medieval and Early Modern Studies*, 26 (1996), 209–53, 215–25 (quote at 216). For Amans's mixing in the business of 'janglers', see *CA* 2. 383–531 (cf. 3. 885–930); but elsewhere Amans seems (more clearly) to be his own toughest opponent (1. 2721–49; 3. 551–92).

[57] The 'seal' meaning is clear in an earlier passage that mirrors exactly the image applied to Danger: False Seeming 'falseth many a covenant, | And many a fraude of fals conseil | Ther ben hangende upon his Seil' (2. 2150–2). See also Angus McIntosh, M. L. Samuels, and Michael Benskin (eds), *A Linguistic Atlas of Late Mediaeval English* (Aberdeen, 1986), i. 511 (map 914, 'well'); iv. 276–7; M. L. Samuels and J. J. Smith, 'The Language of Gower', in J. J. Smith (ed.), *The English of Chaucer and his Contemporaries: Essays by M. L. Samuels and J. J. Smith* (Aberdeen, 1988), 13–22; J. J. Smith, 'Spelling and Tradition in Fifteenth-Century Copies of Gower's *Confessio Amantis*', ibid. 96–113.

[58] Given-Wilson, *Royal Household*, 210.

[59] *MED*, s.v. 'sel(e', n. (1), 1, 2; n. (3), 1(a), 1(b), 3.

Amans by seeming to block out the object of desire, and he ensures that the lady remains an enigmatic absence for Gower's readers as well. Danger is always 'wher as sche was' and 'in hire stede'. He is a fiction of counsel or mediation, a displacement of what is in fact the particular will of the lady. Amans hints extravagantly and comically at this much when he asks how the lady 'mai hirself excuse' (3. 1586) if he were to die in failing to overcome Danger.[60]

The near-identity of Danger and the lady implies a degree of self-abnegation in Danger's service and might suggestively be construed in terms of Fradenburg's formulation of the 'totalized discourse of the sovereign', whereby the servant's subjectivity is nullified by the relationship to the sovereign and the servant represents only the meanings of the master.[61] Danger, however, remains an assertive subject and retains a strong measure of his own will in Amans's distorted perception. It is Danger who is said to have 'englued' the lady and not vice versa, and he is never seen to debase himself. Instead, it is Amans who has found himself repeatedly bowing and beseeching before the counsellor (3. 1551–2). Danger is constructed less in subordinating opposition to the lady than in dominant opposition to the hapless suitor. His role is close to Felicity Heal's conceptualization of household officers' embodying or 'personating' of the authority and qualities of their lord.[62] It is a role he fulfils so completely that Amans, in the very language he uses to express his wish for his own advancement at Danger's expense, is forced to acknowledge that such a change would constitute political breakdown. To counter the strength of Danger's bond to the lady's (or Love's) court, he is obliged to imagine unceasing 'werre' (3. 1565), slaying or utter banishment, and that he might 'dissevere' the counsellor from court (3. 1573).

In the second of the two major accounts of Danger in the middle of the poem, Amans's complaint once again actually works to portray an ideal servant. His previous mood of self-righteous frustration has become

---

[60] At the allegorical level, Danger's role enacts a strategy of gender organization similar to ones detected by critics in courtly love lyric and the *Rose*. These strategies of 'masculinising the beloved' either endow her with powers of lordship or (as in the cases of Bel Acueil and Dangier) displace the lady in favour of a male entity. They thereby demonstrate 'the extent to which "courtly love" is powered by homosocial desire, that is, desire by men for the values (such as status) they find only [or mainly] in other men'. See Kay, *Romance of the Rose*, 45–7 (quotes at 46); Kay, *Subjectivity in Troubadour Poetry*, 83–97; Gaunt, *Gender and Genre*, 131–2, 135–47.

[61] Fradenburg, 'Manciple's Servant Tongue', 89.

[62] Heal, 'Reciprocity and Exchange', 180; cf. Heal, *Hospitality*, 7.

something closer to awe and self-loathing that 'Betwen hire hih astat and me | Comparison ther mai non be' (5. 6597–8), as he acknowledges the baseness of his own motives to 'stalke and crepe' (5. 6638). As a result, the friction between matter and intent in the lover's first exposition of Danger is diminished in the second. An emphatic portrait of integrity and 'trewe' service, the account of Danger as *wardein* neutralizes any lingering suggestions of destructive privacy in the chamberlain. Here, in Amans's despairing, admiring evocation of the 'wonderful' protector of his lady's body, are basic ingredients of an ideal of service that is deeply embedded in Gower's poem. Danger is 'redy ay' to serve in both expositions, and is always attendant upon his mistress 'be nyht or day' (3. 1541). His is a permanent relation grounded on loyalty and adaptable to circumstances, rather than opportunistically formed for particular ends dictated by circumstances. Danger epitomizes *trewe* service.

The *Confessio* argues pervasively that the ideal of personal *trouthe* which Danger embodies (and allegorizes by representing sexual containment) is productive of wider social stability. The imagery with which Amans bemoans Danger's constancy is freighted with this social logic, connecting Danger to the poem's fundamental political vision. Most sententious is Amans's wistful citation of the proverb 'That stronge lokes maken trewe' (5. 6632), which distils a conservative model of social order. It ascribes to Danger—chamberer and female chastity, and the 'strong lock' in question—the responsibility of imposing the image of *trouthe* on society by rendering *untrewe* wills impotent. Earlier, when Danger remains impervious to bribery or eloquence—the lover makes no headway against the chamberlain 'for speche ne for mede' (3. 1543)—he revives memories of the golden age, the nostalgic touchstone of the poem. Then, duplicitous talk (or flattery) and avarice were impossible, and perfect order was underpinned by *trouthe* because speech was always 'lich to the conceite' (prol. 113).[63]

---

[63] Cf. Chaucer's 'The Former Age', in *Riverside Chaucer*, 650–1. See also Chaucer's familiar Platonic aphorism that 'The wordes moote be cosyn to the dede' (*CT* 1. 742; cf. 9. 210), with its ambivalent connotations of proximity without identity. For the likelihood of a (French) word-play in 'cosyn', suggesting deceit, see the articles by Fisher and Taylor cited above, 71 n. 16.

By the same principle, book 7's discussions of rhetoric and flattery cast eloquence as a condition of the post-Saturnian world. Since eloquence's 'goodly wordes' (7. 1561) can work to 'evele' ends (7. 1548–9), it is contingent on the separation of language and *trouthe* after the golden age, whereby 'the word' might now 'to the conceipte | Descordeth' (7. 1554–5).[64] Similarly, the world's original condition of common property at the opening of book 5 precluded bribery. Immune to Amans's 'speche' or 'mede', Danger resembles a fragment of a lost age of 'love' and 'pes' (prol. 109, 115; 5. 12, 14), a bastion of *trouthe* embattled but unbowed by the decline of the world.

The same kind of political affiliation is imputed to Danger by his favourable comparison to 'that Serpent which nevere slepte' guarding the golden fleece of Colchis 'as the tale is told' (5. 6607–9). The tale in which Jason overpowers the dragon and steals the fleece has, in fact, just been told by Genius, but this does not undermine Amans's comparison. Jason wins the fleece with secret magic which betrays rather than compromises the dragon's honest service and strength. Gower's treatment of Jason's contest with the dragon dwells almost exclusively on the 'sorwe' (5. 3700) of the battered and blasted assailant and the impregnability of the guardian, 'scherded al aboute... | Ther mihte nothing go therin' (5. 3707–10). As though an embarrassment to the narrative, the fact that Jason 'overcam' (5. 3718) and 'slowh' (5. 3699) his opponent is sparely reported as bookends to the battle's description. Moreover, Genius expressly confirms that Jason's proper, inherent prowess was no match for the Colchian beast, and that without Medea's multiple and elaborate charms the adventurer 'hadde with that worm be lore' (5. 3716). Gower further shields Danger's exaltation in his analogy to the warden of Colchis by having Amans declare him invulnerable both to conventional weapons *and* to enchantment by 'sleihte of charme' (5. 6618), as if to underwrite his association with the defeated dragon.

Gower's version of the fleece tale stresses an opposition between open, publicly minded *trouthe* and destructive, private self-advancement, with Aeetes and his dragon placed on the side of *trouthe* (see below, 148–51). Genius reads the entire tale, in the light of Jason's sorry ending, as an exemplum against swearing 'an oth which is noght soth' (5. 4224). More broadly, the narrative condemns Jason for abusing Aeetes's hospitality by

---

[64] On the ambivalent profile of rhetoric and eloquence in the *Confessio*, see also Götz Schmitz, 'Rhetoric and Fiction: Gower's Comments on Eloquence and Courtly Poetry', in Nicholson (ed.), *Critical Anthology*, 117–42.

stealing his daughter. When newly crowned king, it behoves Jason to forge
ties with another royal household, but Medea and Jason have undone
Aeetes's daughter's own usefulness to this end. Therefore, Jason's disastrous
marriage to Creusa 'Which dowhter was to king Creon' (5. 4195) both
follows from his unilateral dealings with Aeetes's household and triggers
Medea's attack on Jason's household. Amans's reference to the fleece thus
imports strong associations of order and falseness into his description
of Danger and aligns his lady's servant with a vivid emblem of *trouthe*. It
also, of course, associates Amans with ' "The moste untrewe creature" '
(5. 4213) Jason, and this invidious parallel gains resonance when the lover
relates his own fantasies about using sorcery to steal love's 'Tresor'.

    The ironic hermeneutic according to which Amans's language about
Danger idealizes the chamberer and, furthermore, inscribes in him the
sign of the text's most tenacious hopes for social possibility finds its
apogee in the lover's final, formal complaint. Six stanzas into his
supplication and still baffled by what he supposes to be a uniquely
complete lack of fortune, Amans appeals to the universal mutability
which such a predicament defies:

> I se the world stonde evere upon eschange,
> Nou wyndes loude, and nou the weder softe;
> I mai sen ek the grete mone change,
> And thing which nou is lowe is eft alofte;
> The dredfull werres into pes fulofte
> Thei torne; and evere is Danger in o place,
> Which wol noght change his will to do me grace.

> (8. 2259–65)

The irony here is not just that Amans's own drawn-out lyric shows no sign
of changing suddenly, but that this stanza's imagery recalls very exactly the
paradigmatic political language and theory of 'division' in the prologue.
The force of this parallelism is to juxtapose Danger against the very root of
social imperfection and worldly decline, and to invest him as a symbol of
possible social renewal. The themes of mutability and the 'division' which
is its cause and 'makth the world to falle' (prol. 972) run through the core
of the prologue. Its sections of estates satire (prol. 93–584) operate by
distinguishing the 'daies olde' (prol. 193) from the division-wracked
condition of the present. Subsequently, Gower makes division the main
interpretative principle of his apocalyptic theory of history, which draws
primarily on Daniel 2 and the Gospels. The image of Nebuchadnezzar's
doomed statue with its feet 'departed' between earth and steel serves this

principle admirably. In particular, Gower deploys an extended treatment of division (prol. 849–1052) to gloss the historical conspectus he derives from Nebuchadnezzar's dream and to drive home its apocalyptic import ('Al sodeinly the Ston schal falle, | As Daniel it hath beknowe'; prol. 1038–9). Conceptually and verbally, Amans's stanza on mutability refracts the prologue in miniature. The moon is an emblem of changeability in both (cf. prol. 919), and the conceit that 'Right now the hyhe wyndes blowe, | And anon after thei ben lowe' (prol. 923–4) is compressed into one of the supplication's longer lines (8. 2260).

Especially significant for the supplication's construction of Danger's role is the causality connecting ethics and politics, connecting personal morality and social, even cosmic, conditions. Gower has articulated this causality as part of his theory of division in the prologue. There, we are invited to apprehend the (divided) human microcosm of 'a man in special' (prol. 946) reflected universally, so that 'whan this litel world mistorneth, | The grete world al overtorneth' (prol. 957–8).[65] Danger's immutable resistance to exactly the kind of temporal change by which the prologue characterizes the fallen world, and the end of the world, is in this context highly charged.

Indeed, Danger holds a place in Amans's stanza occupied in the parallel structure of the prologue by none other than the enigmatic, potent figure of Arion's heir. At the very end of the prologue, the narrator briefly, inconclusively, but distinctly reverses its apocalyptic, division-driven movement with an excursus on the unifying power of Arion (who brought all who heard his song 'in good acord'; prol. 1065) and on the narrator's own hope for another who could suspend the world's divisive momentum by which 'reson *torneth* into rage' (prol. 1079, emphasis added). In the supplication stanza's mirrored, miniature-prologue structure, Danger interrupts the 'turning' force which has dominated the preceding bulk of material. This parallelism recognizes in Danger a template for socially regenerative morality, the general or cumulative force of which is symbolized by the figure of Arion's heir. Danger cannot himself produce universal harmony. He lacks an equivalent for Arion's song. But the values which he embodies (and expresses in his own political, service relationships) are those transmitted by Arion's song and might, Amans inadvertently hints, renew the world.

---

[65] Cf. Genius's remarks on the 'kingdom' of the self (8. 2111–36). See also Porter, 'Ethical Microcosm and Political Macrocosm'.

Amans's attempt to petition over Danger's head results in signal disappointment. Cupid and Venus do not join forces against the opponents of the lover's desire, as they do in the *Roman de la Rose*. The supplication instead prompts Venus to expel the lover from her court and to quell his passion. The case of Danger shows just how far the *Confessio*'s poetics and politics have departed from the *Rose*. Gower has turned a tradition of allegory which is immensely indebted to the *Rose* back on itself, and Danger, the opponent of *fin'amor*, is now on the winning side. More significantly, he is not only a defender of a certain aristocratic interest, but a representative of household-based aristocratic relations as well. In this position, he exalts chaste, reproduction-focused love and values of loyalty and *trouthe* which underpin enduring, hierarchically ordered bonds. In the service of such chaste love and the regulation of property transmission and kinship association which it upholds, the *Confessio* transforms Danger from the hectic, beleaguered wild man of the *Rose* into a remote and invulnerable chamberer. He becomes an answer to the magnificent service of vices such as Parsimony, and an adversary who demeans Amans's desire and symbolizes a force of social renewal latent in the great household.

The influence of the household imaginary on the representation of sins and vices and the courtly love allegory of Danger in the *Confessio*'s frame narrative is persistent but uneven. Gower has not extensively and concertedly developed particular personifications among these figures, but the language of service is recurrent. Because of this, the household imagination of the vices and Danger speaks of dispositions and a mode of perception that seem to exceed deliberate, planned, self-conscious poetic agency. It follows that the imagination and politics of the great household might turn up almost anywhere in Gower's text, and that they may regulate the text's more fully developed inventions as well. This is apparent in the frame narrative itself. The expositions and fragmentary narrative of the vices and Danger are contained within material that fashions a sustained narrative of lordship and centres on the relationship between the lover and Venus.

4

Courtly Love and the Lordship of Venus

Gower's lover does not encounter a garden full of allegorical personages (he must settle for a confession full of them), but Danger the chamberlain and Amans himself demonstrate that literary models of courtly love provide rich materials for Gower's politics of the household in the *Confessio*. If it belongs alongside politically interventionary writings such as the appeal of 1388, the *Confessio* also advertises a deep continental poetic heritage. Amans's supplication, like Gower's French *ballades*, shows the poet at home in a continental lyric mode, and the frame narrative as a whole is indebted to Old French lyric and *dits amoreux* (a form that frames lyrics). It should come as no surprise that these forms bring to Gower's poem supple ways to imagine ethical meaning for politics through the theme of love. Critics are now well-accustomed to historical-political interpretations of the troubadours and their inheritors according to which the courtly lover's relationship to the lady and desire can mediate the condition of being at court and in fact negotiate homosocial politics.[1] The previous chapter's discussion of Danger makes an incursion into this territory.

Gower is unexceptional in this context in crafting the court of love with the social imagination and political ideas of the great household. His particular elaboration of courtly love conventions tends to align the lover's desire for the lady with both abject pursuit of and subjection by a

---

[1] See e.g. Simon Gaunt and Sarah Kay (eds), *The Troubadours: An Introduction* (Cambridge, 1999), 4–6; Kay, *Subjectivity in Troubadour Poetry*, 40–9, 111–31; Gaunt, *Gender and Genre*, 10–14, 122–79; Georges Duby, 'Courtly Love', in *Love and Marriage in the Middle Ages*, tr. Jane Dunnett (Chicago, 1994), 56–63. For language and gestures of intimacy between aristocratic men, and their political import, see also Michael Clanchy, 'Law and Love in the Middle Ages', in John Bossy (ed.), *Disputes and Settlements: Law and Human Relations in the West* (Cambridge, 1983), 47–67; Staley, *Languages of Power*, 51–9; Alan Bray, *The Friend* (Chicago, 2003), 13–41, 78–139.

magnificent lord. As such, it exploits the kind of self-absorbed personae ironically voiced by poets such as Guillaume de Machaut (*c*.1300–77) and Jean Froissart (1337?–*c*.1404) to mock subservience and magnificence in the person of Amans. The lady's neglect of Amans is not unethical but proposes the profitlessness of seeking inappropriately calibrated service. At another level of his allegory, Gower's court of love stages a contest between principals who embody magnificent and asymmetric reciprocal economies of rule. Typically of courtly love poetry, the *Confessio's* presentation of Cupid and Venus as lords of love blurs distinctions between love and the language of politics. Gower's narration of their relationship to Amans and to each other goes on to decide superiority between kinds of love and also between rival household modes.[2]

Beyond the metaphorical vicious retinues and factional rancour of Genius and Amans's conversation, Gower's frame narrative is, as a whole, a drama of the great household's mechanisms of informal dispute resolution, of the types of obligation and exchange (of requests, rewards, and worship) that constitute household-based relations. Amans begins the dream vision as a discontented servant seeking redress from his mistress in a quasi-legal dispute. He precipitates the whole narrative by apostrophizing Venus to '"Behold my cause and my querele"' (1. 134) and petitions her that he is:

> 'a man of thyne,
> That in thi Court have longe served,
> And aske that I have deserved,
> Som wele after my longe wo.'
>
> (1. 168–71)

Eventually he will assay a formal, written petition in his cause. The narrative's broadest structure sees a suitor submit to interview with one of his lord's household officers before having his petition, and indeed his membership of the household, swept aside. The poem's fictive representation of love-longing, confession, and moral reform is thus enclosed in a narrative of the practice of lordship. Proper household order becomes both vehicle and end of personal moral reform.

In particular, the frame narrative privileges reciprocalist lordship by Venus as the solution to the lover's complaint and the prologue's crisis sense of 'division'. This is true, I will argue, even though Venus (literally)

---

[2] Revision to the text outside the frame narrative argues for Gower's intent to position his poem still more decisively on this count. See Mahoney, 'Gower's Two Prologues'. For other perspectives on revisions to the *Confessio*, see the studies cited above, 57 n. 106.

stuns her supplicant at the end of the poem by contemptuously declaring her self-interest, dismissing his suit, and banishing him from service. In fact, she is not done with the lover and her magnificent posture at this moment in any case distracts from the first and most painstaking phase of her remedy for his petition, which Genius has just finished. By the confession delegated to Venus's priest and the goddess's own completion of it, Gower extends the competence of imaginary lordship to include radical engagement with a follower's subjectivity. In Genius's and Amans's language, great household discourse makes political meaning parallel with (allegorical) amatory-ethical meaning. The process of Venus's lordship participates in a wider, outright assault on ecclesiastical authority—and corresponding enablement of lay authority—which Larry Scanlon has foregrounded. In his study of medieval exempla, Scanlon argues that 'Gower disenfranchises clerical power by making it entirely spiritual'.[3] On the other side of the same coin, Venus's lordship swallows an ecclesiastical discourse of self-fashioning into the great household symbolic economy. The lover's narrative is at once a complete imitation of penance and a decisive dislocation of it from ecclesiastical and into lay authority. Gower's adaptation of penitential literature's forms appropriates for lay poetry textual authority with ecclesiastical origins. More specifically, by the petition conceit that contains and completes Genius's confession, the poem reimagines the ecclesiastical authority of the institution of penance as lay, household-based authority.

THE LOVER'S CONFESSION
AND THE LIMITS OF GENIUS

The radical competence of Venus's lordship depends upon the long confessional phase of her remedy, without which the lover's productive expulsion from the court of love could not be accomplished. The confession itself is a function of the great household because Genius, ' "myn oghne Clerk" ' (1. 196), is evidently a member of Venus's establishment. Chaplains, who were in some cases priests and in other cases not, were nearly essential to medieval landed households, and Kate Mertes can 'state almost categorically that every noble and gentle [*sic*] had a chapel and at least one chaplain'.[4] In some sense, Genius's household

---

[3] Scanlon, *Narrative, Authority, and Power*, 248–67 (quote at 262).
[4] Mertes, *Noble Household*, 46. For household chapels generally, see Mertes, 46–8, 139–60; Woolgar, *Great Household*, 176–9.

status already blurs his confession's affiliation to the church. Service in a great household complicated a late medieval priest's institutional identity. Especially in all but the largest lay households and in monastic establishments, 'chaplains were expected to be extremely versatile' and might perform the duties of stewards, treasurers, or purveyors, for example.[5] Friar confessors could have highly personal relationships with lords and, along with chaplains, might be part of a circle advising on policy as well as spiritual matters. His obligation to his lord, and his household status and authority, must often have been more immediate for a chaplain and other members of the household than his position in the church, especially if he headed the chapel or another household 'department'. Itinerant households could cross diocesan boundaries, taking chaplains 'in and out of the authority of their spiritual overlords'.[6]

Setting aside questions of intellectual independence or radicalism, however, the religious duties of a priestly chaplain—including confession—obviously associated him strongly with the church. It is in the household role of Genius's lord that Gower decisively annexes penitential practice from the church. Beforehand, Genius tells some stories derogatory of the church's *political* authority, including the Tales of Boniface and the Donation of Constantine in book 2 (ll. 2803–3037, 3187–3496),[7] but he performs (spiritual) ecclesiastic status as well as domestic status throughout the confession.

The status of the confession in this performance is obviously crucial to a reading that places (a laicized institutional) penance at the centre of the *Confessio*'s fictive didactic. Much has been written about Genius's clerical office and its dual service to *fin'amor* and some kind of contradictory, chaste morality.[8] Efforts to specify the tensions investing Genius's priesthood generally focus on the tradition of Geniuses from which he emerges, and especially on Alain de Lille's *De planctu Naturae* (*c.*1160–70) and Jean de Meun's continuation of the *Roman de la Rose* (*c.*1275).[9] Yet no Genius tradition anticipates the extent to which

[5] Mertes, *Noble Household*, 25, 47–8 (quote at 48).

[6] Ibid. 143.

[7] Scanlon, *Narrative, Authority, and Power*, 257–67.

[8] See e.g. George D. Economou, 'The Character Genius in Alan de Lille, Jean de Meun, and John Gower', *Chaucer Review*, 4 (1970–1), 203–10; Denise N. Baker, 'The Priesthood of Genius: A Study of the Medieval Tradition', *Speculum*, 51 (1976), 277–91; Scanlon, *Narrative, Authority, and Power*, 248–9, 255–6; William Calin, 'John Gower's Continuity in the Tradition of French *Fin'Amor*', *Mediaevalia*, 16 (1993), 91–111, 103–4.

[9] But cf. Mary Flowers Braswell, *The Medieval Sinner: Characterization and Confession in the Literature of the English Middle Ages* (Rutherford, NJ, 1983), 81.

Gower uses the figure to gain lay leverage on penitential theory. Gower's departure is to make Genius's priestly role technically confessorial. Both de Meun and Gower were writing after the Fourth Lateran Council of 1215 had brought confession to prominence in the life of the church. The Council made annual aural confession mandatory for all Christians, and instructional treatises for the clergy subsequently established its conventional forms. By the late thirteenth century, vernacular penitential manuals which had evolved from these clerical tracts were becoming popular with lay audiences.[10] Nature's 'confession' in the *Roman de la Rose* comprises no formal elements of confession more notable than Genius's token absolution and penance. These are nothing more than an affirmation of the status quo and are appended after Nature has already dictated the formal outcome of the interview—her excommunication of false lovers and the chaste, and pardon for active lovers.[11] De Meun's confession is basically Alain's complaint against humanity accommodated to the single (if powerful) joke of Nature's purporting to blame herself for that which is incredible to her. In the *Confessio*, on the other hand, Genius relies fully on conventional confessional forms. (If Gower owes any debt to the *Rose* for the imitative use of confession, it is located less in de Meun's Genius than in characters like La Vieille and Fals Semblant, who construct themselves by a sort of confessional method.[12]) Even Genius's detours in the *Confessio* into exemplary and additional expository material agree with the discursive

[10] On the development of penitential literature and practice, and the Fourth Lateran Council, see John T. McNeill and Helena M. Gamer (eds and trs), *Medieval Handbooks of Penance: A Translation of the Principal Libri Poenitentiales and Selections from Related Documents* (New York, 1938), 23–50, 413 14; H. G. Pfander, 'Some Medieval Manuals of Religious Instruction in England and Observations on Chaucer's Parson's Tale', *JEGP* 35 (1936), 243–58 (surveying Latin, French, and English texts); Robert Mannyng of Brunne, *Handlyng Synne*, ed. Idelle Sullens (Binghamton, NY, 1983), pp. xv–xviii. For the popularization of penitential culture from the clerical penitentials, and the development and uses of the vernacular penitential manual, see also D. W. Robertson, 'The Cultural Tradition of *Handlyng Synne*', *Speculum*, 22 (1947), 162–85; Lee W. Patterson, 'The "Parson's Tale" and the Quitting of the *Canterbury Tales*', *Traditio*, 34 (1978), 331–80; R. N. Swanson, 'The Origins of the *Lay Folks' Catechism*', *Medium Ævum*, 60 (1991), 92–100. A history of penance is available in the first 2 vols of Henry Charles Lea's monumental *A History of Auricular Confession and Indulgences in the Latin Church* (London, 1896).

[11] *RR*, ll. 19335–427.

[12] For such observations about the confessional characterization of figures in the *Roman de la Rose*, see Lee Patterson, *Chaucer and the Subject of History* (London, 1991), 393; John M. Ganim, 'Chaucer, Boccaccio, Confession, and Subjectivity', in Leonard Michael Koff and Brenda Deen Schildgen (eds), *The Decameron and the Canterbury Tales: New Essays on an Old Question* (London, 2000), 141.

and catechetical *modus agendi* (or mode of procedure) of vernacular penitential manuals especially (if not with their imagination of an actual confessional dialogue). In shriving Amans by the 'wittes fyve' (1. 296) and by 'an other forme' also 'Of dedly vices sevene applied' (1. 577), Genius is employing standard *formae confitendi* (forms of confessing) of confessional treatises. His principal tool, the account of the seven sins and all their branches, was ubiquitous.[13]

Gower's representation of confession tends towards its desacralization, but does not rely on parody to this end. Eschewing parody, the text retains important elements of confessional structure.[14] Foremost among these are Genius's questions, which elicit a subject-constituting narration of an individual's experience. Confession aims, by managing the self-representation that is a narrative of sins, to discipline and contain the individual, to dissipate the behaviour and intentions represented. The dissipative effects of penance seek to accommodate the penitent to the institutional authority that directs confession. This process can be theorized as the articulation of a complete self corrected of particular defects, or, contrariwise, as the self's alienation when penance homogenizes and assimilates to its institutional prerogatives 'the "individuality" created by the experience of sinfulness'.[15] Formally, the necessary (dissipative) components of non-sacramentalist penance, besides

[13] For the seven deadly sins in vernacular penitential literature, see e.g. *The Lay Folks' Catechism, or The English and Latin Versions of Archbishop Thoresby's Instruction for the People*, ed. Thomas Frederick Simmons and Henry Edward Nolloth, EETS, os 118 (London, 1901), T 447–560; Mannyng, *Handlyng Synne*, ll. 2991–9500; *Jacob's Well: An Englisht Treatise on the Cleansing of Man's Conscience*, ed. Arthur Brandeis, EETS, os 115 (London, 1900), 68–166. See also, Bloomfield, *Seven Deadly Sins*. For the five senses as 'entrees' to a 'pytt, þi body', letting in 'þe dedly watyr of curse', see *Jacob's Well*, 1–2.

[14] Cf. Braswell, *Medieval Sinner*, 81–7; Gerald Kinneavy, 'Gower's *Confessio Amantis* and the Penitentials', *Chaucer Review*, 19 (1984–5), 144–61, 144–56. Gower makes no attempt to follow the Chartrian and de Meun legacies by mingling and blurring clerical and pagan or lay trappings for his priest: cf. Alain de Lille, *De planctu Naturae*, ed. Nikolaus M. Häring, *Studi Medievali*, 3rd ser. 19 (1978), 797–879, 878; *RR*, ll. 19 431–8. There are no traces in the *Confessio* of the sacerdotal vestments and appurtenances which Genius wears in *De planctu* and the *Rose*, nor of the sacral rites he performs in these works.

[15] Ganim, 'Confession and Subjectivity', 131. Cf. Mary Flowers Braswell's reading of Genius's confession as a process that has 'rid [Amans] of all that sinfulness which had made him unique' (*Medieval Sinner*, 87; cf. 12–13). Ganim summarizes various formulations of confession and its cultural impact ('Confession and Subjectivity', 130–3). Michel Foucault locates the influence of power on the self in confession even prior to the question of penitential structures of dissipation. 'Foucault's thesis', as Ganim concludes, 'is nothing less than that the "self" is constructed by the very forces that seek to control the individual subject' ('Confession and Subjectivity', 133; cf. 142–3). See Michel Foucault, *The History of Sexuality*, tr. Robert Hurley (London, 1979–88), i, esp. 58–9.

confession, were contrition and satisfaction.[16] The remission of sins could not occur in the absence of inward contrition, while the penance or 'satisfaction' designated by the confessor served particularly to reconcile the penitent to the church and to embed the moral reform and renunciation of sin taught by preparation for and performance of confession. Vernacular manuals such as *Handlyng Synne* and *Jacob's Well* were most conscientious in keeping the required coordination of contrition, confession, and satisfaction in view. The important, final exemplum position in *Handlyng Synne*, for example, is occupied by the tale of the shriving of a devil ignorant of contrition, not to mention the prospect of having satisfaction imposed. When the frustrated fiend reveals himself, his unflappable confessor explains patiently that the redeemed confessants he wished to emulate ' "are repentaunt of here synne, | And are now come to ryght gode wyl | To do penaunce & no more yl" '.[17]

In the *Confessio*, Amans's language of privation in love mirrors the language of medieval penitential theory and its dramatization in literature such as penitential lyrics. Augustinian theory formulated confession's autobiographical recollection as self-collection, or the 're-collecting' of a self dispersed amongst earthly pleasures by sin.[18] Analogously, Amans's desire is emblematized by Cupid's 'firy Dart' that, thrown 'thurgh myn herte rote' (1. 145), divides the lover to the core. Amans asks Venus whether he shall ' "ben hol or elles dye?" ' (1. 163) and Venus responds by appointing Genius to ' "hier this mannes schrifte" ' (1. 197). The task of the confession is set up as the (re)construction of a whole self, and success is eventually signalled by the return of ' "John Gower" ' (8. 2321). Venus's questions about the lover's identity had originally met with silence or with

[16] A sacramentalist position developed by scholastic theology after 1215 held that the sacrament of penance alone could accomplish justification, and could do so even in a case of attrition, in the absence, that is, of complete contrition. But lay penitential culture had more affinity with a contritionalist stance, and vernacular penitential treatises adopted the theory of writers such as Raymond of Penyafort. These manuals thus held inward contrition to be requisite for the remission of sins. See Patterson, *Subject of History*, 374–7; cf. Scanlon, *Narrative, Authority, and Power*, 73 and n. 34.

[17] Mannyng, *Handlyng Synne*, ll. 12606, 12613–14. For other examples of manuals' prescribing contrition or satisfaction as penitential essentials, see *Handlyng Synne*, ll. 10819–950, 11359–80, 11457–90, 11525–82; *Lay Folks' Catechism*, T 307–14. In the elaborate structuring metaphor of *Jacob's Well* (2, 64–8, 168–216), contrition, confession, and satisfaction are figured as a 'skeet', a 'skauell', and a 'schouele' to remove the 'deep wose' of sin from the body's pit, and the tract treats satisfaction at unusual length (188–216).

[18] See e.g. St Augustine, *Confessionum libri XIII*, ed. Lucas Verheijen, Corpus Christianorum, ser. Latina, 27 (Turnholt, 1981), 2. 1, 10. 11; tr. R. S. Pine-Coffin, *Confessions* (London, 1961); Patterson, *Subject of History*, 66–7.

depersonating or anonymous, relational answers—' "A Caitif that lith hiere" ... "a man of thyne" '.[19]

Immediately before the return of 'John Gower', however, the penitential process seems utterly to have broken down. The confession itself ends in acrimony and Amans's repudiation of Genius as one 'That fielen noght of that I fiele' (8. 2153). The apparent breakdown is not for a lack of confessional sincerity on Amans's part. He not only hopes to attain a ' "hol" ' self from his suit to Venus, but he has fully, technically confessional expectations of his interview with Genius and is prepared obediently to commit himself to his confessor (' "let me noght mistime | Mi schrifte" '), acknowledging that his own ' "wittes ben so blinde, | That I ne can miselven teche" ' (1. 220–9).[20] He even anticipates performing satisfaction, asking of Genius at several junctures how he should 'be peined' (2. 2075) in correction of his error (2. 3508–14, 3. 2740–6). Genius, however, never prescribes a penance. The core disciplinary instruments of contrition and satisfaction will be imposed on the lover, but not by the confessor. When he departs at the end of his dialogue with Amans, the priest's confession is institutionally insufficient, unable to effect the reordering of the self.

The breakdown at the end of the confession and Amans's alteration from more or less uninterrupted compliance to outright defiance are explained by the collision of split penitential paradigms which have until now doubled or overlapped each other in the frame narrative. On the one hand, Amans assumes that the confession's institutional prerogatives

---

[19] See *CA* 1. 153–71. Cf. Paul Strohm, 'A Note on Gower's Persona', in Mary J. Carruthers and Elizabeth D. Kirk (eds), *Acts of Interpretation: The Text in its Contexts 700–1600* (Norman, Okla, 1982), 297; R. F. Yeager, *John Gower's Poetic: The Search for a New Arion* (Cambridge, 1990), 232–7. Genius and Amans's confession can be interpreted as an allegory of the reintegration of a self by an act of confessional self-reflection in an especially strong sense. Readings which emphasize that the confessor's presence in the poem is conterminous with the expression of the lover's malady, and which read Genius and Amans as aspects of a single consciousness, are especially suggestive here. For Simpson's treatment of Genius as the imagination belonging to a soul whose will is embodied in Amans, see *Sciences and the Self*, esp. 167–72, 196–7, 271. Winthrop Wetherbee considers the medieval Genius as an allegory of imagination in 'The Theme of Imagination in Medieval Poetry and the Allegorical Figure "Genius" ', *Medievalia et Humanistica*, NS 7 (1976), 45–64. On late medieval theories of imagination, see also A. J. Minnis, 'Langland's Ymaginatif and Late-Medieval Theories of Imagination', *Comparative Criticism*, 3 (1981), 71–103.

[20] Paul M. Clogan views Amans from a similar but different angle, as a satirized penitent, in 'From Complaint to Satire: The Art of the *Confessio Amantis*', *Medievalia et Humanistica*, NS 4 (1973), 217–22, 220. On Amans's desire-driven response to the confession, cf. Calin, 'Gower's Continuity', 105.

accord with the ' "reverence" ' of love (1. 218). He longs for correction to
assimilate him to the ideal pattern of the courtly lover and equates vice
with that which will hurt his chances in love. He agrees with reading Ovid's
books 'if thei mihte spede | Mi love' (4. 2675–6), and seeks instruction
that he might 'The more unto my love obeie | And puten mi desese aweie'
(3. 636–8). At many points during the confession, Genius colludes in this
conflation of amorous and penitential expectations. He sugars his rebuke
of Amans's murderous hatred for Danger, for instance, with the recommendation 'if thou wolt love and spede' (3. 1641). At a basic level the
confessor's supposition that love is an irresistible force (qualified by him
only very late in the confession) sustains Amans's complacent assumption
that it lies outside the remit of penitential correction, that it 'were an
ydel peine' to read Ovid's books 'if thei techen to restreigne | Mi love'
(4. 2677–8).[21] As late as his discussion of the sixth deadly sin, Genius is
qualifying his discipline with the caveat that 'natheles ther is no wyht | That
mai withstonde loves miht' (6. 317–18).

Conversely, Genius's conclusion to the confession confirms an alternative way of understanding it. Genius has evaded Amans's earlier
requests for penance, stressing instead the imperative of telling 'what
is more, | So that thou schalt the vices knowe' (2. 3520–1). Now, when
Amans requests a final 'hole conseil' (8. 2057), Genius judges not
particular sins in love but love itself as a context for immoral behaviour,
concluding against Amans's desire: 'Be that thou seist it is a Sinne'
(8. 2088). Having straddled the confession's split penitential paradigms
previously, Genius now decisively reorients Amans's confessional self-
speaking, cementing a generalized moral purpose that might be dubbed
'orthodox' in contrast to Amans's amatory moral purpose. In his summing up, Genius takes up the language of division, insufficiency, and
reintegration in plainly penitential and non-amatory terms. He means
'finaly to knette | This cause, where it is tobroke' (8. 2072–3). The
sinner who misrules himself 'lest himself' (8. 2115) and 'Hath noght
himself' (8. 2119), and Amans must 'thiself rekevere' (8. 2129) by
constraining his disparate desiring self 'under that lawe, | The which
of reson is governed | And noght of will' (8. 2134–6). Amans's love has

---

[21] For discussion of the premise that amatory desire cannot be resisted and of its
contribution to 'asymmetries between politics and love', and to the progression of the
Confessio as a whole, see Simpson, *Sciences and the Self,* 144–8, 157–60, 164–5, 179–97,
209, 215–17 (quote at 144). Cf. Olsson, 'Natural Law', 232–4, 250–5; David W. Hiscoe,
'The Ovidian Comic Strategy of Gower's *Confessio Amantis*', *Philological Quarterly,* 64
(1985), 367–85, 381–2.

lost all priestly backing, and the moment has arrived, it seems, for institutionally sanctioned disciplining of desire. But at this point Amans withdraws from confessional speaking. Furthermore, polite deference towards his confessor is replaced by a certain aggression, and Amans then produces his strongest expression of his desire yet— the twelve-stanza rime royal lyric of supplication to Venus (8. 2217– 2300). From Genius's concluding, orthodox perspective, Amans now appears to be the self unmoored to institutional prerogatives and obligations, its desire reinforced, indeed, by the scrupulous self-exam- ination elicited by confession. He is the product of restaged desire without effective constraint. The confessional dialogue has evoked sinful acts and intentions with precision and intensity, and can now be seen to have regenerated rather than dissipated their source. In line with Amans's own theory of delicacy, it has cooked up 'every syhte and every word' in the 'pottes hote' of his imagination (6. 913–21).[22]

According to the orthodox paradigm, Amans lacks contrition.[23] It is this lack first and foremost that enables the lover's confessional narration to recreate rather than dissipate sinfulness. Amans's misconception, encouraged by Genius, has allowed him to believe sinful behaviour to be mitigated by his love or even to stand as proof of virtue.[24]

Having betrayed Amans's understanding of his confession's purpose, Genius is in no position finally to constrain the lover's self-constitution, and he claims no authority to do so ('For I can do to thee nomore | Bot teche thee the rihte weie: | Now ches if thou wolt live or deie'; 8. 2146–8).[25] According to Amans, the only way Genius will be allowed to retain

---

[22] Cf. Simpson, Sciences and the Self, 208–9.

[23] In this, Amans's confession finds one of its closest literary parallels in the fiend's shrift that closes Handlyng Synne (ll. 12507–12626). Both confessants narrate sins 'ful bostly' (Handlyng Synne, l. 12517) because they fail to recognize requirements of contrition about which they will later be informed. Whether 'boasting' of the destruction of thousands (Handlyng Synne, ll. 12519–42) or of tickling a small dog (CA 4. 1187–90), they share equivalent penitential naivety; a naivety that distinguishes their speaking from the confessio ficti of a hypocrite like de Meun's Fals Semblant or Langland's Lady Meed.

[24] See e.g. Amans's extended denials of idleness (4. 1122–1233) and somnolence (4. 2746–2874) which constitute detailed narratives of sin from an orthodox perspective. Genius solicits the first of these directly by asking his charge to tell 'What hast thou don of besischipe | To love' (4. 1119–20). For closer attention to Genius's encouragement of Amans's love, see Simpson, Sciences and the Self, 159–62.

[25] Kinneavy comments that the matters of penance and absolution in the frame narrative 'are handled in a rather complex fashion', but prefers to rescue Genius's clerical authority, by comparing his relationship to Venus to that of 'the priest as intermediary between penitent and God' ('Confessio Amantis and the Penitentials', 151–2). This solution seems to me to produce a somewhat uncomfortable coupling of Venus and God.

legitimacy is by becoming a vehicle of Amans's meanings, carrying to Venus 'Mi lettre' (8. 2209) in his cause of love. Yet Amans is, in due course, reintegrated into a whole self ('John Gower') that abandons his former desire. The reintegration is effected by an institutional agency beyond Genius and invoked at the very moment when Amans rejects the priest's authority. The moment of confessional breakdown, of 'Debat and gret perplexete' (8. 2190), is also the fulcrum for Gower's most incisive transformation of penance.

VENUS'S REMEDY: THE POLITICS OF PENANCE

Escaping the clerical frying pan, Amans does not reckon on the seigneurial fire. His dispatch of Genius to Venus with his petition closes down confessional dialogue emphatically, but simultaneously opens the way to Gower's full appropriation of penitential, and not merely confessional, discourse. Gower expropriates the penitential—in particular the institutional authority finally to discipline sinful intentions and to reintegrate the self—from the clerical and annexes it to lay lordship. Amans's rebellion against Genius extends the penitential beyond the confessional dialogue and (back) into the frame narrative's outer enclosure, namely, the petition narrative of Venus and the lover. When Venus returns to address the lover's written 'Supplicacioun' (8. 2301), she resumes the language of identity and wholeness into which she directed Amans's suit originally, and which Genius came fully to inhabit in his recent summing up. The fulfilment of confession is achieved by instruments of Venus's lordship over her petitioning retainer. The institutional factors that enforce penitential dissipation become functions of exchange effecting reciprocalist lordship, and putting down magnificent lordship.[26]

Venus concludes her response to the lover's petition with a ceremony of four parts which implements the missing disciplinary factors and makes the confession efficacious at last. She anoints the narrator, then presents him with his own (decrepit) image in a mirror, whereupon he submits to her will. Thirdly, he takes his absolution from his confessor, before finally kneeling before Venus to receive a rosary and some instructions for prayer and future living.

---

[26] *Sir Gawain and the Green Knight* also relocates the effects of penance in the aristocratic household through Gawain's relationship with his host and challenger. See further Braswell, *Medieval Sinner*, 95–100.

Venus, which hield a boiste clos,   *jar, box*
And wolde noght I scholde deie,
Tok out mor cold than eny keie
An oignement, and in such point
Sche hath my wounded herte enoignt,
My temples and my Reins also.   *kidneys*
And forth withal sche tok me tho
A wonder Mirour forto holde,

. . . .

Myn yhen dymme and al unglade,
Mi chiekes thinne, and al my face
With Elde I myhte se deface,

. . . .

And thus thenkende thoghtes fele,
I was out of mi swoune affraied,
Wherof I sih my wittes straied,
And gan to clepe hem hom ayein.
And whan Resoun it herde sein
That loves rage was aweie,
He cam to me the rihte weie,

. . . .

'Touchende mi confession
I axe an absolucion
Of Genius, er that I go.'
The Prest anon was redy tho,
And seide, 'Sone, as of thi schrifte
Thou hast ful pardoun and foryifte;
Foryet it thou, and so wol I.'

. . . .

Bot sche, that wolde make an ende,
As therto which I was most able,
A Peire of Bedes blak as Sable
Sche tok and heng my necke aboute;
Upon the gaudes al withoute
Was write of gold, *Por reposer.*
'Lo,' thus sche seide, 'John Gower,
Now thou art ate laste cast,
This have I for thin ese cast,
That thou nomore of love sieche.
Bot my will is that thou besieche
And preie hierafter for the pes,
And that thou make a plein reles
To love, which takth litel hiede

Of olde men upon the nede,
Whan that the lustes ben aweie'

(8. 2816–2917)

The language and function of this episode is strongly penitential, and it completes the technical, institutional competence of Genius's confession. The episode is simultaneously a performance of lay lordship (by a pagan goddess), even though the kind of penitential efficacy it exhibits is usually associated with ecclesiastical social and textual authority.

The encounter with the mirror and old age constitutes the lover's unforgiving passage to contrition. It is reminiscent of the will-breaking use of old age in penitential treatises and lyrics, and in the sprawling *memento novissima* argument of *Vox clamantis* book 7.[27] Venus's use of the mirror in the *Confessio* resembles an inversion or belated application of the process recommended by Alain de Lille in his penitential book, whereby the priest should terrify a recalcitrant confessant into an initial change of heart that might then form the foundation for instruction towards fully fledged contrition and correction.[28] Venus has Genius painstakingly prepare the intellect (in some sense coextensive with himself), and only then does she shock the will into the change necessary for this instruction to take effect. Amans himself has acknowledged that his 'will' is resisting 'techinge of so wis a port' (8. 2191–6). Now, with desire quelled, reason-already-informed suddenly and retroactively comes 'to me the rihte weie'. Gower's frame narrative has the anguish of love-longing do the work of the bitterness of old age in some lyrics, resisting the reintegration of the self before a penitential resolution.[29]

---

[27] *Novissima* refers to the four last things (death, judgement, heaven, and hell). See *Vox*, 7. 863–1106, esp. 919–20, 947 (cf. Psalm 101: 27, Isaiah 51: 6). In the *Confessio*, the emphasis on beholding and seeing as Venus directs Gower's attention to the mirror is suggestive of apocalypse qua vision—the episode is indeed a supernaturally mediated vision of his end. There is, likewise, a strong parallel with the apocalyptic prologue's description of seasonal fluctuations in a divided and senescent world (*CA*, prol. 923–38). On the technical properties of apocalypse, as opposed to apocalyptic, see Bernard McGinn, 'Early Apocalypticism: The Ongoing Debate', in C. A. Patrides and Joseph Wittreich (eds), *The Apocalypse in English Renaissance Thought and Literature: Patterns, Antecedents and Repercussions* (Manchester, 1984), 3–6; John J. Collins, 'Introduction: Towards the Morphology of a Genre', *Semeia*, 14 (1979), 1–20.

[28] See Alain de Lille, *Liber poenitentialis*, ed. Jean Longère, Analecta Mediaevalia Namurcensia, 17–18 (Louvain, 1965), 2. 2. Alain recommends that the confessor inspire 'servilis timor' (submissive fear) by showing the 'aeternitatem' and 'acredinem' (eternity and bitterness) of the pains which await the impenitent sinner.

[29] See e.g. 'An Old Man's Prayer', in Carleton Brown (ed.), *Religious Lyrics of the Fourteenth Century* (Oxford, 1924), 3–7, and the lyric beginning 'In my yowth fulle wylde I was', in Frank Allen Patterson (ed.), *The Middle English Penitential Lyric: A Study*

At the end of the ceremony, Venus confirms the reintegrative and dissipative—that is, penitential—functions of the entire ordeal which she has arranged: '"John Gower, | Now thou art ate laste cast"'. Her richly ambiguous phrase enmeshes the making of a whole self with the 'casting down' of unruly passions (Amans, of course, has disappeared). Her subsequent instructions about the narrator's future mode of living equate to a prescription of satisfaction, behaviour that will reconcile him to her authority, and redress and eschew ('"make a plein reles | To"') his previous conduct.[30]

Here, however, I am principally interested not in the penitential mechanics of the poem's closing ceremony but in their unconventional enclosure within a narrative of lay lordship. Reproducing penitential forms in a petitionary setting, Venus's resolution of the frame narrative laicizes penance and the institutional authority to which the penitent is accommodated. In other words, it makes penitential reform a product of good lordship.

Combining penance and the great household produces a notable doubling of religious and secular symbolism in Venus's presentation of the 'Peire of Bedes' to the narrator. For, if the necklace, its gauds inscribed with gold, is in the first instance a rosary, it can also stand as a livery collar. Remembering the arbitral context of Venus and the lover's entire exchange, and noticing the ceremonial tableau of a regal figure placing a (suitably elegant) decorative article around the neck of another, kneeling, we can recognize the livery in the rosary string.

The whole episode from the removal of the lance of love to Venus's departure (8. 2783–2945) reinvents scenes in which courtly lovers enter the service of Love. Most famously perhaps, in the *Roman de la Rose* (ll. 1681–2764) Cupid shoots the lover, takes him as a vassal (ll. 1955–8), performs a kiss of homage (ll. 1926–58), and presents instruction on a courtly lover's style of living in the guise of terms of service. The amatory allegorical meaning of Gower's scene is opposite, but the lordship imaginary reappears. It is adjusted by historical changes—the *Confessio* imitates a

and Collection of Early Religious Verse (New York, 1911), 57–9; and in Frederick J. Furnivall (ed.), *Hymns to the Virgin and Christ, The Parliament of Devils, and Other Religious Poems*, EETS, os 24 (London, 1867), 35–9. Lee Patterson discusses these lyrics in *Subject of History*, 386–92. See also, in Patterson (ed.), *Penitential Lyric*, 103–8, two 'timor mortis' lyrics, the first of which ('Alas, My Hart will Brek in Thre') ends with the 'Infirmus' narrator suddenly exclaiming, '*In Celum* ther is Joy with the!' (103).

30 Cf. *Handlyng Synne*'s instruction to the penitent-reader 'yn gode wyl ʒow to wyþholde | Fro þo synnes þat byfore are tolde [in his or her shrift or else the tract in hand]' (ll. 12631–2).

livery exchange where the *Rose* mimics homage—but the basic structure, in which a ritualized yet intimate encounter between lord and subordinate yields instruction on a mode of living, is the same. The parallels extend to an ointment that salves the wounded heart (*RR*, ll. 1847–72; *CA* 8. 2811–19). This episode in particular in the *Confessio* hints that Gower had the *Rose* somewhere in his mind when composing the scene and, in echoes of the earlier poem, Gower's Venus seems to be restaging and inverting her predecessor Cupid's lordship. (This reinvention of the *Rose*'s politically imagined brand of courtly love is of a piece with the representation of Danger discussed in the previous chapter.) Taking her ointment from a closed box, Venus echoes Cupid's drawing from his purse ('s'aumosniere') a literalized key to the heart (*RR*, ll. 1999– 2010). Not only is Venus's ointment—'mor cold than eny keie'—sharper than the unguent on the *Rose* Cupid's arrows, its love-expunging sensory thrill plays off Cupid's soft, almost undetectable touch with his love- fastening key (*RR*, ll. 2008–10). Gower's episode turns the *Rose* Cupid's practice on its head, but in doing so, and for all that it is suffused with penitential discourse, its pedigree as a climactic fantasizing of lordship is unmistakable.

This restaging of love-lordship, and the livery aspect of Venus's rosary in particular, are framed by a general laicization of penance in this section of the poem. Venus's ceremony does, it is true, involve pseudo-sacramen- tal elements in the anointing and absolution. At fewer than ten lines apiece, however, these are minor parts of the ceremony account. The absolution, requested by the narrator and conducted in almost embar- rassed haste after eight books of exhaustive instruction, is more interrup- tion than order of business. It is priest Genius's only contribution after the supplication, and reminds us how exiguous his role has become since the confession proper.[31] The closing ceremony as a whole suppresses or diminishes ecclesiastical overtones in its religious elements. As Genius's office has been desacralized by his association with a pagan goddess and lack of emblematic or parodic vestments, so the salvific frame of the sacrament of penance is largely elided by a temporal one in Venus's ceremony. The narrator is moved not by the prospect of Judgement to

[31] Indeed, so marginalized is the confessor at the end of the frame narrative that Gower himself seems to have forgotten that his priest was still around. He only made provision for Genius's exit when he came to revise Venus's valedictory passage including her message to Chaucer: cf. 8. 2940–70* and 8. 2947–50. If Genius is imagined as an aspect of the confession's divided soul, his disappearance from the text can be interpreted in the light of the soul's reintegration and the sublimation of Amans into 'John Gower'. See above, n. 19.

contemplate salvation, but by the prospect of mortal decay to consider a
kind of intellectually active retirement—' "thin ese" ' with ' "thi bokes" '
of lay poetry (*CA* 8. 2910, 2926).[32] The rosary string, meanwhile, refers
to devotional practice that, while entirely orthodox, is also meditative
and autodidactic. Such practice is, crucially, 'extraliturgical . . . and per-
formable in the vernacular', non-expert, and suited to and informed by
the needs of the laity.[33] As an instrument of penitential satisfaction, the
beads dispense with the intermediary agency of a priest, and are to this
extent well-suited to the *Confessio*'s interest in self-reformation as fostered
by lay social relations.

The promotion of lay household authority, as well as private devotion,
is corollary to this cutting off of clerical supervision. Moral reform by
confession and penance has become fully integrated into a larger aristocratic petitionary process. But, it may seem difficult to know if any
particular mode of lordship—reciprocalist or magnificent—is being promoted. Is Venus's treatment of her petitioner finally to be seen as responsible recuperation or arbitrary banishment? The queen of love both
rewards and banishes the narrator. Her lordship is split; it is involved
both with Amans's abject service and unchecked desire, and with the
narrator's release from such desire. Conventional elements of Venus's role
as queen of love suggest an uninterested and magnificent attitude to the
lover. Certainly, Amans cannot have anticipated banishment as a reward
' "deserved" ' (1. 170) for long service and, announcing ' "the fortune of
my whiel" ' (8. 2880), Venus (' "Which al only my lustes seche" '; 8. 2399)
seems wholly contemptuous of her servant's worth. Yet this attitude and
the Cupidean environment with which it is associated are countered by
the action of Venus's lordship towards the reintegration of a whole 'John
Gower'.[34] By penitential process, this dominant aspect of her lordship
produces a healed self, corrected of error and 'hol ynowh' (8. 2869).

[32] Cf., by way of contrast, the salvific objective of the *memento novissima* theme in the
Vox. See e.g. *Vox*, 7. 1463–8, where, concluding a book persistently concerned with
morbidity, the poem recommends penance under the mixed eschatalogical logic of
coming Judgement and current divine retribution.

[33] Anne Winston, 'Tracing the Origins of the Rosary: German Vernacular Texts',
Speculum, 68 (1993), 619–36, 635. Winston discusses the origins, importance, and
popular appeal of the rosary as a 'religious exercise uniquely suited to the needs of the lay
faithful' (619). In *The Rose-Garden Game: The Symbolic Background to the European
Prayer-Beads* (London, 1969), Eithne Wilkins mentions the *Confessio* narrator's 'chaplet'
(47) and goes on to discuss decorative or precious prayer-beads as 'a token of social status
as well as of piety' (47–9, quote at 48).

[34] Richard Firth Green argues that Gower is 'far from uncritical' of the Ricardian
court in placing Venus's rejection of the narrator in a context of loyal service and

Of course, Venus's penitential project itself appears magnificent and oppressive if her interest in the lover is understood to comprise above all the reduction and alienation of his individuality; if the reader, that is, empathizes with Amans and his desire as the narrator's best self, and responds to the cold ointment and mirror as morbid tools that crush out the lover's experiences and personality.[35] The lonely quality of the poem's revised ending ('whanne y sigh non othre weie | Bot only that y was refusid'; 8. 2963–4) can support an argument that the narrative reveals institutional penance to be intrusive and alienating power. It is an argument for the bleaker side of an individual's being ' "cast" '. From this perspective, even power that is ostensibly reciprocalist (in so far as it seeks to enable an individual to signify their own being) is always already totalizing and prepared to allow self-construction only in power's own terms. All this changes if we accept the premise that the narrator's penitential reconstitution is beneficial to him. If we read Venus in cooperation (or collusion) with what I argue to be the socially conservative burden of Gower's text then we are obliged to recognize behind the goddess a positive, enabling view of lordship.

However we assess the narrator's fate, the text depicts a reciprocalist core in Venus's lordship and privileges it over another brand of lordship which is represented by Cupid and his court of love. This lordship is depicted as excessive and magnificent, and quelled by Venus's reciprocalist authority. Venus recognizes an obligation ' "to commune" ' her retainer's ' "desese" ' (8. 2351–5), and she is consistently interested in his significa-tion of himself. The action and language of the frame narrative's resolution reinvoke and close the action and language of its opening in book 1. The lover's ability to name himself recalls Venus's initial interrogation about his identity (1. 153–71) and demonstrates the way that her response to the petition has encouraged the narrator's expression of his own being (and not simply her power) from the outset. She has refused from him self-definition that threatens to submerge his being within signification of a sovereign other. At the appearance of Cupid and Venus at the beginning of the dream vision, Amans anticipates such obliteration of being in

reciprocal duty: 'The *Familia Regis* and the *Familia Cupidinis*', in Scattergood and Sherborne (eds), *English Court Culture*, 92. I find the poem's take on courtly culture in 'Loves Court' (see below, 118–27) ultimately more disparaging than the banishment itself, which can be read as a release from unrewarding, magnificent service.

[35] Braswell, for one, reads the frame narrative's resolution morbidly, in *Medieval Sinner*, 12–13 and esp. 86–7.

magnificence ('Sche cast on me no goodly chiere'[36]). So he is startled and unable to answer when Venus asks suddenly, ' "What art thou, Sone?" ' (1. 154), inviting him to speak for himself, and taking 'riht good kep' (1. 156) of his distress. Venus will refuse to speak for Amans, even though she knows ' "how that it is" ' (1. 191), and her dialogue with the lover and the confession which she appoints continue to advance self-recognition and self-representation until the servant who would subsume himself in her power (' "A Caitif that lith hiere" ' before her; 1. 161) has become able to name himself and be addressed as ' "John Gower" ' (8. 2321, 2908). As 'John Gower' kneels to receive the rosary-livery and is pronounced ' "cast" ', the symbolism of good lordship and penance fuse in a climactic iconic moment. The pronouncement ratifies Venus's lordship's ability to represent the personal meanings and subjectivity of servants rather than to reduce them to otherwise empty signifiers of longing.

The lover arrived with hopes of winning his way into the heart of a court and now 'John Gower' leaves having been won over to the much less concentrated reaches of an aristocratic network. Venus's reciprocalist agency makes exile from service in Love's court the paradoxical reward of a different, enduring kind of bond. As she prepares the narrator for his future life with the presentation of the rosary-livery, her split lordship is intensely conflicted. The Venus of Love's court is extinguishing a relationship with a long-suffering retainer. The Venus of her penitential dialogue with the narrator is completing a reciprocal exchange securing the narrator's benefit and binding him to her authority permanently. Preparing to leave, Venus insists that the narrator allow ' "reson" ' to protect him as a ' "guide" ' (8. 2919) in the course she has laid down for him. In the context of her lordship, this resembles a promise of support of a kind a late medieval retainer must have expected—support derived from the informal social network of the affinity. The rosary-livery emblematizes this exchange of good lordship. Livery collars decorated with a lord's device publicly displayed the wearer's allegiance and might be distributed expediently, to amass or to advertise the lord's power. In this they resembled livery badges and badges' capacity as instruments of magnificent lordship.[37] Yet collars were also suited to reciprocalist use—to signify

---

[36] *CA* 1. 152. The description by the narrator, now stuck with Cupid's lance, recalls the god of love's 'chiere' of 'yhen wrothe' (1. 140–1), and the narrator does not discriminate between the two deities.

[37] Walker discusses the Lancastrian collar of linked SS as a livery badge, and thus, I would argue, tends to elide a generally applicable difference in 'reciprocalist' value between prestigious collars and the more commonplace and expedient livery signs which actually took the form of badges (*Lancastrian Affinity*, 94–6). Walker notes that

desert and to benefit the wearer—in ways that badges were not. Collars were the most prestigious of symbols in the expanding hierarchy of liveries in the late fourteenth century, usually reserved for retainers of high rank or for powerful affines as a sign of mutual respect, or granted as a special reward (whereas robes would be distributed more regularly and systematically).[38]

Superior liveries like the collar, of course, typically designated relationships of enduring or permanent *affinity*, whereas Venus's gift imposes a kind of permanent non-relationship on the narrator, betokening the injunction ' "tarie thou mi Court nomore" ' (8. 2924). Ultimately, Venus cannot be separated from her court. She is irrevocably infected by symbolism of the wilful lover's amatory service and aspiration in the frame narrative. Yet, the resolution of the lover's petition comprises substantive household exchange—of a gift and of particular, positive instruction and obligation for time to come, of gestures of deference and reward. Formalizing the narrator's renunciation of natural love and projecting it into the future, this exchange (re)constitutes a bond even as it dissolves a bond with Love's court. Thus, after she has departed, ' "to comune" ' with the narrator ' "nevere after this" ' (8. 2936–7), Venus's agency lingers. In the revised conclusion to the frame narrative, the narrator's future life will seemingly remain anchored by Venus's gift:

> And in my self y gan to smyle
> Thenkende uppon the bedis blake,
> And *how they weren me betake*,
> For that y schulde bidde and preie.
>
> (8. 2958–61, emphasis added)

The presentation of the rosary-collar has not annulled the bond between Venus and the narrator. Indeed, the queen's language constantly suspends and subverts the annihilation of the bond between herself and him. The early version of the ending, in which the queen bids ' "Adieu" ' but then delegates the narrator to commission Chaucer's ' "testament of

Bolingbroke's receiver-general distributed 192 gilt collars in the summer of 1399. But he also discerns that its distinctive form and use 'invested the collar of SS with a significance that other livery badges lacked' (95), and that the collars 'were at least expensive and desirable objects of display worth, by themselves, a considerable sum' (95–6). For badges as instruments of magnificence, see below, 189–92.

[38] See Nigel Saul, 'The Commons and the Abolition of Badges', *Parliamentary History*, 9 (1990), 302–15, 309–10. For Henry of Derby's grant of a collar of SS to Gower in 1393, see Fisher, *John Gower*, 68 and n. 5. On the prestigious use of the Lancastrian collar generally, see Walker, *Lancastrian Affinity*, 95–6.

love"' (8. 2955*), enacts a slippage back into an active service which is confused between amatory and reformed allegiances. Other claims on the banished retainer survive Gower's revisions and are less equivocal. Banishment is one side of a twofold claim which Venus makes upon her servant at the presentation of his rosary-collar. The other is summed up initially in the instruction to '"preie hierafter for the pes"' (8. 2913), and further specified by delegation to Gower's literary legacy, where '"vertu moral duelleth"' (8. 2925). Venus's instructions, their summary head of the king's peace, and her role as a kind of absentee patron return the narrator, as John Gower, poet, to the theme of political good order and a morally and socially productive function for writing. The content of reward, promise, and obligation in her concluding speech also characterize her lordship as reciprocalist. The narrator is to respect the king's peace, avoid Love's court, and go back to his books. In return, he will have his '"ese"'—consequent upon Venus's favour and the healing of his love malady, and ensured by his use of her gift. As a poet, 'John Gower' will stand apart from the thick of aristocratic politics; but as a peripheral retainer, he will embody the landed household's far-reaching ability to structure society.

MAGNIFICENT CUPID

Proof of Venus's reciprocalist lordship more dramatic than her launching of her retainer into a new mode of living comes by what her lordship negates. For if Venus's lordship is invested in 'casting' a whole self, it is in turn engaged in 'casting down' a rival, magnificent mode of lordship and service. This rival mode is represented by Cupid, by 'Loves Court' as an apotheosis of service in love, and by Amans and his desire. More conspicuously than she answers a literary predecessor (ointment rewriting key), Venus challenges her present partner in Gower's narrative. Amans's conception of reward for his service would entail a place in an eternalized court as a pure signifier of love. Corrected of sins *against* love, and fully assimilated to the pattern of abject lover, the narrator would become a mere cipher for the arbitrary power of Love. The power under which the narrator labours, pierced by Cupid's 'firy Dart', and the service he would enter (dreamed most vividly in the shock of failure and the vision of Love's court) are construed in terms of magnificence. The frame narrative's resolution reveals such lordship and service to be both pervasive and vulnerable, stretched thin, to be shattered by Venus's response to the supplication, which heals the lance's wound and closes off any avenue to service in the companies of lovers.

Certain gestures of contempt and exclusion intersect the productive side of Venus's arbitration. They read like residues from traditions of Venuses and Cupids in which love is figured as a kind of magnificent lordship. Venus's son was especially prone to depiction as an arbitrary, wilful lord, in which guise he features in the *Roman de la Rose*, Chaucer's *Legend of Good Women*, and Clanvowe's *Boke of Cupide*.[39] The *Confessio*'s 'kyng of love' (1. 139) is no exception, and wears his literary heritage of magnificence lightly. Gower's Venus, however, is in significant ways unlike such a Cupid's usual companion. In the effects of her dealings with her petitioner, and even in a certain strictness and kind cruelty in her manner, she finds a better precedent for her role in the Boethian female counsellor and a parallel, indeed, in Thomas Usk's Love in his contemporary *Testament of Love* (1385–7). There, Love welcomes a petitioning servant (and self-confessed ' "caytife" ') ' "into myne housholde... as one of my privy famyliers" ' to take special knowledge and support.[40] Gower's lover treats king and queen as equivalent embodiments of the same authority, quailing before them and directing his supplication to both (8. 2206, 2215, 2305), and some critics have shared his assumption (if not his emotion).[41] Genius, however, makes a material distinction between the pair in his processing of the supplication, taking the bill written 'Unto Cupide and to Venus' directly 'To Venus, forto wite hire wille' (8. 2301–9). There is often a clear separation of status, narrative prominence, and even roles between Cupid and Venus in medieval literature. In Boccaccio's *Teseida* (1339–40), for instance, Cupid is

---

[39] Guillaume de Lorris's Cupid should nonetheless be distinguished in this company. He lectures the wounded lover, ' "Vassaus, pris es... Il est fos qui moine dangier | Vers celui qu'il doit losengier | E qu'il covient a soupleier" ' ('Vassal, you are taken. He is a fool who resists the one whom he should flatter and before whom he would do better to beg'; *RR*, ll. 1884–91). He is also, however, intent upon and interested in his servant in a sense in which Chaucer's, Clanvowe's, and Gower's Cupids are not. His comprehensive terms of service, which demand thought on love 'senz cesser' (l. 2236), also promise reward and include detailed advice about grooming and budgeting (ll. 2141–74).

[40] Thomas Usk, *The Testament of Love*, ed. R. Allen Shoaf (Kalamazoo, Mich., 1998), 1. 315–19, 2. 292–4; cf. *CA* 1. 161–71. Russell Peck reads Venus as a suspicious, courtly parody of Lady Philosophy in *Kingship and Common Profit*, 29–30. Gower has earlier portrayed a grotesquely lascivious Venus in the *Vox*, although she is here figured, with Genius, as an infiltrator of religious houses, not as a lord, magnificent or otherwise. See *Vox*, 3. 1535–42, 4. 257–62, 4. 595–600.

[41] Michael D. Cherniss e.g. states that 'Gower offers no clear indication in the *Confessio* that Cupid is to be distinguished from Venus in concept or function': *Boethian Apocalypse: Studies in Middle English Vision Poetry* (Norman, Okla., 1987), 106.

discovered incidentally, preparing arrows by a spring, as Palemone's prayer proceeds to Venus's temple to discover the goddess deep inside, attended in its ' "più secreta parte" ' ('most secret part') as the focal point of her court.[42] In the *Roman de la Rose*, Cupid does not act alongside Venus until the final stages of the poem, and has a complicated political (and filial) relationship with the queen, ' "Qui ma dame est e ma maistresse" ' ('who is my lady and my mistress') and ' "N'est pas dou tout a mon desir" ' ('is in no way subject to my desire').[43] I know of no case, however, in which the lordships of Cupid and his consort meet in such opposition as they do in the *Confessio*.

This opposition resembles that between Venus's court and Nature's parliament in *The Parliament of Fowls* (?early 1380s), inasmuch as Chaucer's Venus presides impassively over a court of extravagance and sensuality while Nature allows a busy, if shambolic, arbitration-based politics.[44] In fact, Nature is nothing so resourceful as Gower's Venus and is evidently ill-equipped to intervene in the exceptional case of a contested suit; but the contrast between abject temple supplicants and assertive fowls in the *Parliament* is all the more emphatic for that.

Extravagant and sophisticated culture of leisure marks out both the court led about by Cupid in the *Confessio* and the *Parliament*'s court of Venus: it is a shared descriptive signature that smacks of magnificence. Both sites are dedicated to music that challenges earthly measure ('It thoghte as al the hevene cride'; *CA* 8. 2480; 'That God . . . | Ne herde nevere beter'; *PF*, ll. 199–200), to surfeits of 'joie' (*CA* 8. 2490–3; *PF*, ll. 208–9), and to a timeless love-service of dancing. Young lovers leaping and dancing behind Gower's Cupid 'do to love her entendance' (8. 2488), while Chaucer has women attend Venus's temple in a terpsichorean 'offyce alwey, yer by yeere' (*PF*, l. 236). Within Chaucer's temple, Venus herself is revealed to the narrator's greedy eyes amidst luxury which, in fact, makes the leisure of Gower's garlanded and

[42] Giovanni Boccaccio, *Teseida*, ed. Salvatore Battaglia (Florence, 1938), bk 7, stanzas 54, 63–6 (quote at stanza 63); N. R. Havely (ed. and tr.), *Chaucer's Boccaccio: Sources of Troilus and the Knight's and Franklin's Tales* (Cambridge, 1980), 129, 130.

[43] *RR*, ll. 10750–1.

[44] Paul Strohm draws a distinction between Venus's and Nature's sections of the *Parliament*'s garden focusing on the types of love each deity sponsors. He points to Chaucer's adaptation of the two Venuses in Boccaccio's commentary on his own text, whereby Venus in the *Parliament* retains the lustful associations of the *Teseida*'s 'second Venus', while Nature takes up Boccaccio's goddess's (glossed) socially productive aspects. See Strohm, *Social Chaucer*, 126 and n. 39; Boccaccio, *Teseida*, bk 7, stanzas 55–60, and *chiosa* at stanza 50. Gower's Venus combines both sides of the twofold character present together only in Boccaccio's commentary, and distilled into separate personas by Chaucer.

'queintised' youths look spartan and chaste by comparison. The goddess, her hair 'untressed', lies in a 'prive corner', 'on a bed of gold',
beneath 'a subtyl coverchef of Valence' in a stifling atmosphere of
rushing 'sykes hoote as fyr', near-darkness and 'a thousand savours
sote', attended by 'Richesse' and gods of appetite, Bacchus and Ceres
(*PF*, ll. 246–76). This sensual saturation is associated with an absence of
'political' or patronal attention. Thus, the narrator notices two supplicants before Venus, but registers no response to their presence let alone
their suits. The pair seem to be trapped in the same non-progressive
cycle as the dancers outside. The narrator, a tourist beyond the gateway
inscribed with verses of portentous yet conflicted power (ll. 123–61),
seems to have discovered a still centre of suspended authority, uninterested in resolving such a tension. Meanwhile, the painted gallery of
surrendered maidenhood and an 'antihistorical jumble' of unhappy
lovers resembles Gower's company of young lovers (including a considerable intersection of membership) and gives testimony to the arbitrary
power of Venus when she does act.[45]

Cupid's court in the *Confessio* seems similarly saturated and inert
(allowing for Chaucer's descriptive luxury). The company of young lovers
is twice characterized by the 'newe' and combines extreme refinement
with limitless leisure. The courtiers of love are 'queintised' by the high

[45] The description of the temple paintings is Strohm's (*Social Chaucer*, 126). Tristram
and Isolde, Hercules, Paris and Helen, Troilus, Pyramus and Thisbe, Achilles, Dido,
Cleopatra, and Canace feature in both parades. (Of these, only Hercules, Pyramus, and
Thisbe appear in the *Teseida*'s list; Boccaccio, *Teseida*, bk 7, stanzas 61–2.) Gower and
Chaucer may have encountered many such lists or processions in their reading or
listening, including Froissart's 'compagne grande' in *Le Paradys d'amour* or Deschamps's
'tresnoble compaignie' in green in *Le Lay de franchise*. See Jean Froissart, *Œuvres de
Froissart: Poésies*, ed. A. Scheler (Brussels, 1870–2), i. 29–30, ll. 957–1004; Eustache
Deschamps, *Œuvres complètes de Eustache Deschamps*, ed. le marquis de Queux de Saint-
Hilaire and Gaston Raynaud (Paris, 1878–1903), ii. 206, l. 94. Strohm reads Nature's
haunt in the *Parliament* as seemingly 'preferable from almost any perspective to Venus'
statically arrested precincts' (*Social Chaucer*, 126). For diverse interpretations of the
moral and social value of Venus's court and authority, see A. J. Minnis, *Oxford Guides
to Chaucer: The Shorter Poems* (Oxford, 1995), 283–90; J. A. W. Bennett, *The Parlement
of Foules: An Interpretation* (Oxford, 1957), 78–132; George D. Economou, *The Goddess
Natura in Medieval Literature* (Cambridge, Mass., 1972), 135–9 (finding 'destructive
love' and an 'evil Venus'; 137, 138); Elaine Tuttle Hansen, *Chaucer and the Fictions of
Gender* (Berkeley, Calif., 1992), 115–40 ('The garden ruled by Venus and Nature
cultivates nothing but contradiction between and within'; 116); Elizabeth Salter, *Fourteenth-Century English Poetry: Contexts and Readings* (Oxford, 1983), 130–7 ('No breath
of criticism disturbs the still scene'; 136); Michael St John, *Chaucer's Dream Visions:
Courtliness and Individual Identity* (Aldershot, Hants, 2000), 135–45 (opposing the
temple's alienating courtliness to a 'democratisation' of courtly space in Nature's garden).

fashion of Bohemia (8. 2470–2) which, incidentally, signposts an allegory of the royal household of King Richard and Anne of Bohemia.[46] Fashion unites novelty and sophistication in the continually renewed rejection and eclipse of what went before. The leisured conversation of the company mingles the martial and the amorous in a passage evocative of Walsingham's satirizing of Richard II's court as 'knights of Venus rather than Bellona: more effective in the bedchamber than the field':[47]

> The moste matiere of her speche
> Was al of knyhthod and of Armes
> And what it is to ligge in armes
> With love whanne it is achieved
>
> (8. 2496–9)[48]

The difference between 'knyhthod' and 'love' is confused or elided by the ambiguity of the second set of 'armes' and, especially, of the final impersonal pronoun. Knightly exploits are drawn into a lassitude which seems post-coital, depending upon what 'it' is (chivalry or sex) that is 'achieved' or, crucially, *talked about* as a precious goal. Imagining performance as already accomplished, Cupid's court is infused with an air of leisure and enervation.

Nature in the *Parliament* and Venus in the *Confessio*, by contrast, enjoy no sophisticated visual and sensual backdrops, and are primarily defined by arbitral activity performed right before the narrator's gaze. After lingering on Venus and her inner sanctum, Chaucer briskly cites Alain de Lille as a shorthand for Nature's appearance (exquisite as it happens to be in *De planctu*).[49] The elegance of Nature's environs, 'Of braunches . . . | Iwrought after here cast and here mesure' (*PF*, ll. 304–5), is likewise understated. In turn, stasis and non-progression give way to pragmatic bustle (focused on a procreative end). The narrator is

---

[46] See Mathew, *Court of Richard II*, 76; Green, '*Familia Regis*', 91–2; and for 'benevolent Cupid' in a 'commentary on Ricardian kingship', Patterson, 'Court Politics', 11. For Mathew's assessment of the influence of Queen Anne and her retinue on English court culture, see *Court of Richard II*, 1–52, esp. 21, 39–42.

[47] Thomas Walsingham, *Chronicon Angliæ 1328–1388*, ed. Edward Maunde Thompson, Rolls Ser. (London, 1874), 375.

[48] The (lack of) punctuation here is taken from Oxford, Bodleian MS Fairfax 3. Macaulay's comma after 'love' in l. 2499 resolves (or diminishes) the final clause's ambiguity in favour of 'knyhthod'.

[49] *PF*, ll. 316–18; cf. Alain de Lille, *De planctu*, 808–20. Chaucer has earlier supplied three lines of superlative description for Nature (*PF*, ll. 299–301).

impressed mainly by the business of the scene, as the crowds of birds wait 'in [Nature's] presence | To take hire dom and yeve hire audyence' (ll. 307–8). The scene takes on the character of a hierarchically ordered gathering intent on judgement and award.[50] The citation of Alain tidies away descriptive duties so that Nature's activity—bidding 'every foul to take his owne place' (l. 320), ordering and initiating proceedings—can take centre stage. Using legal terminology ('"By my statut . . . my ryghtful ordenaunce"', ll. 387, 390), and always mindful of a proper order of worship, Nature's role is then to direct the spirited avian debate which occupies the remainder of the dream vision.

Intriguingly, Nature fails to make anything of this debate. For all that her 'governaunce' seems easily to provide almost every bird a mate 'By evene acord' (l. 668), she proves to have none of Gower's Venus's procedural wherewithal when the difficult case arises—in particular, when readers are surprised by '*Another* tersel egle' (l. 449, emphasis added) bidding for the one formel and numbers do not fall into place. Nature initiates a consultative procedure for dealing with the case, but eventually gives up in frustration, closes debate and '"opynyoun"' (l. 618), and improvises another procedural amendment (turning the matter over to the formel). By neglecting to frame any terms that the fowls' '"verdit"' (l. 525) should address, she has been partly responsible for the consultation's internally contradicted and inconclusive quality.[51] Nature's failure to settle the three male eagles' dispute, however, is equally testimony to the participatory character of the politics she facilitates. She refuses to compel the formel eagle's choice and her authority permits and invites a plurality of voices.[52] Delegated consultation and personal intervention are more integrated under Venus in the *Confessio*.

Venus especially qualifies a parallel between her own and Nature's roles by entering direct competition with her opposite number (having taken no place in the lover's vision of Cupid's teeming court). Gower's god of love epitomizes magnificence: his lordship is portrayed as

[50] D. S. Brewer points out that the *Parliament*'s French analogues typically involve debates (and arbitration adds Strohm) in the context of a noble council or retinue: Geoffrey Chaucer, *The Parlement of Foulys*, ed. D. S. Brewer (1960; Manchester, 1972), 37; Strohm, *Social Chaucer*, 218 n. 45.

[51] For passages in which Nature displays her consciousness of ' "degre" ' and worship, see *PF*, ll. 390–401, 519–21, 631–7. For her efforts to control the birds' proceedings, see e.g. ll. 446–8, 519–32, 617–37.

[52] On the social drama and politically charged forms of Nature's assembly, see Strohm, *Social Chaucer*, 126–30, 152; cf. St John, *Dream Visions*, 135–45.

arbitrary and unreliable in rewarding service, immune to obligation, and totalizing in its refusal of pluralized discourse and its demand for servants to signify their master's meanings.[53] Such magnificence is the majestic twin of Amans's own politics of irresponsibility, and a psychological reading of Gower's allegory might understand both lover and god as separate aspects of the same person. Looking outside the *Confessio*, magnificence also attaches to Cupid's lordship in *The Legend of Good Women* and Clanvowe's *Boke of Cupide*.[54] The action opening the dream visions in the *Confessio* and the *Legend*'s prologue share some obvious 'Cupidian' affinities. Both narrators find themselves confronted in a meadow or 'grene pleine' by a glowering god of love, who is accompanied by his consort and brandishes a 'firy Dart' or two (*CA* 1. 138–47; *LGW*, G 158–84). Both descriptions create compact gestures of intimidating, arbitrary authority as the narrators focus on the god's hostile gaze and suffer or anticipate harm without knowing cause (*CA* 1. 140–5; *LGW*, G 169–72). More significant parallels, however, are to be found between the *Confessio* and Clanvowe's poem, despite—indeed because of—Love's failure to appear in *The Boke of Cupide*'s narrative. Cupid's fleeting, mute appearance at the start of the *Confessio* mirrors the unreliable authority which Clanvowe attributes to his absent god of love.[55] Both the *Cupide* and the *Confessio* begin with extensive, experientially authorized and ironic praise of love as an all-powerful but unsettlingly capricious lord (*CA* 1. 17–60; *Cupide*, ll. 1–35). Both narrators set about embroidering with imagery and epigrams a conception of love as a lord who cannot be resisted but who applies his will unpredictably, even randomly, and with results that may or may not be beneficial and will surely be drastic and destabilizing. He 'can glade and

[53] See Fradenburg, 'Manciple's Servant Tongue', 88–9.

[54] I am not attempting here to pursue any direct connections between Gower's and Chaucer's vision-framed tale collections. For an ambitious association of the *Confessio* with *The Legend of Good Women*, see Fisher, *John Gower*, 235–50.

[55] The *Cupide*'s few critics have noted its debt to Chaucer, but not enough has been said of possible connections with Gower's English dream vision, which was being composed at the time the *Cupide* appears to have been written (i.e. in the late 1380s or certainly before Clanvowe's death in 1391). It is not impossible that Clanvowe knew Gower's poem as he was composing it, and vice versa. The pair were quite possibly acquainted (both certainly knew Chaucer: Strohm, *Social Chaucer*, 41–6). In any case, the two deploy conventional elements with remarkable similarity of tone and narrative pace in setting up their respective dream visions. For the authorship and dating of the *Cupide*, see V. J. Scattergood, 'The Authorship of "The Boke of Cupide"', *Anglia*, 82 (1964), 137–49; Clanvowe, *Works*, ed. Scattergood, 9–14. See also Strohm, *Social Chaucer*, 78. Scattergood discusses the relationship between Chaucer's poetry and Clanvowe's, for which see also Strohm, *Social Chaucer*, 79–82; Patterson, 'Court Politics', 21–2.

greve whom him lyketh' (*Cupide*, l. 18) and 'yifth his graces undeserved, | And fro that man which hath him served | Fulofte he takth aweye his fees' (*CA* 1. 51–3). The god of love in each vision then fulfils the profile of capricious power spelt out for him by the narrator. Lee Patterson has analysed the nightingale's service and Cupid's lordship in Clanvowe's poem, arguing that Cupid's lordship is shown to be thoroughly unproductive and unreliable, and that eventually 'Cupid disappears from the poem as a figure of authority'.[56] The nightingale's plea for Cupid's assistance to defend love's '"worshipful seruyse"' (*Cupide*, l. 213) against the cuckoo is answered only by the buffoonish narrator, and she can offer him as reward nothing beyond her good wishes and the unsecured promise of her song the following May, providing she is not then '"affrayed"' (l. 235). Gower's Cupid at least puts in a showing in Amans's vision, but he is also unresponsive and unresponsible. Appealed to for pity, he remains silent—as absent in the vocal expression of his authority as Clanvowe's Cupid. His impaling of Amans, narrated after we are told he has cast 'His chiere aweiward' and moved on (*CA* 1. 141–2), seems an afterthought, or absent-minded. One way of reading Cupid and his opaque motives in Chaucer's, Clanvowe's, and Gower's poetry is that they suggest how a magnate or king with major interests centred elsewhere might have appeared to a landed family with a much more localized view of the history of a region's politics and the rights and wrongs of possession.

Cupid's lordship demands everything of its servants, but is at the same time unreciprocal. This magnificence is most vividly and comprehensively depicted in the vision of the court led by Cupid before the swooning lover. The lover has, at this moment, felt the first shock of his petition's refusal by Venus on the grounds of age.[57] Cupid's companies, then, appear as a kind of residual vision of the reward or 'hyre' (8. 2291) that the lover has claimed (8. 2291–3) and is convinced is his due. Despite the lover's wistful belief that 'it was half a mannes hele' (8. 2484) just to overhear the music of the court, however, passing before his head is an epiphany not of reward due and denied but of unaccountable, totalizing power. As in Chaucer's court of Fame, reward bears no relation to merit in Cupid's court, and

[56] Patterson, 'Court Politics', esp. 10–12 (quote at 12). For the conceit of the nightingale's service to Love, also see above, 66.

[57] *CA* 8. 2398–2459. On the problem, or trick, of the lover's age, see Donald Schueler, 'The Age of the Lover in Gower's *Confessio Amantis*', *Medium Ævum*, 36 (1967), 152–8; and (convincingly) contesting Schueler's view, Burrow, 'Portrayal of Amans', 11–16. Cf. Calin, 'Gower's Continuity', 108–9.

Love's appetite for its own meanings is unbounded. Its hyper-refined culture—the unproductive superabundance of wealth, technical expertise, and recreation which I have already discussed in relation to Youth's company—simultaneously constitutes the court's appeal to the lover and its magnificent contempt for the individual identities and deserts of love's servants. All of the 'gentil folk' (8. 2457), young and old, disport themselves in signification of love.

Youth's office as 'Mareschal' (8. 2662), or steward, of the court makes it clear that the narrator fantasizes an institutionally framed, spectacular household ceremony.[58] The festivity is imposed upon the company to magnify sovereign Love, not gifted to it as a reward for service. The singing, dancing, and playing is itself a service or 'entendance' to Love 'After the lust of youthes heste' (8. 2488–9), and it is exclusive of all but its own meanings. The steward is so intent on his signification of love, that he fails to notice the narrator ('So besy... upon his lay | That he non hiede where I lay | Hath take'; 8. 2663–5). The spectacle led by Youth and his 'route' (8. 2465) triumphantly refuses to notice any external voice or reality. Thus, the noise of the first company fills the dream space with a single strain, as if 'al the hevene cride | In such acord and such a soun' (8. 2480–1); there is no song heard that is not 'unto love... touchende' (8. 2475); and the court banishes the rival voice of Care, who is an excluded figure in household society, put 'out of the weie, | That he with hem ne sat ne stod' (8. 2492–3). The narrator, unnoticed, is also excluded by his own incomprehension (8. 2494–9) due to courtly plenitude or excess—either simply that of the lovers' noise or, perhaps, the complex and difficult quality of 'her speche' (8. 2496).

The narrator beholds troops of servants in fossilized service. The unilateral priority of the sovereign Love, that his servants embody and symbolize only his magnificence, pre-empts any concern for the servants themselves.[59] Unlike Gower's court of Love, the world's worth of lovers which trails Cupid

[58] The late medieval steward of the royal household was 'responsible for order, discipline, and over-all efficiency within the *domus*' (Given-Wilson, *Royal Household*, 9).

[59] The violence done to the signification of individual lovers' beings in the service of Love is most pronounced in the second, older company. Sampson and Aristotle e.g. are radically alienated from their respective essences of strength and science (8. 2702–13). The philosopher has featured in the poem up until this point exclusively in his dominant, traditionalist guise of *auctor* and *Secretum secretorum*'s teacher to Alexander. Now he is suddenly and surprisingly forced back on stage in his less familiar fabliau role as grey-bearded dupe and mount to Alexander's queen. The tradition of Aristotle, as careerist counsellor and hence courtier, being humiliated by his master's queen originated in a widely known French fabliau of the thirteenth century. See Henri d'Andeli, *Le Lai d'Aristote de Henri d'Andeli*, ed. Maurice Delbouille (Paris, 1951).

in *The Legend of Good Women* (*LGW,* G 188–92; cf. *CA* 8. 2456–8) comprises only women (purportedly) 'trewe of love' (G 193). This train, however, presents not so much reward but a smooth surface on the magnificent symbolism of Love's power.[60] Gower's court is deeply furrowed with different types of service and different personal feelings where the *Legend*'s company of true women signifies power univocally and with personal fates and demeanours hidden. In the *Confessio*, a pervasive incongruity of universal play and individual moods deconstructs the vision's magnificent imperative. Troilus's forced cavorting, for instance ('althogh he pleide, | Be semblant he was hevy chiered'; 8. 2532–3), distils the fabricated, endless festivity's uncanniness, which is the sign of the gap between Love's meanings and those of his servants. The discrepancy between the spectacular purpose of the court and the diverse and conflicted subject positions which the court attempts to order reveals Love's sovereign desire for its own symbolism as well as the unreliability of this desire as a form of lordship. Untrue lovers, like Theseus, Jason, and Paris, are rewarded, or allowed to prosper; grievances are not redressed; innocent lovers wronged are not relieved. Where the lack of a third party clears the way for joyful reunion, it is in many cases denied, so that Pyramus and Thisbe evidently do their service one apart from the other (8. 2542–3, 2578). Even the exemplary wives, by whose virtue in signifying love 'the Court stod al amended' (8. 2608), are not reunited with their husbands. Their sacrifices stand and win reverence in the court, unqualified by compensatory personal joy.[61]

Curtailing Cupid

Despite the lover-narrator's longing, Venus's exclusion of him from such a situation looks like a reward given the prospect of eternal and thankless service. Banishment from such service is the freedom that the sovereign-subjected will eternally woos but recognizes as death.[62] The court episode becomes the frame narrative's definitive intersection

[60] For the image of suffering itself and their own textual 'rescue' as the reward of 'good women', see L. O. Aranye Fradenburg, *Sacrifice your Love: Psychoanalysis, Historicism, Chaucer* (Minneapolis, 2002), 196.

[61] They experience immediately (or are suspended in) the alienation of Fradenburg's 'rescue' by the reputation for sacrifice (above, n. 60). See also A. S. G. Edwards, 'Gower's Women in the *Confessio*', *Mediaevalia*, 16 (1993), 223–37, esp. 234–5 on Gower's 'male-focused world' (235).

[62] For this conception of service to the sovereign other, and of the 'obsessional text' which 'continues to defer both life and death, preferring to live in death, because it cannot imagine itself without the master: to do so would be to imagine death', see Fradenburg, 'Manciple's Servant Tongue', esp. 103, 109 (quote at 109).

between magnificence and reciprocalism. Whereas sterile service en-
dures at the end of *The Boke of Cupide* and the *Legend* prologue,
Venus finally asserts an alternative to Cupid's magnificence.

The parliament of fowls appointed at the end of Clanvowe's poem to
hear the nightingale's complaint at Woodstock may be offered as some
kind of answer to the flawed authority of Love, and it will seemingly not
be daunted by the nightingale or the authority of her lord. The birds
demur at the nightingale's obsessive, impatient temper with a cool
deferral for ' "good avysement" ' (l. 272) and a hearing for the accused
cuckoo. Nevertheless, Clanvowe (engaged with the Ricardian court, like
Chaucer, in ways that Gower was not[63]) does not offer the assurance of
promoting this conciliar alternative in any definitive competition
against Love's magnificence. After all, the birds' parliament does not
take place in the poem (let alone decide in favour of the cuckoo) and the
narrator is not persuaded of anything. The poem ends with the nightingale still possessed by Cupid, still circumscribed by his signification, as
her final song echoes eerily in the cavernous space of the god's absence
from the text.

Although Chaucer's Alceste may appear to fulfil a role very similar to
that of Gower's Venus, her influence ultimately reinforces rather than
curtails her consort's power. At first it seems otherwise: from the moment
at which she intervenes in his declamation that he will ' "so cruelly" '
(*LGW*, F 340) make the narrator sorry for his literary injury to Love's
worship, Alceste confronts Cupid's anger with rigorous corrective counsel. Locating Alceste as mediatrix within late medieval conceptual structures of queenly influence, Paul Strohm has analysed her 'transformation
from an abject intercessor of royalty to royalty's companion and adviser
and a source of irrefutable authority in her own right'.[64] The queen

---

[63] On Chaucer's social location, see Strohm, *Social Chaucer*, 10–13; Patterson, *Subject of History*, 32–9. On Clanvowe's situation as Ricardian chamber knight, see Given-Wilson, *Royal Household*, 160–74, 196; Strohm, *Social Chaucer*, 39–40. See also McFar-lane, *Lancastrian Kings*, 139–226; W. T. Waugh, 'The Lollard Knights', *Scottish Histor-ical Review*, 11 (1913–14), 55–92, 75–80. Waugh's article remains a useful check on inclinations to define a chamber group by too neatly categorizing the religious beliefs of Clanvowe and his peers.

[64] Strohm, *Hochon's Arrow*, esp. 111–19 (quote at 116). David Wallace includes Alceste amongst Chaucerian representations of the power of feminine rhetoric to avert masculine violence: see *Chaucerian Polity: Absolutist Lineages and Associational Forms in England and Italy* (Stanford, Calif., 1997), 212–46 (esp. 213–14). See also Robert B. Burlin, *Chaucerian Fiction* (Princeton, 1977), 40–3; Judson Boyce Allen, *The Ethical Poetic of the Later Middle Ages: A Decorum of Convenient Distinction* (Toronto, 1982), 267–8. Cf. John Carmi Parsons, 'Ritual and Symbol in the English Medieval Queenship

lectures her consort on mercy in general terms and seeks to constrain his
masculine, sovereign will ('"Leteth youre yre, and beth somwhat treta-
ble"'; G 397). She concludes by proposing a concession of his prerogative
arbitrarily to harm the narrator in return for the narrator's future service at
Cupid's direction:

> 'I axe yow this man, ryght of youre grace,
> That ye hym nevere hurte in al his lyve;
> And he shal swere to yow, and that as blyve,
> He shal no more agilten in this wyse,
> But he shal maken, as ye wol devyse,
> Of women trewe in lovynge al here lyve'
>
> (*LGW*, G 423–8)

Such an exchange scarcely embodies reciprocalism in justice. It assumes
that the narrator has already done offence against Love (G 426) and
makes the avoidance of arbitrary punishment contingent on future
service. If any reward for this service is to be envisaged, it is only in
the negative form of not-harm (albeit the queen later promises to
petition that love's servants '"quite"' the narrator's labour; G 484).
Alceste's intercession thus turns out not so much to diminish the
magnificence of the royal authority facing the narrator as to give it
refined and particular expression. By the time Cupid, to '"save my
degre"' (G 437), has relinquished to his queen the entire matter of
judgement (G 439), Alceste has stepped into his authority to renovate
its magnificence. She has already presumed a '"trespas"' (G 470) on the
narrator's part and is utterly uninterested in his attempt to answer the
charge against him, rebuking him with an uncompromising statement
of sovereign unaccountability: '"Lat be thyn arguynge, | For Love ne
wol nat counterpletyd be | In ryght ne wrong"' (G 465–7). In turning
from Cupid to the narrator, Alceste has become overtly aggressive, and
she abruptly refuses rival speaking.[65] Such peremptoriness agrees with a
totalizing interest in harmony with Cupid's prerogative (so that her

---

to 1500', *Cosmos*, 7 (1992), 60–77; and, on female intercession and mediation more
generally, Carolyn P. Collette, 'Heeding the Counsel of Prudence: A Context for the
Melibee', *Chaucer Review*, 29 (1994–5), 416–33; and 'Joan of Kent and Noble Women's
Roles in Chaucer's World', *Chaucer Review*, 33 (1998–9), 350–62.

[65] On the 'conflicting impulses' of Marian and aggressive characteristics behind the
portrayal of Alceste, see Carolyn Dinshaw, *Chaucer's Sexual Poetics* (Madison, Wisc., 1989),
71–2 (quote at 71). For Alceste's 'participation in the aggressivity of which the God of Love
is such a brilliant image', her eclipsing of rival beauty and goodness, and the instability of her
sublime image, see Fradenburg, *Sacrifice your Love*, 191–5 (quote at 193).

judgement pleases him very well). She has represented the narrator's
worth only in so far as it has assisted Love's sovereign interest, defending
the narrator's ' "makynge" ' to the extent that it ' "furthred wel [Cupid's]
lawe" ' (F 413) and no further (' "Al be hit that he kan nat wel endite" ';
F 414). Having begun by enjoining him to allow the narrator a chance
to ' "replye" ' (G 319), Alceste has actually taken the opportunity of
Cupid's rage to compel a previously free agent and putative ' "mortal fo" '
(G 248) to produce (through her own lethal signification) a totalizing
work in magnification of Love.[66] Where Cupid's magnificent ire was raw,
unfocused, and portended only the exclusion or expunging of the narrator's voice and being, less respected than a worm's (G 243–4), Alceste has
found a means to subdue that voice to the service of Love's meanings
while excluding refutation. Occupying 'irrefutable authority in her own
right', the queen takes inchoate wrath, and gives it shape in a particular
judgement, without unseating its inherently magnificent motivation.
Instead, she modifies raw magnificence according to a less destructive,
more acquisitive totalizing objective.

While *The Boke of Cupide* adumbrates an alternative to the god of
love's authority and *The Legend of Good Women* complicates and modifies his exercise of power through the role of his queen, neither poem
contradicts or replaces the magnificent authority of Love. Returning to
Gower's Cupid and his companies of lovers, we see that the triumphal
last gasp of magnificent love in the *Confessio* is swept away by a process
of 'good avysement' between Venus and her son which prepares the
ground for the full effects of the queen's lordship in the ensuing four-
part ceremony. The aftermath of the festive inertia of Cupid's phantas-
magoric court is a showcase of communicative and deliberative gestures
which contradict wilful magnificence. Venus responds to an appeal to
relieve the narrator's sufferings which is made by old servants of love
who are themselves otherwise subsumed by love's power (8. 2726–9). It
is Cupid, in fact, who then removes the fiery lance which has symbolized
the narrator's suffering under love since the beginning of his dream
vision. Yet this act is inscribed as something quite alien, indeed self-
destructive, to Cupid's lordship, and it signals the banishment of his
power and his courtly entourage from the poem. The result is an
engaging, incongruous portrayal of the god of love which emphasizes
the counter-balancing of his natural, conventional qualities. Compared

---

[66] Dinshaw describes the penance prescribed by Alceste as 'an entirely totalizing
literary activity' (*Chaucer's Sexual Poetics*, 70).

with the initial casting of the dart, Gower expends almost ten times as much verse treating Cupid's painstaking efforts to remove it. Moreover, Cupid is clearly acting here as a delegate of Venus's authority, her supervision (as mother now, rather than regal partner) removing any suggestion of caprice from the endeavour. The god of love eventually and 'Forth with his moder full avised, | Hath determined and devised | Unto what point he wol descende' (8. 2785–7) before he even begins to remove the lance. The passage thoroughly contradicts the anger, haughtiness, independence, speed, and sureness of Cupid's initial exercising of his prerogative (which it expressly recalls). It then concludes by effacing this power altogether, as Cupid and the court depart the poem in an instant, 'As this was do' (8. 2801).

Venus's arbitral lordship counters Cupid's power and its eternal deferral of reward, the suspension of being in this power's spectacle of itself. Venus then completes the penitential rehabilitation of the narrator, securing his rescue from unproductive, unrewarding service and equipping him for a politically responsible life. She does so by enabling Genius's confession's protracted informing of the narrator's reason, opening his will to occupation by the confession's expository and exemplary instruction. This instruction supports the same reciprocalist and anti-magnificent political principles that Venus's management of the lover's petition has dramatized. At the return of 'Resoun' to the narrator the arbitration has finally produced an intellectual environment conducive to the reciprocalist content of Genius's confession and its 'Ensamples . . . many on' (8. 2137).

5

Women as Household
Exchange in Genius's Tales

Daughters and wives cover a good deal of ground in *Confessio Amantis*, and their stories entrench the poem's politics. Gower's frame narrative offers allegorical abstraction and intimate petitioning combined. The numerous tales retold by Genius to Amans during the confession provide wider and more variegated perspectives on great household economies. These tales recount household exchanges more concrete and literal than Venus's moral remedy, although sensational plotting and exotic settings grant them a certain symbolic quality. The exempla are the substance of the lesson that Venus finally embeds in her retainer, and they sponsor the aristocratic reciprocal principles which she personally dramatizes. They are persistently interested in the exchange of women.

Women who are not stopped dead in their tracks criss-cross the classical world, from Persia to Northumberland and from Pentapolis to Tyre, and pepper it with a multitude of more localized movements. The transmediterranean adventures of Constance, Medea, and the pairing of the princess of Pentapolis and Thais dominate respectively the first half of book 2 (ll. 587–1603), the middle of book 5 (ll. 3247–4229), and the bulk of book 8 (ll. 271–2008). The poles of the poem's female traffic, whether it occurs between neighbouring towns and dwellings or between the ends of the earth, are aristocratic households. Her father's household is almost always the woman's starting point and her story is invariably one of sexual possession (sometimes thwarted). Most commonly, another 'worthi kniht' or lord figure will challenge the father's possession and, usually, effect the daughter's removal by marriage, flight, or abduction.

The usefulness of this kind of narrative to Gower and Genius in putting together a compendium addressing amatory woe is fairly obvious. Less obvious is the deep political structure that is shared by these tales of daughters, fathers, suitors, and rapists, and which refracts that of the poem

as a whole. Claude Lévi-Strauss and his critics (including Gayle Rubin and
Eve Kosofsky Sedgwick) have taught us to examine ways in which cultural
productions can reinforce a male prerogative to transact women with other
men, whereby a woman's erotic association structures power relations
between the men who control it.[1] Situated in the great household in
Genius's narratives, Gower's rendition of the exchange of women system
gains distinctive social contours, and structures a particular type of masculine power. The marriages and less legitimate exchanges of women in the
exempla epitomize the ordering and disordering of a much larger set of
relations constitutive of the great household. Tales of sex and love, in other
words, enact and map the modes of household-based exchange that are
available in the poem, and which it deems supportive or disruptive of
aristocratic power. Gower's exchange of women narratives engage his most
fundamental and urgent propositions about this competition over the
proper disposition of the great household.

  The *Confessio*'s exemplary women function as signs of the great household's political economy, its modes of deploying landed power and sustaining aristocratic pre-eminence. Marriage had a major role in the late
medieval landed hierarchy's circulation of wealth and power. Marriage
portions (often worth many hundreds of pounds among the English
nobility), procreation, and their own inheritances, jointures, and dower
rights, involved women in the transmission of real property between
families and generations.[2] Moreover, marriage not only enabled the household systems by which patrimonies themselves were distributed and transmitted. It also conveyed political capital. It was a potent mechanism for
producing bonds and conduits for further exchange between households,
and thus for conserving or dissipating wealth and power. The exchange of
women, among other types of exchange represented in the *Confessio*,
describes a paradigm for proper (reciprocalist) or improper (magnificent)
lordship, positing norms for the spheres of association orbiting the landed

  [1] Claude Lévi-Strauss, *The Elementary Structures of Kinship*, tr. James Harle Bell, John
Richard von Sturmer, and Rodney Needham, rev. edn (London, 1969); Gayle Rubin,
'The Traffic in Women: Notes on the "Political Economy" of Sex', in Rayna R. Reiter
(ed.), *Toward an Anthropology of Women* (New York, 1975), 157–210; Eve Kosofsky
Sedgwick, *Between Men: English Literature and Male Homosocial Desire* (New York,
1985). Sedgwick discusses Rubin's critique of Lévi-Strauss at 25–6.
  [2] See McFarlane, *Nobility*, 64–6, 84–8; Holmes, *Estates*, 41–57; J. M. W. Bean, *The
Decline of English Feudalism 1215–1540* (Manchester, 1968), 104–79; Scott L. Waugh, *The
Lordship of England: Royal Wardships and Marriages in English Society and Politics 1217–
1327* (Princeton, 1988), esp. 15–63; Carpenter, *Locality and Polity*, 97–119, 211–22, 246–
56; Payling, 'Economics of Marriage'.

household. Women become central to (and marginalized by) Gower's preoccupation with landed social relations.

Despite its status as amatory compendium, the *Confessio* evinces little interest in female protagonists qua protagonists. With some notable, complicated exceptions (including Canace, Rosiphelee, Medea, and Apollonius's wife and daughter), Gower's translation of tales rarely pays attention to the personal suffering or desire of women. A. S. G. Edwards remarks that the *Confessio*'s women 'seem . . . to be of significance primarily as aspects of male-focused narratives' and viewed 'as important in functional rather than intrinsic terms'.[3] The great household is the dominant referent of these functional terms. Women linked to great households are important in the poem but their agency is severely restricted. Sometimes they are blank characters who describe and enable property systems crucial to the great household, and act as narrative chits to trace the various modes of power wielded by heads of great households in relation to each other and to their assumed responsibility for social order. Even characters such as Medea and the princess of Pentapolis prove to be exceptions which obey the larger rule of household significance. Their agency and psychological interiority represent certain patterns, vulnerabilities, or renegotiations of the aristocratic politics which the *Confessio* untiringly exhibits and evaluates.[4]

The principal manifestation of women's exemplary function *vis-à-vis* the conduct of lordship in the poem is the narratives' assumption that their will ought to be subsumed in the prerogatives of the household and its lord. Even when women are lords themselves they do not enjoy the range of power of Venus or their male counterparts. Women at all levels of society in medieval England enjoyed much greater independence outside marriage than within it. Wives could act influentially in partnership with their husbands and deputize for them at the head of the household. They were also expected to supervise the internal workings of the household, and in these ways a lady of the manor could influence important exchanges in the household economy. At levels below the aristocracy in the late fourteenth century, wives are increasingly found trading independently of their husbands, as *femmes soles*. Aristocratic wives, however, were most comprehensively subordinated to their husbands by property law and

---

[3] Edwards, 'Gower's Women', 224.

[4] Cf. Kellie Robertson's assessment of the 'cultural preconceptions that underlie the medieval household, particularly the unacknowledged ideological contradiction of female household labor that makes its existence possible' (*Laborer's Two Bodies*, 142).

gender ideology. They were subsumed within their husband's public identity in the control and alienation of land and in politics; and even as independent heads of their own households women were excluded from public office except where they inherited a family position. Stereotyping of femininity as weak and unreliable supported wives' subordination and could interfere with an independent woman's efforts to adopt public roles, which were understood in masculine terms.

If an aristocratic woman experienced at all the adult independence of the unmarried it would probably come *after* marriage since she would likely be married as a teenager. While married status was not the only obstacle to political activity for a woman, widowhood was significant as a means to independent control of a household, especially where there were no heirs of age. Even where a son had come into his inheritance, a widow would retain control of her own property, and custom and common law entitled widows to recover their inheritances, marriage portions, and dowers if, when alive, their husbands had alienated these.

For aristocratic women, widowhood meant lordship. Jointures (husband–wife joint tenancies in survivorship), which were widespread by the fourteenth century, set up landholding wives for widowhood more securely at law—but not necessarily more generously—than the customary dower right. Widows became full partners in household exchanges. Prospective second husbands meanwhile stood to benefit from a widow's remarriage, as did other men (especially kin or superior lords) who persuaded her to this transaction. On the other hand, remarriage complicated matters of inheritance for children of an earlier marriage (the new husband could have rights to his wife's property for his lifetime after her death if their marriage produced a child), so that, as a future male lord of her estate, a son could be strongly interested in protecting his mother's widowhood. Magna Carta had promised to safeguard women against pressure to remarry and, in the fourteenth century, entails excluded prospective heirs from subsequent marriages. Widows were often able independently to manage their estates and the future of their family.[5]

---

[5] For aristocratic women, marriage, and widowhood in medieval England, see Peter Coss, *The Lady in Medieval England 1000–1500* (Stroud, Glos., 1998), esp. 115–49; Caroline M. Barron, 'Introduction: The Widow's World in Later Medieval London', in Caroline M. Barron and Anne F. Sutton (eds), *Medieval London Widows, 1300–1500* (London, 1994), pp. xiii–xxxiv; Payling, 'Economics of Marriage'; Rowena E. Archer, 'Rich Old Ladies: The Problem of Late Medieval Dowagers', in Tony Pollard (ed.), *Property and Politics: Essays in Later Medieval English History* (Gloucester, 1984), 15–35. On jointures and their use, see Given-Wilson, *English Nobility*, 139–40 and n. 52.

There are women in charge of great households in the *Confessio*, but the poem delivers conflicting messages on female political independence in this role. Venus stands out as a powerful female lord (whose position is analogous to a widow's by virtue of Cupid's filial status and, more importantly, his inattentive or absent lordship). Amans's lady also seems to enjoy esteemed independence. Certainly, both recognize the superiority of their own leadership to Amans's politicking. Amans's perspective, however, reveals little clearly of his lady's family circumstances or whatever seigneurial role she may be imagined to have. Venus, and perhaps the lady, remain exceptional in the poem because Genius's tales do not rest easy with the idea of women becoming lords on a permanent basis.

The tales are, in the first place, preoccupied with women subordinated to fathers or husbands. This narrative preponderance conveys a normative vision of a society more fully patriarchal than history, and the uncertainties of birth and survival for one thing, allowed. Secondly, tales of independent women often celebrate their compliance with patriarchal imperatives of marriage or imply that they are not suited to leading a great household. The exempla thus reinforce the aristocracy's interest in marrying its daughters and offer no meaningful support for the possibility (most typically manifest in widowhood in actuality) of female lords' exercising enduring political power. For all the heiresses we encounter in the tales, there are few widows and these, including Constance's mothers-in-law and Florent's nemesis, are marginal and threatening or, like Alcione and Dido, suspended in suffering or between two marriages.[6] In book 4 there are several striking examples of women (Dido, Phyllis, and, in effect, Rosiphelee) independently at the head of great households and central in a tale. Their tales give us a sense that this is unsatisfactory, as though the female-led household were in a retracted or incomplete state, waiting to be reawakened by appropriate male occupation. Virtuous heiresses take some measures to 'remedy' this state, but their proper sphere of activity seems to be limited to their own household and, indeed, to the objective of handing power on to a man. Their tales speak to anxieties about the transference of patriarchy in the absence of paternal authority.

Before turning to these female lords, however, it is worth considering the poem's imagination of dependent heiresses, since their situations— as daughters and wives—reflect ones preliminary to the experience of

---

[6] On the symbolic legacy of widows and dowagers in late medieval literature, see Patterson, *Subject of History*, 292–6.

independent household power of most women who became lords in late medieval England, since they are more representative of Genius's tales, and because they surround the tales of female lords with assumptions about the importance of marriage and male authority to the success of the household.

DAUGHTERS DISENFRANCHISED
AND SELF-EXCHANGING WOMEN

When an aristocratic daughter was an heiress she became upon marriage a conduit not only of social obligation and the material capital of a marriage portion or dowry, but potentially of a patrimony (which in fact counted against the marriage portion). Most of the aristocratic daughters who feature in Genius's narratives are apparently brotherless, implying their suitability for the most important of exchanges and their ability to configure exempla around the household. In this chapter these heiresses will be represented by Leucothoe, Virginia, Dido, Phyllis, Rosiphelee, Medea, the princess of Pentapolis (bride to Apollonius of Tyre), Jephte's daughter, and Rosemund. S. J. Payling has explored the 'special significance of the heiress' in the late medieval landed economy, especially during the plague-induced 'crisis in male succession' that beset at least the greater landowning families in late medieval England and was at its height in the 1370s and 1380s.[7] It is tempting to see a connection between this peak and the attention to the abduction or 'ravishing' of women in complaints about private franchises and avoidance of the common law during Richard II's reign.[8] It is (also) hard to say that Gower was responding directly to this particular demographic pressure in the *Confessio*, given the longer term importance of heiress marriage and the preponderance of such stories in other periods, but the prominence of heiresses (in jeopardy) in Genius's tales is unquestionable.

Medieval English rules of inheritance meant that daughters posed various problems as heirs. Gower's lone heiresses eschew the problem of dismembering patrimonies among multiple inheriting females. In addition, Genius's exempla reflect no obvious anxiety that heiresses can carry patrimonies out of a family unless excluded from inheritance. In this they agree, it seems, with actual heads of families who, for instance, did not typically make use of the new legal devices of inheritance to

[7] Payling, 'Economics of Marriage' (quote at 415); Payling, 'Social Mobility' (quote at 54).
[8] *PROME* iii. 42–3, 62, 81, 139–40, 201.

exclude daughters in favour of older male cognates, and who commonly married hieresses to younger sons in anticipation that such a groom would not inherit his own father's patrimony. This would preserve the separate identity of the bride's patrimony.[9] This kind of thinking in book 8 makes the destitute but 'gentil' Apollonius of Tyre an appealing marital prospect because he will be able 'to governe' the inheritance falling to the princess of Pentapolis (*CA* 8. 939–47). If an heiress's family had reason to blame their luck in the inheritance stakes, other families and those with a sense of the wider economic health of the landed class would sympathize with narratives encouraging daughters to inherit and marry.[10]

The experience of dependent heiresses in the *Confessio* is representative of the exchange strategies pursued (or neglected) by the lords responsible for them, and so epitomizes the whole spectrum of the great household's exchanges. It is no accident, therefore, that episodes of the great household's hospitality frequently rub shoulders with issues of marriage or sexual alliance in Genius's narratives. The largesse of the medieval *hospicium*— the physical and logistical domestic structure serving the lord—provided a platform or context for further acts of aristocratic exchange. Exchanges organized by the *hospicium* were a primary means by which the social bonds of the great household were forged, reinforcing and reforming the conduits along which future exchanges would flow. Preliminary, hospitable exchange in the great household repeatedly provides the context for Genius's treatment of amorous exchanges made for better and worse. Entertaining Jason in the hall, Aeetes calls for his daughter Medea, who comes to sit with Jason during the feast. Eventually, the pair abscond together. Echoing Aeetes's intent to make a guest 'glad' (5. 3367, 8. 735) Archistrates invites Apollonius into his hall in the confession's final exemplum and sends his daughter to the prince. Eventually, the pair are married and journey onward. The Lombard king Alboin's marriage to Rosemund disintegrates after a great feast hosted by the king (1. 2459–2646). The Persian sultaness seizes on the connection of betrothal and feast to destroy both in the tale of Constance (2. 656–713). Minos treats Theseus both to

---

[9] See Payling, 'Economics of Marriage', 417–18, 424–6. Carpenter discusses the importance of the integrity of estates and perpetuation of family arms to the late medieval conception of lineage apart from a name alone (see *Locality and Polity*, 246–56; cf. McFarlane, *Nobility*, 72–3).

[10] Nonetheless, Payling notes that heiresses were not automatically the most desirable targets, especially for well-established families, who might eschew a *potential* stake of inheritance in favour of the immediate and sometimes very substantial benefit of a portion: 'Economics of Marriage', 419–20, 422.

his gruesome parody of hospitality and, like Aeetes, to genuine 'gret chiere' (5. 5375) that allows his guest the opportunity to form a secret bond with his daughter. The long tale of Apollonius can be divided into two overlapping sections, containing movements from stability through flux to new stability, each bounded by episodes of hospitality and espousal. Antiochus's vexed reception of Apollonius is redeemed by welcome and marriage at Pentapolis, and Athenagoras's 'hihe festes of Neptune' (8. 1614) and his marriage to Thais eventually repair the calamities which have befallen since the departure from Pentapolis.

The disparate sexual liaisons which share narrative space with acts of hospitality are influenced by the same stuff of lordship which determines those hospitality events. The Lévi-Straussian rereading of Marcel Mauss illuminates the synthesis between hospitality and the matter of love by interpreting women as that which is exchanged when marriages take place. Lévi-Strauss sees marriage as the most powerful of exchanges between men.[11] Gayle Rubin has drawn out and underlined the implications of this theory of the patriarchal ordering of kinship structures:

Kinship is organization, and organization is power. But who is organized?

If it is women who are being transacted, then it is the men who give and take them who are linked, the woman being a conduit of a relationship rather than a partner to it. The exchange of women does not necessarily imply that women are objectified, in the modern sense, since objects in the primitive world are imbued with highly personal qualities. But it does imply a distinction between gift and giver. If women are the gifts, then it is men who are the exchange partners.[12]

Medieval lords commonly gave their daughters in marriage to forge enduring links with high-status grooms and their families. Rather than partners in exchange practice, this rendering of marriage relations reduces dependent women to the function of sign. A discourse according to which women may not normally give themselves away refuses them the position of one who exchanges, and the benefits and meanings created in an exchange.[13] Where this system of exchange finds its

---

[11] See Lévi-Strauss, *Elementary Structures*, esp. 63–8. See also Mauss, *The Gift*.

[12] Rubin, 'Traffic in Women', 174.

[13] Rubin, 'Traffic in Women', 175, 201, discussing Lévi-Strauss's discomfort with and efforts to deflect or camouflage the implications of his theory (201); cf. Dinshaw, *Chaucer's Sexual Poetics*, 97–9. Having earlier stated that 'the woman herself is nothing other than [a gift]' according to the exchange system (*Elementary Structures*, 65), Lévi-Strauss attempts to mitigate the stark implications of his analysis at the end of his work. He spends a paragraph arguing that 'woman could never become just a sign and nothing more, since even in a man's world she is still a person' (496).

narrative representation in terms of love and desire, lust (or improper desire) becomes the symptom of agencies of illicit exchange and political instability.

Before their exchange, many of the *Confessio's* dependent heiresses are blank signs, full of potential symbolic capital realizable by and for the men who inscribe them in giving and receiving them. These characters facilitate the poem's most transparent appropriations of women and their sexuality as traffic in the great household's political economy. As Carolyn Dinshaw puts it, describing Chaucer's Host's conception of female virginity: 'a woman's "maydenhede",... is a literal blank, an empty space, an "O" that is valued precisely in its being void of spot, of any mark'.[14] This blankness allows the woman legitimately exchanged in Gower's narratives to become a sign of her husband's worship and of his obligation to her father's family and household.

In Genius's treatment of robbery and 'micherie', the status of a 'maidenhede' as property and a valuable blank is especially pronounced. Cornix's body or genitals are 'the cofre' from which Neptune will 'stele' (5. 6177–9). The pregnant Calistona is cast off by Diana as the broken object or contaminated void that ' "hast take such a touche, | Which nevere mai ben hol ayein" ' (5. 6278–9). The tale of Leucothoe narrates such property as an effect of lordship. Reworking Ovid, Gower highlights the affinities between this tale and that of Virginia (7. 5131–5306). In the *Confessio*, both narratives are about a father's endeavour to preserve his daughter's virginity, and result in her death at his will. Gower shifts the focus of Ovid's tale more squarely onto Orchamus and his daughter. He omits material on Phoebus, flattening him in the process, from smitten deity to generic 'lurkende' thief of maidenhood in accordance with Genius's theme of avarice. This moves Leucothoe into the narrative's central position.[15] Yet, Gower simultaneously effaces her Ovidian personality. Ovid twice pictures Leucothoe in attitudes of fear, before the sun god and before her father, her fingers limp ('digitis... remissis'; *Meta.* 4. 229) or her hand outstretched ('tendentemque manus'; 4. 238). His narrative is interested in her helplessness at the moment of rape and allows her to protest her innocence as a counterpoint to her father's

---

[14] Dinshaw, *Chaucer's Sexual Poetics*, 94 (and see further 234 n. 24).
[15] Clytie is also sidelined. Cf. Ovid, *Metamorphoses*, 4. 167–273, ed. and tr. Frank Justus Miller, rev. edn, Loeb Classical Library, 42–3 (Cambridge, Mass., 1977), i. 190–6. For related changes as clues to Gower's use of Pierre Bersuire's *Ovidius Moralizatus*, see Conrad Mainzer, 'John Gower's Use of the "Mediæval Ovid" in the *Confessio Amantis*', *Medium Ævum*, 41 (1972), 215–29, 222. Mainzer acknowledges (215) that such details may have been available to Gower from glosses in copies of Ovid.

heedless rage (*Meta.* 4. 238–9). None of these representations of Leucothoe remains in Gower's narrative.[16] She is without voice or action. She is represented exclusively in relation to her father and his will to preserve her virginity—as the 'doughter, that was kept so deere' (*CA* 5. 6729)—and by her physical beauty (5. 6733–9).[17] This is not to say that Ovid sketches a very particularized or idiosyncratic female character, and Orchamus's revenge in the *Confessio* allows some pathos for Leucothoe because it is unattractively, expediently god-fearing (5. 6765–6). But by muting all of Leucothoe's personal action and describing only her external appearance, her 'feture' (5. 6739), Gower enhances the narrative's capacity to represent the daughter as her father's beautiful possession. Leucothoe must stand in my argument as a representative instance of a tendency in the *Confessio* to deflect narrative efforts away from female personality.[18]

As Orchamus has done in book 5, so Livius Virginius in book 7 will destroy his daughter when confronted by the loss of her maidenhood. Both fathers prefer a dead daughter to a dishonoured one. Virginius's circumstances and his self-justification at the time of killing—especially the consideration 'that Ilicius was weyved | Untrewly fro the Mariage' (7. 5238–9)—reveal the logic of exchange and worship which remains concealed in Orchamus's action. Orchamus seems to be guarding his daughter's maidenhood as an end in itself, indefinitely 'fro yer to yeere' (5. 6730), whereas Virginius has already arranged to exchange his daughter with another 'worthi kniht of gret lignage' when his tale

---

[16] Leucothoe's fear is also lost in translation in the early fourteenth-century *Ovide moralisé*. See *Ovide moralisé*, ed. C. de Boer (Amsterdam, 1915–38), 4. 1432–4. The translation's chamber scene, replacing fear with hope or expectation ('espaourie'), depicts Leucothoe listening attentively rather than transfixed with terror (4. 1411–14). A common thread in the chamber and death scenes is the translator's eschewing graphic and sexualized descriptions of the female body vulnerable to (male) violence. The modifications, regardless, attenuate Leucothoe's personality and limit pathos (albeit not so completely as Gower's departures do). On the tradition of the 'moralized Ovid', see Lester K. Born, 'Ovid and Allegory', *Speculum*, 9 (1934), 362–79. For its possible influence on Gower, see Mainzer, 'Gower's Use of the "Mediæval Ovid"'; Alastair Minnis, '"Moral Gower" and Medieval Literary Theory', in Minnis (ed.), *Responses and Reassessments*, 56–7.

[17] Leucothoe (as distinct from her 'feture') is only twice a grammatical subject, and in active voice (when 'sche sprong up'; 5. 6779) only in the form of a flower. Her counterpart in a tale of 176 lines in book 7, Virginia, is a grammatical subject four times (7. 5149, 5182, 5231, 5237), and then only twice of an active verb. These (technically) active verbs in fact describe things (wedding and wronging) done *to* Virginia, as 'sche stod upon Mariage' (7. 5149) and 'hadde wrong' (7. 5231).

[18] Edwards examines Thisbe, Constance, Lucretia, Virginia, and Phyllis to similar effect in 'Gower's Women'.

opens. Virginius is interested in protecting Virginia's maidenhood exactly in relation to and to the point of exchange. Virginia is 'good' for exchange only as a maid, and if she is to be misexchanged to the detriment of her father's worship, she is better destroyed, her status as empty sign preserved at the cost of all her being. The treatment of Leucothoe and Virginia as signs of aristocratic worship subsumes them in a household discourse of worship-generating exchange.

Independent heiresses produce more complex negotiations between female subjectivity and the idea of lordship in Genius's tales. The queens Dido and Phyllis are not objectified and the subjectivity of a woman becomes the main matter of the tale of Rosiphelee when a vision of ladies dramatizes the heiress's withdrawal 'To thenke what was in her wille' (4. 1296). Still, the way in which the narratives inform these women's wills subtly but insistently subjects them to a version of the household that they are not permitted to own. Virtuous men, of course, are also constrained by narratives which serve household interests, but these interests augment a man's seigneurial identity while the independent heiresses' tales have an appetite for the end of a woman's political importance in her own right. Virtuous ladies seek a surrender of agency and a limiting of personal worship which anticipates the political alienation of the suffering 'good women' in Cupid's court at the end of the poem (see above, 126–7).

In stark contrast to Leucothoe and Virginia, fatherless Phyllis and widow Dido are free from the power of male kin and have narratives devoted to their own emotions and their own attempts to further their causes in love. These exempla nevertheless also end in the heiress's demise and the implication that the household suffers as a result of the miscarried exchange of a woman. Dido and Phyllis win sympathy from readers, but not in the capacity of independent lord. Bestowing sympathy on the suicides, the tales blame negligent men for allowing great households to decline into paralysis. Aeneas's and Demophon's international military interests are demeaned against the opportunity to take over a woman's household.[19] The pining, politically inert behaviour of the love-lorn queens amounts to an abdication of lordship over their own households. Phyllis, in particular, cuts a pathetic, inactive figure as she 'The tyde awayteth everemo' (4. 808) and is drawn to the remote

[19] On Troy, Rome, and critique of chivalry in the *Confessio*'s tales, see Wetherbee, 'Classical and Boethian Tradition', 192–6.

reaches of her castle and a beacon 'on hih alofte | Upon a Tour' (4. 818); but Dido's more agitated longing also suggests that her lordship may otherwise be atrophying. Phyllis's transformation into a filbert-tree at one level symbolizes that household organization risks decay into a state of nature under (protracted) female leadership.

Even in pursuit of transferring lordship to a man, each queen's power is severely limited. Once her guest has departed, she writes an (ineffectual) personal letter but does no more. She delivers no commission under her seal and summons no friends or allies to support her cause. Despite the queens' minimal political efforts (and leaving aside Phyllis's granting Demophon 'al that he wolde'; 4. 770), Genius can heap the shame of events on the negligent males because of the restricted bounds within which even independent women might be expected to operate. If Dido and Phyllis are pitiable and not blamed for failing to cement a marriage it is because, in the tales' world-view, they lack acceptable avenues of public power.

Rosiphelee

The tale of Rosiphelee is more optimistic about an independent heiress's initiative, but it works from the same premise that this initiative should be directed towards securing a husband. It is more explicitly concerned than the tales of Dido and Phyllis with what is at stake in female independence and, in a manœuvre akin to those tales' dislocation of lordship into love, it misrecognizes its male-centred household imperative by means of a symbolic fiction of female community (the vision of ladies).

Among all of Genius's heiress tales, that of Rosiphelee is perhaps most acutely concerned with women as conduits of patrimony. Venus and Cupid object to Rosiphelee's general lack of 'lust', that she 'Desireth nother Mariage | Ne yit the love of paramours' (4. 1268–9), but Genius's moralization narrows the onus to marriage alone (4. 1480–92) and privileges an imperative of procreation ('whiche the world forbere | Ne mai, bot if it scholde faile'; 4. 1496–7). Genius glosses the tale, in other words, as an exemplum for marriage in the service of population. In the symbolism of Rosiphelee's vision, however, children do not explicitly figure, and Genius also classifies the exemplum's target audience as knightly (1. 1456–7). The admonitory difference between the liveried 'Servantz to love' who 'trowthe beere' (4. 1376) and the hapless trailing woman is marked by household material and symbolic capital: clothing and equipment, and the status they represent. The 'route' of ladies comprises a group of the more prestigious members of a single retinue, a fact evinced by their uniform mi-parti livery robes (vertically divided into two colours; 4. 1306–17).[20] Their prestige is advertised by their well-fed horses, jewelled saddles, precious crowns ('As ech of hem a qweene weere'; 4. 1324), and the embroidering 'overal' (4. 1319) of their livery robes.[21] The woman who comes along behind the ladies is, in contrast to them, noticed for the ragged condition of her horse and clothes. When she laments her lot to Rosiphelee, she confirms herself as belonging to the same imaginary household as the ladies and construes her suffering as a lack of rank and position in that household:

> And I mot nedes suie here route
> In this manere as ye now se,
> And trusse here haltres forth with me,
> And am bot as here horse knave.
> Non other office I ne have,
> Hem thenkth I am worthi nomore,
> For I was slow in loves lore
>
> (4. 1396–402)

Moreover, Rosiphelee can understand herself to be ' "riht in the same cas" ' (4. 1440) as the 'horse knave' because this woman too was the daughter of a king and she laments not only a lack but a loss of status. The groom princess suffers not because she has lost her blood-tie to nobility or been transformed into one lowly born, but because she has lost worship, and in particular the esteem of the ladies, who ' "thenkth I am worthi nomore" '. Horse, clothing, and worship are in a state of severe decay, as opposed to original insufficiency. Crucially, this decay evidently took hold after her death (4. 1412–29). Again, this explains Rosiphelee's identification of her 'same cas' in the horse knave's. As heiress, Rosiphelee can expect to enjoy until her own death the trappings of the Armenian royal household.

What is at stake in 'loves occupacion' (whose end is marriage according to Genius's revisionism) is worship, as sustained by and sustaining the patrimony. The horse knave failed to secure by her marriage her father's patrimony, and so her decayed state symbolizes the fate of this

[20] For systems and the significance of colours in livery cloth in the late Middle Ages, see Lachaud, 'Liveries of Robes', 289–92.

[21] The sumptuary ordinance of 1363 restricted embroidered ornament to its most privileged social category, namely the wealthier of two strata of knights and ladies (*SR* i. 381).

patrimony in the generations after her death. Her incongruous 'riche bridel' (4. 1353), in turn, is a token of her belated and insufficient obedience to love. It indicates that she needed to do more than ' "love a kniht" ' (4. 1417) to secure all the signs of worship. It is not her personal association or partnership with a knight that finally counts but her ability, by marriage and 'charge... | Of children' (4. 1495–6), to act as a conduit for patrimony. This counterpoint to the church's exaltation of virginity seeks a particular kind of demographic continuity. The anxiety conveyed by tale and moral together is that aristocratic lineage, not 'the world' in general, 'scholde faile' (4. 1496–7).

Rosiphelee's father, King Herupus, disappears from her tale after the opening sentence (4. 1245–52), leaving her in the position of a lord, preserver of patrimony. The duty incumbent upon Rosiphelee as head of household and conduit of patrimony is to exchange herself. The text hedges Rosiphelee's lordship around with elements that blur the impression of her independent agency. Self-determination is figured as the imposition of external force—the power of Cupid or love that 'overtorned' Rosiphelee's 'mod' (4. 1280) and 'overcame' her counterpart, the horse knave—and María Bullón-Fernández has argued that Genius acts as a kind of surrogate father, who could oversee Rosiphelee's exchange in Herupus's absence.[22] Most subversive of Rosiphelee's representation of female desire in charge of a household's interests, however, are the exemplary ladies of her vision. Undistinguished one from another and voiceless, these ' "Servantz" ' never signify themselves, but signify only the authority and work of love. Their livery robes 'With alle lustes that [Rosiphelee] knew |...enbrouded' (4. 1318–19) may, indeed, be decorated with a kind of heraldry of their lord, although the relevant phrase is vague. Through the lens of Genius's definition of 'honeste' love, the exemplary ladies appear as personally empty signs of marriage. A notion of the independent heiress determining the future of her household remains intact, but Rosiphelee's vision sets a limit to this independence and promises to erode it after marriage. To serve household interests with her own will is to write herself out of household activity after marriage. Rosiphelee's vision instructs her to decide to become a sign of the bond by which patrimonies are transferred and men achieve lordship.

---

[22] Bullón-Fernández, *Fathers and Daughters*, 177–89.

MEDEA'S SELF-EXCHANGE

Gower's exemplary narratives in the *Confessio* tend to adopt a functional approach to the question of female desire in relation to the requirements of their exchange between households. This means that, where they anticipate patterns of stable household exchange, female protagonists' will and desire are elided in favour of a father's or husband's, are responsive to male desire, or (as in the case of Dido and Rosiphelee) internalize the great household's interests.[23] In these cases, even when independence enables proactive desire, agency is circumscribed. When proactive desire and decisive agency combine in a woman in Genius's exempla they tend to violate the norms of household exchange. Such desiring agency is symptomatic of more general disordering tendencies in the household. It marks out an authority vacuum or some kind of impolitic lordship in pursuit of singular profit or treasonous ends. The narratives stigmatize politically expansive female desire accordingly.

The longest tale in book 5 represents female desire which neither originates in a superior household authority nor conforms to household interests. The tale of Jason and Medea features a self-determining heiress who eludes the position of household sign despite the presence of her father. In doing so, however, she does not claim a role for female will as a locus of household personality either before or after marriage. On the contrary, her independence of desire and action is figured as transgressive of household order and she is associated with natural and social disorder.[24]

Another only daughter and dependent heiress of the *Confessio*, the princess of Colchis is profoundly the opposite of Leucothoe, Virginia, or Constance.[25] Far from appearing as the instrument of other wills, Medea

[23] For homosocial discourse's idealizing imperative that female desire must always only be 'responsive' to male desire, and thus only and always able to reinforce the course of transactions determined by men, while pre-empting coercion, see Rubin, 'Traffic in Women', esp. 182. Cf. Dinshaw, *Chaucer's Sexual Poetics*, 107.

[24] Edwards demurs at readings by Derek Pearsall and Linda Barney Burke to interpret this tale as an 'ambivalent acknowledgement of female power' ('Gower's Women', 231–3, quote at 231). The ambivalence he finds seems to depend upon a perceived incongruity between the two main parts of the narrative, whereby Gower (inadvertently, Edwards suggests) suppresses in the earlier part the negative implications of his source. I find more consistency in Gower's handling of his sources, since his narrative seems to be implicitly critical of Medea's desire from the outset, preparing for the second part to expose an anxiety already present in the first.

[25] Constance is a heroine set adrift from paternal and spousal control in one of the *Confessio*'s major tales, but I will not treat Gower's accommodation of her to masculine exchange prerogatives here. For Dinshaw's discussion of Constance's 'pure instrumentality'

endeavours to become a full partner in exchange with Jason. Far from being represented as surface and sign for inscription by male desire, her personality and will dominate the tale. Gower's retelling of the legend consistently attends to her subjectivity at the expense of the objectifying descriptive and behavioural conventions he applies to other maidens in other narratives. In particular, his adaptations of Benoît de Sainte-Maure's *Roman de Troie* (*c*.1160) in the first, Colchian part of his tale eschew a static external gaze and instead animate Medea's psychological being, as when she is introduced to us through her contemplation of her father's Greek visitor and the stirring of desire in her.[26] Gower also adds to his French source passages concentrating on Medea's powerful emotion both at Jason's departure for the isle of the fleece (5. 3634–47), and during his absence as she 'stod upon a Tour alofte' praying 'Al prively withinne hirselve' for her lover's success (5. 3735–51).[27]

Resembling the institutionally correct will of Rosiphelee or Dido, but without match anywhere in the poem, Medea's antiresponsive desire is no projection of male 'heart' or will. Desire springs internal, and mutually between Medea and Jason: 'Here hertes bothe of on acord | Ben set to love' (5. 3390–1).[28] Moreover, it is Medea who supplies most of the initiative and momentum to the pair's affair until it is established. She is purposeful and commanding where Jason is vacillating and steerable. On meeting, Medea, conscious of Jason's fame, controls her gaze and 'gan hir yhe impresse | Upon his face and his stature'

in Chaucer's version of the narrative, see *Chaucer's Sexual Poetics*, 110–12 (quote at 110). Cf. Edwards, 'Gower's Women', 226–8. Winthrop Wetherbee finds Chaucer's Constance 'as nearly as possible inoperative in social terms' in comparison to Gower's 'unwavering and resourceful' heroine ('Constance and the World', 70, 75). The contrast seems to me to illuminate the possessive Man of Law's resistance to his heroine's involvement in the world (so that he actually disguises her own agency and attitudes), rather than revealing an active social role for Gower's Constance. A comparison of texts reveals a matter-of-fact narrative of submission in Nicolas Trevet's chronicle and Gower, in contrast to a more unsettled interplay of plot and narration in Chaucer. The instances of Constance's agency which Wetherbee discovers in the *Confessio* tend to be wholly private or exclusively to concern spiritual matters: her activity here in no way impinges on male prerogatives of household organization.

[26] *CA* 5. 3372–92; cf. Benoît de Sainte-Maure, *Le Roman de Troie*, ed. Léopold Constans, SATF (Paris, 1904–12), ll. 1213–90.

[27] Cf. Medea's exchange with her go-between handmaid, elaborating Benoît's and Ovid's remarks on her secret desire to kiss Jason: *CA* 5. 3789–800; Ovid, *Metamorphoses*, 7. 144–6; Benoît de Sainte-Maure, *Roman de Troie*, ll. 2007–14.

[28] Cf. e.g. the generation of (male) desire in the tales of Constance and Leucothoe, where Allee 'al his hole herte he leide | Upon Constance' (2. 896–7) and Venus 'Phebum to love hath . . . constreigned' (5. 6719).

(5. 3378–9), while Jason, passive and captured by Medea's beauty, 'mihte noght withholde his lok' (5. 3383). Medea lies awake all night resolving 'Hou sche that noble worthi kniht | Be eny weie mihte wedde' (5. 3424–5); Jason is unfocused, 'stered to and fro | Of love, and ek of his conqueste' (5. 3412–13). Medea proposes the exchange of a ' "covenant | To love" ' (5. 3449–50) and her own supervision of Jason's venture. With betrothal by this covenant (specifically intended by her 'For sikernesse of Mariage'; 5. 3483), Medea becomes a full, indeed the dominant, partner in a domestic transaction elsewhere in the poem reserved for men and heads of households.

Medea and Jason's association resembles household exchanges represented elsewhere in the *Confessio*, but their relationship is formed outside a household structure. The pair's defiance of household channels and expectations of social exchange is conspicuous in the sequence beginning when they whisper together in hall, then 'spieke aloud for supposinges | Of hem that stoden there aboute' (5. 3848–9). Jason then 'stalkende al prively' (5. 3861) while the rest of the household sleeps, comes to Medea and they plan to remove from the household altogether (5. 3872–3). Quickly they have embedded a secret set of exchanges within the quasi-public web of decorum and gossip by which great households partly regulate themselves.

Medea's behaviour and perspective especially are at odds with public, visible signs of household order. Her policy conflicts with the king her father's from the outset. Where Medea freely exchanges information and artefacts with Jason for his success in pursuit of the fleece, Aeetes gives him only warnings, to 'dredde him of his harmes' (5. 3360) with 'many a dredful sawe' (5. 3680). Medea's personal desire is attentively represented in the narrative, but, particularly from the point of the betrothal onwards, it exhausts her internal life, excluding external considerations of the household. Jason, conversely, maintains a greater responsiveness to external demands.[29] Upon his return to Colchis with the fleece, Jason accepts the public welcome of his host and companions and prepares for a banquet with the king and 'his knihtes alle' (5. 3773–3816). At this moment, however, Medea's mind is otherwise engaged ('Sche wolde have kist him wonder fayn'; 5. 3789). She later bestows her kiss on her maid, displacing her emotional commerce within the private world of her chamber. The same discrepancy between Medea's exhaustively private desire and Jason's public consciousness is earlier evident when she

[29] See e.g. *CA* 5. 3737–9, 3789–92, 3896–8.

bids him farewell. Her perspective is consumed by him ('al hir world on him sche sette'; 5. 3637), but he remains aware of other, worship-determining factors and so acts as 'he wolde kepe hir name' (5. 3660). The difference is symbolized in household material culture when the pair rise after their first night together to complete the binding exchange of love and artefacts:

> Jason his clothes on him caste
> And made him redi riht anon,
> And sche hir scherte dede upon
> And caste on hire a mantel clos,
> Withoute more and thanne aros.

> (5. 3554–8)

While Jason makes ready as though for public activity, Medea is unmindful of the world outside the chamber and sets about the exchange of artefacts only cursorily dressed.

Medea's independent desire (which is the same thing in this narrative as a private desire which excludes the household) is also imagined (in both parts of the tale) as a transgressive desire, overreaching the natural order. Despite Genius's interpretation of Jason's loss of his wife and sons—as penalty for his being forsworn (5. 4223–9)—Medea's associations with *prive*-ness and unnaturalness mean that the tale's final episode also demands to be read in terms of female desire. Genius's tales of independent heiresses argue that female lordship is safe so long as, with access to power, it has internalized patriarchal imperatives of marriage and patrimony. The tale of Medea avows the case of the dependent but wilful heiress to be potentially much more threatening. Medea's desire not only cannot be accommodated by household structures, but is radically destructive of them. Her farewell speech and gestures in Colchis exemplify her transgressiveness. Love supersaturates her consciousness as she devotes 'al hir world' to Jason: 'thurgh nome' (overwhelmed), she finally falls 'On swoune' (5. 3634–7). This excessive devotion is manifest in an unreal multiplication of gesture and a layering of utterance exceptional by Gower's economies of dialogue:

> Sche tok him in hire armes tuo,
> An hundred time and gan him kisse,
> And seide, 'O, al mi worldes blisse,
> Mi trust, mi lust, mi lif, min hele'

> (5. 3640–3)

In strong contrast in another tale, Constance's speech upon her public reunion with her father is well described as 'terse'.[30]

Sorcery is associated with *prive* thought and *prive* space in Medea's transgressiveness. With Medea absorbed in 'prive' reverie on the tower, Genius speculates (and it is Gower's addition to his sources) on the transgressive energy of her desire:

> If that sche hadde wynges tuo,
> Sche wolde have flowe unto him tho
> Strawht ther he was into the Bot.
>
> (5. 3749–51)

The speculation adumbrates the actual transgression of the natural order achieved by Medea when she summons Hecate's dragon-drawn chariot (5. 3988–93). The second part of the narrative (after the return to Greece) is more transgressive in this fashion, more supernatural, by virtue of Gower's sources (and the shift from Benoît to Ovid in particular). Having said this, Gower does not shy away from Ovid's extensive, detailed description of Medea's midnight magic,[31] and he seems careful to incorporate the episode into his own narrative whole. The magical fleece lore and protective items exchanged in Medea's bedchamber, along with Genius's early reference to 'wynges', have already prepared some ground in which the supernatural can be embedded. So much more emphatically does Gower's abridgement of Medea's incantation to Hecate (selecting only the goddess's help with the fleece)[32] serve to link her late personal unnaturalness back to the earlier part of her story and compose in her a coherent figure of transgression.

Medea's macabre and esoteric necromancy, drawn from Ovid, would automatically place her outside ordinary society. But the way that Gower supplements his source suggests that Medea's exclusion is the principal design behind his deployment of the episode.[33] Twice Gower reads Ovid's descriptions of Medea's sumptuary disorder (her feet bare

---

[30] Edwards, 'Gower's Women', 227; *CA* 2. 1513–17.

[31] *CA* 5. 3957–4174; cf. Ovid, *Metamorphoses*, 7. 179–293.

[32] *CA* 5. 3983–6; cf. Ovid, *Metamorphoses*, 7. 191–219.

[33] Medea's treatment of Aeson was not automatically read as improper in Gower's age. Faced with the challenge of integrating not distinct narrative sources but sensational pagan material and an edifying Christian framework, the author of the *Ovide moralisé* wedges into the translation a remarkable allegorization of the sorcery in terms of the Incarnation and Redemption (*Ovide moralisé*, ed. de Boer, 7. 1081–1246).

and hair loose) with bestial analogy.[34] She seems 'torned in an other kynde' (5. 4084), and soon Gower warms to his task: Medea abandons humanity linguistically and bodily in lines reminiscent less of Ovid than of Gower's own anxiety-ridden metamorphism of the rebels of 1381 in *Vox clamantis* (where rural folk appear 'in diuersas species bestiarum domesticarum transmutatas'[35] and grow wild):

> Bot tho sche ran so up and doun,
> Sche made many a wonder soun,
> Somtime lich unto the cock,
> Somtime unto the Laverock,
> Somtime kacleth as a Hen,
> Somtime spekth as don the men:
> And riht so as hir jargoun strangeth,
> In sondri wise hir forme changeth,
> Sche semeth faie and no womman
>
> (5. 4097–105)[36]

This late dehumanizing of Medea ironizes Genius's homily on Jason's ingratitude for 'thing non other womman couthe' (5. 4184). It also amplifies the reproach in elements common to both sections of the tale and contextualized in Medea's father's household in the first.

By the time, then, that Medea has killed Jason's family and flown 'Unto Pallas the Court above' (5. 4219), she has come to dominate the third largest narrative of the *Confessio* as an example of independent female will. Without seigneurial responsibility, such will has been figured as profoundly transgressive, its exceeding of, and otherness from, household order inextricable from disruption of the natural order.

The exemplary scheme of female sexuality in the tales of the *Confessio*'s first seven books is often unaugmented in the sense of doing little ostensibly to separate good (dependent) women from other objects of

[34] *CA* 5. 3966–7, 4084. The first of these images ('Al specheles and on the gras | Sche glod forth as an Adre doth') is evidently a reapplication (deliberate or otherwise) of the description of a stream at the equivalent point in Gower's source: 'nullo cum murmure serpens | sopiti similis per gramina labitur amnis' (without sound like a sleeping serpent, the stream glided through the grass). See Ovid, *Metamorphoses*, 7. 186 and the edn's note to this line.

[35] *Vox*, incipit at 1. prol. (transformed into different kinds of domestic animals).

[36] Medea's shimmering feyness echoes one of the *Vox*'s bands of mutant rebels in particular, which has changed into 'auium ... domestica turba' (a domestic flock of birds; 1. 517) led by a cock and a gander. For the inarticulate noise of the rebels as a device common to late fourteenth-century attempts to inscribe the purposes of the 1381 revolt as incomprehensible, see Justice, *Writing and Rebellion*, 193–254 (discussing the *Vox* at 207–16).

exchange. There it conforms so closely to the requirements of household exchange as implicitly and often explicitly to sanction coercion. It is also strongly patriarchal. Widows are seldom seen and never lionized. Unmarried heiresses with absent fathers generally have a limited appetite for power and discover desire for (superficially) appropriate marriages. These tales transfigure a generalized cultural coercion as love or (in Rosiphelee's case) a personal, visionary meditation. The tales of dependent women tend to pre-empt coercion by subsuming female subjectivity within paternal or spousal will and exchanges between men. Where men cooperate, female tokens of exchange are used, not forced. Despite Venus's and Amans's lady's liminal presence in the confession, the tales refuse to bring self-enhancing female public power within their positive exemplary horizons.

Dependent women, even so, are not all quiescent Constances or rebellious Medeas in Genius's tale horde. The poem's final book supplies its most substantial complication of the functional binary of usable and wilfull women.

NEGOTIATING FEMALE WILL AND DESIRE IN THE EXCHANGE OF THE PRINCESS OF PENTAPOLIS

The tale of Apollonius of Tyre is the lone major exemplum of the *Confessio*'s eighth book and approaches twice the length of the poem's second longest tale. It has reasonably been read as a 'kind of "exemplary summa"', a careful counter-weight to the vice and moral disorder which has gone before.[37] Repetition and epic scope achieve the graft of atonement which is required if the threats to moral order upon which the confession has dwelt are to be taken seriously and yet challenged with a vision of positive moral conduct.[38] In this light, it makes sense that the tale includes the poem's most involved treatment of a courtship leading to marriage. After Apollonius has undone (and been undone by) Antiochus's courtship trial, he faces at Pentapolis another contest for an

---

[37] Yeager, *Gower's Poetic*, 218.

[38] For Larry Scanlon's comments on the narrative's impression of 'epic scope' by way of 'extreme compression' see 'Riddle of Incest', 115–18 (quotes at 115). Cf. Elizabeth Archibald, *Apollonius of Tyre: Medieval and Renaissance Themes and Variations* (Cambridge, 1991), 12–14.

unnamed royal heiress. Here again he is privy to 'privete' between father
and daughter. The secret incest is paralleled by the second princess's
secret letter.[39] Apollonius's betrothal to Archistrates's daughter is to this
extent a mirror of the earlier courtship and asks to be read as a corrective
to Antiochus's sin. As such, it must address the issue of the daughter's
coercion because the opening episode has exposed the reach and destructive force of paternal power underwritten by rules of household
economy. The courtship of Apollonius and Archistrates's daughter
redeems household relations from the unchecked violence of Antiochus,
without ultimately undermining their foundation in paternal power.

Where Antiochus, with 'leisir at his wille | With strengthe' (8. 298–9),
utterly overmasters his daughter's will, Archistrates accommodates his
daughter's will. Indeed, he abides by her written ultimatum:

> Bot if I have Appolinus,
> Of al this world, what so betyde,
> I wol non other man abide.

> (8. 898–900)

We have been prepared for this decisive expression of will by representations of the princess's introduction, courtship, and desire which resemble nothing more closely in structure and narrative focus than
equivalent episodes in the tale of Jason and Medea. Aeetes's daughter
is, by the structure of her courtship and its control by her will, the
princess's closest counterpart from anywhere within Genius's tales.

Is the 'wylde fader' (8. 309) of Antioch to be redeemed by a daughter
whose forerunner in the confession is the 'wylde' (5. 4081) sorceress of
Colchis? Both Medea and the princess of Pentapolis are introduced to a
visiting prince (to 'make him glad'; 5. 3367, 8. 735) as a gesture of
hospitality by their fathers. Each pairing of guest and daughter sits
together in hall at a feast, and meets the next day more privately. Each
daughter subsequently withdraws from the public life of the household
to her chamber, her thoughts overcome by love. Medea, in shirt and
mantel 'Withoute more', is isolated in *prive* dealings with her handmaid
or, even outside her chamber, in secret thoughts and secret prayers. The
princess of Pentapolis would rather think than eat and 'hield hire ofte
times stille | Withinne hir chambre, and goth noght oute' (8. 862–3).
The sequence of interaction and desiring is assigned the same narrative
focus in each case as well, privileging the princess's perspective and

---

[39] Scanlon, 'Riddle of Incest', 116.

emotions. Just as we see Medea beginning to desire Jason and then 'thurgh nome | With love' (5. 3635–6), so we follow the impression Apollonius makes on Archistrates's daughter (8. 784–94) until 'Then-kende upon this man of Tyr, | Hire herte is hot as eny fyr' (8. 845–6). Both daughters assess their fathers' guests and are then, exceptionally, driven by and 'obeie' (8. 841) their own passion.

Yet one wilful daughter is anathema to the economy of the great household, the other its exemplary support. The defining difference between the princesses is twofold. First, Archistrates's daughter's desire is subordinated to and subsumed by her own reasonings securely aligned with the interests of the great household. She is made safe by her own landed habitus. Secondly, her will and desire are further contained by household authority and the possibility of paternal force. Medea's will and desire are not separated, and the latter springs from the former. She sets her gaze on Jason (5. 3378) and then her heart 'to love' (5. 3390–1). At Pentapolis, conversely, love is something external to the princess and her (rationally constrained) will:

> love hath mad him a querele
> Ayein hire youthe freissh and frele,
> That malgre wher sche wole or noght,
> Sche mot with al hire hertes thoght
> To love and to his lawe obeie
>
> (8. 837–41)

Love seems equally (if not more) unstable in this tale in comparison to the earlier one. It throws the princess into psychological flux and extremity 'Riht after the condicion | Of hire ymaginacion' (8. 845–50). Unlike Medea's will, however, the princess's contests and qualifies the influence of love and is itself accommodated (as Amans / Gower's will finally be) to reason—specifically to aristocratic principles which anchor exchanges in the great household.[40]

Jason's worship (his 'name' for 'worthinesse'; 5. 3376–7) is a catalyst for Medea's desire, but the main reaction is based on 'his face and his stature' (5. 3379). It is a reaction seated in the imagination, and the pair's desire is unmediated by language ('Thus ech of other token hiede, | Thogh ther no word was of record'; 5. 3388–9). It is also (more or less) temporally immediate. In complete contrast to Medea and Jason's pre-verbal love at

---

[40] On Gower's conception of the imagination and its relation to will and reason in the *Confessio*'s moral theory, see Simpson, *Sciences and the Self*, 135, 167–72, 254–71.

first sight, Archistrates's daughter responds to Apollonius in ways which are heavily mediated by language and art, and are initially without sexual desire. She does not contend with love at their first encounter, or even their second, but 'With leisir and continuance' (8. 835) of contact.[41] Her eventual response, though 'Withinne hir herte' (8. 788), is partly an exercise of reason ('wel supposed') and intellectual appreciation. She responds to his music and 'vois celestial' (8. 780), to his polite conversation (8. 787) and 'the wisdom of his lore' (8. 791), and these attributes ultimately form the basis of her love (8. 808–42).

These attributes themselves are signs of an underlying quality associated with ideal landed economics. The princess herself construes them in this way, inferring from them Apollonius's 'gret gentilesse' and 'gentil blod' (8. 789, 794). Her desire is thus rooted in territory shared with the calculative principles of household exchange. Underlining this congruence, the princess's heartfelt supposition about Apollonius is echoed precisely by a *familia* (or at least family) consensus evaluating the guest and the betrothal in terms of the household's ongoing interests:

> For noman knew the sothe cas
> Bot he himself, what man he was;
> And natheles, so as hem thoghte,
> Hise dedes to the sothe wroghte
> That he was come of gentil blod:
> Him lacketh noght bot worldes good,
> And as therof is no despeir,
> For sche schal ben hire fader heir,
> And he was able to governe.
>
> (8. 939–47)

Both daughter and parents work from 'dedes' to 'gentil blod' to approve a union. Moreover, a public, worship-centred perspective not only precipitates the princess's love, it controls this desire once it has taken hold. In a particularly resonant contrast to Medea's story, the princess's

[41] This is much deferred from the onset of passion in what was probably Gower's main source. Although the princess of the Latin prose 'Apollonius', like Gower's, falls passionately in love because the prince shows that he 'omnium artium studiorumque esse cumulatum' (was full of every kind of talent and learning), all of this occurs at the banquet after a single dazzling variety performance by the prince. See the text of the 'Historia Apollonii regis Tyri' printed by Elizabeth Archibald in *Apollonius of Tyre*, 109–81, 128 (16/19–17/2). On Gower's use of sources for this tale, see Macaulay, iii. 537–43; H. C. Mainzer, 'A Study of the Sources of the *Confessio Amantis* of John Gower', D.Phil. thesis, University of Oxford, 1967, 155–7; Archibald, *Apollonius of Tyre*, 192.

will (informed by her reason in the shape of considerations of worship) ultimately rules her desire and imagination.[42] It takes up the part alien to Medea and played by Jason's public consciousness, which would restrain desire in order to 'kepe [Medea's] name' (5. 3660):

> Bot evere among hire thoghtes alle,
> Sche thoghte, what so mai befalle,
> Or that sche lawhe, or that sche wepe,
> Sche wolde hire goode name kepe
> For feere of wommanysshe shame.

> (8. 851–5)

In the earlier scene, between Jason and Medea, female desire and a consciousness constraining the self to worshipful behaviour belong to separate minds and go unreconciled. In the tale of Apollonius, the two are united in the princess, who thus owns the mental aspect which belonged to the male (Jason) in the previous disposition. And it is this aspect that is dominant in the princess.

On the one hand, therefore, the princess's independent desire, informed as it is so thoroughly by considerations of 'gentilesse' and worship (or its antithesis, 'schame'), is in fact a product of male-dominated discourse. On the other hand, by internalizing this discourse, she is 'freed' from paternal coercion. This freedom, however, is in a (further) significant sense illusory. For around the edges of its representation of the princess's will and desire, the text subtly but insistently demonstrates that paternal coercion is an absent presence which guarantees the effect of internalization.

To take the princess's patriarchal disposition first: her idealized wilfulness acts to secure household order by effecting the transfer of male authority (Apollonius will be 'able to governe') which Dido and Phyllis sought in vain. As exemplary order is confirmed at the close of the tale, Apollonius learns that Archistrates has died and he travels to Pentapolis 'his regne to receive' (8. 1974). At his (and his wife's) coronation 'alle goode him was fuisouned' (8. 1992). Here, the calculation of 'worldes good' and governance is fulfilled (notwithstanding Apollonius's existing wealth), and the princess's will is justified by the elision of her own role as household head. The wilful daughter and heiress performs as the sign of a transaction between men, inscribing herself as a conduit of social relation (guest becomes son-in-law) and property (guest also becomes heir). The text has come to terms with the authority of an heiress through that authority's own pre-emptive self-effacement.

The princess of Pentapolis's self-effacing role is similar to that of Peronelle, princess of the Three Questions (1. 3067–402). Peronelle is a wise and assertive intercessor, as authoritative and tactically astute as Chaucer's Prudence in 'Melibee'. She leads her own father by the hand before a king, answers riddling questions, and manoeuvres to marry the king (by claiming a peerage for her father as her reward). Equally, Peronelle's self-assertion presents an idea of feminine power serving the ultimately male household. The tale does not imagine female lordship (as a solution to the tale's male aggressiveness or otherwise). Standing for humility or self-effacement itself, Peronelle determines her own household status (and transfers her dependence from one man to another) in order to reconfigure the political relationship between king and knight. The king's magnificent rebuke of Pedro's past service challenges the knight either to respond with a new, unilateralist kind of exchange of his own (as the public expect) or to submit (fatally) to the impossibility of obliging the king. Instead, Peronelle provides the means to circumvent this impasse, to undo magnificence and re-establish mutuality on a new footing when her reward and her person are converted into her father and her new husband's political capital.

The agency of the princess of Pentapolis and of Peronelle conforms to a discursive structure which will deny them power. Each princess authorizes her own exchange in demanding to marry a certain prince. The second part of this construction (exchange) circumscribes the first (authority). Her demand confirms (however much on her own terms) her position in a process which has been conducted between the prince and her father (antagonistically and blindly in the earlier tale, cooperatively in book 8). For the tale of Apollonius, I will continue to call this process—from meeting in the hall to betrothal—a 'courtship', even though Apollonius shows no initiative in the matter and we do not even glimpse his thoughts on the princess until he is told she wishes to marry him. In each case, the princess's will bridges a circumstance (King Alphonse's magnificence, Apollonius's apparent poverty) that would render the demand presumptuous in the mouth of a prospective (male) partner to the exchange.

Self-effacing before the conventions of sex and status, Archistrates's daughter's agency is also always contained by her father's agency. Larry Scanlon finds a 'radically antithetical double meaning' at the crux of the courtship, in the king's disclosure to Apollonius of 'The lettre and al the privete, | The which his dowhter to him sente' (8. 918–19):

> On the one hand, it is an assertion of patriarchal privilege of the most brutal and naked sort. He displays his daughter's 'privete' as if she were livestock at auction. On the other hand, this gesture also constitutes a radical abdication. The king reduces his role to that of obedient go-between. He becomes the transparent signifier of his daughter's desire. Neither of these meanings can be subsumed by the other; they are irreducible components of the same act.[43]

I would argue, however, that, if the first part of these meanings does not subsume the second, then it is nevertheless a pressure behind it and lies closer to the essence of the act. For the text makes patriarchal privilege and not female desire the perimeter and bedrock of the 'courtship' process. The king's privilege has constantly been felt as latent and final determinant in the courtship narrative.

Along with the princess's conforming will, Archistrates's direction of the courtship crucially differentiates it from the parallel episode in the tale of Medea and ensures that this courtship proceeds as part of his household's culture and economy. Aeetes summons his daughter to meet his guest (5. 336–69) and thereafter takes no part at all in their relationship. His inattention throws into relief the abiding narrative presence of Archistrates's will and his organization of his charges within household structures. The princess initially stands 'ate bord before' (8. 732) the king, more a device of his hospitality than a participant in the feast. She is deployed to cheer Apollonius at her father's bidding and 'on his message' (8. 734) not only in the first instance, but again (with harp) when the king decides that a new strategy is in order:

> The king, which therof tok good kepe,
> Hath gret Pite to sen him wepe,
> And for his doghter sende ayein,
> And preide hir faire and gan to sein
> That sche no lengere wolde drecche,
> Bot that sche wolde anon forth fecche
> Hire harpe and don al that sche can
> To glade with that sory man.
>
> (8. 751–9)

---

[43] Scanlon, 'Riddle of Incest', 121. Georgiana Donavin, following Peter Goodall, 'John Gower's *Apollonius of Tyre: Confessio Amantis*, Book VIII', *Southern Review*, 15 (1982), 243–53, 244, discusses the act in terms of Archistrates's submission to his daughter's will alone, differentiating this from Antiochus's abusive power. See *Incest Narratives and the Structure of Gower's Confessio Amantis* (Victoria, BC, 1993), 79–80.

Where Jason and Medea are lost to observation in their own wordless empathy, Apollonius and the princess's first encounter operates by a peculiar triangulation in which the princess is a vector and instrument for her father's responses to the prince. Throughout their interview, we are aware of no reaction to the prince on the part of the princess. Meanwhile, the king is taking 'good kepe' of his guest's demeanour, and reacts with 'gret Pite' and an emotional 'heste' (8. 760) to his daughter. The interaction between prince and princess functions through the father's gaze.[44]

Similarly, access to space, so important in the politics of high-status buildings, is more evidently controlled by the lord and focused on him at Pentapolis than Colchis. When the hall empties in Colchis, all go their separate ways (an arrangement which will later facilitate a secret rendezvous between Jason and Medea). Archistrates, in contrast, organizes a chamber for Apollonius 'Which nyh his oghne chambre be' (8. 803),[45] and when his daughter now seeks another meeting with the prince she seeks it through the king, who permits it and oversees its arrangement (8. 808–19).

After the king has sought his daughter's opinion on her suitors, it is himself and Apollonius who 'With good herte and with good corage | Of full Love and full mariage | ... ben hol acorded' (8. 923–5). The princess's growing desire and written assertion of will are thus enveloped by her father's decisions and his sympathies with the prince. The text underscores Archistrates's role as partner in his daughter's exchange (obscured by his passive acceptance of her demand) by usurping for him her emotional prerogatives at its instigation and resolution.

More importantly, the king's accession to his daughter's will is only ever a suspension or abeyance of coercion (which hovers in his wish for the queen's 'good assent'; 8. 931) and does not entail the subordination of his will. When the king reads the princess's ultimatum, we are told that 'whan that he it understod, | He yaf [her suitors] ansuer by and by'

[44] The dynamic between father, daughter, and guest also differs from that in the Latin prose story ('Historia Apollonii', ed. Archibald, 126–8). There, we see Archistrates cajoling his miserable guest to '"meliora de deo spera!"' (hope for better things from God) at the moment that his daughter enters and inquires after the stranger of her own volition. The scene describes a king who is either supremely knowing and crafty or slightly complacent. In any case, Gower's retelling makes the king's attention to his guest much less enigmatic and the princess's status as her father's instrument unmistakable. On this last point, cf. Bullón-Fernández, *Fathers and Daughters*, 51.

[45] Again, the king's control is much more obvious than in the Latin history, where it falls to the princess, already burning with love, to suggest Apollonius's lodging with the king: 'Historia Apollonii', ed. Archibald, 130 (17/12–19).

(8. 906–7). Gower's version of the episode persistently resists implications that the king's will is constrained by his daughter's request. Gower enhances the king's understanding of his daughter's demand. The Latin prose narrative from which he seems to have known the episode of the letter has the princess singling out a 'naufragum' (ship-wrecked one) without naming him, and her father unwittingly inquiring for this man amongst the suitors before turning to Apollonius to see if he can make sense of the note.[46] Archistrates is subordinated to his daughter's will by his (tacit) accession to it in ignorance of its particulars, and is thus much more a dogsbody between the princess and Apollonius here than in the *Confessio*. Gower's alteration puts the king in a position to mediate the expression of his daughter's will, rather than to transmit it transparently. He now restricts knowledge of the letter to Apollonius alone and he ensures that the suitors surmise no impairment of his authority, by giving them answer 'prively, | That non of othres conseil wiste' (8. 909). The king proceeds with full knowledge and accedes to nothing without it. He now purposefully reveals Apollonius's marriage option to him rather than inadvertently allowing the letter to do so, becoming the active agent by whom the marriage is 'acorded' (8. 925). When finally enlightened in the Latin narrative, Archistrates declares, '"Quod filia mea cupit, hoc est et meum votum"' ('what my daughter wants is my wish too'), and then consults his daughter further in private about her desire.[47] Because he is pleased with the match, this behaviour is surrounded by ambiguity as to how far his will has been subsumed by or merely coincides with his daughter's. The *Confessio*'s pared-down narrative is much less equivocal. Archistrates makes no such reference back to the princess's wishes, and once the letter is in hand, the business of 'full Love and full mariage' (8. 924) is neatly achieved between himself and Apollonius alone. Gower's king sanctions his daughter's choice, rather than her right to choose. The tale of Apollonius, capping Genius's collection, has represented marriage as a subtle, supple production within the great household's economy. The tale produces a careful deflection of independent female will towards male aristocratic prerogatives, and an extremely measured reconciliation of female desire to the great household's demands on the female as conduit of male will and worship.[48]

[46] 'Historia Apollonii', ed. Archibald, 132–4 (quote at 21/1, 11). The three suitors do not appear in Godfrey of Viterbo's versification of the tale in his *Pantheon*.

[47] 'Historia Apollonii', ed. Archibald, 134 (21/13, 22/1–17).

[48] In the end, we must look outside Genius's exempla, to Venus as she appears to the poem's narrator, if we are to discover an independent female will freely (and legitimately) wielding lordly or household authority.

THE SINS OF THE FATHERS: INCEST,
NEGLIGENCE, AND MAGNIFICENCE

The exemplary difference between Aeetes and Archistrates is one of paternal control. The household discourses of the *Confessio* value dependent daughters according to their conformity to an exchange system the bottom line of which is their signification of paternal will. Much more is at stake in this valuation than the question of compliance or non-compliance with a father's choice. The paternal will itself is revealed and measured against the political economy of the landed household. The exemplary fates of daughters highlight certain patterns of lordship and principles of exchange, and contend that these patterns will enhance or injure (or destroy) a household. Exchange of women narratives open, focus, and quicken the whole discussion of good and bad lordship in the *Confessio*, which I understand as a competition between reciprocalism and (primarily) magnificence. The poem's reciprocalist ethic holds that aristocratic daughters are meant to circulate among households already linked by networks of previous exchanges.

The trajectory between men travelled by both the princess of Pentapolis and Medea, in fact, describes the ideal use of women found throughout the *Confessio*'s assorted tales, as well as the first (extensiveness) principle of reciprocalist lordship. Each woman leaves her father's household with a man 'of gentil blod' of another household. The flaw in Medea's movement is not that it is misdirected but that it is not anchored in her original household. Aeetes is not involved in her transference, so the goal of inter-household traffic in women—a bond between households—is not attained. Aeetes's fruitless search after his daughter's disappearance with the Argonauts signifies the void, the absence of connection, between the two households in question.

Medea's attempt to exchange herself is consequently proven to be hollow by Jason's subsequent pursuit of precisely this reciprocalist goal. Medea provides for Aeson (and Jason) 'thencress of his lignage' (5. 3941), but she can offer no alliance with another great household. So Jason's personal betrayal of Medea is couched in the context and terms of household exchange. When Jason himself takes charge of his lineage's patrimony, and 'bar corone on his hed' (5. 4188), he looks to cement a bond with another lord and, transacting a valid exchange, 'he an other hath received | Which dowhter was to king Creon' (5. 4194–5). Similarly,

Archistrates's supervision and the calculative elements of 'gentilesse' and 'good' informing the betrothal ensure a valid, reciprocalist inter-household exchange when Apollonius comes to Pentapolis.

The parallel between Aeetes and Archistrates instructs Aeetes not that he should have prevented the outward movement of his daughter, but that he should have supervised it and validated it as his own act. The problem with his lack of paternal control is not that it allowed a man, or even the wrong kind of man, access to his daughter, but that it did not order this access and capture it within his household's economy.[49] The same lesson is taught, for instance, by pairing the fathers of Leucothoe and Virginia. Orchamus despairs of the task of keeping a daughter in a state of pure potential ('"Lo, what it is to kepe a Maide!"'; 5. 6764). Virginius is an example to him. His daughter (as her name suggests) is a totem of sexual blankness, but unlike Orchamus, Virginius recognizes this blankness as an ideal of potential and protects it by fulfilling it. It is only a slip between cup and lip, permitted by the delay caused by his military campaign 'er the cause fully spedde' (7. 5154), that undoes his management.[50]

The model of paternal use of daughters which these tales recommend, then, is outward-facing and inter-household, and so accords with reciprocalist lordship. The value of this model is confirmed throughout Genius's narratives by the negative, vicious representation of threats to its operation. Sexual vices and misconduct in the text are sites of anxiety

---

[49] To extend this reading speculatively, there is a suggestion in Aeetes's highly deferential hospitality to Jason (he greets him 'ate paleis gate | So fer the king cam on his gate'; 5. 3329–30) and in his fear of the Greeks (5. 3355–60) that he may not attend to Medea's relations with Jason because his sense of inferiority excludes the possibility of exchanging his daughter with the house of Pelias and Aeson. Greeting at the gate removes the lord from the courtyard, the central stage that usually most fully displays his house (see Johnson, *Behind the Castle Gate*, 77).

[50] This is one of several incidents in Genius's tales in which military enterprise conflicts with and compromises patriarchal domestic interests or duties. Others include Aeneas's leaving Dido to 'ryde' in Italy (4. 95), Ulysses's and Demophon's commitment to the Trojan war (4. 147–233, 731–878, 1825–99), Jephte's campaign against the Ammonites (4. 1508–23), Minos's absence from Pasiphae (5. 5274–96), and Philip of Macedon's absence from Queen Olympias (6. 1789–2366). For comments on Gower's or his text's position on warfare in the light of some of these narratives, see Peck, *Kingship and Common Profit*, 93 (Ulysses and Nauplius); Bullón-Fernández, *Fathers and Daughters*, 152–3 (Virginius); Lauren Kiefer, 'My Family First: Draft-Dodging Parents in the *Confessio Amantis*', *Essays in Medieval Studies*, 12 (1995), www.luc.edu/publications/medieval/vol12/kiefer.html. See also, more generally, Yeager, '*Pax Poetica*', 97–108; Wetherbee, 'Classical and Boethian Tradition', 192–6.

about (and because they are about) inter-household relations and inter-household exchange. This makes sense of Gower's particular choice of incest as the thematic vice of book 8 (beyond the need to avoid repetition in treating the deadly sin that has been the umbrella theme of the confession as a whole). Scanlon has explained this choice incisively in terms of household relations.[51] It is worth briefly returning to the matter to remind ourselves that incest belongs at the opening of the book because it is the most insidious (and inherent) threat to the exchange of women between households.[52] The poem's climactic tale is predicated on incest for the same reason, taking its departure from the vice exhaustively to assert an oppositional, outward ideal of household-based relations. Genius explains the historical development of exogamous laws of marriage demographically, 'For ther was poeple ynouh in londe' (8. 101) by the time of Abraham for 'Sosterhode of mariage' (8. 103) to be avoided. Augustine, further expounding the same demographic explanation, had much earlier spelt out the reason that populousness should be exploited to avoid incest:

... nec essent ulli homines, nisi qui ex illis duobus nati fuissent: uiri sorores suas coniuges acceperunt; quod profecto quanto est antiquius conpellente necessitate, tanto postea factum est damnabilius religione prohibente. Habita est enim ratio rectissima caritatis, ut homines, quibus esset utilis atque honesta concordia, diuersarum necessitudinum uinculis necterentur, nec unus in uno multas

---

[51] Scanlon, 'Riddle of Incest'. Other commentators suggest that the text construes incest as a crime against the common weal but do not often dwell on why it should do so and how the sexual and the political are connected in this crime. See e.g. Peck, *Kingship and Common Profit*, 165–6; Goodall, 'Gower's *Apollonius of Tyre*', 248–9; Porter, 'Ethical Microcosm and Political Macrocosm', 160; C. David Benson, 'Incest and Moral Poetry in Gower's *Confessio Amantis*', *Chaucer Review*, 19 (1984–5), 100–9, 106; Yeager, *Gower's Poetic*, 217–18; Kurt Olsson, *John Gower and the Structures of Conversion: A Reading of the Confessio Amantis* (Cambridge, 1992), 215–17. Donavin, *Incest Narratives*, 10–11; Elizabeth Allen, 'Chaucer Answers Gower: Constance and the Trouble with Reading', *ELH* 63 (1997), 627–55, 631–2; and Bullón-Fernández, *Fathers and Daughters*, 18–19, 22–4, all lay the theoretical groundwork for a political interpretation of the incest taboo similar to Scanlon's, but do not take up the household-based implications of this analysis. In turning to Gower's text, they suggest that incest functions as a (somewhat opaque) metaphor of kingship. Thus, Allen introduces Augustine's and Aquinas's arguments that incest limits the formation of social bonds and finds that it also 'represents other misuses of power' and that 'Incestuous kingship ... figures a possessive and tyrannical failure of government' ('Chaucer Answers Gower', 632). Cf. Donavin, 72–3; Bullón-Fernández, 24–5, 57–64.

[52] See Lévi-Strauss, *Elementary Structures*, esp. 478–81: the incest taboo is the 'supreme rule of the gift' (481), obliging the woman to be given to others. Cf. Rubin, 'Traffic in Women', 173.

haberet, sed singulae spargerentur in singulos ac sic ad socialem uitam diligentius conligandam plurimae plurimos obtinerent.

But there were then no other human beings apart from those who had been born of the first two. Therefore, men took their sisters as wives. In ancient times, this was acceptable, because done under the compulsion of necessity; now, however, it is damnable because forbidden by religion. For affection is now given its proper place, so that men, for whom it is beneficial to live together in honourable concord, may be joined to one another by the bonds of diverse relationships: not that one man should combine many relationships in his sole person, but that those relationships should be distributed among individuals, and should thereby bind social life more effectively by involving a greater number of persons in them.[53]

Modern discussions of medieval restrictions on marriage involving non-biological relations—that is, marriage with 'affinal, or fictive, relatives' such as relatives by marriage as well as adopted children or godchildren—underline the implication that exogamy laws were concerned to prohibit marriage where a similarly powerful bond was already established.[54] Drawing attention, meanwhile, to what the theologians take for granted—that incest prohibitions focus on the prerogatives of men and tend to address which categories of women they should be denied—David Herlihy concludes that 'the incest rules, in sum, primarily affected the movement of women among...households'. The prohibitions 'assured that women would circulate among households and across kindreds'.[55] The laws of monogamy and exogamy were about extending the formation of social bonds and the circulation of

---

[53] St Augustine, *De civitate Dei*, ed. B. Dombart and A. Kalb (Turnholt, 1955), 15. 16/4–12. The translation is from *The City of God against the Pagans*, tr. R. W. Dyson (Cambridge, 1998), 665. Aquinas, similarly, recognizes the historical contingency of ecclesiastical marriage regulation and describes the wider promotion of social ties as the rationale for the prohibition of consanguinous marriages: 'per accidens finis matrimonii est confoederatio hominum, et amicitiae multiplicatio; dum homo ad consanguineos uxoris, sicut ad suos, se habet' (the accidental end of marriage is the alliance of men and the extension of friendship: for a husband regards his wife's kindred as his own). St Thomas Aquinas, *Summa theologica* (Turin, 1933), suppl. Q. 54. 3, quoted and tr. Scanlon, 'Riddle of Incest', 102. Cf. *Summa theologiæ* (London, 1963–76), 154. 9.

[54] See James A. Brundage, *Law, Sex, and Christian Society in Medieval Europe* (Chicago, 1987), 193–5 (quote at 193). Joseph Lynch, in *Godparents and Kinship in Early Medieval Europe* (Princeton, 1986), observes that baptism created a 'spiritual' kinship that was 'the mirror image of the natural family' (275).

[55] David Herlihy, 'Making Sense of Incest: Women and the Marriage Rules of the Early Middle Ages', in A. Molho (ed.), *Women, Family and Society in Medieval Europe: Historical Essays, 1978–1991* (Providence, RI, 1995), 105, 108.

land between landed households, preventing the accumulation of women and lines of inheritance in the most powerful households.[56] As a dimension of lordship, these laws articulate a particular obligation to give. Incest violates reciprocalist principle by retaining possession of the woman.[57] Akin to magnificence, it is one-sided and exclusive, a narrowing or inward turn of the exchange system. Antiochus's crime, then, subverts a particular construction of household authority, a norm which Apollonius's story reasserts. Events at Pentapolis correct the pattern of their subversive precedent, the redemption confirmed by news upon their conclusion of divine retribution against Antiochus and his daughter (8. 998–1002). The second part of the story then tests and reaffirms Apollonius's achievement mainly through the experience of his own daughter and his relationship with her, as the potential (and hence the principle) of exogamous exchange is protected through bewildering vicissitudes and afterwards finally realized in Thais's marriage to Athenagoras.[58]

Other exempla, not involving father–daughter incest, embellish the poem's dominant ideal of lordship in the same spectrum of exemplary outwardness, similarly presenting abuses of paternal authority by retention of possession. The successful exchange of Archistrates's daughter can be read as antidote not only to Antiochus's incest but to Aeetes's

[56] They were not, as Herlihy makes clear in contesting Jack Goody's explanation of incest prohibitions in *The Development of the Family and Marriage in Europe* (Cambridge, 1983), about stifling inheritance, as part of a church strategy to siphon patrimonies into its own endowment ('Making Sense of Incest', 103–4). Brundage's analysis of the church's regulatory activity includes the aim of breaking up the nobility's power base of landholdings, and to this extent agrees with Herlihy's theory (*Law, Sex, and Christian Society*, 192–3). For widely differing accounts and explanations of medieval exogamy laws and practices, see Georges Duby, *Medieval Marriage: Two Models from Twelfth-Century France*, tr. Elborg Forster (Baltimore, Md., 1978), esp. 8–10, 21, 53–4; Constance B. Bouchard, 'Consanguinity and Noble Marriages in the Tenth and Eleventh Centuries', *Speculum*, 56 (1981), 268–87; Lynch, *Godparents*, esp. 258–81; Mayke de Jong, 'To the Limits of Kinship: Anti-Incest Legislation in the Early Medieval West (500–900)', in Jan Bremmer (ed.), *From Sappho to De Sade: Moments in the History of Sexuality* (London, 1989), esp. 45–54; Elizabeth Archibald, 'Incest in Medieval Literature and Society', *Forum for Modern Language Studies*, 25 (1989), 1–15; and *Incest and the Medieval Imagination* (Oxford, 2001), 9–52.

[57] Dinshaw, *Chaucer's Sexual Poetics*, 102.

[58] A number of critics have observed that undertones of incestuous desire and violence return during the crucial trial of Apollonius in this part of the story (when Thais, unrecognized, endeavours to coax him from his *prive* lassitude in his ship's cabin; 8. 1649–747). See Wetherbee, 'Constance and the World', 87–9; Scanlon, 'Riddle of Incest', 122–3; Bullón-Fernández, *Fathers and Daughters*, 52–9; Donavin, *Incest Narratives*, 83; Allen, 'Chaucer Answers Gower', 638–9.

negligence as well. Aeetes, Orchamus, and even Virginius partake in some sense of Antiochus's guilt, even if their guilt is much diluted due to the difference between commission and omission. The failing of Aeetes and fathers like him requires the intervention of an active misdoer before it becomes destructive. These lords do not conclusively retain possession—they do not spoil their virginal property. But they fail to manage its exchange. Their insulated paternalism permits the active transgressions of household order of a Medea, a Phoebus, or an Appius Claudius. Antiochus's culpability is all his own, although it taints his daughter and (like Leucothoe and Virginia) she is struck down for his crime. His sin of commission also raises the issue of coercion inside the discourse of paternal authority and so demands a complex reshaping of that discourse in response.

Jephte and his daughter

The tale of Jephte and his daughter bridges the gap between omission and commission (negligence and incest) in insulated paternal lordship. Gower makes the Old Testament story (Judges 11) a narrative wholly about household liquidity and the circulation of aristocratic women. The biblical narrative falls into three parts, in which Jephte is successively and primarily outcast, prince-commander, and father. Gower elides the complicated prehistory of Jephte's battle against the Ammonites (Judges 11: 4–28) and he simplifies Jephte's own personal history (Judges 11: 1–3), making him a straightforward exemplum of aristocratic (mis)conduct, unencumbered by abnormal kinship relations. The biblical son of a harlot excluded by his legitimate brothers becomes simply 'A noble Duck' (*CA* 4. 1507). Gower then expands the final section of the biblical story (Judges 11: 25–40), in which Jephte assumes the role of father. He elaborates its suggestions that the fate of Jephte's daughter—victim of her father's vow to sacrifice the first to come out of his house upon his return from victory—is the result (and price) of her virginity (Judges 11: 37–40). He overtly links virginity and misfortune when Jephte's daughter seeks

> That sche the whyle mai bewepe
> Hir maidenhod, which sche to kepe
> So longe hath had and noght beset;
> Wherof her lusti youthe is let,
> That sche no children hath forthdrawe

In Mariage after the lawe,
So that the poeple is noght encressed.

(4. 1565–71)

This demographic logic has already been introduced in the moralization of the foregoing tale of Rosiphelee (and so served as the premise for Genius's telling of the present exemplum). The household imagery of that tale, as I have argued, encodes the imperative of 'encres' in terms of aristocratic lineage and patrimony. Gower thus appropriates pre-Christian scripture to underwrite a secular aristocratic scheme of values, silencing the medieval church's own celebration of absolute chastity.

Genius expressly blames Jephte's daughter for her own death because she has not left her father's household, as normative expectations of exchange require. But the rest of the story seems to place the blame elsewhere. For Jephte's daughter, innocent of the deadline created by her father's vow, behaves as a passive victim of paternal righteousness, her suffering parallel to that of Leucothoe and Virginia. She conforms wholly to her father's will, strengthening and then modifying rather than opposing it when she knows he is bound to kill her. If she is guilty of preventing exchange, then so is he. As in Leucothoe's tale, so here Gower makes the exemplum's central speech an utterance by patriarchal authority about itself. Gower replaces the biblical Jephte's exclamation against his daughter—that she 'hast deceived me' (Judges 11: 35)—with an apostrophe to God in which cause is deferred ('"Mi joie is torned into sorwe"'; 4. 1545) and then ascribed to himself ('"Thurgh min avou"'; 4. 1549). The alteration suppresses an original mitigation of Jephte's responsibility. The speech (in both versions) also, of course, notes the most obvious aspect of Jephte's responsibility for the familial disaster, namely, his rash promise to God. In this rash promise, Jephte is suspended between errors of omission and commission. The pathos in his daughter's eager welcome depends upon knowledge of Jephte's vow which the reader shares with the duke.

Sche waiteth upon his cominge
With dansinge and with carolinge,
As sche that wolde be tofore
Al othre, and so sche was therfore
In Masphat at hir fader gate
The ferste...

(4. 1529–34)

Dramatic irony and pathos stem from Jephte's oversight. The harshest, most ironic (and most exemplary) reading of the welcome, indeed, reveals Jephte's seigneurial irresponsibility as the cause of ruin. The biblical text explains Jephte's daughter's fateful position only by her lack of siblings ('for he had no other children'; Judges 11: 34). Gower's description (illuminated by the moralization on the retention of 'maidenhod') ascribes it to a narrowness and exclusivity underlying the father–daughter relationship and pointed up 'at hir fader gate'. Neither father nor daughter appreciate the danger in time to avert disaster. The maiden's unexpected (because abnormal) pre-eminence in household space is a symptom of insularity, and becomes the fatal symbol of the relationship's improper, transgressive nature.

Alboin and Rosemund

Many of the exemplary (mis)doings of lovers or the lustful in Genius's narratives pose a threat to household order more radical than the neglectful or incestuous lord. Thieves of love, like Mundus, Amphytrion, Theseus, Tereus, Phoebus, and Arruns, who spoil other men's women, enact a basic threat to reciprocalist exchange because they hold in contempt the seigneurial authority (paternal and spousal) which enables reciprocal ties.[59] Paternal incest and neglect privilege the giver's authority while effacing responsibility. Interlopers abrogate the possessor's authority to determine exchange, resulting either in the utter degradation of exchange or in an approximation of magnificence. Where rape and spoilation of a woman do not take possession of her, but simply ruin her as a token of exchange and worship, they are external and wholly detrimental to household structures and exchange practices.[60] Jason's treatment of Medea, when he abandons her for

[59] When Theseus abandons Ariadne for her sister (5. 5395–483) and Tereus carries off a second daughter from Pandion (5. 5551–6047), this disregard for paternal prerogative is coupled with affinal incest, doubling the counts on which these princes subvert the reciprocalist economy. Carolyn Dinshaw discusses the incestuousness of Tereus's rape in 'Rivalry, Rape and Manhood: Gower and Chaucer', in R. F. Yeager (ed.), *Chaucer and Gower: Difference, Mutuality, Exchange* (Victoria, BC, 1991), esp. 136–7. Cf. Archibald, *Incest and the Medieval Imagination*, 89–91.

[60] Cf. Dinshaw, *Chaucer's Sexual Poetics*, 103: 'But the threat of father-daughter incest does not violate the mechanism of the rule of exchange of women: father-daughter incest creates a trade imbalance, but it does not violate the power and prerogative of males to determine the destination of the female and, consequently, of feminine desire.' Dinshaw goes on to consider 'potentially incestuous' desire of mother for son as posing 'a radical threat to masculine prerogative'.

Creusa (obtained in a legitimate exchange), recognizes that he has effaced the exchange system and its benefits as they apply to the house of Aeetes, collapsing the conduit of benevolent obligation which legitimate marriage could have secured. But Jason does retain possession of Medea long enough to attain or approximate one benefit of exchange— the extension of his lineage—without any capital, symbolic or otherwise, accruing to Aeetes. In this, his story moves closer to the transformation of exchange rather than its effacement. Other vicious figures, in other narratives, similarly enact usurpations of paternal authority which locate them within the one-sided, magnificence paradigm of household relations. Like incest, acquisitive, usurping violence seeks to preserve the work of exchange while aggregating it to a single household. Its concern is to augment (with perfect conservation) rather than (incestuously) to freeze that household's worship. It is the expansionist flipside to the incestuous, isolationist coin of magnificence. Under the *Confessio*'s master imperative of outwardness and reciprocity, these strategies spiral inward into ruin.

When the Lombard king Alboin kills his enemy, King Gurmond, and marries Gurmond's daughter, Rosemund, he embarks on such an expansionist path to ruin. His tale is a study of magnificence embodied by exotic luxury culture—in particular, a gem-encrusted cup which excludes would-be beneficiaries (and, in Rosemund's case, an actual recipient) from informed, enabled participation in exchange. Husband and wife actually 'love ech other wonder wel' (1. 2489) and Alboin eventually looks to realize some social capital from his possession of the king's daughter by holding a feast 'for his wyves sake' (1. 2500).

Unlike Theseus, Tereus, and even Jason, Alboin obviates paternal authority but also seeks to use the daughter within the aristocratic social economy, deploying hospitality as a context in which to realize worship. His feast looks like a parallel to the wedding feast at Pentapolis, where 'al aboute | Of gret worschipe, of gret noblesse | Ther cride many a man largesse | Unto the lordes', namely Archistrates and Apollonius (8. 960–3). Yet Alboin's feast signals the collapse of his household from 'al his welthe' to woe.

The flaw in Alboin's political economy is emblematized by his gruesome trophy cup; it is the faultline in the feast which will shake the household to its foundations. The king offers his wife the jewelled cup made out of Gurmond's head and bids her ' "Drink with thi fader, Dame" ' (1. 2551). Then he announces the vessel's origins to all assembled. Genius, fitting the story into his *forma confitendi*, draws from the story a lesson against the vice of 'Avantarie' or boasting, of representing one's 'oghne pris' (1. 2649). The confessor says that self-representation can jeopardize the exchange of worship (a boaster 'mai lihtliche his thonk tobreke'; 1. 2650). Yet Archistrates, or any model lord, is not to be faulted for displaying his own wealth and power in feasting. Rather, Alboin's error lies in the substance of his self-representation, and not in the fact or degree of it. Alboin boasts of the 'prouesse' through which 'He hath his wyves love wonne' (1. 2560–1). The skull-cup, 'soth witnesse' (1. 2559) of this prowess, exposes the one-sided origins of Alboin's marriage—an exchange between great households based on the obliteration of one household's personality and authority. The transformed skull's parodic resonance with sacramental rite in turn evaluates this mode of exchange, underscoring its 'vaunting' excess. Obliging his wife to consume from her father, Alboin imposes on her a grotesquely banal parody of the eucharistic consumption of her Father. Alboin's magnificence is so unruly, so expansive and exclusive, as to encompass not only another individual patriarch but, symbolically, the analogical source and 'originary status' of all patriarchal authority.[61]

As well as being a totem of totalizing ambition, Alboin's cup, 'policed ... so clene | That no signe of the Skulle is sene', *sublimates* the violent origins of the king's new household. This effect of the cup crowns several ways in which Gower's English narrative puts more distance between war and marriage than his likely source or his own Latin gloss. In the gloss, as in Godfrey of Viterbo's *Pantheon* (Gower's probable source), the marriage happens not once violence has 'ate laste' (1. 2486) been repressed, but as its direct continuation: 'insuper et ipsius Gurmundi filiam Rosemundam rapiens, maritali thoro in coniugem sibi copulauit' (and moreover, seizing the daughter Rosemund of Gurmond himself, he bound her to him in wedlock on the bridal bed).[62] In the English

---

[61] For the metaphorical substitution of a human patriarch for God as securing an 'originary status' for patriarchal authority, see Glenn Burger, *Chaucer's Queer Nation* (Minneapolis, 2003), 132. Noting Gower's allusion to the mass, Bullón-Fernández reads Alboin's feast as a kind of wedding ceremony which enacts the king's 'narcissistic' assumption of the roles of 'husband, father, and priest/Father' (*Fathers and Daughters*, 125). Cf. the funeral custom of the islanders of Ryboth described in *Mandeville's Travels* as parody or parallel of the Christian mass: a father's skull is made into a cup, shared amongst select guests, and then kept by the son 'to drynken of all his lif tyme in remembrance of his fadir'. See *Mandeville's Travels*, ed. P. Hamelius, EETS, os 153–4 (London, 1919–23), i. 205–6 (quote at 206).

[62] Gloss at 1. 2462; cf. Godfrey of Viterbo, *Gotifredi Viterbiensis opera*, ed. George Waitz (Hanover, 1872), 213–16: 'Albinus filiam Cunimundi occisi nomine Rosimundam deduxit captivam. Quam quia Glotosinda, filia regis Glotharii, prior scilicet uxor sua, iam obierat, ipsam captivam in suam perniciem, sicut postea patuit, duxit uxorem' (213/35–7). On sources for Gower's tale, see Macaulay, iii. 476–7.

narrative, time, the apparent absence of coercion, and the household trappings of hospitality disguise the unilateral origins of the marriage. Yet the disguise (in which Latin gloss and skull-cup are cracks) slips. Alboin's unilateralism, manifest in warfare, is shown to be always present in his household practice. In the skull-cup, in particular, the repressed returns (and then breaks out). The household's violent origins are completely submerged and yet visible transformed into magnificent artifice and ornamentation.

> [The cup] was with gold and riche Stones
> Beset and bounde for the nones,
> And stod upon a fot on heihte
> Of burned gold, and with gret sleihte
> Of werkmanschipe it was begrave
> Of such werk as it scholde have,
> And was policed ek so clene
> That no signe of the Skulle is sene,
> Bot as it were a Gripes Ey.

(1. 2537–45)

Gower's description of the great cup emphasizes its considerable sophistication and exoticism, comparing it to curios supposedly fashioned from griffins' eggs.[63] The cup is a wonder to set Alboin apart and it signifies his power without offering anything to those who gaze on it— no collateral protection and certainly no direct gift of or from it.

There are traces of magnificence in the rest of the feast as well. Where Archistrates's wedding feast is carried off with exemplary, moderated largesse, made with 'every thing which was honeste | Withinnen house and ek withoute' (8. 958–9), Alboin's celebration is characterized by the extravagance of 'many a perled garnement | Embroudred . . . ayein the dai' (1. 2510–11), especially for the occasion and for his own household. The detail of the host household's dress suggests its members' function primarily as signs of Alboin's wealth, and (juxtaposed with the 'beste arrai' of the guests; 1. 2512) indicates that the feast is a spectacle designed to outmatch the guests' worship before it contributes to it. The feast is, after all, held for the sake of Alboin's power alone, and there is

---

[63] John Burrow relates the cup to precious goblets that were typically made out of ostrich eggs and adorned with gold and gems: 'The Griffin's Egg: Gower's *Confessio Amantis* I 2545', in Toshiyuki Takamiya and Richard Beadle (eds), *Chaucer to Shakespeare: Essays in Honour of Shinsuke Ando* (Cambridge, 1992), 81–5. He notes (83) that, in the 1380s, Charles V of France owned at least three such treasures and Durham cathedral apparently housed no fewer than ten.

the suggestion of compulsion and the arbitrary composition of an audience in the classification of those invited (or summoned) as lords 'That were obeissant to [Alboin's] heste' (1. 2502). The celebration itself partly prefigures the stagnant magnificence of Cupid's court at the end of the poem, especially (and with verbal resonance) in the troped description of the participants' speech: 'Al was of armes and of love' (1. 2528; cf. 8. 2496–9).

The tale's exemplary fault relates not to any possible coercion of Rosemund (nor to initiative in the exchange on her part), but to the usurpation of her father's authority to exchange her. Alboin's celebration of his marriage yokes, and condemns, multiple aspects of household exchange under the same principle of magnificence. Unilateral violence (behind the exchange of a woman) returns through one-sided display (in hospitality and household ornament) and an entire mode of household management becomes the exemplary destruction of a household.

6

Justice and the Affinity

Daughters were among the most valuable items of exchange in the aristocratic household, not only because they could be heiresses but because the kind of tie forged by their exchange—kinship—was charged with an insistent and long-lived species of obligation. The tactical business of political conflicts amongst the aristocracy was more obviously about converting obligation than creating it. Nonetheless, aristocratic marriages themselves usually fulfilled complex sequences of obligation or careful evaluations of mutual interest, and exchanges of political support created new balances of regard and indebtedness between households.

Aristocratic disputants in late medieval England could hope for assistance from their networks of friends, connections, and powerful supporters in ways, persuasive or intimidatory, that would forestall violence, and conflict (so often about land) rarely became violent beyond repair. Of course, this condition itself reflected that force, gestures of force, and the possibility of force shaped political decisions by gentry neighbours and rival magnates alike. In the *Confessio*, violent retribution is fully implicated in the negotiations in Genius's tales of proper forms of household relations and exchange. Vicious protagonists commonly suffer retribution for violating reciprocalist values of household exchange—namely, that exchanges should be ordered by shared expectations derived from a sense of social hierarchy and existing networks of personal relations. The narrative fact of retribution establishes the moral, instructive value of the conduct that calls it forth, and retribution itself stands or falls by reciprocalist values.

The magnificent, one-sided actions of vicious protagonists often, by the text's sense of moral proportionality, trigger spirals of violence within the protagonists' own households. When Jason attempts to reverse his approach to marriage, his family implodes around the vestige of his unilateral dealings with the house of Aeetes (namely Medea). Elsewhere, Tereus, Alboin, and their families are all eliminated from society when the lords' unilateral interventions in the system of exchange (of women) come to light. In these cases, justice or retribution is a visceral matter. It is revenge simple, unstructured, and unrestorative. It again indicates that the poem's investment in household order is secured outside the will and conduct of female victims of household wrongs like Rosemund, Procne and Philomela, or Medea. The kind of justice which these women enact does not serve them as victims; rather it engulfs and erases them. Becoming agents of revenge, they are tainted by the original wrongdoing and suffer further for it. Rosemund and her co-conspirators are poisoned by the duke of Ravenna, Medea must abandon earthly society, and, with greater symbolic impact, Tereus, Procne, and Philomela are all transformed into birds. This Ovidian metamorphosis results in a political null state. Procne and Philomela, made 'felle' by Tereus's 'grete wrong' (5. 5880–2), become the hapless instruments of a natural justice that balances wrong by wrong and sustains no social constructs. Agents of retribution in other tales, however, do not share in the fates of the malfeasants they pursue. Wrongs in these tales are corrected to leave political order intact and reinforced.

Distinguishing between stable and unstable, destructive and constructive outcomes is the starting point for an attempt to classify the *Confessio*'s politics of retribution. Certain portions of Genius's narrative repertoire (including episodes of tales specifically altered by Gower and several whole tales) function principally to outline a conception of the redress of wrongs, which in turn belongs to a larger field of late medieval ideas about conflict resolution and reciprocalist lordship. The concept of redress, for instance, most readily makes sense of the otherwise baffling tale of Orestes, which I will examine in depth at the end of the next chapter. Derek Pearsall contends that 'Gower is simply not equipped to cope with' his source material for this tale, and he finds it 'difficult to know... exactly what lies behind [Gower's] telling of the story... Purportedly an exemplum against murder, it fails completely to make its point or even to extract any single story line.'[1] I would suggest that only from the perspective of household relations can a single main story line be brought into focus in the Orestes narrative and that its point (while not the one against murder that Genius adduces) is an exemplary demonstration of conflict resolution through good lordship. The tale opens with adultery and the murder of a father and it follows Orestes as he 'wroghte mochel schame | In vengance of his fader deth' (3. 1960–1). His revenge on his own mother is especially grisly. So far, so much in common with the wrongs and retributions of the stories of Rosemund and Procne. Yet the tale closes with Orestes solemnly

---

[1] Derek Pearsall, 'Gower's Narrative Art', *PMLA* 81 (1966), 475–84, 483.

crowned king by the Greeks. The tale presents a scheme of conduct that thoroughly describes the poem's operative distinction between illicit and licit retribution, between Rosemund's and Procne's failures and Orestes's success.

The text's model of legitimate retribution again privileges reciprocalist lordship and does so not only because legitimate retribution supports such lordship but even more importantly because it constitutes the performance of such lordship. The great household's social economy contains the licit forms of justice available to agents in the poem's narratives. For this reason, female agents of retribution are consumed by their own pursuit of justice. Within the exchange parameters of reciprocalist lordship, women who are not lords cannot call directly on inter-household obligations, and publicly can only properly be signs and victims, acted upon. The moment they act wilfully in Genius's narratives, they transgress the norms of good lordship (and suffer the consequences). Unless they happen to be lords, no licit (and therefore productive) form of justice is immediately available to them.

JUSTICE AND THE GREAT HOUSEHOLD
IN THE LATE FOURTEENTH CENTURY

In the 'complaint poetry' of the *Confessio*, Gower joins a mainstream of late fourteenth-century complaint attacking lords and their household retinues for illegitimately 'maintaining' their friends' causes:

> Touchende of the chevalerie,
> . . . .
> . . . of here large retenue
> The lond is ful of maintenue,
> Which causith that the comune right
> In fewe contrees stant upright.
> Extorcioun, contekt, ravine
> Withholde ben of that covyne,
> Aldai men hierin gret compleignte
> Of the desease, of the constreignte,
> Wher of the poeple is sore oppressid
>
> (8. 3007–19)

This passage chimes with a volume of parliamentary complaint linking retaining and 'oppression' by maintenance. Poem and petitions reach for the same terminology and triangulation of corrupt or lawless practices, retaining, and the common good. A general petition on public order set before the commons at Cambridge in 1388 more specifically deems it maintenance when, for instance, 'any maintain or retain about them (*mayngtenent ou retiegnent devers eux*) any persons indicted or outlawed for felony or any common thieves, murderers, or other felons, so that the king's, officers . . . dare not perform their offices . . . for fear of their maintenance and support' (*WC* 358). The opening provision of this petition calls for the abolition of 'all the liveries called signs (*signes*)', including the king's, 'and all other lesser liveries, such as hoods (*menuz liverees come chaperons*)' (*WC* 356). The restriction of liveries (and especially the livery of signs, badges, or 'company') because they abetted maintenance was a persistent demand of the commons from the beginning of Richard's reign to somewhat beyond its end.[2]

At first sight, both Gower's and the commons' complaint against 'maintenue' suggest a vivid and familiar pattern in which localized power (in the 'contrees') perverts a norm of stability and justice available from centralized authority (and embodied by the king's officers). Livery and lawlessness, however, were not equated wholesale in aristocratic discussions about justice. Gower's poem and the parliamentary gentry's petitions on livery and maintenance in fact represent contemporary thinking about justice that is heavily invested in uncentralized power and allocates the great household a great deal of room to operate as a user of law rather than an object to be controlled by it. Justice in these texts is not a binary matter in which law and central legal procedures are grouped against the great household, its livery exchange and illicit local power bases. Commons that supported legislation on liveries were archreciprocalists: evidently what alarmed them was not unofficial force *per se* but that privileged relationships (represented by liveries) were breaking free from a household economy structured by aristocratic status and slow-burning relationships.

The *Confessio*, similarly, is committed to a discourse of interpersonal relations organized by the great household for its imagination of social

---

[2] *PROME* iii. 23 (Oct. 1377); *SR* ii. 74 (1390): the king's lieges to have access to the law without being 'oppressez par maintenance'; *SR* ii. 113 (1399): badges banned 'pur ouster meintenance' (to eschew maintenance); National Archives, SC 8/100/4985 (unenrolled petition), printed in Saul, 'Abolition of Badges', 314: retainers by signs 'maintaining most heinous quarrels (*maigntenauntz tresmalveys quereles*), oppressing your [the king's] loyal lieges, and disturbing the right and common law of your land as well for doubt of the friends (*doute de laliance*) of them who bear these signs aforesaid as for the anger of the lords who give them'.

process and stability, and this commitment extends to issues of law and the administration of justice. The poem's epilogue's complaint against maintenance quoted above (8. 3007–19) and the prologue's allegiance to conciliatory or unofficial justice are entirely compatible articulations of this household discourse. Even given the epilogue's synthesis with currently popular protest against noble retinues, Gower's text is not opposed to certain forms of maintenance or informal dispute resolution, for which the parliamentary commons themselves were endeavouring to preserve a zone of legitimacy. Certainly, the implicit investments of the poem are aligned with household-based (as opposed to centralized) forms of justice.

A reciprocalist imaginary held that the operations of the law should be conditioned by the great household's political economy. Both lordship and law, retainer and justice, became outrageous when they failed to register local networks of worship and histories of power. Indeed, given the overlap of personnel and indeed places between the justice system and political elites in the localities, an attempt generally to disentangle the operations of the common law from local landed interests in late medieval England would ultimately be wrongheaded.[3] Within the many layers of the fourteenth-century justice system, however, it is realistic to arbitrate between particular developments on the basis of their relationship to centralized and uncentralized power, and whether they seem more or less responsive to patterns of authority at a local level, within and between great households.

The innovation in civil procedures under Henry II, the critical mass of standard writs being produced by Edward I's chancery which stranded it at Westminster, and the explosion of new types of writ in the early fourteenth century were watersheds in the development of an astonishingly comprehensive centralized system of royal justice in medieval England.[4] The Angevin innovation in common law procedures worked by greatly expanding the jurisdiction of the royal justices in eyre. Yet the common law civil procedures appealed to landowners above all because they could be used to protect their overriding (and local)

---

[3] See Walker's comments in 'Yorkshire Justices', 310–11. For architecturally inflected 'intermeshing' of royal and local interests when royal judicial sessions were held in privately owned venues, see Anthony Musson, 'Legal Landmarks: The Architecture of Justice in Late Medieval England', *Australia and New Zealand Law and History E-Journal*, 2 (2006), paper 15 (quote at 9), www.anzlhsejournal.auckland.ac.nz; and 'Court Venues and the Politics of Justice', in Nigel Saul (ed.), *Fourteenth Century England V* (Woodbridge, Suff., 2008).

[4] Clanchy, *Memory to Written Record*, 62–8.

interests in the possession and transmission of land.[5] Prominent in baronial opposition to Angevin prerogative rule was protest against being bound to expensive (and arbitrary) personal royal justice and denied access to the routine procedures initiated by the common law writs 'of course'. Common law reproduced basic 'feudal' customs of inheritance and reinforced these with speed, cheapness, and the gentry's own involvement as jurors. These qualities made the procedures attractive *as part of* the aristocracy's equipment of dispute resolution, the efficiency of which was ultimately bound up with local social relations and therefore the great household.[6] Furthermore, the common law overlapped the category of custom by way, for example, of the so-called 'laws of Edward the Confessor'. Custom was held to be immutable and able to constrain present royal authority. The common law did not provide support for ideas of majesty like that available in Roman law doctrines.

The aristocracy seem to have found the apparatus of civil pleas at common law, state-like and blank to local contours of power as it was, welcome and 'inscribable' with these contours where other versions of crown authority which were more majestic or imposed more heavily on local political society appeared more threatening. Thus, the crown pleas—or criminal law—business of the eyre, unlike its supervision of civil pleas, was extremely lucrative for the crown and *was* viewed as exploitative and a threat to centrifugal power. Its expansion met with aristocratic resistance in the twelfth and thirteenth centuries. Here the centralizing impetus of the general eyre explains its decline during Edward I's reign and the discrediting as overweening of the single-purpose commissions which filled the space it left (including oyer and terminer, and trailbaston but excepting assizes). The peace commissions, with strong local aristocratic representation helping sitting justices in a locality–centre linkage, and magnates associated as buttresses for the commission's authority, emerge as the centrifugal and most successful successors to the general eyre in the fourteenth century. The professional lawyers who served as justices on the commissions could themselves be local landholders.[7]

The extent to which the gentry advanced a consensus policy on justice in the fourteenth century is debatable, but even if its role in specific

---

[5] Harriss, 'Political Society', 49.   [6] Ibid. 50.

[7] Ibid. 45–8; Musson and Ormrod, *Evolution of English Justice*, 69, 73; Walker, 'Yorkshire Justices'. For a view that crown administration of criminal justice in the fifteenth century was weak even when local peace-keeping agencies worked free of faction, see S. J. Payling, 'Murder, Motive and Punishment in Fifteenth-Century England: Two Gentry Case-Studies', *EHR* 113 (1998), 1–17.

institutional changes was no more than opportunistic, mainstream gentry representation showed itself persistently eager to promote local input into judicial processes.[8] In particular, this was the case in what Gerald Harriss describes as 'half a century of argument and experiment' that formed the peace commissions of Gower's day.[9] The common law courts and delegated crown authority, moreover, did not exclusively set the horizons for land-holders' pursuit and protection of their interests in land and family. The gentry were also impelled to preserve their own position in non-state mechanisms of dispute resolution, including, at the least official end of the spectrum, retaining and 'good lordship' or maintenance. These mechanisms could take account of factors beyond the common law. Common law, for instance, could not easily address deep-rooted assumptions about patrimony and inalienability of estates. Rights of use and entail with reversion to the primary line of a family involved legal alienation of the property by the landholder and were used to negotiate between demands of patrimonial continuity and more present concerns (such as providing for younger sons). These devices were judiciable only in developing courts of 'conscience' or 'equity', not under common law.[10] They could also be defended by less official local processes, such as various forms of arbitration, which sought conciliation rather than legal exactitude and completeness.

More generally, as Harriss notes, litigation was not the aristocracy's 'sole or even principal means for resolving a dispute' (even if it was popular and the 'most obvious' one).[11] Access to the centre was jealously guarded, but it was also important that law or influence brought to bear in this way conformed to local political topography. Litigation often served as a tool to advance a dispute rather than a final resort to finish it, and Christine Carpenter insists that:

It is indeed becoming a commonplace that conflict and litigation cannot always be taken at face value, that law itself settled nothing among the gentry, and that a real settlement could only be reached by more informal means: arbitration before

---

[8] Anthony Verduyn argues against a commons 'policy' on local justice under Edward III in 'Early Justices of the Peace'.

[9] Harriss, *Shaping the Nation*, 51.

[10] For entail and enfeoffment to use, see McFarlane, *Nobility*, 61–82; Given-Wilson, *English Nobility*, 138–53. For equitable jurisdiction, see J. H. Baker, *An Introduction to English Legal History*, 4th edn (London, 2002), 97–126, 248–57; T. S. Haskett, 'Conscience, Justice, and Authority in the Late Medieval Court of Chancery', in Anthony Musson (ed.), *Expectations of the Law in the Middle Ages* (Woodbridge, Suff., 2001), 151–64.

[11] Harriss, *Shaping the Nation*, 197, 198.

a case ever went to law or after it had reached the law courts. Moreover, resort to law was in itself the sign of a local breakdown, and no permanent agreement could be achieved without the restoration of some degree of local harmony.[12]

Historians continue to develop a picture of arbitration's enduring appeal to the aristocracy.[13]

Late fourteenth-century arbitration may have become increasingly formalized and reliant on written records of settlement in response to legal constraints.[14] The habits of consumers of justice to view conciliation and litigation as interlacing paths to justice also stand as caution against binary approaches to the subject. Nevertheless, (relatively) informal arbitration outside the king's courts remained a viable (if complicated) mode of dispute resolution in Gower's time, and could be *represented* as an ideal of 'love' and custom somehow separated from and implicitly opposed to centralized law.

In late medieval terms, the opposition is between 'love' and (formal) 'law'.[15] 'Love' encompasses unofficial and customary methods of dispute resolution structured by the great household and manorial courts, such as

---

[12] Carpenter, 'Gentry and Community', 355. See also Edward Powell, 'Arbitration and the Law in England in the Late Middle Ages', *TRHS* 5th ser. 33 (1983), 49–67, 56–62; and 'Settlement of Disputes by Arbitration in Fifteenth-Century England', *Law and History Review*, 2 (1984), 21–43, 39–40; Carpenter, 'Law, Justice and Landowners'.

[13] See e.g. Clanchy, 'Law and Love', 57–61; Ian Rowney, 'Arbitration in Gentry Disputes of the Later Middle Ages', *History*, 67 (1982), 367–76; Powell, 'Arbitration and the Law'; and 'Settlement of Disputes'; Carole Rawcliffe, 'The Great Lord as Peacekeeper: Arbitration by English Noblemen and their Councils in the Later Middle Ages', in J. A. Guy and H. G. Beale (eds), *Law and Social Change in British History* (London, 1984), 34–54; and 'Parliament and the Settlement of Disputes by Arbitration in the Later Middle Ages', *Parliamentary History*, 9 (1990), 316–42; Simon J. Payling, 'Law and Arbitration in Nottinghamshire 1399–1461', in Joel Rosenthal and Colin Richmond (eds), *People, Politics, and Community in the Later Middle Ages* (Gloucester, 1987), 140–60; David Tilsley, 'Arbitration in Gentry Disputes: The Case of Bucklow Hundred in Cheshire, 1400–1465', in Diana E. S. Dunn (ed.), *Courts, Counties, and the Capital in the Later Middle Ages* (Stroud, Glos., 1996), 53–70. For a contrary argument that lovedays were a judicial irrelevance and 'a burlesque' by the late fourteenth century, see Thomas J. Heffernan, 'A Middle English Poem on Lovedays', *Chaucer Review*, 10 (1975–6), 172–85, 175. Richard Firth Green briefly surveys much of this arbitration research (*Crisis of Truth*, 178–9). For manorial jurisdiction and dispute settlement, see Lloyd Bonfield, 'The Nature of Customary Law in the Manor Courts of Medieval England', *Comparative Studies in Society and History*, 31 (1989), 514–34; Janet Williamson, 'Dispute Settlement in the Manorial Court: Early Fourteenth-Century Lakenheath', *Reading Medieval Studies*, 11 (1985), 133–41; Carlin, *Medieval Southwark*, 112–16.

[14] See Powell, 'Arbitration and the Law', 62–3; and 'Settlement of Disputes', 33–5; cf. Green, *Crisis of Truth*, 181.

[15] For Michael Clanchy's seminal discussion of medieval law and justice in these terms, see 'Law and Love'.

lovedays and parliamentary arbitration. The term 'loveday', it seems, could refer to a hiatus in legal proceedings enjoined by a court, seigneurial or crown, to facilitate an informal settlement or, more specifically, to a customary mechanism of aristocratically led arbitration or mediation. These two senses of the term are not, of course, mutually exclusive. In its occasional sense, the loveday aimed to cement a restored order of worship before representatives of the local polity. It might conclude with a kiss of peace or some other sign (at least) of the harmony Carpenter mentions.[16]

Arbitration and amicable settlements offered all the disadvantages as well as the advantages of informality and flexibility, including compromise and the scope for household-based networks and power relations to influence outcomes. Consensual settlement is fundamentally desirable practice for the observer who, like Gower, has faith in the great household and assumes that, *trouthe* prevailing, its political economy tends to produce conciliation and stability rather than inequity, factionalism, and violence. Simon Walker describes a long-running dispute which involved as principals Thomas Molyneux of Cuerdale and Henry Chaderton, John of Gaunt's 'delinquent bailiff' in west Derbyshire.[17] The conflict illustrates the kaleidoscopic quality of aristocratic politics (at least as they appear in texts). Viewed one way, the dispute tells a story of Molyneux and his associates operating as a lawless and violent band unchecked by judicial authority. Turned another, it looks like a history of local gentry who resort to their own networks to seek justice against murder and abuses of their worship when the common law courts have failed them. Another turn, and the different episodes of the decade-long contest fragment into a confusing array of circumstance and social structure, principle and expedience.

Richard Firth Green suggests that most English historians themselves display an optimistic bias in evaluating the actual impact and justice of late medieval arbitration. Many broadly approve of arbitration as a cheap, efficient, and honourable option for local gentry.[18] Conversely, Green notes, Michael Clanchy suspects that 'in the later Middle Ages procedure by love seems to have become as embroiled in faction as the ordinary processes of law'.[19] Clanchy resists definitive evaluative comparisons of love and law, however, and his examination proceeds from a

---

[16] Josephine Waters Bennett, 'The Mediaeval Loveday', *Speculum*, 33 (1958), 351–70.
[17] Walker, *Lancastrian Affinity*, 165–7 (quote at 165).
[18] e.g. Rowney, 'Arbitration in Gentry Disputes', 370–1, 376; Payling, 'Law and Arbitration', 147, 157; Tilsley, 'Arbitration in Gentry Disputes', 69–70.
[19] Clanchy, 'Law and Love', 61, quoted in Green, *Crisis of Truth*, 179.

recognition of love's (reciprocalist) grounding in local power relations, bonds of publicly recognized affection and mutual obligation, as opposed to the abstract principles of law.[20] Likewise, my argument does not ultimately turn on whether love or law offered the more effective or just methods of dispute resolution, but on the distinction and tension between concepts and social forms associated with each system, and on the political logic of a gentry interest in love.

Reciprocalist discourse best served groups interested in sustaining close ties of mutual dependence between different levels of the aristocracy. Reciprocalist positions on legal and extra-legal political intervention shared concerns for worship-building histories and their asymmetries. Naked, past-blind law, which does not recognize the great household's role in the local polity, is condemned as intrusive. By the same values, lordship becomes overmighty maintaining when it is out of step with local expectations and assessments of worship.

TROUTHE AND LAW

Green distinguishes two complexes of ideas about 'trouthe' and justice that are related to 'love' and 'law' and conflicted in the late fourteenth century. With an established and 'ethical' notion of *trouthe* as a personal quality of integrity and fidelity, Green associates a traditional conception and system of law that is oral, local, communal, and consensual.[21] These terms require qualification before they are matched to late medieval practice. In a culture of commissions, letters, and the personal seal, unofficial methods of dispute resolution were hardly independent of writing. Local power structures were not isolated, but were connected to the royal centre in formal and informal ways. The 'communal' and the 'consensual' are idealizations that disguise social hierarchies and suppressed tensions. Nevertheless, this set of terms represents important aspects of a medieval political imaginary, and Green suggestively discusses fourteenth-century practices of maintenance (in a broad sense) as a legacy of a 'personal *trouthe*' tradition.[22] At a loveday, settlement took the form of *pactum* or trothplight and was therefore insured in the first

---

[20] Clanchy, 'Law and Love', 47–52, 54, 61, 64.

[21] For the semantic variations of 'trouthe' and their coexistence in the late fourteenth century, see Green, *Crisis of Truth*, 8–28. Green discusses the traditional system of 'trothplight' and the 'folklaw' in his second and third chapters (ibid. 41–120).

[22] Ibid. 165–205.

place by personal *trouthe*. With an emergent and 'intellectual' meaning of *trouthe* as objectifiable fact, or 'sooth', Green associates a newly dominant legal system (in the royal courts of common law in particular), literate, centralized, narrowly formal, and authoritarian, for which he adopts the shorthand 'the king's law'.[23]

Green ascribes to many poets contemporary with Gower, including Langland and Chaucer, an alienation from established mechanisms of amicable settlement. Such poets' texts, he argues, make gestures of 'profound respect for just that spirit of generosity, toleration, and forebearance that the loveday was supposed to embody', but these gestures remain hollow because of the texts' hostility towards and 'skeptical view of lovedays'.[24]

Gower, however, resists any final scepticism about household-based justice. Regardless of the actual state of arbitration in the late fourteenth century, and underlying a surface disappointment at present corruptions of love and maintenance, the *Confessio* registers a deep conviction in the superiority of the loveday and an associated ideal of informal aristocratic dispute settlement somehow recoverable even in the degraded present. The poem makes explicit statements that privilege personal *trouthe* as the supreme value underwriting society, and which (in consonance with Green's oppositions) bifurcate this *trouthe* and writing. In the prologue, for instance, Gower imagines as part of the golden age a kind of pure *trouthe* and proto-linguistic personal integrity:

> Of mannes herte the corage
> Was schewed thanne in the visage;
> The word was lich to the conceite
> Withoute semblant of deceite
>
> (prol. 111–14)[25]

---

[23] Ibid., esp. 121–64. See also Clanchy's admonition that, 'Law and government in medieval England have been surveyed too often from above, from the unique viewpoint of the king', and his criticism of those who, trapped by assumptions about 'the "state"' and royal dominance implicit in such surveys, become 'King's Friends' ('Law, Government, and Society', 75, 77). Cf. Powell, 'Settlement of Disputes', 21–4, against the tendency to regard medieval informal dispute settlement as an 'aberration from the norm of litigation within a well-regulated and efficient legal system' and 'a temporary expedient forced on litigants by the failure of judicial institutions' (24).

[24] Green, *Crisis of Truth*, 175–9 (quotes at 176, 179). Green goes on to imply that this hostility stems from contemporary conciliatory methods' entanglement in formalized law after 'the disintegration of the folklaw' (183).

[25] Cf. Chaucer's 'The Former Age', in *Riverside Chaucer*, 650–1. In this golden age, 'Doublenesse, and tresoun' were similarly unknown, and the hearts of people 'were al oon withoute galles' (ll. 47, 62) (although, the primitive, pre-commercial status of the

The prologue's vision of the golden age further coordinates *trouthe* and ideal law intimately with one another, to posit a working justice of love now lost (prol. 115–92). This vision rescues ideal law from concepts of complex, formalized legal procedure, which carry connotations of four-teenth-century developments in the king's law. In the Latin verse accompanying this section, a line which anticipates the English text's fusion of emotion and expression, thought and word, leads into a peculiar description of golden age law:

> Progenuit veterem concors dileccio pacem,
> Dum facies hominis nuncia mentis erat:
> Legibus vnicolor tunc temporis aura refulsit
>
> (prol. at 92 (3–5))
>
> Harmonious love begat the ancient peace,
> When yet man's face was herald of his mind:
> The air of that age shone, one-hued, with laws[26]

The legal image is not only grammatically linked to that of unmediated personal *trouthe*, but resonates with it in the shared conceit of abstractions made visible. Law, somehow suffusing the very atmosphere, is construed as something 'grounded ... upon nature' like the true alchemists' craft. The image resists formalism, suggesting an ideal of monovalent and universally accessible law. The resistance to formalism is compounded later in the verse by the extension of colour imagery, when the law of the present is contrastively described as 'Chameleon-like' ('Instar... Cameliontis'; prol. at 92 (9)). The image of non-intrinsic, unstable colouring is associated with legal innovation ('noua iura'; prol. at 92 (10)), and both are aligned with the political fragmentation and instability of the decayed present. Gower is recycling the device of the chameleon from *Vox clamantis*, where its cosmetic meanings of colour and formal non-essentiality are made explicit.[27] In this light, the unusual phrase 'Legibus vnicolor' and the image of the reactive chameleon might refer most particularly to the developing legal

---

Saturnian society is closer to *CA* 5. 1–21 than to the prologue's idyll of 'astat'). See also *CT* 1. 742, 9. 210; above, 94 n. 63.

[26] Siân Echard and Claire Fanger, *The Latin Verses in the Confessio Amantis: An Annotated Translation* (East Lansing, Mich., 1991), 5.

[27] *Vox*, 4. 825–6: 'Aspiciens varias species variatur et ipse | Camelion, et tot signa coloris habet' ('The chameleon looks at varied colors and is varied, | Having the mark of all colors upon itself'; tr. Echard and Fanger, *Latin Verses*, 5 n. 6).

practice of 'colour' in pleading (the technical detail being reserved for the erudite voice of the Latin apparatus). Apparently an invention of the early fourteenth century, giving 'colour' was, by the end of the century, increasingly a process of inventing and revising legal fictions in the common law courts.[28] The operation of this process is counter-intuitive and need not be elaborated here. Suffice it to say that giving colour was a technical, procedural expertise rooted in the conception of law as a given form to be left materially unaltered but mediated by the organs of the king's law.[29] Gower's Saturnian closing down of colour, then, represents the ideal of law as something prior to the mechanisms of the king's law and implies that the (literate) expertise required by these mechanisms is something dangerously fractured and polysemous.

At the other end of the prologue's apocalyptic teleology, informal, non-litigious methods of dispute resolution are bound up with the necessary conditions for a period of quasi-chiliastic grace before the End of History. The milieu of Arion is evoked as a prefiguration of a restored golden age preceding divine judgement. The harper figure primarily signals the potential of lay poetry to generate personal moral reform which will pre-empt social disorder and dispute. I would argue further that at the level at which Arion's successor can be read as a mediator of disputes, who 'myhte availe in many a stede | To make pes wher now is hate' (prol. 1074–5), he emblematizes social systems which would maintain order in a future golden age, just as Arion

> ... the comun with the lord,
> And lord with the comun also,
> He sette in love bothe tuo
> And putte awey malencolie
>
> (prol. 1066–9)

Green identifies Arion as a supreme mediator and hence something of an anomaly amongst contemporary writings that do not translate *trouthe* rhetoric into support for unofficial justice and instead see love-days and 'less formal modes of dispute settlement in general' as untrustworthy, corrupting, and intimidatory.[30]

---

[28] Donald W. Sutherland, 'Legal Reasoning in the Fourteenth Century: The Invention of "Color" in Pleading', in Arnold et al. (eds), *On the Laws and Customs of England: Essays in Honor of Samuel E. Thorne* (Chapel Hill, NC, 1981), 182–94; cf. Green, *Crisis of Truth*, 147–8.
[29] See Sutherland, 'Legal Reasoning', esp. 191–2.
[30] Green, *Crisis of Truth*, 175–8 and n. 9 (quote at 176); cf. Heffernan, 'Lovedays', 175–6. Green thus seems to acknowledge some distance between Gower and his non-provincial

Certainly, the lines before the advent of Arion encourage us to associate his ordering influence with institutions of love. The end of the prologue presents as alternatives Judgement and its deferral through 'acord' such as the poet-harper Arion inspired. The categorical and final nature of Judgement is thrown into relief against the loveday:

> And every man schal thanne arise
> To Joie or elles to Juise,
> Wher that he schal for evere dwelle,
> Or straght to hevene or straght to helle.
> In hevene is pes and al acord,
> Bot helle is full of such descord
> That ther may be no loveday:
> Forthi good is, whil a man may,
> Echon to sette pes with other
> And loven as his oghne brother;
> So may he winne worldes welthe
> And afterward his soule helthe

(prol. 1041–52)

The reference to lovedays foregrounds temporal mechanisms of justice as a layer of meaning in this passage. Earthly history is characterized by the opportunity to take advantage of conciliatory forms of justice and social ordering before they are rendered obsolete by the all or nothing of eternity. The ensuing description of Arion's milieu and its unifying 'acord' (as prototype for quasi-chiliastic renovation) takes up these meanings. If we recall the prominence in the golden age of 'lawe' and 'governance' coupled with 'charite' and 'pes' kissed by 'ryhtwisnesse' (suggestive of the kiss of peace; prol. 102–10) then we should read not just spirit but social substance into the later passage. The contrast between Judgement and loveday aligns divine justice with categorical, formal law. The time of the future Arion, as a pre-empting and forestalling of such justice, thereby becomes the envisaged fulfilment of conciliatory institutions which operate before and alongside authoritarian legalism.

The *Confessio*'s investment in personal *trouthe*, then, does not stop short before the territory of political relations, and at least begins to construct a language of informal justice. The prologue's composite Saturnian and apocalyptic theory of history privileges *trouthe*-based or

literary peers, but his particular reading of the tale of the False Bachelor aligns Gower with the momentum of the king's law and abandoned faith in love's mechanisms (*Crisis of Truth*, 271–2; cf. below, 222, 231–2).

'love' mechanisms of order and justice, and imagines ideal society as space constituted by their operation.

What, then, of the revised epilogue's flat statement against maintenance? The epilogue's complaint and the prologue's commitment to household-based justice dovetail in seigneurial authority and a particular (reciprocalist) order of privileged relations structured by the great household. These elements are present in both prologue and epilogue, are further tested (and transformed) in Genius's narratives, and operate also in the parliamentary texts on livery and maintenance.

The prologue's overview of golden age social stability joins a legal ideal to a compact hierarchical conspectus of secular society:

> Justice of lawe tho was holde,
> The privilege of regalie
> Was sauf, and al the baronie
> Worschiped was in his astat;
> The citees knewen no debat,
> The poeple stod in obeissance
> Under the reule of governance
>
> (prol. 102–8)

Golden age law was justly administered, the passage alleges, whereas now, it follows, law functions corruptly. (Amalgamating 'Justice' and 'lawe' in line 102 distinguishes more starkly between a past of effective law and a present of legal desuetude.) As I have discussed, the corresponding Latin head verse has suggested a gap between a 'vnicolor' age of law simple and a present of complicated applications of the law. This English passage writes conventional, limited social hierarchy into the age of law simple. Similarly, orderly human society under Arion's influence is represented by 'love' between 'the lord' and 'the comun' (prol. 1062–9), and the epilogue's complaint against maintenance is made within an estates satire structure under the section treating the secular aristocracy (8. 3005–19). The implication common to these passages is that public order is properly articulated through the aristocracy (and especially the nobility). The apposition of aristocracy and good order, however, remains opaque. The order-bringing function (and its relationship to the law) is transferred to the enigma Arion and the love he inspired, or otherwise goes unexplained. Genius's narratives and the commons' discussions of livery and maintenance fill in some of the blank.

THE LIVERY AND MAINTENANCE DEBATE

The commons of Ricardian parliaments, like Gower, were interested in defining a sphere of legitimate lordship, and their texts on livery and maintenance draw on a broader seam of household discourse than that condensed into the *Confessio* epilogue's related complaint. These texts in turn illuminate how Genius's tales expand the *Confessio*'s reference to legitimate lordship by promoting a reciprocalist model of household exchange that encompasses justice and retribution. Exempla and parliamentary texts participate in the same discourse of household-based relations and exchange.

Through the commons texts, a social logic which also underpins the exemplary imagination of dispute resolution and civil order in the *Confessio* can be scrutinized. The legislation's treatment of disorder and retaining (as an aristocratic activity) is informed not by a dual opposition between lawlessness and the enforcement of law, but by a triangulation of the law and different unofficial types of intervention in civil order. The petitions on maintenance and retaining resort to the centralized legal system not to substitute its authority for that of the magnate and the power structures enabled by his household organization, but to reorder (and retrench) those power structures according to the asymmetric patterns characteristic of reciprocalist lordship. They seek to eliminate neither all local, unofficial interventions in the operations of justice nor all forms of liveried retaining, but precisely those that exceed or impinge upon the structures of lordship assumed to be normative.

The Ricardian commons that debated livery expressed anxiety about the failure (especially on the part of the nobility) to contain powerful modes of household exchange according to shared and enduring expectations about social order. That such anxiety belongs above all to the gentry is suggested by the livery petitions' imagination of legitimate (privileged) retaining relationships and also by the influence of the gentry in the late fourteenth-century commons.[31] The 1388 Cambridge petition's definition of maintenance is likewise concerned with exchange (of political and sometimes armed support) which is not channelled by established (and hierarchically ordered) relations. The commons' livery legislation is focused mainly on lesser types of livery,

[31] For the commons' gentry voice, see the works by McFarlane, Richardson, and Wood-Legh cited above, 34 n. 23.

rather than the more prestigious, traditional *liveree de draps*, the livery of cloth or robes.[32] In 1377, a petition against retaining for the purpose of maintenance produced a statute against liveries of hats (*chaperons*) in particular.[33] According to the Westminster chronicler, the commons at Salisbury in spring 1384 turned their attention to the novel livery of the badge or sign of company, which remained a bugbear until the turn of the century.[34] Commons petitions were interested in abolishing or radically restricting only these *lesser* liveries.[35] The conservative partitioning of livery exchange is drawn most vividly, and along a perspective common to Gower's prologue, in an undated, unenrolled petition.[36] The text is structured by a commanding vision of past unity (in the time of the present king's 'most noble progenitors') counterposed with present division. Livery of cloth is assigned a privileged, golden age status in the nostalgized past, when the people were ruled 'saunz desseverance entre eux faitz par conisance du signes ou autre liveres *forpris* livere de vesture' (without division among them made by recognizance of badges or other liveries *except* livery of cloth).[37]

Seeking to (re)contain seigneurial exchange practice, the commons petitions define its acceptable boundaries by traditional forms of livery, by social condition, and by established relations based in the great household. A 1390 petition dealing in particular with livery of cloth

---

[32] Genius uses a stratified livery metaphor to emblematize the 'double grace' of material and spiritual capital that rewards aristocratic giving: 'the cote for the hod/ Largesse takth' (5. 7716–17). The image may also apply to largesse's asymmetrical worldly returns that the confessor goes on to proverb.

[33] *PROME* iii. 23; *SR* ii. 3.

[34] *WC* 80–2. The commons' complaint was not enrolled. Badges were again the focus of complaint at Cambridge in 1388, Westminster in 1390, 1393, and 1397, and (alongside livery of cloth) in Henry IV's first two parliaments. See *WC* 354–6; *PROME* iii. 265, 307, 345, 428, 477–8; *SR* ii. 113–14, 129–30. An unenrolled petition calling for the abolition of badges (below, n. 36) also belongs to this period. Saul considers September 1388, but favours a date of 1401 ('Abolition of Badges', 303).

[35] A petition of January 1390 does seek regulation of the superior livery of cloth and Carpenter suggests that the commons responsible may have been packed. She adduces its commune petition as 'almost uniquely subservient to the crown' ('Law, Justice and Landowners', 231). Nonetheless, the petition on cloth seeks only to contain the livery strictly within an aristocratic household system, and is separate from the session's much more stringent proposal on badges (*PROME* iii. 265, 266). Walsingham reports that there was pressure on the magnates to give up badges entirely: *Historia Anglicana*, ed. Henry Thomas Riley, Rolls Ser. (London, 1863–4), ii. 195–6. Tuck mistakenly claims that the commons sought 'the total abolition of all liveries' (*Richard II and the English Nobility*, 148).

[36] National Archives, SC 8/100/4985, printed in Saul, 'Abolition of Badges', 314–15.

[37] Ibid. 314 (emphasis added).

attempts to describe a stable set of household-based relations as the limits of legitimate exchange. A lord may only distribute livery to the 'familiers de son hostelle, ses parentz et alliez, ses seneschalle, son conseille, ou a ses baillifs de lour manoirs' (familiars of his household, his kin and kin by law, his steward, his counsel, or to his bailiffs on their manors; *PROME* iii. 266). This petition and the more numerous ones which target badges are especially concerned to exclude recipients of less than aristocratic status unless they are connected to a household by a secure tie. Divisions are drawn and redrawn at about the level of 'vadletz' and (lesser) esquires, at the base of the armigerous strata.[38] A badge-wearer must additionally be retained by life indenture (1390, *PROME* iii. 265) or be 'meynal et famulier, ou officer continuel de son dit Seigneur' (domestic and familiar, or permanent officer of his said lord; 1397, *PROME* iii. 345). Complementary provisions aim to obstruct the extension of liveried forms of association to (urban) milieux outside the orbit of the great household. The 1390 bill on cloth singles out guilds and fraternities for livery prohibition (*PROME* iii. 266), and a 1393 badges petition recites urban professions—summed up as 'artificers, vitaillers, et autres' (*PROME* iii. 307)—as a chief concern.

The current distribution of badges, and other improper forms of retaining, are thus conceived as an abnegation of noble responsibility to modulate exchange according to social hierarchy and established relations. Hence, the Westminster chronicler's summary of the complaint at Salisbury against 'potentes homines in partibus dominantes' (certain locally powerful persons; *WC* 80) describes the domineering retainers in question as 'nimis elati' (overmuch lifted up; *WC* 82) by receiving the badges and favour (*favore*) of lords (cf. *WC* 354). The phrase registers an anxiety that these lords are neglecting presupposed constraints of social degree and permitting the social order to be transgressed. Simon Walker concludes of the commons' campaign on public order in the 1380s that its 'real target . . . proves to be less the abuse of maintenance than its practitioners—the *gentz de petit garisons* . . . who were using the cloak of magnate authority to challenge the pre-eminence that the established gentry families had long enjoyed at county level'.[39]

---

[38] See *PROME* iii. 265, 266, 307, 345. The category of 'vadletz' (valets or grooms) is associated with archers or 'gentils', and, in a 1397 bill, specified by the phrase 'vadletz appellez yomen' (valets called yeomen; *PROME* iii. 345). On the significance of these status divisions see Saul, *Knights and Esquires*, 6–29; and, in the context of household rank, Mertes, *Noble Household*, 27–31.

[39] Walker, *Lancastrian Affinity*, 260.

An ordinance promulgated by Richard's council in May 1390 responds to the social logic of the complaint against badges in two directions, adapting the January 1390 commons' two-pronged approach (which addressed badges and cloth separately).[40] The ordinance bans the distribution of badges by non-nobles, and limits the nobles' legitimate exchange partners by class and by extant relationship (of kinship or service).[41] When later legislation comes to regulate livery of cloth, it follows the same principles of lordship channelled by degree and existing personal ties.[42]

The retaining legislation construes illicit retaining (which enables the abuse of the common law) as a kind of magnificence, a lordship without respect for external pressures and prerogatives. The livery badge, indeed, was a form of exchange that tended to the totalizing signification of the lord's power and the exclusion of the recipient's worship, the evacuation of the recipient's selfhood. Unlike liveries of cloth, badges or signs were gifts which had minimal inherent value and which identified the bearer's lord. Woollen liveries of cloth were valuable in themselves as expensive suits or material for clothing.[43] They could also represent the status of their wearers without subsuming it in signification of the lord. Because liveries of cloth were not designed to identify their provider, and did benefit and enhance the worship of the recipient, I would differentiate them from a Lacanian reading of livery such as Fradenburg's.[44] Late medieval sumptuary legislation indicates the capacity of clothing to signify social status, and points to the concomitant requirement of traditional retaining (by robes) to recognize the status of the retainer.[45]

[40] *PROME* iii. 265, 266; and see above, 189 n. 35.

[41] *SR* ii. 75.

[42] *SR* ii. 113–14 (1399), 129–30 (1401), 155–6 (1406).

[43] See Lachaud, 'Liveries of Robes', 287–8. Giles of Rome registers the practical usefulness of robes and the expectations of a prince's servants when he stipulates that the livery handed out should accord with the relevant custom of the country and time of year. See Giles of Rome, *D. Aegidii Romani archiepiscopi Bituricensis ordinis fratrum eremitarum Sancti Augustini de regimine principum libri III* (Rome, 1556), 232 (cited in Lachaud, 'Liveries of Robes', 291 n. 5). On the value of silk, woollen, and linen robes, see Dyer, *Standards of Living*, 78–9.

[44] Fradenburg's contention that, 'The wearing of livery aptly expresses the alienation of the servant's being, the alienation which the subject suffers in becoming a signifier for the other' ('Manciple's Servant Tongue', 89) seems to me well suited to badges, but less so to cloth. On the capacity of livery cloth to represent the status of the retainer, see Lachaud, 'Liveries of Robes', esp. 288–9.

[45] The most comprehensive sumptuary legislation passed in England was the ordinance of 1363 which restricted expenditure on material, ornamentation, and types of cloth across ten social and economic categories and subcategories (*SR* i. 380–2; *PROME* ii. 278–9).

Variations of colour and pattern within particular liveries (that is, distributions of cloth to a household) could also designate status and rank within the household. At the same time, such variations were not heraldic and did not identify the lord of the household.[46] Badges, on the other hand, were easily and cheaply produced and, 'bearing various decorations' (*ornamentis*; *WC* 82) of particular lords—such as Richard II's famous white hart—were effectively labels indicating the lord's possession. Indeed, badges seem to have originated in the early fourteenth century as marks attached to valuable household property.[47]

As well as being a one-sided sign, the low-cost badge was also suited to forming new and short-term bonds of loyalty.[48] Such practice converges with commercial exchange, collapsing the deferrals and sequences of inexact reciprocation that lie behind Bourdieu's diagnosis of misrecognition in gift exchange.[49] It is opposition to this mode of association that seems to lie behind the legislative provisions designating existing and (effectively) permanent relationships as prerequisites for the granting of badges and cloth. As Paul Strohm's careful reading demonstrates, the same anxiety about associations unchannelled by hierarchical and enduring networks of relations informs the 1388 Cambridge petition's definition of maintenance.[50] The extensive definition falls into broad sections. The first involves opportunistic, non-violent manipulations of legal process, motivated (commercially) by a specific exchange.[51] The

[46] See Lachaud, 'Liveries of Robes', 289–97. Lachaud discusses an instance (at London in 1321) when an innovative livery was evidently designed to be emblematic of particular lords (295–7). She notes, however, that chroniclers' terms for the dress (*cotuca* and *cote-armur*) suggest that it was recognized as a light, military dress rather than woollen livery robes (296 and n. 6).

[47] Saul, 'Abolition of Badges', 307–8. On Richard's introduction of the white hart livery at Smithfield in 1390, and its reduction of individuation in the household group beneath the king, see Sheila Lindenbaum, 'The Smithfield Tournament of 1390', *JMRS* 20 (1990), 1–20, 4–5, 16–17. For badges' tourneying use individually to identify their *wearers*, see Juliet R. V. Barker, *The Tournament in England 1100–1400* (Woodbridge, Suff., 1986), 183–6.

[48] Richard II's attempts at such expedient retaining in eastern counties (with a badge representing a crown) met with blunt resistance in 1387 (*WC* 186). Cf. the commons' concern with established types of retaining bond (above, 189–90).

[49] Bourdieu, *Theory of Practice*, 5–6, 171.

[50] Strohm, *Hochon's Arrow*, 60.

[51] A maintainer is one of any degree who 'takes up or supports another's quarrel to which he is not a party by reason of blood or marriage (*partie cosyn nalye*), in order to have the whole or a part of that which is claimed, or instigates or procures for reward, gift, or promise the passing of inquests in quarrels to which he is not a party' (*WC* 358). Cf. the 1390 livery of cloth petition's delimiting of a proper sphere (including 'parentz et alliez') for the distribution of cloth (*PROME* iii. 266).

second section covers the use (or threat) of violence by 'great routs and multitude of people in excess of their degree and condition' (*outre lour degre et estat*; *WC* 358); and the third, the retaining of felons 'so that the officers of the king . . . dare not perform their offices' (*WC* 358). Strohm provides this analysis of the definition:

Some of the points of particular concern here . . . are that such associations involve alliance of persons not otherwise related, that they represent a temporary and voluntary association for concerted action, and that they seem to involve transgression of the normal constraints of personal degree.[52]

The petition implicitly leaves inside the realm of legitimate practice a full range of unofficial mechanisms of justice and interventions in legal process. These types of intervention are available to socially respectable retainers and associates and can turn on obligations forged by household-based exchanges (or exchange histories).

The parliamentary texts on retaining and maintenance instantiate a discourse about lordship operating in the late fourteenth century to draw only certain types of household-based social organization under the cloud of social instability and the abuse of law. This explains the intensive definition of maintenance in the 1388 petition and the divergent attitudes towards badges and livery of cloth respectively. By the same token, these texts reveal a concern to reserve privileged forms of household relation for the socially privileged, and to reserve unofficial mediation of the law for those privileged forms of relation. The texts delineate two opposing spheres of personal relations. Both spheres accommodate and produce unofficial, non-centralized practices mediating the law. One sphere, however, comprises collusive, short-term associations for concerted ends and associations unconstrained by social degree, and is aligned with illicit, oppressive practices. The other sphere, largely by contrary implication, involves enduring, asymmetrically ordered household-based obligation, which is aligned with legitimate, stabilizing practices.

[52] Strohm, *Hochon's Arrow*, 60.

7

Retribution as Household Exchange in Genius's Tales

I want to suggest that the very same discursive dynamic operates in the parliamentary livery and maintenance texts and the short narratives of *Confessio Amantis*; that the same basic criteria of personal association inform these texts' imagination of licit and illicit approaches to justice. In depicting acts of wrongdoing and the forms of association which orbit them, the confession's narratives bear little superficial resemblance to the parliamentary complaints. Psychologically detailed descriptions of sins of lust are more common than general references to the dispossession of landholders. It is worth noting, however, that, in early Ricardian parliaments, the 'ravishing' of aristocratic women was a recurrent element in complaint about evasion of the common law.[1] Moreover, like the petitions, the tales work over types of unofficial dispute resolution and attempt to draw lines between the licit and illicit according to modes of lordship, service, and household exchange. In each type of text, these lines run along the same principles of outward exchange that recognizes the worship of a deserving community. Again in the *Confessio*, therefore, the boundary of legitimacy (and the social good) is the boundary between reciprocalist lordship and magnificence.

The poem's conception of justice and the preservation of social stability is intimately bound up with its preoccupation with personal *trouthe*. Public order, that is, is produced by the quality that underwrites lasting personal bonds, and which (persistently determinative of worship in the poem) also belongs primarily to an aristocratic honour society. The corollary of personal *trouthe*'s political pre-eminence, then, is that justice and public order must be imagined as sustained by

---

[1] Most of this was down to complaint about private franchises, which by January 1380 was leading with the palatine jurisdiction of Cheshire: *PROME* iii. 42–3, 62, 81, 139, 201. But see also a separate bill for a remedy when women are complicit in their own ravishing: ibid. 139–40 (Oct. 1382; *SR* ii. 27).

a system of enduring, hierarchically privileged personal relations. Against this, the poem depicts opportunistic, collusive association (especially for personal retribution) as destabilizing, motivated by the antithesis of common profit—singular profit.

The confessor's narratives define a sphere of licit unofficial mediations of law most conspicuously through negative example. The disruptive retributive actions of Rosemund, Medea, and Procne all share essential characteristics, and map the negative image of proper dispute resolution. The discursive landmarks in this territory of the improper and destructive are also those of the parliamentary complaint against livery and maintenance, and the Appellant representation of courtier enemies (above, 43–9). In other words, what the *Confessio* assumes to be wrong in the wronged wives' revenge mirrors what the parliamentary texts assume about the lawlessness and oppressions of retainers, maintainers, and counsellor-traitors.

'AND IN HIR CHAMBRE PRIVELY': THE HOUSEHOLD CONTOURS OF RETRIBUTION IN GENIUS'S TALES

Prive is a term central to the *Confessio's* representation of improper retribution. It goes hand in glove with covin, a concept which signals collusion and personal bonds (commercially) strengthened or created for the particular, concerted end at hand. These *prive* connections are dislocated from a wider social context, removed from the constraints of degree and from matrices of worship connecting multiple households. In book 3's tale of Nauplius and the Greeks, the vengefulness of Nauplius is called a 'prive hate' (3. 1015, 1027). The collocation contaminates *prive*-ness with the vicious connotations of the noun to which it is bound. The narrative allows that King Nauplius has been wronged by 'tresoun' (3. 1010) against his son, so its exemplary impetus is directed against his method of retribution rather than his desire for retribution *per se*. The same quality of narrow (or non-existent) socialization, or *prive*-ness, is the key to the self-destructive justice of Rosemund, Medea, and Procne. It is definitive also, for that matter, of the disruptive behaviour of the mothers-in-law in the tale of Constance. The justified vindictiveness of the wronged wives is thus collapsed by their conduct into the wholly unjust vindictiveness of the sultaness and

Domilde. The sultaness embodies envy that works 'prively' (2. 642) and collusively until, 'With fals covine' drawn together for the purpose (2. 674–6), 'Hire clos Envie tho sche spradde' (2. 683–4). The covin, in the *Confessio* and in the livery and maintenance complaint, epitomizes forms of association inimical to good order.[2]

When Rosemund and Procne are confronted by their husbands' sin, their responses are immediately *prive* and collusive misappropriations of *trouthe*. They forge exclusive bonds—or covin—by oath for the specific end of revenge. Their responses are characterized by the private setting of the chamber, and by the narrow containment of knowledge of (and thus responsibility for) their actions. Having concealed during the feast her thoughts about Alboin's grotesque vaunting, Rosemund 'goth to chambre and hath compleigned | Unto a Maide which sche triste, | So that non other wyht it wiste' (1. 2572–4). The pair make 'covenant' for the purpose of revenge (1. 2575–86). From this point onwards, the tale's initial ambience of masculine spectacle and public society is exchanged for one of close feminine intrigue. The lists and the great hall buzzing and glittering with 'perled' garments and the bejewelled skull-cup give way to 'A chambre derk withoute liht' (1. 2603). Similarly, when Procne learns of her sister's plight, her first thoughts are of vengeance and of a covin within the household 'that noman withinne, | Bot only thei that were suore, | [her plan] scholde knowe' (5. 5798–5800). The two sisters are reunited 'In chambre' (5. 5807) and, while setting her revenge in motion, Procne keeps to 'hire chambres' (5. 5873), killing her son 'in hir chambre prively' (5. 5895). The final macabre act of the revenge (discovering it to Tereus) is played out 'at board', but with no indication of a 'public' audience, and too late for any to intervene.

The *Confessio*'s imagination of *prive* revenge intensifies a politics of space in the late medieval great household that has a wider application in reciprocalist discourse and practice. The hall was the focus of the medieval great house. As a site of meals, justice, rest, entertainment, and ceremony, its layout shifted with the various faces of lordship and its

---

[2] See e.g. the Appellants' accusations of 'covyn' and 'meyntenance' against Richard II's adherents in 1388 (*WC* 242, 248, 254); the king's own promise the following year to suppress 'congregaciones, oppressiones, manutenencias, seu conventicula illicita' (*Rot. parl.* iii. 404); and the indictment before king's bench in 1393 of a self-liveried band operating in Yorkshire and comprising named individuals 'with other malefactors of their covin (*de eorum couina*) to the number of eighty' (*KB* vii. 83). Strohm discusses the Yorkshire band in *Hochon's Arrow*, 180–2. For discussion of the negative associations of 'covin' in relation to the 'Good' and Merciless Parliaments' attacks on courtiers and their associates, see above, 46–8, 87.

architecture and routines were crucial to the naturalizing of aristocratic and royal power.[3] Matthew Johnson notes that castle halls were always placed to be visible to the visitor on entry to the courtyard.[4] In Michael Camille's words, the hall's 'symbolic power... continued to dominate both real and imagined domestic architecture' in the late Middle Ages, but high-status domestic buildings increasingly included more exclusive spaces that competed with the hall for political and recreational functions.[5] These spaces, including chambers linked to gardens and chapels, were often for women's use, reinforcing the kind of public/private gender norms that Gower's tales sponsor.[6] But reciprocalist dispositions were challenged when spatial changes impaired the hall as an arena of lordship and the representation of the community that lordship produced. One such change that may have taken hold in the fourteenth century was a tendency for aristocratic families to use chambers for meals and entertainments, separating themselves and their guests from the main body of the household.[7] The withdrawal from the hall could be represented as a kind of insidious privacy and neglect of seigneurial responsibilities. Such critique is expressed in a well-known complaint by Langland's Dame Studie against parsimony:

> 'Elenge is the halle, ech day in the wike,
> Ther the lord ne the lady liketh noght to sitte.
> Now hath ech riche a rule—to eten by hymselve
> In a pryvee parlour for povere mennes sake,
> Or in a chambre with a chymenee, and leve the chief halle
> That was maad for meles, men to eten inne,
> And al to spare to spille that spende shal another.'[8]

---

[3] See Johnson, *Behind the Castle Gate*, 66–70, 78–80, 83–4.

[4] Ibid. 76.

[5] Michael Camille, *Mirror in Parchment: The Luttrell Psalter and the Making of Medieval England* (London, 1998), 120. See also Johnson, *Behind the Castle Gate*, 80–2. Given-Wilson, *Royal Household*, 29.

[6] Johnson, *Behind the Castle Gate*, 81; Roberta Gilchrist, *Gender and Archaeology: Contesting the Past* (London, 1999), 123–8, 138–45, remarking that 'the ideology of female seclusion' diminished once a woman 'had fulfilled her obligation to produce the heir apparent' (142). Arlyn Diamond, focusing on female heirs, argues that 'the division between public and private which the chamber is taken to represent... is a misleading opposition' for actual households and some romances; but in a different context (more closely aligned with heir production), W. M. Ormrod indicates that the bedchambers of royal women had 'more intimate and explicitly sexual' associations than those of royal men: '*Sir Degrevant*', 94–7 (quote at 96); cf. Ormrod, 'In Bed with Joan of Kent', in Wogan-Browne et al. (eds), *Medieval Women: Texts and Contexts* (Turnhout, 2000), 280–4 (quote at 282).

[7] Heal, *Hospitality*, 39–44.

[8] William Langland, *The Vision of Piers Plowman: A Critical Edition of the B-Text*, ed. A. V. C. Schmidt, 2nd edn (London, 1995), 10. 96–102.

Dame Studie uses a language of free and inclusive largesse. She makes the withdrawal of the rich to the 'pryvee parlour' a subject of blame by attributing it to their contempt for the poor (10. 99), and attributes to the hospitality of the 'chief halle' ('maad for meles') an inherent inclusiveness. Gower's villainous Duke Mundus conspires with priests by inviting them to dine and giving them 'mete in prive place' (*CA* 1. 815). Hospitality in the great hall registered social status during large-scale *gesta* or tenant feasts, the entertainment of individual guests and their entourages, and routine meals attended by those who enjoyed bouche of court.[9] Most schematically, it did this by hierarchically ordered seating arrangements. Certain duchy of Lancaster deeds grant retainers seat allocations at particular tables in hall.[10] The chamber and its exclusive (if not necessarily intimate) meetings had much less scope to stage lordship with reference to an expansive community.

The hall holds its ground in the *Confessio*. In a domesticated body politic metaphor, for instance, the lordly regal heart's servant-organs gather their strength for service by 'eating' together in the metaphorical hall (7. 463–89). Apollonius begins his journey back to high status when Archistrates summons him to his hall ('At Souper time'; 8. 705). The sorcerer Nectanabus's transgressiveness is (for readers) amplified and (for spectators in the narrative) publicly afforced by his shape-shifting spectacle in Philip of Macedon's hall, 'In sihte of alle men aboute' (6. 2195). Aeetes in Colchis and Lucretia at Rome receive guests honourably in the hall and are betrayed by them in the chamber. In the tale of the Trump of Death (1. 2021–2253), the king of Hungary's brother gives foolish, jealous counsel in the king's chamber and receives his object lesson in the hall. Medieval audiences of the poem would also presumably have taken the hall for granted as the unspoken setting in numerous scenes of seigneurial public–private practice. The vindication of Florent (1. 1628–64), the marriage feast of Constance and the sultan (2. 681–700), the alliance of Orestes and the duke of Athens (3. 1984–92), and many other adjudications, entertainments, parliaments, councils, and coronations belong most obviously in a great hall. In the flow of these narratives, the hall is so automatic to the political imaginary as to have the status of *doxa*.[11]

---

[9] On the tenant feast, see Heal, 'Reciprocity and Exchange', 183.

[10] National Archives, DL 25/929, 2026, cited in Woolgar (ed.), *Household Accounts*, pt 1, 9. On hierarchical seating, see also Johnson, *Behind the Castle Gate*, 79–80.

[11] For *doxa* as undiscussed, undisputed norms, see Bourdieu, *Theory of Practice*, 164–71, and above, 62. For the place of great halls in a fourteenth-century 'proliferation of

Authority in the great hall—the right to command the dais—authorizes retribution in the *Confessio*. The poem's discourse of collusion and
prive revenge (like the corresponding discourse in the parliamentary
texts) works to restrict the kinds of person who can properly enact
retribution, mediate the law, and organize force through unofficial
personal relations. Not all unofficial force is stigmatized. *Prive* revenge
defines by contrast a field of *legitimate* action. The wronged wives are
excluded from this field because, in the first place, they are not household lords. Legitimate unofficial retributive practices are enacted by the
head of a household, and they are defined by outwardness and worship.
They engage established personal relations that are structured by and
represent worship, and form networks along which justice is implemen-
ted openly—publicly in terms of an aristocratic community. Retribution becomes inclusive of and validated by that community, which
stands as a quantity external to the particular will to retribution,
generalizing retribution's significance. The law (as a universal quantity
ultimately independent of the mechanisms of the king's law) can also
contribute to external validation, and is associated with communal
retribution.

Mundus and Paulina

The first major tale of the *Confessio*—that of Mundus and Paulina—
enacts both sides of the opposition between socially destructive and
productive modes of association. Duke Mundus's covin threatens social
order, but their victim's husband responds through reciprocalist household politics. Mundus's activity is not performed in the pursuit of
justice, but it fits the profile of illicit retributive acts and so further
infects them with resonances of (punished) vice as they occur later in the
poem. Mundus's behaviour is characterized by *prive* collusion. At his
private meal, the normal gift exchange mechanisms of household bond-
ing are perverted as the duke compresses (or commercializes) them in
order to create short-term bonds with the priests of Isis for a particular,
limited purpose:

> This Duck, which *thoghte his love gete*,
> Upon a day hem tuo to mete
> Hath bede, and thei come at his heste;

venues for gaol deliveries and sessions of the peace', see Musson, 'Legal Landmarks'
(quote at 8); and 'Court Venues'.

> Wher that thei hadde a riche feste,
> And after mete in prive place
> This lord, *which wolde his thonk pourchace,*
> To ech of hem yaf thanne a yifte,
> And spak so that be weie of schrifte
> He *drowh hem unto his covine,*
> *To helpe and schape* how he Pauline
> After his lust deceive myhte.
> And thei here *trowthes bothe plyhte,*
> That thei be nyhte hire scholden wynne
> Into the temple...

> (1. 811–24, emphasis added)

Mundus commercializes gift exchange by his expectation of an immediate and specified return on his 'gifts' to the priests.[12]

The duke's misuse of systems of exchange and personal relations is
ultimately redressed by monarchical prerogative (1. 1008–10) and 'be
lawe resonable | Among the wise jugges there' (1. 1030–1), who counsel
the emperor (1. 1018–19) and thus seem to fill a role occupied by the
justices of the king's bench in Gower's time. In the first place, however,
the abuse is countered, and the solution of imperial redress enabled, by a
contrary reliance on personal relations. Against the damage done by
Mundus's collusion, Paulina's husband takes up the potential in existing
social networks. As in the case of Rosemund and Procne, Paulina's resort
upon discovering the tale's sin is the chamber (1. 952–5). Here, however, she turns to her husband and head of her household (who is
wronged rather than the wrongdoer). In his wife's chamber, his thoughts
(again, like Rosemund's and Procne's) turn at once to vengeance. But
the retributive dynamic which he instigates moves outwards from the
chamber from the first:

> His herte stod in sori plit,
> And seide he wolde of that despit
> Be venged, how so evere it falle,
> And sende unto hise frendes alle.

> (1. 989–92)

The friends gather and offer counsel. The patience and measure of this
approach is underlined by the two-day delay before this network acts

---

[12] For the importance to gift exchange of the deferral of counter-giving, enabled by
misrecognition, see Bourdieu, *Theory of Practice*, 4–7.

against Mundus (1. 997–1007). They act by supporting the couple's quarrel with the weight of their worship or *worthinesse*:

> The thridde day sche goth to pleigne
> With many a worthi Citezeine,
> And he with many a Citezein.
>
> (1. 1005–7)

Justice in the tale of Mundus and Paulina depends upon mobilizing a community of worship (Paulina's husband's friends) in witness of established worship (his own).[13]

The tale of Constance

In the following book of the poem, another lord and husband whose wife has fallen prey to deception and dishonour enacts retribution on his own authority. King Allee in the tale of Constance conflates the roles of victim and monarch that are separate in the tale of Mundus and Paulina. Allee also entirely subsumes the role played by the emperor's judges in the earlier tale. Gower, referring to Nicholas Trevet's French chronicle (*c.*1334), has Allee's vengeful wrath explode upon Domilde:

> And lich the fyr which tunder hente,
> In such a rage, as seith the bok,
> His Moder sodeinliche he tok.
>
> (2. 1274–6)

Allee promises her that '"I schal be venged er I go"' (2. 1285), and Domilde is soon dead. In Trevet's 'bok', Alle's retribution against his mother is private and unmediated. He confronts her while she lies naked in her bed and hacks her to death on the spot. In the *Canterbury Tales*, Chaucer more or less follows Trevet, ignoring Gower's extensive modifications to the *Chroniques*' account of the episode. The Man of Law leaves out the domestically and sexually charged site of Alla's revenge, but what sense of privacy is lost with the omission of the vivid image of intimate violence is compensated for by the obscurity

---

[13] Faced with the 1388 Cambridge petition's definition of maintenance, encompassing any who 'takes up or supports another's quarrel to which he is not party by reason of blood or marriage, in order to have the whole or a part of that which is claimed' (*WC* 358), Paulina's husband might object in mitigation that the support is supplied by existing relationships (albeit ones weaker than kinship) and is executed with a lack of acquisitive interest.

in which the narrator cloaks the event (and the absent presence of the fatal bed) with protestations or fillers of conjecture and reportage.[14]

All three accounts—Trevet's, Gower's, and Chaucer's—represent Done-gild/Domilde's death within a household frame, but only Gower fully authorizes the killing. The Ricardian poets replace or elide the bed, and qualify the old woman's death with charges of 'treason' against her bonds of kinship (*CA* 2. 1281; *CT* 2. 895). Nevertheless, neither Trevet nor Chaucer defends the manner of Donegild's death as just. Trevet vividly emphasizes the immoderate anger of the wronged king ('com homme hors de sens'; like a man out of his wits),[15] while Chaucer has the king set out on pilgrimage in repentance particularly of his mother's slaying and 'his wikked werkes' (*CT* 2. 994). Gower, conversely, takes special care to rewrite Domilde's end. Having brought the queen to the brink of destruction in something of the rush of Trevet's account—the command to 'caste hire inne' the fire being issued hard on the heels of her accusation—Gower suddenly holds up, even reverses the momentum of the narrative in order to buttress Domilde's demise with proofs of her guilt:

> And [the king] let a fyr do make tho,
> And bad men forto caste hire inne:
> Bot ferst sche tolde out al the sinne,
> And dede hem alle forto wite
> How sche the lettres hadde write,
> Fro point to point as it was wroght.
> And tho sche was to dethe broght

---

[14] 'But in what wise, certeinly, I noot'; 'out of drede'; 'that may men pleynly rede' (*CT* 2. 892–4). This narratorial hedging enshrouds the incestuous image at the centre of Alla's revenge. The Man of Law's impulse to suppress the incestuous resonances in his tale are much discussed: see Wetherbee, 'Constance and the World', 68–70; Dinshaw, *Chaucer's Sexual Poetics*, 88–90, 100–2; Peter Goodall, '"Unkynde abhomynaciouns" in Chaucer and Gower', *Parergon*, NS 5 (1987), 94–102, 99–100; R. A. Shoaf, '"Unwemmed Custance": Circulation, Property, and Incest in the *Man of Law's Tale*', *Exemplaria*, 2 (1990), 287–302, 295–6; Elizabeth Scala, 'Canacee and the Chaucer Canon: Incest and Other Unnarratables', *Chaucer Review*, 30 (1995–6), 15–39, 21–3; Scanlon, *Narrative, Authority, and Power*, 246–7. Readings that find incest (maternal or paternal) to be a significantly absent presence in Gower's version of the tale include: Margaret Schlauch, *Chaucer's Constance and Accused Queens* (New York, 1927), 132–3; Donavin, *Incest Narratives*, 44–6, 59–62; Allen, 'Chaucer Answers Gower', 641–6; Bullón-Fernández, *Fathers and Daughters*, 75–101.

[15] Margaret Schlauch (ed.), 'The Man of Law's Tale', in W. F. Bryan and Germaine Dempster (eds), *Sources and Analogues of Chaucer's Canterbury Tales* (London, 1941), 176–7 (quote at 176). Schlauch has excerpted the chronicle narrative here (165–81) as 'Trevet's Life of Constance'.

And brent tofore hire Sones yhe:
Wherof these othre, whiche it sihe
And herden how the cause stod,
Sein that the juggement is good,
Of that hir Sone hire hath so served;
For sche it hadde wel deserved
Thurgh tresoun of hire false tunge,
Which thurgh the lond was after sunge,
Constance and every wiht compleigneth.

(2. 1286–1301)

Gower transforms the killing he found in Trevet into a case of explicitly just retribution. The renovation produces public signification for the queen's offence and her son's violent response. Allee's now exemplary vengeance nonetheless remains unsupported by official apparatus. Domilde's secret, private guilt is given communal resonance by a new punishment, and by her own confessional declaration, which 'dede *hem alle* forto wite' (2. 1289, emphasis added). Allee's 'juggement', in turn, is ratified by an informal and presumably affinity-based group (2. 1294–7). It is unclear where all this takes place, but a chamber seems an unlikely venue for a pyre.

Gower's revision (so that death in bed becomes death by burning) further means that Domilde suffers the manner of death usually reserved for treasonous women in the late fourteenth century.[16] Without representing legal process, Gower is able to invoke the public meaning which the criminal law attaches to private acts in the punitive displays it organizes. Similarly, the import of Domilde's admission and the witnessing group's ratification of her doom is diffused 'thurgh the lond' by gossip. As Patricia Meyer Spacks contends, gossip functions as an unofficial interface between public and private, able to give 'private detail general meaning'.[17] Gower makes a significant number of adjustments

[16] See *WC* 322–3 n. 7; Barbara Hanawalt, 'The Female Felon in Fourteenth-Century England', *Viator*, 5 (1974), 253–68, 265; W. R. J. Barron, 'The Penalties for Treason in Medieval Life and Literature', *Journal of Medieval History*, 7 (1981), 187–202, 190; Strohm, *Hochon's Arrow*, 122 and n. 1.

[17] Patricia Meyer Spacks, *Gossip* (New York, 1985), 262. Strohm connects Spacks's explanation of gossip specifically to a case of domestic treason and the burning of an unfaithful wife (*Hochon's Arrow*, 122). On gossip, see also Susan E. Phillips, 'Gossip and (Un)official Writing', in Strohm (ed.), *Middle English*, 476–90; and *Transforming Talk: The Problem with Gossip in Late Medieval England* (University Park, Pa, 2007).

to his source which produce a legitimation of Allee's unofficial retributive behaviour. All operate by projecting the private and chamber-bound outwards, but none violates or replaces the unofficial personal relations which frame the episode. Rather, the witnessing of Allee's act incorporates a stabilizing breadth of such relations beyond the tale's fractured bond of kinship.

The False Bachelor and the chamber

One of the *Confessio's* most involved illustrations of the importance of household-based relations to public order and social structure occurs in book 2 shortly after the tale of Constance. The tale of the False Bachelor is fundamentally an exemplum about the coordination of socially constitutive exchange by household-based relations and the importance of the principle of outwardness and wide networks of support in protecting these exchange operations. So much is intimated by the classification of the tale's evildoer alone. At the narrative's determining moment, when the emperor's son, adventuring incognito, imparts the 'conseil' (2. 2659) by which his confidant will betray him, this confidant-knight is called a 'Bacheler'—the title by which he will be known from this point in the tale onwards. Described at the outset as a member of the prince's household ('A kniht of his to whom he triste'; 2. 2525), the knight is subsequently identified by a particular kind of household position the defining characteristic of which is intimacy. Gower's text tends to equate such intimacy with dangerous *prive*-ness and, accordingly, this false bachelor's household position comes to emblematize his narrow, destabilizing politics.

J. M. W. Bean distinguishes three major semantic strands operating within the term 'bachelor' during the fourteenth century.[18] Two, closely related to each other by common connotations of youth, carry meanings of marital status and social rank. The bachelor, where these senses apply, is a young man belonging to the aristocratic social stratum but unmarried or on the threshold of the rank of knight (perhaps enjoying sufficient social status and means to make a knightly identity without having been knighted).[19] The third strand of meaning available in

[18] J. M. W. Bean, ' "Bachelor" and Retainer', *Medievalia et Humanistica*, NS 3 (1972), 117–31, esp. 123–4.

[19] Bean notes that the threshold sense of proximity to a ceremony of knighthood does not exclude knightly status (ibid. 118, 123). The estates taxonomy of the poll tax of 1379 groups the category of bachelor with that of esquires with sufficient resources to become knights, in a 20s band below the 40s tier of barons, bannerets, and wealthy knights (*PROME* iii. 57–8). On the incentives for landowners eager to claim knightly status

'bachelor' pertains to a household relationship. In the household registers of John of Gaunt and the Black Prince, the term designates a
knightly retainer belonging to the lord's chamber. Bean surmises from
these records that the duke's and prince's bachelors comprised a distinct
inner group of household knights enjoying a position of intimacy and
special trust in relation to their lord, and occupying key administrative
posts as stewards, constables, and chamberlains.[20] In the retaining
discourse of the registers, this household status is definitive, and can
exclude connotations of youth, marital status, and economic resources
belonging to the other semantic strands of bachelorhood. A chamber
bachelor, in other words, could be a married, knighted landowner.

According to Bean, the household-chamber sense of 'bachelor' was
not current in textual matrices outside the administrative records of
great households. In poetic texts of the late fourteenth century, 'bachelor' tended to be used according to its sense of youth, social rank, and
spousal eligibility, as well, possibly, as secondary connotations of frivol-
ity or rashness. Gower is certainly able to deploy it in this way. The lover
Acis, like Chaucer's twenty-something pilgrim squire, is 'A Bacheler in
his degree', a 'yonge knyht' and 'lusti'.[21] The collocation of 'lusti' and
'bacheler', with its overtones of youthful exuberance, was commonplace, and Chaucer's 'lusty bacheler' Squire has another Gowerian
counterpart in the 'lusti Bacheler' Pyramus (*CA* 3. 1343). Where such
youths are described by a bond with another knight or a noble, the bond
is typically one of kinship and not formal service. Both Pyramus and the
Squire are identified as sons.[22] Chaucer, however, seems also to use
'bachelor' in the household sense in 'The Clerk's Tale' when Marquis
Walter entertains 'of his retenue the bachelrye' at his wedding feast along
with invited 'Lordes and ladyes in his compaignye' (*CT* 4. 267–73).
Bean himself provides further evidence that this sense penetrated texts

nevertheless to avoid being knighted (involving military and official service obligations),
see Carpenter, *Locality and Polity*, 39–40.

[20] Bean, '"Bachelor" and Retainer', 119–22; and see e.g. *Register of Edward the Black
Prince* (London, 1930–3), i. 128–9; ii. 45–6, 182 (600 mark annuity to Sir James de
Audeley); iv. 12; Sydney Armitage-Smith (ed.), *John of Gaunt's Register (1371–1375)*,
Camden Soc. 3rd ser. 20–1 (London, 1911), i, nos 819, 849, 855 (Sir Walter Blount; cf.
the reference to Blount as 'nostre tres cher bacheler' at ii, no. 1179); Lodge and
Somerville (eds), *John of Gaunt's Register, 1379–1383*, pt 1, nos 24, 40; 'Unpublished
Indentures', in Walker, *Lancastrian Affinity*, 292–303, nos 2, 5.

[21] *CA* 2. 124–31; cf. *CT* 1. 79–80: 'With hym ther was his sone, a yong Squier, | A
lovyere and a lusty bacheler'.

[22] *CA* 3. 1343; *CT* 1. 79. Cf. *CT* 1. 99–100: the Squire is 'servysable' (1. 99) in the
role of courteous son rather than retainer.

other than domestic records. In Chandos herald's life of the Black Prince (*c.*1385), another lord is attended by household knights at a major station on life's journey. Bachelors are included in the select group of adherents, 'Counte, baron et bachiler', who surround the prince at his deathbed.[23] Sometimes Gower, too, uses *bacheler* primarily in its household sense. The false bachelor of book 2 is introduced by his relationship and bond of service with the prince (2. 2525), and is designated 'seruus' (servant) in the Latin summary of the tale (gloss at 2. 2503). His youth is indicated (2. 2537), but no emphasis is laid on his (initial) unmarried status. Household position is again the material qualification of *bacheler* status for one Taliarchus, who is in the service of King Antiochus in the tale of Apollonius of Tyre (8. 503). Both the false bachelor and Taliarchus are essentially intimates of their respective lords and exchange counsel with them (8. 504–12). Indeed, as I have noted, the Roman bachelor is first labelled as such on an occasion of close counsel.

What is noticeable about Gower's chamber-knight bachelors, beyond their relationship of intimate service, is first that they are essentially vicious characters, and secondly that their viciousness is bound up with the exclusiveness of their mode of service. When Gower attaches the unmarried sense of *bacheler* to a negative exemplar in Pyramus (3. 1343), the youth's 'folhaste' is not so knowing, blameworthy, or sinister as the evil will of the false bachelor and of Taliarchus (sent to poison Apollonius). The chamber knights are at once extremely socially disruptive and wholly representative of the major service discourse that the poem attacks. Their designs of disordering are enabled (if not finally achieved in the case of Taliarchus) by the exclusive, intensive, *prive* service relations and collusion which the poem opposes to extensive household connections and networks.

Momentarily, there is exact linguistic convergence between Gower's poem and contemporary complaints about livery and maintenance when Taliarchus is dubbed a 'feloun bacheler' (8. 503), summoned by his lord to an urgent criminal task. He fits the bill, so to speak, of the felonious retainers who were objects of legislative efforts by the Cambridge commons in 1388—the 'persons indicted or outlawed for felony (*felonie*), or common thieves, murderers, or other felons' (*WC* 358) who were supposedly retained to impede the king's justice and administration.

---

[23] Chandos herald, *La Vie du Prince Noir by Chandos Herald*, ed. Diana B. Tyson (Tübingen, 1975), l. 4133; cf. ll. 612, 2978 (where bachelorhood seems to indicate youth and knightly promise); Bean, ' "Bachelor" and Retainer', 118.

Usually with less specific overlap with parliamentary discourse, the chamber relationship is the common site of anxiety about exclusive lordship and service across a number of tales in the *Confessio*. The chamber-knight bachelor did not belong by definition to a truncated household structure, but Gower's chamber malefactors thrive (or survive) on sealed-off social clusters or nodes. Antiochus colludes with 'his prive consailer' (8. 504) and inauthentic social contact on Taliarchus's secret mission emphasizes the inaccessibility of the pair's relationship: 'for he wolde noght be knowe, | Desguised thanne he goth him oute' (8. 520–1). In another galley journey arranged by 'prive conseil' (2. 2538), the false bachelor is the only companion taken east by his prince, who takes no larger retinue. Like Taliarchus, the prince's bachelor is deceptive, and 'feigneth with a fals visage | That he was glad, bot his corage | Was al set in an other wise' (2. 2671–3). The two servants depend in different ways upon deception to protect and to exploit the exclusive nature of their lord–bachelor bonds, preventing the exchange of knowledge beyond that privileged relationship.

The service of bachelors and chambermaids embodies suspect *priveness* in the *Confessio*. The bachelors' special service relationships resemble those enjoyed by the chamber servants of Rosemund (the chambermaid Glodeside) and Medea. All four servants pursue highly exclusive and collusive 'prive' behaviour, all of which goes amiss, and which in three cases (excepting Taliarchus's) leads to ruin. The introductions of Glodeside and the false bachelor share a formula. Rosemund complains

> Unto a Maide which sche triste,
> So that non other wyht it wiste.
>
> (1. 2573–4)

The emperor's son confides in

> A kniht of his to whom he triste,
> So that his fader nothing wiste.
>
> (2. 2525–6)

Medea's maid is a constant go-between, facilitating the secret liaisons of Jason and her mistress at Colchis.[24] Rosemund and Glodeside add another layer to the impression of the chamber bond as dangerously intensive and subversive when their conspiracy ensnares Helmege, 'Which was the kinges Boteler, | A proud a lusti Bacheler' (1. 2593–4). In accord with

[24] See e.g. *CA* 5. 3495–7, 3648–9, 3794–3800, 3860–3.

other fourteenth-century suspicion of the chamber as social space, all of these privileged, intimate servants, and their tales, argue that the chamber is an extension of a lord or lady's *prive* intent and too narrow a platform for the great household's action in society.

The False Bachelor and the community of worship

The tale of the False Bachelor is in the first place an exemplum about the importance of *trouthe* in maintaining household relations. The bacheler 'Is swore' (2. 2536) to support the prince in his knight errantry. But the tale is also about the proper structure and reach of systems to which these relations belong. The bond between the emperor's son and his bachelor breaks down internally, whereas other chamber bonds in the poem (such as Rosemund and Glodeside's) project disorder from a fused core. Nonetheless, the prince and bachelor's bond is subversive because of the suspect narrowness that it shares with these other relationships. The prince's dying words tell only part of this story, explaining that he has been undone and supplanted 'for that he his conseil tolde' (2. 2724–5). The prince and sultan's marriage plan is thwarted because it was disclosed to one, untrue confidant (his bachelor), but equally because it is divorced from a local network of relations that would support the prince's worship.[25] The marriage of the sultan's daughter is decided before a Persian community of worship, comprising the lords of the sultan's court (2. 2685–9). The slain sultan had secretly bequested his daughter's ring to the emperor's son as a sign of his choice in her marriage. Displaced from his own supporting networks, however, the unknown Roman visitor can find no help in taking 'Querelle ayein his oghne man' (2. 2703) when the bachelor flourishes the purloined ring before the court. The prince is without anyone else who might have known of his receipt of the ring or, more pointedly, would know his worship and the topsy-turvy disruption of preferring his servant to him. As things stand, he has no purchase in the community of worship that confirms the sultan's daughter's match and 'He mihte as thanne noght ben herd, | So that his cleym is unansuerd' (2. 2705–6). In the absence of established networks of worship and personal relation, extra-legal contestatory processes that resolve disputes and guarantee proper social order cannot operate.

[25] On Lévi-Straussian social theory and women's status as objects of exchange within patriarchal gift economies, see above, 132–72.

Eventually, the bachelor's offence *is* addressed because of the recognition of worship by the aristocratic community. With his erstwhile chamber knight 'coroned Lord and Sire' (2. 2710), the Roman prince finally represents his salient credentials to the locally powerful:

> He sende for the worthieste
> Of al the lond and ek the beste,
> And tolde hem al the sothe tho,
> That he was Sone and Heir also
> Of themperour of grete Rome,
> And how that thei togedre come,
> This kniht and he . . .

(2. 2717–23)

It comes too late for the dying prince, but his credentials are confirmed and the intervention of the Persian nobles corrects the bachelor's 'tresoun' and ensures that it does not produce a lasting fissure in the normal social and moral order. The intervention is underpinned by a universal belief in the personal quality of *trouthe* as the fundamental guarantor of exchanges and relationships, and it encompasses the restoration of the dislocated community of worship. Once the 'worthieste' of Persia have acted, and arrested the knight, there is a general acceptance 'Thurghout the lond' that 'His oghne untrowthe him schal depose' (2. 2748–50). The discovery of this 'untrowthe' is a process saturated with worship. The Persians approach the Roman emperor 'With honour and gret reverence' (2. 2752), and he dispatches an embassy of 'many a worthi Romein' (2. 2761). The presence of this worshipful body reimposes a prior order of status and reputation on the 'liege tretour' (2. 2762), and is sufficient to secure his capitulation and resubordination of himself to 'his worthi lord':

> And whan thei thider come were,
> This kniht him hath confessed there
> How falsly that he hath him bore,
> Wherof his worthi lord was lore.

(2. 2763–6)

The make-up of the Roman embassy, which retraces at the end of the tale the path between Rome and Persia taken by the prince at its beginning, is particularly significant. An antidote to the prince's *prive* and perilously exclusive party, the embassy is led by the emperor's own 'Stieward . . . | With many a worthi Romein eke' (2. 2760–1). Given the comparable and sometimes overlapping household positions of bachelors and stewards observable in late fourteenth-century administrative records (and recalling also Helmege's steward-bachelor position in Gower's poem), the detail is particularly resonant. The second, corrective Roman party to Persia replicates the prominence of a lord's privileged servant, reintegrating the role in an extensive, worship-marked group.

THE PLACE OF THE LAW: UNOFFICIAL AND OFFICIAL JUSTICE IN LIVERY AND MAINTENANCE PETITIONS

The corrections of domestic treason and *prive* collusion staged in the *Confessio* are not in themselves independent of law. The false bachelor is executed in Rome only after an excursus into a kind of comparative law, whereby some 'founden such a weie | That he schal noght be ded in Perse' (2. 2768–9), and a change of jurisdictions is required. Duke Mundus's priestly co-conspirators are condemned, as we have seen, 'be lawe resonable | Among the wise jugges' (1. 1030–1) of the emperor's court and counsel. The principles of justice and public order bound up in the discourse of reciprocalist lordship do not exclude the common law or a surrogate for it (such as the central and secular law of Genius's Rome or Persia). The reciprocalist great household discourse imagines the law as a basically unified and unchanging authority that is always mediated by (and thereby subordinated to) personal *trouthe* according to certain normative forms of personal relation and local networks of worship.

The law's administration, therefore, is the most significantly contested ground between reciprocalist lordship and a discourse which sponsors the centralized mechanisms of the king's law. Within the representative confines of the household, the extensive, hierarchically ordered personal networks of reciprocalist lordship are most obviously opposed to *prive* collusion and the treason that subverts household ties. In particular relation to law, on the other hand, reciprocalist lordship is defined against and threatened by notions of central legal bureaucracy—a system outside and enveloping the great household. With its primary reliance on the technology of writing, on documentary evidence, on universal, literal interpretative principles, and on objective standards of truth (or 'sooth'), this system cannot accommodate aristocratic reliance on worship and bonds of personal *trouthe*. Green has extensively analysed the tensions and conflict in fourteenth-century England between traditional conceptions of law and the centralized king's law in terms of the latter's literate character. He argues that the consolidation of bureaucratic support for written law during the period enhanced the sanctity of the letter of the law and entrenched a positivist, literal formalism in its interpretation and administration.[26]

The written law administered in the royal courts and by central commissions like those of trailbaston, constrained all consumers of justice within a single, literate, and literalist 'straitjacket'.[27] It made no allowance for local conditions and intra-community power balances, and it produced absolute results, inhibiting mediatory strategies and flexible solutions.[28] Contemporary reaction to the king's law and its centralized mechanisms did not attack the notion of law *per se*, but often expressed dissatisfaction with the justice brought from Westminster by the king's officials, in the form of a nostalgia for an imagined past in which the legal order recognized *trouthe*. Gower's imagination of the golden age in the *Confessio*'s prologue suggests in its perfect 'vnicolor' laws and identity between 'word' and 'conceite' (prol. 113) an interpretative univocality which necessarily corresponded to *trouthe* and so produced 'ryhtwisnesse' (prol. 109). The revised epilogue extrapolates this logic into a degraded present in which *trouthe* and laws are sundered:

> And forto lokyn ovyrmore,
> Wher of the poeple pleigneth sore,
> Toward the lawis of oure lond,
> Men sein that trouthe hath broke his bond
> And with brocage is goon aweie,
> So that no man can se the weie
> Wher forto fynde rightwisnesse.

> (8. 3029–35)

Now the laws, their administration no longer mediated by personal virtue, have become instruments of injustice.[29]

Writing and law

Literate technology was yoked to competing traditionalist and progressive agendas in relation to the production of law. The conservative position,

---

[26] Green, *Crisis of Truth*, esp. 137–41, 288.   [27] Ibid. 133.
[28] Ibid. 127–33.   [29] See also ibid. 165–205.

according to which personal *trouthe* and not legal innovation enabled justice, emphasized for writing the function of preserving laws in the written record rather than that of creating new laws. Landlords adopted manor court rolls by the end of the thirteenth century to record tenancy changes, dispute settlements, and declarations of estate custom.[30] Along this line of thinking, the role of the king as a supreme central power was not to make law but to guard it as an absolute and unchanging value.[31] The coronation oath which Richard II first swore in 1377 and renewed eleven years later seems to have drawn a deliberate distinction between the established laws, customs, and franchises of Edward the Confessor and earlier kings on the one hand, and modern statute law on the other. The first promise of the oath is to preserve the earlier laws. The fourth and final promise is to observe and enforce the laws that the commonalty has chosen or will choose.[32] H. G. Richardson has argued that the first promise refers to a particular legal collection (or type of collection) in circulation in the fourteenth century, which comprised the Confessor's laws and other Anglo-Saxon and ancient collections.[33] The oath could thus be appealed to in order to privilege a set of fixed earlier laws over modern legislation, constraining new legislation by the implication that it must not abrogate the ancestral laws. Meanwhile, prejudice against central lawmaking (at least without the initiative of the commonalty) might be inferred from the fourth promise, which is the oath's only direct reference to the creation of new laws.

The *Confessio*, similarly, valorizes scholarly and poetic writing as preservational. Dominant medieval ideas about authoritative knowledge or *auctoritas* venerated the distant past, and Gower is unusual in degree, not kind, in his strategy of authorizing his writing by its strong connection to 'olde bokes'. His major project in English embraces a less authoritative language than his earlier long poems in French and (especially) Latin, but it scaffolds the English verse with Latin and remains profoundly engaged

---

[30] Clanchy, *Memory to Written Record*, 97–8.

[31] See Green, *Crisis of Truth*, 237–47; cf. Carpenter, 'Law, Justice and Landowners', 210–11. Green remarks that 'while societies are in a state of transition from memory to written record . . . the threat that writing poses to their customary law will often appear far less serious than the promise it holds out of being able [to] protect such law against change' (*Crisis of Truth*, 240).

[32] For texts of Richard's coronation oath, see *Fœdera*, iii/3. 63; *Anonimalle Chronicle*, ed. Galbraith, 109–10. For his renewal of the oath in 1388, see *WC* 294, 342. On the possible relationships of the oath to the king's legislative authority, see H. G. Richardson, 'The English Coronation Oath', *Speculum*, 24 (1949), 44–75; Green, *Crisis of Truth*, 241–2; Saul, *Richard II*, 25.

[33] Richardson, 'Coronation Oath', 60–4.

with *auctors*: in terms of medieval models, Gower's role in making the *Confessio* is most openly that of guiding, transmitting compiler rather than truth-making *auctor*.[34] Although King Richard, in an early version of the poem, is said to have asked Gower for 'Som newe thing' directed at the king's 'hihe worthinesse' (prol. 49–53), the poem opens with a different view of writing. Gower locates his book in a continuum beside the books 'Of hem that writen ous tofore' (prol. 1), and presents himself less as writing new matter than as writing old, authoritative material '*of newe*' (prol. 6, emphasis added)—in a currently accessible manner that includes the use of English (prol. 22–4). The explanation introducing the tale of Dives and Lazarus—placed there because Gower is about to present Gospel material in English—can stand as a statement of the poem's general purpose in translating biblical, classical, and more recent matter. English is written 'for the more knoulechinge | Of trouthe' (6. 982–3). The purpose of *compilatio* (the new transmission of authority) is to recover universal truth from the past for the degraded present.

The present is far gone in decline, the prologue especially insists, and a diminished regard for authoritative writings is one grave symptom that the world is 'lassed' (prol. 56) from the 'daies olde, | Whan that the bokes weren levere [more dear]' (prol. 36–7). The falling off of learning means, for instance, that now 'fewe understonde' the natural truths of alchemy transmitted in the books of Avicenna (Abu Ali Sina; 980–1037) and, it seems, other alchemists (4. 2606–32). These books are misunderstood, Genius says, 'pleinli as thei stonde' (4. 2613)—an ambiguous phrase suggesting that the books require glossing or other mediation but also that they carry *auctoritas* openly and truly (for a competent reader).[35]

---

[34] For contemporary ideas of writerly roles, including *auctor* and *compilator*, see A. J. Minnis, *Medieval Theory of Authorship: Scholastic Literary Attitudes in the Later Middle Ages*, 2nd edn (Aldershot, Hants, 1988), 94–103; Wogan-Browne et al. (eds), *The Idea of the Vernacular: An Anthology of Middle English Literary Theory, 1280–1520* (Exeter, 1999), 4–12, 19–105, 331–52. For Gower's writing in this context, see Minnis, *Theory of Authorship*, 168–90 (demonstrating Gower's 'claim of limited *auctoritas*' and self-fashioning as a 'modern author'; 190, 209). For the *Confessio*'s self-authorizing Latin apparatus, including commentaries, see also Derek Pearsall, 'Gower's Latin in the *Confessio Amantis*', in A. J. Minnis (ed.), *Latin and Vernacular: Studies in Late-Medieval Texts and Manuscripts* (Cambridge, 1989); Siân Echard, 'Glossing Gower, in Latin, in English, and *in absentia*: The Case of Bodleian Ashmole 35', in Yeager (ed.), *Re-Visioning Gower*, 237–9 and n. 3.

[35] Cf. the conjunction of (ethical) *trouthe* and *plein* (spoken) language in the politically inconclusive exemplum of the trial of Catiline's conspirators in book 7 (ll. 1595–1628).

Failures of enthusiasm and competence in modern 'lore' only underline writing's ability to preserve ancient historical and philosophical truth. They tease at a great furtive hope implicit in Gower's project—that if 'a burel clerk' (a lay or merely 'common' clerk; prol. 52) can release such truth 'of newe', then he may just prove to be 'An other such as Arion' (prol. 1054) and usher in a new golden age.

Ideas of law in the *Confessio* are equally nostalgic. The concept of a kingship that preserves a fixed and monumental body of law, and guarantees this preservation by the power of sworn *trouthe*, finds an apotheosis in the tale of Lycurgus retold by Gower in book 7 of the *Confessio*. The tale opens with a vision of an Athenian society reminiscent of the prologue's golden age in its combination of law, *trouthe*, and hierarchy:

> In a Cronique I rede thus
> Of the rihtful Ligurgius,
> Which of Athenis Prince was,
> Hou he the lawe in every cas,
> Wherof he scholde his poeple reule,
> Hath set upon so good a reule,
> In al this world that cite non
> Of lawe was so wel begon
> Forth with the trouthe of governance.
> Ther was among hem no distance,
> Bot every man hath his encress;
> Ther was withoute werre pes,
> Withoute envie love stod;
> Richesse upon the comun good
> And noght upon the singuler
> Ordeigned was, and the pouer
> Of hem that weren in astat
> Was sauf: wherof upon debat
> Ther stod nothing, so that in reste
> Mihte every man his herte reste.

(7. 2917–36)

The uncontested authority of those who are 'in astat' ensures that laws scarcely need administering (in the absence of 'debat'). Lycurgus then executes a ruse of 'rihtwisnesse' on the Athenians, having them swear an oath to keep his laws until he returns to Athens, before leaving the city forever 'So that Athenis, which was bounde, | Nevere after scholde be relessed, | Ne thilke goode lawe cessed' (7. 3004–6). The tale then precipitates a glorious commemorative listing of originary lawmakers, 'Of hem that ferst the lawes founde' (7. 3023) in various civilizations, which includes Lycurgus and Athens (7. 3040–61). The tale and the celebration of lawbringers locates ideal legislative activity in the past. Kingship is construed as a limitless power of self-restraint, able through its own self-legitimating discursive strategies (Lycurgus secures his aim by counterfeit divine sanction for his laws) to fix the character and to guarantee the continuity of law. The king of Athens seeks an eternalization of law, hoping by his trickery 'For evere after his deth to rihte | The cite which was him betake' (7. 3016–17) with law that 'Mihte afterward for evere laste' (7. 2945).[36] The attitude to law foregrounded by the exemplum is extremely conservative. The law preserves social stasis; legal change and innovation are imagined only as a detrimental taking away. Lycurgus's anxiety is that '"mi lawe | Amonges you ne be with-drawe"' (7. 2983–4), and the narrative entertains no concept of legislative incrementation.

The livery ordinance of 1390

Turning once more to the late fourteenth-century parliamentary public order debates, I would suggest that they illuminate conservative four-teenth-century discourses of justice. These discourses direct suspicion towards the mechanisms of the king's law, both judicial and legislative. In so far as the writing of law is valuable, it is as a cultural and social preservative, fixing established laws and crystallizing or making more clearly manifest and enforceable established customs. The commons' petitions on livery and maintenance, and related legislation, demon-strate a local lordship discourse and its constitutive assumptions in collision with a discourse of central, official legal authority. While any appeal to statute-making draws concern for public order into the orbit of the king's law, the commons' legislative approach to the question of maintenance and forms of association in the 1380s is notable for its decentralizing and even nostalgic attitude towards the written law. Indeed, as Christine Carpenter has remarked, the dominant character of commons petitions dealing with the administration of justice during the period was that of efforts to roll back royal justice from the provinces,

---

[36] For a fuller reading of the tale as an exemplum of unlimited royal authority, see Scanlon, *Narrative, Authority, and Power*, 287–90.

to exclude and fend off the intrusions of officers and arms of the king's law into the localities.[37]

Commons under Edward III made determined efforts to keep the king's general commissions of trailbaston and oyer and terminer, the eyre court, and the itinerant king's bench at their distance, or even to eliminate them. This antagonism survived into Richard II's reign at a level of abiding wariness, after much had been done to reduce such machinery or to assimilate it to the control of local men of substance.[38] Foremost in this assimilation were the peace commissions. By the 1380s and 1390s, commissions composed of magnates, professional lawyers, and gentry meant that local landed interests were well represented in shire-level administration of the common law.[39] The composition and jurisdiction of the commissions were still contested. Magnates and their stewards were excluded in 1387 until their restoration in 1389, apparently with the design of reducing external or deputized influence where great lords were absentees or did not have their major estates in the region. Further reform, addressing the quorum in 1394, aimed to make local men of law more independent in the trial of felonies. The gentry in parliament also continued in this period to seek expanded authority for the peace commissions, especially over determination in felony cases (which gentry JPs enjoyed again in 1380–2 and 1389–94). The 1388 Cambridge petition seeks for JPs the authority to determine in maintenance cases, and similar efforts are made in livery petitions of the 1390s.[40] Alterations of membership and authority notwithstanding, the

---

[37] Carpenter, 'Law, Justice and Landowners', 228–9. On the impact of the central machinery of law in the localities, of which the commons petitions in question are repercussions, see Clanchy, 'Law, Government, and Society', 77–8; and 'Law and Love', 64–5; Richard W. Kaeuper, 'Law and Order in Fourteenth-Century England: The Evidence of Special Commissions of Oyer and Terminer', *Speculum*, 54 (1979), 734–84 (which assumes firmly, however, a 'background of disorder endemic in medieval society'; 735); Nigel Saul, 'Conflict and Consensus in English Local Society', in Taylor and Childs (eds), *Politics and Crisis*, 48–52; R. L. Storey, 'Liveries and Commissions of the Peace 1388–90', in Du Boulay and Barron (eds), *Reign of Richard II*, 133–4; Green, *Crisis of Truth*, 182–6.

[38] See *PROME* ii. 128, 141, 148, 202, 286, 305; iii. 18 (against forest and exchequer officials, and the Marshalsea), 119, 140, 200, 223, 267, 468–9, 472. On the late medieval expansion of local government, and its transfer to local control, see Carpenter, *Locality and Polity*, 41–2, 44, 48, 348; Saul, 'Conflict and Consensus', 51–2; cf. Kaeuper, 'Law and Order', esp. 749–74.

[39] On the fourteenth-century peace commissions, see Storey, 'Liveries and Commissions of the Peace', and the works cited above, 178–9 nn. 7–9.

[40] *WC* 358; *PROME* iii. 307, 345. Saul discusses the authority to determine as part of a thirteenth- and fourteeth-century gentry 'strategy designed to assert control over the very

peace commissions had by now superseded general commissions and the eyre visits of central justices in the administration of the common law, and were often working in tandem with those justices when they toured on assize and gaol delivery.

When concern with local lawlessness intensified in Richard II's parliaments, the same principles of local aristocratic justice preferred to intervention by central government remained intact and influential. In fact, the most persistent sequence of protest about unpunished oppressions and extortions was directed principally (and somewhat forlornly) at the royal palatine jurisdiction of Cheshire.[41] These petitions allow that marcher and palatine lords should be the ones to enforce (and profit materially from) justice against their own adherents (especially *PROME* iii. 201, 308). The commons' approach to the twinned problems of new liveries and maintenance, meanwhile, was fundamentally directed at defending an assumed customary responsibility of the nobility as the guarantors of good order at a local level. The 1388 Cambridge petition stands out for the lengths to which its drafters went to define unlawful maintenance without impinging on unofficial interventions in the law's operations under the umbrella of established aristocratic networks, but it is only explicitly stating assumptions that are shared by other commons legislation (above, 192–3).

The livery and maintenance petitions view the written law as a means to protect this aristocratic order. They imagine it as a formally non-complex preservative, a vehicle for restating an existing set of customs. New law should refound these customs against erosion by innovative social practices without enhancing the central legal bureaucracy most closely associated with the literate technology of law. The 1388 Cambridge petition and the unenrolled petition against badges, which may also belong to the 1380s,[42] presuppose an authoritative model of justice by reciprocalist lordship. Most strikingly, the unenrolled petition's assumptions are encoded in a

[Crown] institutions that threatened them' ('Conflict and Consensus', 51–2, quote at 51). Verduyn is more sceptical that the parliamentary gentry had any consolidated approach to mid-fourteenth-century jurisdictional changes but finds a feature of their petitions to be 'general support for gentry involvement in judicial commissions' ('Early Justices of the Peace', 92).

[41] *PROME* iii. 42 (Oct. 1378), 62 (Apr. 1379), 81 (Jan. 1380), 139 (Oct. 1382), 201 (Nov. 1384), 280 (Nov. 1390), 295 (Nov. 1391), 308 (Jan. 1393), 440 and *SR* ii. 118–19 (Oct. 1399). For Richard II and Cheshire, see Saul, *Richard II*, 172, 392–4; Davies, 'Richard II and the Principality of Chester'.

[42] See above, 189 n. 34.

restricted focus on livery badges and an uncomplicated view of the law. These elements are thrown into relief when read against a text that contributes to the same public order debate but was produced by Richard II's royal government outside parliament. This livery law of 1390 was an ordinance of the king's council and takes the form of proclamations from the king to individual sheriffs.[43] It contains elements that contradict the dominant assumptions informing the commons' petitions on the same issues—specifically, a wider concern with all forms of liveried retaining, a blanket formulation of maintenance in strict opposition to formal law, and a direct emphasis on the operations of that law.

Whatever the correct date of the unenrolled petition, both it and the ordinance clearly belong to the same discursive matrix of public order and justice. Each speaks the same language, recognizable in protest against the oppression of the commons and in complementary appeal to the singular standard of the law. But visions of the law differ. The unenrolled petition rhetorically quarantines good law against present innovation. It repeatedly yokes the health of 'la ley de la terre' (the law of the land) to the threatened unity and peace of the past.[44] The substance of its request is that the king refortify the nostalgized past and the law it contains, purging the traces of the contaminated present:

> [liveries of badges] ought to be annulled and withdrawn in preservation (*adnulles et retretez en sustenance*) of loyal allegiance to your righteous laws and customs which were held and used without division among your liege people and the commonalty in the time of your most noble progenitors.[45]

The ordinance of 1390 is much more interested in a technology of law, current and complex. It opens with a purposeful royal acknowledgement of recent complaints about lawlessness, expressly mentioning the Cambridge and Westminster parliaments of autumn 1388 and the winter just passed (*SR* ii. 74). Yet the ordinance by no means simply rubber-stamps the petitions it adduces to authorize itself.[46] It pays far more attention to the secure administration of the law, far less to any acts or ambience of public disorder itself. Where the livery petitions reiterate a trope of 'great and unbearable oppressions and extortions' (*PROME* iii. 265), and the bills on the effects of palatine franchises recite violent litanies of robbery, beating, burning, ravishing, maiming,

---

[43] Storey, 'Liveries and Commissions of the Peace', 144–6. See *SR* ii. 74–5 for the text of the ordinance.
[44] National Archives, SC 8/100/4985, printed in Saul, 'Abolition of Badges', 314.
[45] Ibid. 315.   [46] *WC* 356; *PROME* iii. 265, 266.

and destroying, the ordinance features a conspectus of ways in which the workings of the legal system can be perverted. Its villains are not felons and brigands but 'diverses maintenours menours barettours procurours et embraceours de quereles et enquestes en paiis' (diverse maintainers, instigators, barrators, procurers, and embracers of quarrels and inquests in the country; *SR* ii. 74). All these terms carry a sense of fraudulent instigation or manipulation of legal process.

The livery petitions scarcely imagine legal process. The ordinance's much more detailed texture evinces a correspondingly greater interest in formal legal process, along with a distinct bias in its favour. In the petitions, maintenance explains the main evil—intolerable disorder. For the ordinance, however, the manipulations of legal process it cites *are* the 'evil deeds' to which the possession of livery emboldens retainers. Indeed, the intent behind the ordinance seems to be to denounce any possible form of non-formal interference with legal process, violent or otherwise, carried on by persons of any social status beneath the nobility.

Of course, much of the discrepancy between the language of these texts comes down to the expertise brought to bear in the drafting of each. The petitions betray few signs of legal expertise, whereas the drafting of the ordinance was obviously completed or assisted by legal professionals serving the king's council. This observation, however, simply affirms the contention that social structures reproduce themselves in cultural practice or 'the regulated improvisations of the habitus'.[47] Legal and seigneurial languages are the first clues to the differing priorities embodied in the texts and the assumptions upon which they are based. 'Tacitly laying down the dividing line between the thinkable and the unthinkable', the texts' representations of social relations sanction either lordship or the rule of the king's law as the norm.[48] The effort punctiliously to categorize maintenance in the ordinance, for instance, may stem from the definition of maintenance provided by the commons in 1388, but if so, it has drifted to comprehensiveness from precision and retains none of that definition's implied restrictions touching social degree and non-violent good lordship.

Better to illustrate the phrasing and concepts peculiar to the 1390 ordinance as a 'centralist' royal text on public order, I will quote from the preamble at some length:

Whereas by the laws and customs of our realm, which we are bound, by the oath made at our coronation, to preserve, all our lieges within the same realm,

---

[47] Bourdieu, *Theory of Practice*, 21.   [48] Ibid.

as well poor as rich (*sibien povres come riches*), ought freely to sue, defend (*franchement suer defender*), receive, and have justice and right, and the accomplishment and execution thereof, in any of our courts and elsewhere (*en quelconqes noz Courtes et aillours*), without being disturbed or oppressed by maintenance, menace, or in any other manner; . . . whereof many [maintainers etc.] are the more encouraged and bold in their maintenance and evil deeds aforesaid because they are of the retinue of lords and others of our said realm by fees, robes and other liveries called liveries of company.[49]

Sharing the language of commons petitions on the topic, and rewarding hope recorded at successive parliaments that the king's council would address the problem of liveries, the ordinance appears to constitute a new solicitude on the part of the king for the commons' position on public order. But the ordinance also appropriates the commons' discourse of peace and good order to promote the extension of central legal authority. Richard's deference to the coronation oath at the opening of the law looks like an attempt to fashion himself as an exemplary exponent of public order in consonance with the commons' concerns. The king had recently renewed his coronation oath at Westminster, at the conclusion of the Merciless Parliament, and after a performance as mediator between commons and lords at Cambridge a few months later, he was able confidently to carry his public order persona into his resumption of sole personal rule in May 1389.[50] Again, in the announcement of this resumption, stress is laid on the 'pacem, quietem, et tranquillitatem' (peace, quiet, and tranquillity; *Rot. parl.* iii. 404) of the realm against illicit modes of association and maintenance. The 1390 ordinance, promulgated a year later, completed this trajectory, formalizing a compromise between the abolition and the unregulated use of badges that had been worked up at Westminster during the winter.[51] Yet the ordinance's preamble asserts a role for the king under the coronation oath not as a guardian of the laws and customs guaranteeing the 'peace' of the gentry's continued enjoyment of social privilege, but rather as a champion of central, status-blind legal authority. Hence the call for universal access to justice (for 'touz noz lieges . . . sibien povres come riches') and the conception of justice primarily as access

[49] *SR* ii. 74–5.
[50] See *WC* 356; Strohm, *Hochon's Arrow*, 63–5.
[51] *PROME* iii. 265; cf. 266.

to the law courts.[52] The language of legal process in the 1390 ordinance is unfamiliar, assembling totalizing groupings of actions that are redolent of formality and dignify the law of the royal courts ('noz Courtes').

The ordinance sets out a much broader and inherently formal vision of central justice than anything contained in livery and maintenance petitions of the period. I have already mentioned the 'public–private' quality of medieval politics, and Carpenter's argument that, amongst the late fourteenth-century aristocracy in England, there was a fundamental acceptance of the influence of private relations (like those between lords and retainers) in the public sphere and, consequently, on public justice and its supreme concern to protect land.[53] The 1390 ordinance is premised on no such acceptance. Instead, with a centralist vision which precludes local private relations, it claims a right of access to impartial, court-administered justice for all ('freely to sue and defend'). Furthermore, while its only particularized provisions deal with badges, it backs its claim up by demanding (rather optimistically) a purge of all interferers with the legal system from any retinue and by otherwise proscribing any such interference or maintenance in the context of all retaining. The ordinance does not share the commons' concern with restricting the benefits of livery to an aristocratic and non-urban sphere. It even seems to envisage some residual, unmediated imposition of the most central brand of authority, for while it makes no real provision for the enforcement of its measures, it reserves the right of discretionary punishment to the king and his council (*SR* ii. 75).

The Ricardian commons' discourse on new liveries and maintenance appeals to and harnesses written law in opposition to the centralized, bureaucratic legal machinery that writing also enabled, and which the 1390 ordinance places at the heart of its vision of the common good and a unified realm. The uncentralized political-legal imaginary favoured by the commons is also refracted in the narratives arranged by Genius's confession.

---

[52] Cf. the bifurcated concept of justice in the badges debate at Cambridge, as recorded by the Westminster chronicler. The badge-wearing retainers are ' "pauperes in curiis principum et aliorum ubicumque dilaniant et confundunt, mediocres vero et alios indifferenter in quibuscumque locis ubi jus redditur jure suo expoliant et enervant" ' (fleecing and discomfiting the poor in the courts of the greatest and others, and indiscriminately robbing the middling sort and others of their rights and reducing them to helplessness wherever justice is dispensed; *WC* 354). The Cambridge commons would have the poor protected by the operations of lordship, and confine the legal system to the protection of their own interests. They are concerned, in turn, to protect their access to the law particularly from the interference of lesser sorts—those ' "lifted up" ' (*elati*; *WC* 354) by their new badges.

[53] Carpenter, *Locality and Polity*, esp. 284–6, 351–9; cf. Carpenter, 'Gentry and Community', 355, 369.

THE UNWRITTEN COMMUNITY OF
WORSHIP: UNOFFICIAL AND OFFICIAL
JUSTICE IN GENIUS'S TALES

As the parliamentary bills (with the notable exception of the 1388 Cambridge petition) minimize or ignore the technical capacity of written law and collapse it between the complaint rhetoric of past custom and the will of magnates or the king, so Genius's tales manifest an uncertainty about writing as a reliable means of communication (the exchange of authority). Just as the petitions seek to produce written law without limiting unofficial and local modes of justice and dispute resolution, so the tales stigmatize centralized, writerly legal administration as a system unable to respond to or take the imprint of personal *trouthe* and worship.

A corollary of Green's argument that (most) Ricardian poets' profound respect for *trouthe* did not translate into support for unofficial mechanisms of dispute resolution is the contention that writing and formal mechanisms based upon it were superseding alternative modes of resolution.[54] Thus, while he finds in Arion an appeal to a traditional and relatively informal institution of mediated settlement, Green later reads in Gower's tale of the False Bachelor the recognition of the functional superiority of written communication (as the basis of non-mediatory justice) over the relic of an eclipsed *trouthe*-based system of justice and social relations. He identifies the sultan's daughter's ring, which the sultan bequeaths to the Roman prince, as a symbolic wed—a token designed to communicate and memorialize the daughter's sworn commitment to its bearer.

We should not suppose that the legal weight accorded this 'so sufficant' token is entirely a matter of romance hyperbole, for as I have been at some pains to suggest, Gower's world had yet fully to transfer its allegiance from the machinery of preliterate trothplight to that of the written indenture.[55]

Green argues that the success of the cheated suitor's letter from his deathbed in facilitating the bachelor's arrest, contrasted with the miscarriage of the ring wed, 'pointedly underlines' the superiority of the literate mechanism over the non-literate one.[56]

---

[54] Green, *Crisis of Truth*, 175–81 (but cf. 281–2). Also see above, 182–3.
[55] Ibid. 272.   [56] Ibid.

I would locate the tale of the False Bachelor, however, in the order of narratives that imagine household- and worship-based foundations of justice and owe full allegiance to unofficial relations and extra-literate exchange. These narratives characteristically model justice by negation, which includes the depiction of destructive unofficial retribution. Yet, these failures speak not of the unworkability of the model but of decay from its ideal fulfilment. There is symbolic simplification at work. In the relationship between the tales' imaginary and actual social structures, representations of extra-literate practice seem broadly to correspond to unofficial processes that, in reality, made some use of writing. As the great household's commercial practices are ignored in favour of its persona of gift exchange, so writing is subsumed in the imagination of more personal interaction. Reflecting anti-centralist dispositions, the narratives symbolically construct written communication and literate means of dispute resolution as fundamentally unreliable and inadequate.

Tarquin, Arruns, and Brutus

Genius supplies perhaps his most emphatic and potentially subversive narrative doctrine apropos of the king's law towards the end of the confession. The double exemplum of Tarquin and Arruns (involving the hapless Gabines and Lucretia) combines with the Tale of Virginia at the conclusion of book 7 to form a major statement about just retribution. The justice imagined is strikingly uncentralized: it includes the deposition of a monarch and excludes official legal administration. The retribution against Tarquin and his son is a primarily, though not wholly, implicit refutation of literateness and formalism. It is symbolically burdened with the organic, the paganistic, the plenary and inclusive, and it alienates the official or the formally, intellectually precise as meaningless and absent. The dual tale reproduces some of the elementary components of the *Confessio*'s moral political semiotics. Both of Arruns's climactic acts of violence are acts of personal treason which strike at the core of aristocratic households, effacing worship, threatening lineage, and disrupting the transmission of patrimony and the exchange of power. He first destroys the lords of Gabii, having earlier sworn 'trouthe' to them, by which treason the city's society unravels and 'al was wonne' (7. 4647–8, 4694–5). Then, exploiting obligations created by kinship, 'As he that was cousin of house' (7. 4921), Arruns is received in the 'worthi knyht' (7. 4776) Collatinus's hall (7. 4946–7) and betrays the hospitality of his cousin's household by attacking and ruining his most honourable possession—his wife.[57]

In each section of the exemplum, violation of household order emanates from the poem's characteristic conjunction of private household space and socially dubious conduct. Arruns prepares his ruse of self-mutilation for the Gabines 'at hom | In Rome' in 'a prive place... | Withinne a chambre' (7. 4613–15). To set about their fatal competition, he and Collatinus first 'come | Al prively withinne Rome... | And take a chambre' and stay 'out of sihte' (7. 4789–92). The tale thus offers a twin sequence of a pattern that is familiar in the *Confessio*; but in this case it is to be knitted up with correction and restored order.

As at first sight of the livery and maintenance complaints, it looks like Gower diagnoses the problem as uncontrolled power, the solution (we might expect) royal authority and law. As I have argued, however, the *Confessio* seems to me normally to speak for those landed interests that say that the problem is improperly networked households, the solution mutually obliged, status-sensitive great households. A shorthand for good order is visible, public–private interactions between great households. In other words, the hall trumps the chamber and the law court.

In the Tarquin and Arruns tale, there is a kind of quilted correction, proleptic then performed, and each layer is unapologetically contrary to the literate, official, and centralized. When Tarquin orders a sacrifice to celebrate the victory enabled by his son's destruction of Gabii's lords, it is obliterated by 'An hidous Serpent' which then returns 'Into the depe ground ayein' (7. 4710, 4715). The assembled Romans are unable to read and to interpret this mysterious, non-verbal message and express confusion. In answer they receive a verbal gloss from Apollo, in 'gastly [spiritual] vois' (7. 4721). The god interprets the serpent's wasting of the sacrifice as a consequence of Tarquin and Arruns's 'unrihtwisnesse' (7. 4724), and then goes on to prophesy a sign of retribution:

> And seith that which of hem ferst kisseth
> His moder, he schal take wrieche   *vengeance*
> Upon the wrong: and of that speche
> Thei ben withinne here hertes glade,
> Thogh thei outward no semblant made.

> (7. 4730–4)

---

[57] The outcry provoked by the offence significantly assails both '"lecherie and covoitise"' (7. 5119).

The Romans are literalists. And their literalism threatens to lead them along a path of false retribution, turning them into isolated, *prive* revengers. Satisfied that the enigma of the serpent has been unequivocally decoded by Apollo, they rush to kiss their own mothers when they return home (7. 4746–50). The Romans' inept interpretation of the oracle is geared to cause further social fragmentation. It steers them towards gestures confined to single households (perhaps with vaguely incestuous overtones) and, competing 'To be the ferste upon the chance' of vengeance (7. 4751–2), they are already prompted to *prive* secrecy and dissimulation, concealing self-satisfaction and anticipation at the temple (7. 4733–4). Exploiting the post-Saturnian divide between heart and countenance (which 'outward no semblant made'), their manner recalls the prologue on the *trouthe*-less present, fallen from the age when 'Of mannes herte the corage | Was schewed thanne in the visage' (prol. 111–12, and above, 182–5). Meanwhile, their literalism is shown to be comically insufficient when they mistake Brutus's response to the oracle—he kisses the earth—guessing only 'that he hadde sporned [tripped] | Per chance, and so was overtorned' (7. 4739–40).

Brutus, of course, perceives beyond the literal surface of the sign. He finds a 'gastly' meaning that defies formalistic interpretation and official channels of power alike. Kissing the ground (as 'Moder'; 7. 4744) and the serpent's disappearance 'Into the depe ground' are signs of the earth, evoking its primal, pagan meanings of universal life and death. Ordinarily inscrutable, they are invoked against the formal, ritualized symbolic language and authority of central sovereign power. The serpent snuffs out the 'sollempne Sacrifise' incorporated in a 'riche feste' (7. 4702–3) and Brutus's gesture is also antithetical to the king's ceremony: spontaneous and direct, it is performed 'with al the haste he myhte' (7. 4736) and even mistaken as involuntary by onlookers. The matrix of signs which predicates retribution is pre-institutional and, in the case of the earth as universal mother, underwrites the individual's act of 'wrieche' with inclusive, communal representativeness.

At the end of the next and concluding section of the exemplum, the signs of Apollo's temple legitimate and are fulfilled by a great, rebellious, and almost bathetically well-ordered process of unofficial retribution. After hearing Lucretia's lament, Brutus translates the primal symbolic into socially inclusive, yet hierarchically ordered, political action:

> Bot Brutus, which was with hem there,
> Toward himself his herte kepte,

And to Lucrece anon he lepte,
The blodi swerd and pulleth oute,
And swor the goddes al aboute
That he therof schal do vengance.
. . . .
And Brutus with a manlich herte
Hire housebonde hath mad up sterte
Forth with hire fader ek also
In alle haste, and seide hem tho
That thei anon withoute lette
A Beere for the body fette;
Lucrece and therupon bledende
He leide, and so forth out criende
He goth into the Market place
Of Rome: and in a litel space
Thurgh cry the cite was assembled,
And every mannes herte is trembled,
Whan thei the sothe herde of the cas.
And therupon the conseil was
Take of the grete and of the smale,
And Brutus tolde hem al the tale;
And thus cam into remembrance
Of Senne the continuance,
Which Arrons hadde do tofore,
. . . .
So that the comun clamour tolde
The newe schame of Sennes olde.
And al the toun began to crie,
'Awey, awey the tirannie
Of lecherie and covoitise!'
And ate laste in such a wise
The fader [Tarquin] in the same while
Forth with his Sone thei exile,
And taken betre governance.

(7. 5082–5123)

Swearing on the sword, Brutus makes it a symbol of his personal *trouthe*,
and from this point, he goes fully and rapidly public. He does this first
through an elementary kinship network, rousing Lucretia's husband and
father, before generalizing the bloody sword's significance completely
with 'cry' in the quintessential public space of the marketplace. Brutus's
retributive method is unofficial and extensive, operating through
unofficial personal relations (with Lucretia and her family), by rumour,

informal 'conseil', and 'the comun clamour'. It also results in the undoing of royal absolutism.

The clamour of Brutus's rebellion has everything to do with justice and order. Yet earlier in the same book, and vividly in *Vox clamantis*, the common voice is inarticulate noise and fearful. It destabilizes Roboam's kingdom by deposing him and is likened to the 'salvage' sea under the 'wilde wode rage' of a storm (7. 4111–12).[58] The Roman clamour produces a univocal, articulate attack on 'tirannie', and far from triggering chaos, it brings about positive change and the end of the narrative with scarcely a whimper. With extreme narrative economy, the tale muffles the disruptive resonance and potential of popular revolt. The colourless rebellion is achieved without apparent violence and accomplishes the transition from retribution to new, 'betre' political order from one line of verse to the next, allowing almost no space into which disruption may be read. In the opaque phrase 'betre governance', Gower neatly by-passes the constitutional bombshell that Tarquin's fall marks the end not just of a Roman king but of kingship in Rome.[59] The tale's focus in portraying unofficial and communal retribution against a corrupt centre is rather on the hierarchy and ordering principles which shape it. For the retribution is always led by the aristocratic Brutus, whose special authority has been inscribed much earlier, at the tale's midpoint.[60] Brutus's revenge project is contained within a hierarchical order even, and most notably, when it expands into the public sphere at the marketplace—the Bakhtinian site of collapsed difference and, according to the Cambridge commons of 1388, gatherings of 'great routs of people in excess of their degree and condition' (*outre lour degre et estat*; *WC* 358).[61] The Roman assembly's counsel is differentiated according to the degrees of 'the grete' and 'the smale'. And the assembly

---

[58] In his menagerie of transformed rebels in the first book of the *Vox*, Gower devotes an extended passage to the 'rudis clangor' of their new voices—braying, bellowing, grunting, barking, wailing, cackling (1. 797–820). For late fourteenth-century writers' memorialization of the 1381 rebels as inarticulate and insane, see Justice, *Writing and Rebellion*, 193–254 (and 207–16 for the *Vox* in particular). In 'Chaucer's Trivial Fox Chase and the Peasants' Revolt of 1381', *JMRS* 18 (1988), 195–220, Peter W. Travis remarks that the chroniclers of the revolt were apparently 'as disturbed by the revolting noise of the peasants as by the fact that the peasants were revolting' (217).

[59] Cf. Scanlon, *Narrative, Authority, and Power*, 293–5.

[60] In contrast, Roboam 'Which rihtfull heir was be descente' (7. 4129) is replaced by the initiative of 'the poeple', and then only with 'A povere knyht' (7. 4127) whom they acclaim.

[61] See Mikhail Bakhtin, *Problems of Dostoevsky's Poetics*, tr. R. W. Rotsel (Ann Arbor, Mich., 1973), 105–7.

remains unified and responsive to Brutus's authority, interpreting justice from the 'sothe' of his 'tale', and from the general memory he activates (7. 5109–14).

Virginius

Formalism again comes up short against informal retributive power as Genius runs the exemplum of Tarquin and Arruns together with the tale of Virginia (7. 5124–30). This tale intensifies the political resonance of the previous narrative, embroidering the pattern of treason and revenge with detail of bureaucratic justice administration in collision with aristocratic worship and, ultimately, communal retribution. The structure of retribution echoes the previous exemplum from the point at which Virginius, having slain his own daughter, rides out to the Roman 'chivalerie' at war:

> And with his swerd droppende of blod,
> The which withinne his douhter stod,
> He cam ther as the pouer was
> Of Rome, and tolde hem al the cas,
> . . . .
>   Of this merveile which thei sihe
> So apparent tofore here yhe,
> Of that the king him hath misbore,
> Here othes thei have alle swore
> That thei wol stonde be the riht.
> And thus of on acord upriht
> To Rome at ones hom ayein
> Thei torne, and schortly forto sein,
> This tirannye cam to mouthe,
> And every man seith what he couthe,
> So that the prive tricherie,
> Which set was upon lecherie,
> Cam openly to mannes Ere;
> And that broghte in the comun feere,
> That every man the peril dradde
> Of him that so hem overladde.
> Forthi, er that it worse falle,
> Thurgh comun conseil of hem alle
> Thei have here wrongfull king deposed,
> And hem in whom it was supposed
> The conseil stod of his ledinge
> Be lawe unto the dom thei bringe,

> Wher thei receiven the penance
> That longeth to such governance.
>
> (7. 5263–300)

Once again a 'worthi kniht' brandishes a 'naked swerd' (7. 5243; cf. 7. 5066) wet with the blood of a woman killed to preserve honesty and honour as a potent token which will translate individual revenge into a public enterprise. Once more, the retributive project is accomplished along unofficial channels by a combination of aristocratic leadership, sworn oath (7. 5280), an unofficial and unwritten, non-technical call for justice (7. 5266–76), popular communication or rumour (7. 5285–9), 'comun conseil', and the apparently non-violent deposition of a monarch.

Virginius is able to accuse Appius Claudius of 'tricherie' or treason, so that the text propagates a concept of treason based on violation of *reciprocal* obligation. Larry Scanlon sums up a reciprocalist reading of the tale when he says that Appius is 'deposed, just as Richard will be, for his failure to embody the common interest—a common interest which...has been defined as the patriarchal privileges of his knight-hood'.[62] A mutually obliging concept of treason was increasingly under threat in the fourteenth century. The statute of treason of 1352 extended the formal definition of treason to include the killing of certain types of person to whom a potential traitor 'doit foi et obedience' (owes faith and obedience), namely a master, husband, or prelate.[63] The provision is significant in terms of reciprocalist notions of lordship because it abrogates reciprocity in framing a form of treason that is only possible against social superiors.[64] The statute originated in a commons petition which was principally interested in limiting the scope of treason, to rein in the reach of forfeitures and royal jurisdiction.[65] The provision on what would come to be called 'petty treason' in the fifteenth century, however, broadens the range of treason and, by writing over the mutuality of a bond of *trouthe* or trust, serves the authoritarian interests of a centralized bureaucracy endeavouring to entrench unilateral rights for the crown.[66] During the second half of

[62] Scanlon, *Narrative, Authority, and Power*, 295.

[63] *SR* i. 320. The phrase is applied to the category of prelate only, but, as Strohm observes, it reveals 'the logic behind the entire provision' (*Hochon's Arrow*, 124).

[64] For more involved discussion of the statute and the concepts of treason which surround it, see Strohm, *Hochon's Arrow*, 123–8; Green, *Crisis of Truth*, 206–30.

[65] Bellamy, *Law of Treason*, 79–85.

[66] Green, *Crisis of Truth*, 217–19. For the benefit to royal authority of a strong model of hierarchy attached to lower levels of society, see Strohm, *Hochon's Arrow*, 125.

the fourteenth century, then, the written law, by formal designation, competed with more traditional notions of treason organized by the principle of mutuality and reproduced in Gower's poem.

Virginius's tale's promotion of a two-way concept of duty—up and down the hierarchy of the elites—contains a particular rebuke for formalist, centralized, unilateral legal authority. For the treason that is corrected by Livius Virginius and his supporters is specifically carried out through the litigation of a (supposed) 'covenant' (of service between Virginia and the governor-king's brother, Marcus Claudius) and the abuse of central judicial authority. Virginia is summoned 'After the lawe which was tho' (7. 5180) to appear before Appius in his capacity as judge, and the king eventually 'Yaf for his brother the sentence' against which there is 'non Appel' (7. 5224, 5233). Virginius defends his daughter according to the fact- or sooth-based requirements of law:

> Wher al that evere reson may
> Be lawe in audience he doth,
> So that his dowhter upon soth
> Of that Marchus hire hadde accused
> He hath tofore the court excused.
>
> (7. 5212–16)

But his efforts are to no avail against an arbitrary, unilateral implementation of the law. This arbitrariness is contrasted with the use by Virginia's 'frendes' of the 'comun lawe' (perhaps itself to be contrasted intrinsically with 'the lawe which was tho', exploited by the brothers) (7. 5185–8). Where Appius uses the law as an arbitrary vehicle of private desire, these supporters appeal to the common law as a guarantee of worship, claiming that it should protect a 'noble worthi knyht' from being 'harmed' or 'schamed' (7. 5189–95). Ultimately, Appius's privately motivated use of the law is conclusively opposed to another, larger group of extensive interpersonal bonds which manifests the value of (sworn) *trouthe* and also reintegrates the law into this system of relations and values when the rebel network brings the deposed king's counsellors 'Be lawe unto the dom' (7. 5298).

The rise and fall of the False Bachelor

The False Bachelor exemplum in book 2 insists that there can be no good justice in the absence of *trouthe* and suggests that formal law, and the literate technology and literalist hermeneutic which underwrite it,

cannot guarantee the transmission of *trouthe*. The tale represents unofficial structures—the extensive personal bonds that constitute a community of worship—as the guarantee of *trouthe*. Formal law, which is not
intrinsically capable of registering worship (itself a product of *trouthe*),
becomes unreliable when it is divorced from a sufficient community of
worship. The Roman prince's good fortune begins obviously to unravel,
as Green remarks, with the miscarriage of an exchange in which the
sultan's daughter's ring (mal)functions as a simple symbolic wed. The
failure of this exchange, however, is neither predicated on the absence of
writing nor redeemed by its new prominence. The wed malfunctions
not because such signs of interpersonal bonds and the *trouthe* which
should fix them are inherently flawed. It malfunctions in the first place
because of the failure of *trouthe* endemic to the age which the *Confessio*
hopes (ambitiously) to redeem. Treason is always already couched in this
zeitgeist, and tends to be let loose by *prive* relations. Thus, a more
immediate cause for the wed's failure, based on the prince's particular
social circumstances, is its divorce from the necessary support of community and extensive personal networks. The ring as a mechanism of
exchange is underwritten by personal *trouthe* because it works upon the
daughter's sworn oath to accept its bearer (2. 2608–16, 2642). Crucially, however, this *trouthe* is not secured within a community of
worship. The ring wed mechanism is set up with the daughter 'in gret
privete' (2. 2606) and then likewise with the prince, 'that non it wiste'
(2. 2640). In the systemic vocabulary of trothplight and weds, the
mechanism lacks a borrow.

Green explains the *borh* or borrow not only as a surety but as an
evidentiary agent of *trouthe*:

> Borrows were originally the primary witnesses to contracts—people trusted by
> both parties to give a reliable account of what had been agreed should there later
> be a dispute—and the token was handed to them because it was their memory
> that would preserve the agreement and their testimony that might be needed to
> enforce it.[67]

The wed mechanism fails because it is partial—stripped, in an environment of *untrouthe*, of its unofficial public or communal dimension. It is
instead introduced to a formalist structure which cannot supply this lack.

---

[67] Green, *Crisis of Truth*, 66 (see also 64–70). Amans (*CA* 4. 960) and Jason (5. 3416)
take God and St John respectively 'to borwe' as guarantors or witnesses of their *trouthe* in
making oaths. On the use and applicability of supernatural borrows, see Green, *Crisis of
Truth*, 67–8.

The Persian court ratifies the betrothal of the sultan's daughter, and thus the succession, 'upon the lawe' (2. 2698). This law comprises a literal interpretation of 'The charge which [the sultan] bad' (2. 2693) within the limits of which 'The tokne was so sufficant' (2. 2700) as to advance the prince's bachelor, as the person 'Which thilke same Ring to honde | Hire scholde bringe after [the sultan's] deth' (2. 2614–15). The court must function (and abet injustice) as a formal, literalist legal mechanism because it is disempowered as a community of worship. It cannot function as such a community in relation to the wed because the prince and his worship have no established place within it and because it lacks knowledge of the sultan's final exchange, which would have established and extended the prince's worship. Shorn of such resources, the court reads the wed according to the narrow, literal principles of the king's law and upholds the ringbearer's claim. Employing a mechanism which is unable to transmit or to access *trouthe* and worship, the court's reading is found wanting.

Nor is writing wholly or even mainly responsible for the recuperation of this situation. The arrival of the Roman embassy which ensures retribution against the bachelor-sultan depends upon a letter written by the dying prince to his father the emperor. But as an instrument which facilitates a much larger recuperative process, the letter is only enabled by the restoration of a social *trouthe*-bearing structure in the form of unofficial, worship-based networks. The Persians send the letter to Rome only after the prince has located himself within a recognizable field of worship (revealing to the 'worthieste' Persians 'That he was Sone and Heir also | Of themperour of grete Rome'; 2. 2720–1) and so gained access to a Persian aristocratic network of political action. Even before the letter is sent, then, the Persian community of worship has embraced the prince and acted on its perception of his *trouthe* through his worship by arresting and imprisoning their new ruler (2. 2744–5). Once the letter has been sent, it is still not the case that writing produces retribution and the resolution of the disorder wrought by the unsupported wed. The letter only enables and instigates the further restoration of worship-based networks which themselves accomplish resolution outside, and indeed against the grain of, formal law. The letter is dispatched along an extension of the Persian network (lately encompassing the Roman prince) to the Roman emperor so that an expanded and knowledgeable community of worship (represented as we saw earlier by the Roman embassy[68]) can be organized around the bachelor.

[68] See above, 209–10.

By this means, worship will once again become an active factor in judgement liberated from the formalist constraints of the dead sultan's precept, and the bachelor's 'oghne untrowthe him schal depose' (2. 2750). Furthermore, the newly constituted, worship-based mechanism of justice and retribution is brought into direct conflict with and overcomes formal law when it comes to the punishment of the confessed supplanter:

> Tho seiden some he scholde deie,
> Bot yit thei founden such a weie
> That he schal noght be ded in Perse;
> And thus the skiles ben diverse.
> Be cause that he was coroned,
> And that the lond was abandoned
> To him, althogh it were unriht,
> Ther is no peine for him diht;
> Bot to this point and to this ende
> Thei granten wel that he schal wende
> With the Romeins to Rome ayein.
> And thus acorded ful and plein,
> The qwike body with the dede
> With leve take forth thei lede,
> Wher that Supplant hath his juise.

> (2. 2767–81)

The strict and somewhat convoluted requirements and 'skiles' of the Persian law are circumvented by a simple—'ful and plein'—and apparently informal agreement (2. 2776–8). The agreement shifts the Persian legal technicalities, indeed, to enable the performance of justice within the fully restored Roman social context, the abandonment of which made the destructive impact of *untrouthe* possible in the first place.

'THE WREECHE WHICH HORESTES DEDE': AN EPITOME OF UNOFFICIAL RETRIBUTION

The vision of justice as reciprocalist exchange, a product of extensive and worship-ordered household-based relations, circulates throughout Genius's exemplary material. Having examined several aspects of it, from Paulina and her husband's rallying of support for a direct appeal to the emperor against a powerful magnate, to Virginius's winning of the Roman knighthood's sworn support against their prince, it is worth closing this chapter with one of the poem's most comprehensive statements of this vision. Like other classical retellings to come (especially in book 5), book 3's tale of Orestes is one of grisly retribution within a family. Yet, as I noted at the beginning of the previous chapter, Orestes does not suffer any exemplary judgement resembling that of Procne and Philomela, or Medea. Set in the midst of a discussion of homicidal wrath, the Orestes exemplum might be expected to condemn his brutal matricide (3. 2070–8). But Orestes is crowned king in response to his bloody deed—a reward which Gower's narrative endorses with the just and 'wonder' self-destruction of Erigone, the offspring of the adulterous liaison he has avenged (3. 2170–95). Pearsall has suggested that the tale is singularly wanting as an exemplum against murder or indeed as a coherent narrative.[69] Nevertheless, the puzzling discrepancy of fortune between Orestes and the *Confessio*'s disgraced avengers is exactly the feature that seems to call forth the tale's single story line in Gower's exhaustive attention to aspects of Orestes's retribution. The narrative painstakingly distinguishes Orestes from illicit killers, and in so doing creates a *positive* exemplum less against murder than *for* the ordering powers of reciprocalist lordship.

The tale, for which Gower relies predominantly upon Benoît de Sainte-Maure's Troy poem,[70] takes its starting point in domestic treason. Clytemnestra and Aegisthus's 'love untrewe' (3. 1898) leads to Agamemnon's murder. The crime triggers a sequence of events which culminates in the death of the lovers when 'Horestes with hise hondes | Climestre his oghne Moder slowh' (3. 2110–11) and Aegisthus is hanged (3. 2103–6). The surrounding plot is occupied by details of Orestes's personal pursuit of justice and eventual vindication.

The household revenge premise is transformed into positive exemplary ground by established, status-ordered personal networks. Orestes's personal retribution is germinated by kin and household, and his cause grows beyond anger and vengeance to find authority in a less ambivalent political objective, namely the recovery of patrimony. From the outset, Gower's retelling registers the importance of such networks and obligations. Idomeneus of Crete is obliged to take ward of the infant Orestes in the first place 'So as he was of his lignage' (3. 1944), a detail from

[69] Pearsall, 'Gower's Narrative Art', 483; and see above, 174–5. Cf. Charles Runacres, 'Art and Ethics in the "Exempla" of *Confessio Amantis*', in Minnis (ed.), *Responses and Reassessments*, 124.

[70] Macaulay, ii. 499–500; Benoît de Sainte-Maure, *Roman de Troie*, iv, ll. 27925–90, 28155–283, 28339–402.

Guido Delle Colonne's *Historia destructionis Troiae* (1287) that Gower added to his main source material.[71] The king undertakes not only to protect and to nurture the child, but to do so that he might 'venge him at his oghne wille' (3. 1957). By the time Orestes receives divine licence at the Athenian temple, the assimilation of vengeance to worshipful politics has advanced:

> He was ansuerd, if that he wolde
> His stat recovere, thanne he scholde
> Upon his Moder do vengance
>
> (3. 1997–9)

This authorizing version of Orestes's enterprise subordinates revenge to patrimony as means to objective. The earlier emergence of his vengeful purpose has been associated with the development and outward display of his worship through knighthood and retinue, and has included a gesture to that worship's core element of patrimony:

> And he began to clepe and calle,
> As he which come was to manne,
> Unto the King of Crete thanne,
> Preiende that he wolde him make
> A kniht and pouer with him take,
> For lengere wolde he noght beleve,
> He seith, bot preith the king of leve
> To gon and *cleyme his heritage*
> And vengen him of thilke oultrage
> Which was unto his fader do.
> The king assenteth wel therto,
> With gret honour and knyht him makth,
> And gret pouer to him betakth,
> And gan his journe forto caste
>
> (3. 1966–79, emphasis added)

Orestes sets out 'As he that was in herte wroth' (3. 1982). Despite the 'time of yeres' (3. 1962) that has passed since Clytemnestra's crime, his will to vengeance seems to have something like the urgency of Rosemund's or Procne's. Yet its first manifestation here is a projection into the public sphere and the masculine, rather than a *prive* containment which is feminine. As wronged wives, Rosemund and Procne have no

---

[71] Macaulay, ii. 499; Guido Delle Colonne, *Historia destructionis Troiae*, ed. and tr. Mary Elizabeth Meek (Bloomington, Ind., 1974), 32. 144–53.

resources for justice and fall back on the chamber and collusion. Orestes's accession to manhood (3. 1967), conversely, empowers his vengefulness and gives it an extroverted voice (to call out; 3. 1966) by wedding it to worshipful social rank and (putatively) to the position of householder. This position can validate a variety of exchanges, including the exchange of force. Through knightly status, revenge borrows the trappings of 'gret honour' and its conventional material power or manpower. At the same time, this passage seamlessly yokes revenge to the more soundly legitimate purpose of the restoration of Agamemnon's household and inheritance (3. 1973–5).

Subsequent steps in the narrative extend and reinforce the public but unofficial aristocratic configuration of Orestes's retribution. It becomes a conglomeration of noble power based on free allegiance and shared griev-ances. Political support is exchanged as part of an aristocratic gift econ-omy—according to self-interest perhaps, but always non-commercially. The support of the duke of Athens 'and his pouer' (3. 2020) is contextual-ized only in the broadest terms of open hospitality towards Orestes:

> Unto the Cite of Athene
> He goth him forth and was received,
> So there was he noght deceived.
> The Duc and tho that weren wise
> Thei profren hem to his servise

> (3. 1984–8)

At the next city Orestes visits, the lord Phoieus is eager to join the band because of his own household, marital grievance against Aegisthus (this of the 'damaged goods' variety after Aegisthus married, 'Forlai', and abandoned the lord's daughter; 3. 2029–32). Aegisthus's *untrouthe* in exchanges with his neighbours tells in the end. Crucially, Phoieus proffers his help 'withouten hyre' (3. 2024). No commercial or expedi-ent paradigm applies to Orestes's gathering of his 'host' (3. 2036). Its assembly is predicated on hierarchy and interpersonal ties that are already established for a larger range of purposes. Each principal shares noble standing or (in Orestes's case) has a claim to such standing sponsored by a king. The body of the host comprises pre-existing retinues alongside Orestes's 'pouer', which has been royally bestowed as an adjunct of knighthood and not simply as an instrument of his immediate cause.

Phoieus's response to Orestes, and the similarity and accretion of his own grievance to Orestes's cause, demonstrates that, in relation to

Aegisthus at least, this cause has a validity outside the potentially *prive* confines of a single household. The legitimating power of this multiplication or public diffusion of Aegisthus's viciousness is represented in the narrative by gossip. The re-emergence of Phoieus's grievance stimulates gossip, the generalizing function of which enhances the communal credentials of Orestes's campaign:

> Men sein, 'Old Senne newe schame':
> Thus more and more aros the blame
> Ayein Egiste on every side.
>
> (3. 2033–5)[72]

Aegisthus's final confrontation with justice is, indeed, a markedly public affair as he is 'forth broght' (3. 2095) after his capture and hanged 'above alle othre' (3. 2105) as part of a mass execution of his party. Legal, judicial language authorizes Orestes's practice (without representing it as legalistic). The narrator ascribes the term 'tresoun' or 'tretour' to Aegisthus four times in twenty-one lines, amply reinforcing the significance of the method of his punishment. Moreover, this punishment is explicitly made a matter of rational judgement—of 'deeming' or 'dooming' and 'ordaining' —and Aegisthus suffers under 'sentence' and 'be the lawe' (3. 2099–2103). At the same time, the only agency explicitly identified in connection with the retributive process here is Orestes and 'a gret partie' of his men (3. 2088). No official judicial mechanisms are appended to Orestes's use of household force 'in buisshement' (3. 2089), and the passage's legitimating import accrues wholly to his personal lordship.[73]

The text is notably less at ease, of course, about the process and symbolism surrounding the death of Orestes's other and earlier victim. The premeditated tearing off of Clytemnestra's breasts and abandonment of her corpse 'Unto the hound and to the raven' (3. 2077) is not accommodated by any legal punitive paradigm. It is a radically personal, unofficial retribution. The text impresses this upon the reader with

---

[72] For the generalizing function of gossip, see above, 203 and n. 17, and cf. the generalization of Brutus's cause as 'the comun clamour tolde | The newe schame of Sennes olde' (*CA* 7. 5115–16); and above, 226–8.

[73] Cf. the unofficial retribution in the tale of Boniface—one of the usurpation narratives which envelope the tale of the False Bachelor in the previous book. Boniface, like Aegisthus, is taken by a party of retainers or 'men of Armes' (2. 2998). Scanlon has discussed the tale, and the episode of Boniface's ambush in particular, with regard to the negotiation of ecclesiastical and lay political authority and material power (*Narrative, Authority, and Power*, 258–62).

evenly spaced repetitions of certain phrases, so that Orestes's doing 'juise' with 'his oghne hondes' for Clytemnestra's 'oghne lord' works as a kind of refrain in the tale.[74] Nevertheless, an emphasis remains on the retribution's difference in kind from *prive* revenge. Orestes deliberately accuses and kills his mother at Mycenae 'tofore the lordes alle | And ek tofor the poeple also' (3. 2052–3). The killing itself is also, moreover, a stark confrontation with taboos of *prive*-ness. Orestes himself defines his act as unnaturalness answering unnaturalness:

> Unkindely for thou hast wroght,
> Unkindeliche it schal be boght,
> The Sone schal the Moder sle
>
> (3. 2065–7)

The deed and devouring at the heart of the tale thus have the same capacity for scandal and destructive domestic internalization, and are as radically subversive of gender and familial boundaries as the acts 'ayein kinde' (5. 5905) orchestrated by Procne. Clytemnestra's punishment not only exiles her from the human, it also, as scandalous 'juise' at 'His oghne hond' (3. 2142), poses the extreme test of the personal, unofficial process by which Orestes seeks to redress his grievance.

Supernatural authority supports the manner of Clytemnestra's death. The three elements of 'Pappes', 'hors', and carrion are doubled in each detail in the instructions received by Orestes in the temple at Athens and in these instructions' execution (cf. 3. 2010–15, 2070–8). Yet, the gods are not an unproblematic source of legitimation (and indeed hardly a source of legitimation at all) in Genius's tales. Orestes himself 'Was nothing glad' (3. 2005) of the divine recommendation that he do cruel vengeance on his own mother. His retributive project instead escapes taint courtesy of unofficial and communal processes akin to those by which it was achieved. The medieval versions of the story which Gower follows collapse a classical sequence according to which Orestes is pursued by furies after the slaying of his mother and is then cleared of guilt in an Athenian tribunal (often very narrowly). Euripides has Orestes doomed to death by the citizens of Argos before his Athenian reprieve.[75] Gower's

---

[74] *CA* 3. 2003–11, 2059–70, 2142, 2162.

[75] Euripides, *Orestes*, ed. and tr. M. L. West (Warminster, Wilts., 1987), ll. 857–956 (Orestes and Electra have been condemned by an assembly of citizens, despite the vigorous defence of an honest farmer from outside the city). Cf. Delle Colonne, *Historia*, 33. 89–124. For a brief summary of ancient Greek versions of the Orestes tale, see Aeschylus, *Eumenides*, ed. Alan H. Sommerstein (Cambridge, 1989), 4–6.

tale provides no such opportunity for ambivalence or disapproval about Orestes's deed (albeit Euripides's play is chiefly concerned with the cynicism and hypocrisy of Orestes's accusers). The Athenian tribunal, now a 'parlement' (3. 2130), meets after little narrative space, on the back of the spread of ill 'fame' (3. 2107) and rumour. Before it is called, the narrative has already framed the assembly's task as the vindication of Orestes, characterizing accusations against him as a kind of 'worste speche' credited 'til it be ansuerd' (3. 2121–2).

The 'parlement' itself is unlike its classical ancestors in that it is a baronial forum of arbitration rather than a civic court (such as the Athenian Areopagus, the homicide jurisdiction of which was supposed to date to Orestes's trial[76]). All of the separate *parlements* that feature in the tales of the *Confessio* have more in common with English parliaments of the thirteenth century than with either ancient civic and judicial institutions or, more pertinently, the parliaments of Gower's own day.[77] Genius's *parlements* are, almost invariably, noble councils or of unspecified composition while dealing with similar business.[78] The *parlement* that judges Orestes's right to reign is certainly made up of 'lordes' (3. 2129, 2146). On one hand, it is undertaking to authorize kingship (much as most of the other *parlements* in the *Confessio* are summoned in order to ratify or acclaim a transference of monarchical power). At the same time, however, the *parlement* is also undertaking to resolve the question of a particular offence (judged in the language of 'wreeche' and 'vice'; 3. 2147, 2157, 2161). The ultimate arbitration of justice in the tale is thus effected by a community of worship, and not by any instruments of central government or the king's law.

---

[76] See Aeschylus, *Eumenides*, ed. Sommerstein, 5, 16–17, and ll. 674–710; Laura Carrara, 'Il processo Areopagitico di Oreste: le *Eumenidi* di Eschilo e la tradizione Attica', *Philologus*, 151 (2007), 3–16.

[77] For the development of the medieval English parliament from an informal baronial council to a two-tier institution including the house of commons, see Richardson, 'The Commons and Medieval Politics', 25–8; Holt, 'Prehistory of Parliament'; G. L. Harriss, 'The Formation of Parliament, 1272–1377', in Davies and Denton (eds), *English Parliament*, 36–7, 41–2, 50, 53–4. For parliament's aristocratic arbitral function, see Harriss, 'Formation of Parliament', 49–50; Rawcliffe, 'Parliament'. See also Matthew Giancarlo, *Parliament and Literature in Late Medieval England* (Cambridge, 2007).

[78] See e.g. *CA* 2. 2650–3, 2685–9 (the *parlement*, or 'Court', of 'lordes' which establishes the Persian succession on the False Bachelor); 5. 7299–7306, 7319–7440 (a Trojan *parlement* where 'ben the lordes alle and some'); 2. 1549–54 (the Roman *parlement* which establishes Mauricius as heir in the tale of Constance); 8. 1914–18 (Apollonius's *parlement* which crowns Thais and Athenagoras). But cf. 7. 2949–97 (Lycurgus's *parlement* 'of grete and smale'), and 7. 4029–64 (Roboam's acclamation by 'The poeple upon a Parlement').

Orestes's vindication, moreover, relies upon the system of traditional conflict resolution which Green opposes to centralized law, and it hinges on the stability and recognition of personal *trouthe* and worship. Menestheus, who is introduced with a trope of worship, offers a defence of Orestes that relies (beyond 'Ful many an other skile'; 3. 2156) on the honour proof of trial by combat (3. 2143–54).[79] Menestheus's commitment of his own *trouthe* and honour to Orestes's worship satisfies the aristocratic community of worship and its curiosity 'To knowe hou that the sothe was' (3. 2133). It does so without bureaucracy or explicit reference to the king's law and Orestes is restored to his patrimony. The restoration completes the resolution of a conflictual process which has expanded from an originary (and now remote) offence to a complex, multilayered structure filling a substantial exemplum. This process is repeatedly and consistently constituted by acts of personal, aristocratic management of justice enabled by household bonds and their extensive coordination.

Orestes's uncontested coronation attests that the unofficial but public (public–private) strategies of redress which he has pursued (from the deployment of knightly status and retinue to the coordination of noble support and the public execution of his enemies) are productive of social stability. The social and moral superiority of such a system of justice is subsequently restated and enhanced in the uncanny duplication of its effects. Having repaired the offence against Orestes, the coronation produces a final erasure of that offence's lingering household legacy by Orestes's half-sister's suicide 'Whan sche herde how hir brother spedde' (3. 2177). Erigone's self-destruction occurs almost magically, as a remote function purely of Orestes's repute (3. 2177):

---

[79] On the medieval trial by combat, see Green, *Crisis of Truth*, 78–92; V. H. Galbraith, 'The Death of a Champion (1287)', in Hunt et al. (eds), *Studies in Medieval History Presented to Frederick Maurice Powicke* (Oxford, 1948), 283–95; Frederick C. Hamil, 'The King's Approvers: A Chapter in the History of English Criminal Law', *Speculum*, 11 (1936), 238–58, 243–7, 255–7; J. G. Bellamy, 'Sir John de Annesley and the Chandos Inheritance', *Nottingham Mediaeval Studies*, 10 (1966), 94–105; M. J. Russell, 'Accoutrements of Battle', *Law Quarterly Review*, 99 (1983), 432–42; and 'Trial by Battle Procedure in Writs of Right and Criminal Appeals', *Tijdschrift voor Rechtsgeschiedenis*, 51 (1983), 123–34. For the 1388 Appellants' offer of their own trial by combat as security in the Merciless Parliament, see *WC* 234. In *Fourteenth Century Studies* (Oxford, 1937), 134–6, M. V. Clarke views this as evidence that the appeal was to be conducted under the aegis of the court of chivalry; but see Rogers, 'Parliamentary Appeals', 96–103.

> So that be goddes juggement,
> Thogh that non other man it wolde,
> Sche tok hire juise as sche scholde
>
> (3. 2188–90)

The stress on the absence of external human agency underscores the legitimacy of Orestes's retribution not only with divine sanction but by contrastive household dynamics. The generalization of Orestes's grievance into the public sphere and the expansion of his worship has become the guarantor of (and is reflexively legitimated by) the tendency of *prive*, intensive household conduct towards inward collapse and a self-eliminating spiral of violence.

Actual late medieval landholders were doubtless unaccustomed to marshalling political support by waving bloody swords. I am put in mind, however, of Earl Warenne's famous rusty sword and of less well-known, fourteenth-century symbolic interventions that concentrated complex meaning during disputes. The Westminster chronicler, for example, selects such gestures as pivotal points in a narrative of a dispute between men of the bishop of Exeter and men of the archbishop of Canterbury. After the archbishop's messenger is forced to eat a visitational summons, 'certain members of the archbishop's household' and others corner one of the bishop's squires at a fair and attempt to force him 'to chew and swallow the tips of his own shoes'.[80] Less mimetically, the *Confessio's* repeated opposition between formalist and household-based systems supports ideas of independence for the great household's networks in controlling its tenants, patrimony, and local relations. Yet the *Confessio* carries itself like a majestic work. Even the consistently grand production of early copies seems to hint that this poem will not finally rest easily with its universal ideal of social order entrusted to a many-centred latticework of misrecognized exchange. In book 7, the poem's attempt to anchor this latticework for good places it under severe stress.

---

[80] *WC* 84 (1384). For Earl Warenne and his sword, see *The Chronicle of Walter of Guisborough*, ed. H. Rothwell, Camden Soc. 3rd ser. 89 (London, 1957), 216; Clanchy, *Memory to Written Record*, 35–43.

8

Total Reciprocity and
the Problem of Kingship

When Genius completes the sixth book and sixth sin of his confession with the tale of Nectanabus and Alexander the Great as the book's last major exemplum, Amans presses his confessor to expound Aristotle's instruction of the conqueror in 'al that to a king belongeth' (6. 2413). The confessor protests that the request lies outside his expertise and, once Genius has done his best with Aristotle's wisdom 'In boke as it is comprehended' (6. 2435), Amans and he agree that it is time to return to the 'schrifte' 'as we begonne' (7. 5435, 5423). The participants in the confession themselves thus frame book 7 as a conspicuous annex to the poem's main structure.[1] In the context of discourses of lordship, how-ever, the book is no detour in the poem (yet is simultaneously a serious complication). It attempts to anchor the household-based system of political authority by the superior and analogous authority of the king. Yet the impetus to construct an absolute guarantee for 'good order' (that is, an order constituted around reciprocalist lordship) reveals at certain points a non-reciprocalist discourse of sovereignty that resists and subverts book 7's own theorized claims to reciprocity.

The book on kingship does not disrupt the structure of the *Confessio* as much as Genius and Amans's conversation suggests. In relation to the principal *forma confitendi* of the deadly sins, it draws a line between the six books dealing with sins with an intermediate connection to the matter of love and the final book on lechery. Book 8 (redundant as it would have been as an examination of a heading already unpacked

---

[1] For some attempts to address the particular status of book 7, and its relationship to the rest of the *Confessio*, see Porter, 'Ethical Microcosm and Political Macrocosm'; Simpson, *Sciences and the Self*, 198–229; Copeland, *Rhetoric, Hermeneutics, and Translation*, 211–12; M. A. Manzalaoui, ' "Noght in the Registre of Venus": Gower's English Mirror for Princes', in P. L. Heyworth (ed.), *Medieval Studies for J. A. W. Bennett* (Oxford, 1981), 159–83.

during the preceding portion of the confession) is thereby marked out in the position of a summary coda. As an exposition of all three sciences and the branches of knowledge contained therein, book 7 fits into a penitential-instructional pattern of encyclopedic lectures by Genius which includes the discussion of diverse labours and lores in book 4 (ll. 2363–2671) and the history of religions in book 5 (ll. 747–1959). Most important, with regard to the text's political imagination, is book 7's discussion of kingship, which occupies the bulk of the book and the third primary division of philosophy ('Practique'). This discussion contributes the final component to a developing scheme of lordship before this scheme is recombined and embodied in the long exemplum of Apollonius of Tyre.[2]

The lordship discourse which operates across the narratives of the confession imagines and endorses a social order and system of justice which always registers and reproduces worship. Within this system, the function of the monarch is that of guarantee and last resort. The king stands at the apex of the entire hierarchical social structure and all of the networks of lordship it contains. As legitimation of their landed wealth and political actions, and as their final point of reference, royal authority moors the manifold social matrices which gather around and between the noble heads of great households. As Carpenter states, 'When [the nobility] looked upwards in the hierarchy of deference, it was straight to the king.'[3] What the nobility, and the lesser aristocracy, looked for from the king, above all else, was justice. The king, in other words, was to provide for the protection of their interests, both by preserving the common law against which they could resolve their own disputes and by offering direct redress of grievances when such methods proved unworkable or undesirable.[4] The king's duty to provide justice tended to mean different things to nobility and gentry. Carpenter again:

While the nobles, despite making use of the law-courts, would normally look to the king to intervene personally in a major internecine feud, the gentry relied on a more complex interweaving of public and private processes. In this the king's

---

[2] Cf. above, 152 and nn. 37–8.

[3] Carpenter, *Locality and Polity*, 616.

[4] For evidence of the importance of the king's role in the context of Henry VI's disastrous failure to fulfil it during one fifteenth-century dispute, see S. J. Payling, 'The Ampthill Dispute: A Study in Aristocratic Lawlessness and the Breakdown of Lancastrian Government', *EHR* 104 (1989), 881–907.

law, the king himself, the magnates and their own peers and neighbours all played a part.[5]

According to aristocratic expectations of reciprocalist lordship, the king's performance of justice should adequately represent the worship of all those nobles and lesser landowners for whose stable relations he is responsible, whose own worship sustains order away from the centre, and whose disputes he has the authority to determine. He acts not simply as the pre-eminent magnate, the greatest householder among great householders, for he is responsible for the stability of the entire realm and thus a great multiplicity of social groupings, not a single (if complex) affinity. But he is to act and to guarantee order according to the same principles—the same obligation to worship, to the recognition and conservation of social structure—that ideally animate the reciprocalist lordship of his magnates and those beneath them. Royal redress, in this view, is based on the implementing of permanent law mediated by 'reason'. Reason here constitutes the recognition of the disputing parties' respective *trouthe*, which is knowable by, and so becomes discursively equivalent to, their worship.[6]

Royal authority could accommodate the worship of magnates and other landowners both directly, in particular performances of redress, and indirectly, in the protection of an environment in which landowners are allowed to order their own affairs. Such reciprocal kingship aimed to intervene in landed society's protection of the king's peace only to correct a lapse in this responsibility and then with sensitivity to the worship values and power balance of the local aristocratic social nexus.[7] Late medieval English magnates commonly enjoyed a duty and privilege of serving the king as the pre-eminent agents of justice in the localities. This authority conforms to a reciprocalist model of uncentralized administration of justice, with local politics regulated in the first place by relationships between local notables from the ranks of the gentry and nobility.[8] The reciprocalist, redresser-king is less concerned to make law that might be imposed with blank impartiality by his official judicial

---

[5] Carpenter, *Locality and Polity*, 616–17; see also 351–2, 616–29.

[6] On the significance and theorized range of reason as a kingly attribute, see Watts, *Henry VI*, 28 n. 82, 71. Cf. Carpenter, *Locality and Polity*, 623.

[7] See Harriss, introduction, pp. xxi–xxii.

[8] Comparing the informal arbitral modes of twelfth-century France with the (relatively) formal ones of fifteenth-century England, Edward Powell reckons that their most important common characteristic is the 'central role played by members of the local community in promoting the resolution of disputes by compromise' ('Settlement of Disputes', 35).

mechanisms than he is to conserve the law that nobility and gentry cooperate to uphold. He will safeguard the law as a predictable instrument of aristocratic and unofficial mechanisms of dispute resolution, recognizing and supporting the special role of those who have worship in maintaining social stability and good order.

In England from Edward III's time until late in the fifteenth century, it is commonly argued, a decentralized order obtained, heavily dependent on the nobility and their local relations with the gentry. Carpenter considers that during this period 'the royal government in the localities expanded enormously and, at the same time, was devolved to the local landowners, who exercised it with an almost unprecedented lack of supervision'.[9] Anthony Musson and W. M. Ormrod argue that the judicial system emergent in the fourteenth century was 'much less obviously and self-consciously "devolved" than is usually assumed'.[10] They offer a valuable challenge to those who would underestimate the extent to which an integrated system of central, touring courts and local commissions operated in England in the late fourteenth century. They stress, however, the role of landholders (especially on commissions of the peace) as royal agents, where I am inclined (following Carpenter, Simon Walker, Gerald Harriss, and others) to see these agents first as gentry and magnates with their own, local interests.[11] In this light, the *Confessio's* prevailing idea of kingship appears to validate royal power in the service of steady landed hierarchies.

Yet an axiom of royal authority as total, unified safeguard for all lordship is, in a deep sense, at odds with reciprocalism. The very effort to reproduce for kingship an authority able to place reciprocalist aristocratic relations beyond hazard makes totalizing modes accessible for this authority. The threat of non-reciprocalist kingship becomes more pressing in proportion to such effort. Totalizing, magnificent tendencies inherent in the concept of sovereignty may be bound to emerge even within discourses which seem to allay or prohibit them. Gower's treatment of kingship and some of the commons' legislative efforts seemingly unwittingly provide royal government with symbolic means to enhance its authority without heed to aristocratic interests.

---

[9] Carpenter, *Locality and Polity*, 348; cf. 41–4; see also 28–88, 347–60, 633–40. For a summary of debates about the impetus to and desirability of decentralization in this period, see Harriss, 'Political Society', 28–32. See also above, 177–82, 188–93.

[10] Musson and Ormrod, *Evolution of English Justice*, 74.

[11] See above, 15, 178–9 and nn. 3, 7.

A king whose unofficial justice is unilaterally informed acts magnificently. A king who takes justice into the undiscriminating ambit of a central legal bureaucracy enables commercial (that is, overtly, impersonally calculated) judicial exchanges. In either case, the nobility and local gentry are disenfranchised as agents of public order. Rather than preserving law for the aristocracy to employ, centralizing kings will tend to innovate to legislate their own power (magnificently) or to create law as the formal extension of centralized, bureaucratic power. The latter approach broadly speaking commercializes royal power, so that the administration of justice responds only to the formal dictates of the law and makes no discrimination on the basis of the *trouthe* or worship (that is, the accumulated, misrecognized social capital) of its consumers. If the king also has total power over lawmaking, then this judicial commerce is itself illusory or vulnerable to magnificent royal constructions of its base (the law). Carpenter argues that Richard II's reign represents a failed challenge to the relatively uncentralized status quo that had emerged over previous decades, which anticipated the eclipse of this status quo at the end of the following century. In the context of tensions between 'love'—justice that reflected local balances of power—and 'law' or centralized public authority, 'the real litmus-paper reign is that of Richard II . . . for it is apparent that, even in the 1380s, Richard was trying to establish the kind of rule by "law" that was to be the norm by the sixteenth century'.[12] Such rule by 'law' was increasingly firmly situated in autocratic or majestic kingship.[13]

The expectations of the commons' petitions on new liveries and maintenance during Richard's reign, however, seem to match a reciprocalist model of obligation and redress. As I have said, for example, the petitions of 1388, 1393, and 1397 ask that the king's authority enhance the localities' responsibility over livery and maintenance by means of jurisdictional empowerment for commissions of the peace.[14]

[12] Carpenter, *Locality and Polity*, 637. See also Clanchy, 'Law and Love'.

[13] For the development of Richard's majestic, legally authoritarian kingship, see Saul, 'Vocabulary of Kingship'; Storey, 'Liveries and Commissions of the Peace'; Caroline M. Barron, 'The Quarrel of Richard II with London 1392–7', in Du Boulay and Barron (eds), *Reign of Richard II*; Given-Wilson, *Royal Household*, 213–26, 248–51, 258–67. For the Tudor monarchy as a new, one-sided inflection of service to the crown, whereby a magnate could no longer claim a right to serve but waited instead wholly on royal pleasure, see Harriss, introduction, pp. xxv–xxvii. Harriss argues that this change was facilitated by the gradual decline of noble power, and by the independence from this power of gentry who looked instead to the centre for office and advancement.

[14] *WC* 358; *PROME* iii. 307, 345; and see above, 216 n. 40.

Richard himself lived up to these expectations to some extent with his performance in the Cambridge parliament of 1388. In the speech in which he resumed his position as head of government the following spring, he would spell out a prescription of rule in which justice (against 'manutenencias' and other oppressions) was to feature as a duty and not simply a power.[15] His intervention as mediator between commons and lords in the Cambridge parliament seemed to promise that the mode of justice envisaged would be conciliatory and reciprocalist. The Westminster chronicler relates that, as the commons responded to the lords' sidelining of their concerns over livery badges, the king 'out of desire for domestic tranquillity (*affectans ut tranquillitas foret in regno*), for the sake of the peace, and in order to set an example to others, offered to discard his own badges' (*optulit se deponere sua signa*; WC 356). Although Richard's offer came to nothing, the chronicler represents it as a laudable gesture and the king as a successful mediator between lords and commons.[16] In the end, Richard sanctioned the status quo until the next parliament. Nothing substantive was achieved, but Richard and the chronicler represented the king as a source of final authority, which takes the imprint of both lords' and commons' interests (but is capable, as Strohm points out, of making ' "concessions" ' to the lords though previously excluded from the business of government).[17]

Other formulations of Richard's duty of justice, however, were to suggest that the aristocracy lacked an automatically privileged position within it, and with particular regard to the law. An appeal by localized interests to a final and universal source of authority creates a tension between, on the one hand, the claim of those interests to be recognized by (and thus to constrain) that authority and, on the other hand, the appeal's construction of the authority as final and universal. The relationship between the commons' petitions on livery and maintenance of 1388 and 1390 and the royal ordinance on the same matter promulgated in May 1390 reveals this tension, and its pull towards central authority. The ordinance fashions itself as an instrument of justice and redress by identifying the commons'

---

[15] *Rot. parl.* iii. 404; *Fœdera*, iii/4. 37–8. See also Tuck, *Richard II and the English Nobility*, 148; Storey, 'Liveries and Commissions of the Peace', esp. 135–6; Strohm, *Hochon's Arrow*, 64.

[16] *WC* 354–6. For assessments of the episode as a decisive piece of royal self-representation, see J. A. Tuck, 'The Cambridge Parliament, 1388', *EHR* 84 (1969), 225–43, 235; and *Richard II and the English Nobility*, 134–7; Storey, 'Liveries and Commissions of the Peace', 135–40; Strohm, *Hochon's Arrow*, 63–70.

[17] Strohm, *Hochon's Arrow*, 64. Cf. *WC* 356: 'Rex . . . concessit dominis sepedictis uti eorum signis usque in proximum parliamentum' (the king allowed the lords to go on using their badges until the next parliament).

petitions as its own origins, referring to them as the 'grevous pleint' (*SR* ii. 74) of both lords and commons. It thus appropriates the commons' discourse of justice and the common weal to its own formulation of official, centralized justice, which aggregates the operations of justice to the centre and the king's law.[18] The ordinance's articulation of ideal justice as something available to 'touz noz lieges... sibien povres come riches' (all our lieges as well poor as rich; *SR* ii. 74) and its construction of injustice primarily as the abuse of formal legal procedure efface external claims of worship and social status and the prerogative of the aristocracy as privileged agents and consumers of justice. By turning to Richard to address threats to their exclusive status as mediators of justice at a local level, the gentry, through the commons, provided the king with an opportunity to reconfigure their call for order in general terms—terms which privilege the law over *any* uncentralized set of interests seeking to claim its protection.

MERCILESS PITY: SLIPPAGE TO THE SOVEREIGN IN *CONFESSIO AMANTIS*, BOOK 7

Similarly, Gower's text struggles and, at certain stages in book 7, fails to exclude from kingly redress the totalizing voice of sovereign authority. The commercial, exactly calculating pressure of the law poses little overt challenge to reciprocalism in this part of the poem. Royal power *magnificently* conceived disturbs the *Confessio*'s political logic much more thoroughly. In its own pursuit of an uncompromised guarantee for its vision of reciprocalist, worship-based social relations, the poem's drift towards absolutism is so pervasive that it colonizes even ostensibly reciprocalist discourses, including that of pity.

In book 7, pity is pivotal to Gower's rendition of an orthodox contemporary approach to the problem of unified but representative authority. This orthodoxy was most expressly formulated in treatises on rule such as Giles of Rome's *De regimine principum*, the pseudo-Aristotelian *Secretum secretorum*, and (especially) Brunetto Latini's *Li Livres dou Tresor* (1262–6), and Gower's reworking of these writers belongs in this group.[19] John Watts has analysed the constitutional force of the

---

[18] See above, 218–21.

[19] For Gower's use of Latini, Giles, and *Secretum secretorum* (itself claiming to be Aristotle's correspondence course on kingship for Alexander the Great), see Mainzer, 'Study of the Sources', 34–48; Copeland, *Rhetoric, Hermeneutics, and Translation*, 207–11.

orthodoxy in question, which locates the regulation of royal power finally within the king himself.[20]

The reason why virtue was so important, then, was that it bound the king *internally* to exercise his powers according to the common interest. . . . Just as the Bractonian king was released from the bonds of law partly because he was internally bound to justice, so the four cardinal virtues justified the king's sovereignty by making him inherently responsive to the common interest of the people.[21]

Instead of the four cardinal virtues of prudence, justice, temperance, and fortitude, Gower, loosely following *Secretum secretorum*, presents five core virtues of policy: truth, largesse, justice, pity, and chastity (*CA* 7. 1704–5397). These direct kingship in basically the same manner as the cluster of virtues used as an example by Watts. That is, they are to guarantee 'sovereign representativeness'. The orthodoxy of virtue-led sovereignty granted kingship 'a monopoly of legitimate power' on the assumption that the king would be conditioned to use that power only in the common interest, which in turn he would discover in the counsel of subjects (especially the great). Ideals of counsel refracted a widely supported 'residual belief in the principle that what affected all should be advised by all'.[22] The king's authority was conceived as representative and sovereign because his will alone determined which policy drawn from his own and (especially) public opinion (counsel) was in the common interest.[23]

The 'main endeavour' of this orthodoxy, according to Watts, 'was not to restrain, or to divide, [society's] executive, but to direct it' (*Henry VI*, 21). The danger for reciprocalism was that emphasis on the undivided quality of authority would subsume efforts of direction. The royal act of will that reduces sectional interests to singularity and authorizes opinion as representative policy is made responsive to the common interest by the king's personal virtues, and more generally by reason.[24] As a personal attribute, reason equips the king to identify the common interest and disposes him to act for it. As a propositional category, reason

---

[20] Watts, *Henry VI*, 13–51. The following paragraphs are strongly indebted to Watts's study.

[21] Ibid. 25 (emphasis original). For 'Bracton' (*Bracton on the Laws and Customs of England*; 1220s–1230s), see *Bracton de legibus et consuetudinibus Angliae*, ed. George E. Woodbine, ed. and tr. Samuel E. Thorne (Cambridge, Mass., 1968–77); Brian Tierney, 'Bracton on Government', *Speculum*, 38 (1963), 295–317.

[22] Watts, *Henry VI*, 17, 25–6.

[23] Ibid. 17.

[24] For the orthodox role of the king's will in counsel and rule, see ibid. 27.

becomes 'a coded term for the common interest' and is that which the king draws from counsel and his own informed wisdom.[25] The personal (and sovereign) can thus be conflated with the representative in a single term. In the *Confessio*'s seventh book, kingship is held to be directed by reason in both of these senses, and reason underwrites the directive force of virtues, including pity.

While stresses between sovereign will and reciprocalist virtues are fully exposed in Gower's discussion of pity, he does manage to set down some relatively unimpeded statements about ideal reciprocalist kingship. The model of king as reciprocalist redresser, whose justice recognizes the relative worship of those who seek it just as their obedience ensures his worship and the obedience of others, underpins the theoretical commentary for the largest section by far of book 7's philosophical *divisio*. The section (7. 1641–5397) treats the political science of 'Practique', and in particular the subcategory of Policy, and it comprises a treatise on kingship. In this treatise, reason authorizes a king's adherence to virtues: Genius concludes Aristotle's teaching on policy by counting off the five virtues a king 'oghte of reson' to have (7. 5391). Reason also features in its overtly representative guise in a warning against unresponsive administration of justice and 'the lawe of covoitise' (7. 2754), which, implicitly, ignores local balances of power. By way of antithesis, Genius emphasizes that if 'the lawe is resonable, | The comun poeple stant menable' (7. 2761–2), uniting reason with the common interest and stable hierarchy. Later, in the tale of Roboam, an archetypal embodiment of constitutional theory sees the people in parliament ask their new king that he '"grante ous that which reson wile"' (7. 4037) against innovative law (his father's levies, '"Thing which men nevere afore knewe"'; 7. 4044).

Reason and pity are almost interchangeable as legitimating modifiers of sovereign justice in book 7's constitutional theory. They are ordinarily imbued with reciprocalist meaning. The Latin verse introducing the 'policy' subsection on pity, for instance, combines reason and pity as symmetrical contraries of tyranny: 'Having no reason (*Nil racionis habens*), a tyrant's will strips bare the kingdom . . . But Pity, and the kingdom it will preserve for eternity, pleases not only the people but God' (at 7. 3103; cf. 7. 3520–3). When Tarquin slaughters the Gabines, his failure of reason and pity means that he ignores social structure. He acts 'Withoute reson or pite, | *That* he ne spareth no degre' (7. 4699–4700, emphasis added).

[25] Watts, *Henry VI*, 28 n. 82.

Again the implication is that pity and reason, like 'love', determine justice with reference to social standing (which presumably indicates political responsibility in this tale's context of war).[26] Other statements about policy also suggest the inherently reciprocalist character of its sovereign representativeness. Genius's opening remarks on the subject describe the community in whose interest policy and 'O lawe mot governe' (7. 1696) in a thickly classified way, so that this interest of the people—'Of clerk, of kniht and of Marchant, | And so forth . . . | Withinne Burgh and ek withoute' (7. 1687–90)—is always already 'After thastat' (7. 1698). The common interest is merged with the interest of the aristocracy in the tale of Lycurgus, for the king achieves perfect order without 'debat' because 'Richesse' is 'Ordeigned' according to the 'comun good' and 'the pouer | Of hem that weren in astat | Was sauf' (7. 2930–6; cf. prol. 93–110).

Justice and the common interest are, similarly, socially stratified under the head of policy's second virtue, largesse. Indeed, royal justice is here construed as (household) exchange designed to protect aristocratic power. Glancing back towards the lost stability of an age when property (and the people's interest) was really 'comune' (7. 1991), Genius identifies the originary purpose of kingship to be to reconcile ('appesen'; 7. 2006) conflict over property and, specifically, to regulate the transmission of patrimonies amongst the aristocracy ('lignages'; 7. 2007–8). Such justice is to be moderated by, or adjudicated in the spirit of, largesse (7. 2014–24). In this sense, kingship becomes an extension of reciprocal lordship's essential economic mode.

The goal of a final authority that is somehow at once representative and sovereign, accommodating and supreme, is clear enough in glimpses in book 7. Genius gives a forcefully economic authorization of pity, thick with language of (inexact) obligation—of being 'holden'—which states that a king owes his subjects pity in return for obedience (albeit this is divinely required of them; 7. 4173–80). Explicit theoretical statements and narrative illustrations (including the tales of Julius and the Poor Knight, and Maximinus; 7. 2061–2114, 2765–79) posit a model of royal authority limited by considerations of deferred counter-giving, social degree, and external, localized worship. These limitations are powerfully reasserted in the major late exempla (of Tarquin and Arruns, Lucretia, and Virginia) in the final, fifth section of the policy lecture (on chastity). The king is described as the highest authority in a static hierarchical structure, but his authority depends upon his preservation of that structure.

---

[26] Cf. ibid. 71.

Magnificent pity

Gower's apparent concern to ensure such authority, however, transmutes it into a vision of unqualified monarchic power. Making the monarch the unchallengeable site of justice and social power promises fixity and closure, and this promise seems to lead Gower's text towards the legitimation of totalized royal authority. Of Gower's five virtues of policy, truth and pity may seem most obviously disposed to construct kingship as responsive and representative in the way I have been discussing. In fact, by the economic logic of patrimony, the exempla of chastity house the poem's most radical assertions of royal obligation. Despite, or perhaps because of, appearances, the totalizing logic of the apex makes itself felt most strongly in the section on pity (7. 3103–4214). The earlier section on a king's *trouthe* (7. 1711–1984), by comparison, is brief and abstract. It glosses the crown as a sign that the coronation oath obliges a king to act in the common interest, that he should 'holde trewly his beheste | Of thing which longeth to kinghede' (7. 1764–5). But the discussion surrounds this proposition with the crown's symbolism of supremacy (7. 1745–74) and displaces the most vivid illustration of *trouthe* as unrestricted obligation onto a self-sacrificing wife (Alceste; 7. 1917–43). This kind of muffling of reciprocalist regal principles is much more sustained and striking when Genius comes to the topic of pity.

The pity discussion dissolves reciprocalist substance in virtue-governed sovereignty in three related ways. Most simply, caution that pity should not diminish sovereign authority leads to explicit qualifications against 'excess'. More curiously, pity is represented as an instrument rather than a modifier of power, and the defence of pity—even its enactment—is represented by extreme vengeance. Both kinds of representation render pity a species of magnificence.

The cross-current that warns against submerging justice in excessive pity and mercy is focused on a discussion of 'Pusillamite' (7. 3518–3880) and includes the subsection's longest narrative, the tale of Gideon (7. 3627–3781).[27] Demonstrating that pity, or the avoidance of force, should never be a matter of expedience, and that good order flows from force, God helps Gideon to prune his army of the weak and weary, and to press on with those willing and able to use violence. The energy of such qualification in this section of the poem is remarkable because it is

---

[27] In the absence of the excised tale of the Jew and the Pagan (7. 3207–3329*, 123 lines), the tale of Gideon is by far the most substantial of the pity narratives at 155 lines (excluding its moralization).

pushing at an open door. Pity is eclipsed by its own qualification because its representation as *curtailment* of royal power has been outstandingly weak to begin with. Cautions against pusillanimity and representations of pity itself turn out to be closely related in Genius's learning since both chiefly promote unfettered power.

The entire discussion of pity takes for granted the self-regulating quality of kingship, which secures sovereignty and is aligned with Walter Ullmann's 'theocratic' model of monarchy.[28] The virtues directing the king are authorized by God. Nothing external and temporal restrains the king, and unilateral royal authority is analogously legitimated by another unilateral lord and patriarch.[29] On the other hand, in so far as pity effects obligation to the common interest and especially to custom and law, it accords with Ullmann's 'feudal' type of monarchy. Even within this resemblance, however, the difference is that restraint is internal not external, and royal self-curtailment paradoxically totalizes royal authority as the only authority capable of constraining itself.[30] If there were an external, temporal authority that limited such kingship, it belonged to the makers and inculcators of virtue-based orthodoxy, including the (mainly clerical) handlers of treatises of princely instruction.[31]

'Theocratic' justice is divinely sanctioned and comes directly to the king without the mediation of counsel. Its effects are totalizing, felt as the expunging of contrary signification. This is the kind of justice that operates in book 7's section on pity. In particular, a strong symbolic nexus links God, the king, and the images of the lion and the champion, producing a theocratic and magnificent version of royal justice. As signs in this nexus, both lion and champion share reference to God and king. This linking authorizes kingship by proximity to divine authority, and associates royal justice with the unanswerable power of God. God the champion 'Whos strengthe mai noman withstonde' (7. 3253), is yoked to the wartime king, who must 'Be to the poeple a champioun | Withouten

[28] See Walter Ullmann, *The Individual and Society in the Middle Ages* (London, 1967), 66–9.

[29] Cf. above, 170 and n. 61. See also Strohm, *Hochon's Arrow*, 125 and n. 4, quoting Jean-Louis Flandrin, *Families in Former Times: Kinship, Household and Sexuality*, tr. Richard Southern (Cambridge, 1979), 119–20.

[30] Cf. Scanlon's analysis of kingship—its 'public dependence' and its authority's 'absolute singularity'—and 'the image of the self-regulated royal body' in book 7 of the *Confessio* (*Narrative, Authority, and Power*, 282–97, quotes at 296). For the idea that royal self-curtailment strengthens royal power by enhancing subjects' loyalty and obedience, see *CA* 7. 3138–41; Watts, *Henry VI*, 29–30.

[31] For the clerical claim to this kind of authority, in which lay writers such as Gower and Thomas Hoccleve intervened, see Scanlon, *Narrative, Authority, and Power*.

eny Pite feigned' (7. 3538–9). The lion appears three times in the pity section in an early version of the *Confessio*. In the tale of the Jew and the Pagan (7. 3207–3360*), omitted after revision, the lion represents the instrumentality of God's justice. Later, the lion figures the just prince (7. 3387–3403, 3532–9). Lion and champion—adjacent in the sketch of the wartime king—coordinate divine and regal authority. The lion, especially, brings together pity and a resistance to pity on a shared ground of totalizing authority.

Even when the lion or another agent exercises pity as a conspicuous abeyance of force, book 7 supports Andrew Galloway's analysis of pity as a 'palpable' instrument of power; and for palpable we can frequently read magnificent.[32] Thus, the lion that Gower uses to emblematize the natural justice of mercy and the unnaturalness of tyranny more persuasively figures magnificent power:

> Of the natures this I finde,
> The fierce Leon in his kinde,
> Which goth rampende after his preie,
> If he a man finde in his weie,
> He wole him slen, if he withstonde.
> Bot if the man coude understonde
> To falle anon before his face
> In signe of mercy and of grace,
> The Leon schal of his nature
> Restreigne his ire in such mesure,
> As thogh it were a beste tamed,
> And torne awey halfvinge aschamed,
> That he the man schal nothing grieve.
> Hou scholde than a Prince achieve
> The worldes grace, if that he wolde
> Destruie a man whanne he is yolde *has yielded*
> And stant upon his mercy al?

(7. 3387–3403)

'Mercy' and 'grace' here are not recognition of another's worth (much less worship). They are only significations of absolute power that are alternative to physical death, but nonetheless operate by the exclusion of another's being. The lion's destructive 'ire' is only restrained when the man has disavowed his being by falling to the ground in abject submission. Analogously, the representation of power remains totalized when a

---

[32] Andrew Galloway, 'The Literature of 1388 and the Politics of Pity in Gower's *Confessio Amantis*', in Emily Steiner and Candace Barrington (eds), *The Letter of the Law: Legal Practice and Literary Production in Medieval England* (Ithaca, NY, 2002), 95.

prince might grant mercy because the subject is already 'yolde'. Destruction would be a redundant doubling of the totality of power. Here pity is no less unilateral and scarcely less oppressive than 'tyranny'.

The magnificent pity of Pompey (7. 3215–44) resembles the lion's. In one sense this tale reverses the pity of the previous exemplum, in which the exemplary *pitous* King Codrus of Athens inverts the totalizing sovereign principle by choosing (like Alceste) 'himselve to be ded' (7. 3199) in order to save his people from defeat. Codrus obliterates his own being in favour of his subjects', while Pompey restores another's power as a sign of his own.[33] In the exemplum of Pompey's *pitous* restoration of the defeated king of Armenia, the narration is of *Pompey's* practice above all. The restoration may recover the king's 'astat al full and plein' (7. 3235), but it also recontextualizes it and alters its signs, so that Pompey's act of pity first of all represents his own power. Pompey, raised on his dais

> Tofore al Rome in his Paleis,
> As he that wolde upon him rewe,
> Let yive him his corone newe.

> (7. 3232–4)

The setting expresses Pompey's pre-eminence and the passage denotes the 'coronation' as Pompey's exchange (the king of Armenia is not named or titled in the passage), and as 'newe', divorced from the prisoner king's previous authority. The *rewe/newe* rhyme tacitly associates pity with freedom from exchange histories and the obligation they produce. Pompey's act of pity answers a lack of further exchange instead of a substantive challenge. Like the lion, Pompey responds to the Armenian prisoner's abjection, his 'ful gret humilite' (7. 3227). This ostentatiously unbalanced sequence not only emphatically disavows obligation to the vanquished king, it possesses him by imposing on him an undefrayable capital of obligation (since he cannot hope ever to bestow on Pompey a comparable increase in power). Pity's unanswerable gift doubles the overmatching exchange of military power and extends its effects in 'final pes' (7. 3241). To paraphrase Bourdieu,

[33] A more complicated reading of the tale of Codrus, however, might take a lead from Ernst Kantorowicz's famous discussion of the premise that the status of a king's subjects as 'his poeple' (7. 3195) itself signifies the king just as the status of 'his body' does (7. 3192). In this case, Apollo offers Codrus only alternative paths to the injury of his own being, and the one he selects does more to preserve and enhance the signification of his kingship (and kingship generally through the representation of the choice in an exemplum), even though it involves his physical death. See Ernst H. Kantorowicz, *The King's Two Bodies: A Study in Mediaeval Political Theology* (Princeton, 1957).

Pompey's pity perpetuates a relationship of utter domination and returns the recipient to an environment in which debt can be (intermin-
ably) repaid not just by peaceful 'humilite' but in more useful forms of
political cooperation.[34]

Magnificence is rarely so non-violent in Genius's discussion of pity.
Gower's lion and champion are parts of a pattern of totalizing but also
actively violent 'pite'. Far from acting only as a caveat to the main theme
of the section, the violence of justice threatens wholly to occupy the
theme of pity and to overturn its perlocutionary force. Galloway has
argued that the *Confessio* advances 'a sense of true "pite" as including,
indeed mainly being, justice, vengeance, even extreme violence'.[35] As
well as being a fearsome emblem of 'mercy', the lion turns killer in
support of pity in the tale of the Jew and the Pagan, leaving the bullying
Jew 'Al blodi ded upon the gras' (7. 3322*) in demonstration that 'what
man that to pite serveth, | . . . | God schal hise foomen so represse, | That
thei schul ay stonde under foote' (7. 3332–5*). A cluster of five narratives in the middle of the subsection (from the tale of Leontius to the
tale of Spertachus and Thamaris; 7. 3267–3517) further develops the
violent magnificence associated with pity.

When the discussion turns from Pompey's pity to consider 'crualte' and
its by-product, 'tirannie' (7. 3249–50), Genius hints that his lecture will
now illuminate pity *in opposition to* tyranny, which God always throws
down (7. 3254–61). The exempla that follow, however, are much more
interested in showing tyrants 'overladde' (7. 3255) than in counterpoint-
ing their example with one of pity. The lesson that kingship guided by
pity is superior to tyranny is left entirely implicit, and is actually threatened by narrative specificity which celebrates absolute, unilateral, and
violent justice. This justice is itself defined by its very lack of pity.
A general statement about justice against tyranny sums up the pure
retributive economy common to the four preceding brief exempla:

> Bot hou so that the wrong beginne
> Of tirannie, it mai noght laste,
> Bot such as thei don ate laste
> To othre men, such on hem falleth;

[34] Bourdieu, *Theory of Practice*, 189; for possessing by giving, see 195.
[35] Galloway, 'Literature of 1388', 95. Galloway's study is more widely concerned than
mine with an ethic of pity in the *Confessio* and Gower's *Cronica tripertita* (86–104), and
attaches Gower's interest in pity directly to Ricardian politics, especially those of the
Merciless Parliament of 1388.

> For ayein suche Pite calleth
> Vengance to the god above.
>
> (7. 3376–81)

Tyranny is to be met with tyranny, and 'Pite' is not to qualify sovereign force but to underwrite an even more totalized 'Vengance'. The vocabulary of 'Pite' and 'Vengance' which initially divided competing models of power is now mingled.

The exempla themselves have shown 'pite' as the mirror image or twin of tyranny. Leontius overthrows Justinian and cuts off his nose and lips. God 'which is al merciable' (7. 3276) addresses this evil by ordaining a repeat sequence of deposition and cruelty. Leontius is 'schoven out of his empire' (7. 3280) and, with Tiberius in turn leading Rome 'after his will' (7. 3282), suffers the loss of his nose and lips. Only as a coda to the tale does Genius assert that 'Pite was set up ayein' as a result of this sequence, with Justinian returned to power (7. 3289–94). Justinian's restoration is not presented as a correction to Tiberius's will.

In the following narrative, one Berillus, counsellor to the tyrant Siculus, designs a brass bull as an instrument of torture and execution and ends up the chamber's first victim by sleight of 'The devel' and 'for a trespas which he dede' (7. 3325–7). The bull's special attribute is its ability to transform the 'criinge' of its victims into 'A belwinge in a mannes Ere' (7. 3322–3). The device totalizes Siculus's power, destroying the victim and permitting his voice to signify nothing of human status but only the 'peine' (7. 3319) that is the manifestation of the tyrant's might. The moralization of the tale attributes Berillus's fate to God's abomination of 'tirannie and crualte' (7. 3333–7). It follows that the magnificent will of Siculus, 'whom no Pite myhte areste' (7. 3298), acts as an instrument of divine justice even as it totalizes its own representation. Siculus, effecting God's justice, wholly appropriates the brass bull by expunging its inventor instead of signifying Berillus's own being—his cruelty and 'oghne ymaginynge' (7. 3312)—with the 'likinge' (7. 3311) which his gift sought.[36] Two further exempla in which pitilessness answers

---

[36] When Hoccleve retells this popular exemplum in his own manual of kingship, he more clearly makes the (earthly) cause of the counsellor's falling victim to his own cruel invention the tyrant's totalization of majesty and corresponding antagonism against any competing claim to that majesty's central facet of cruelty. See Thomas Hoccleve, *The Regiment of Princes*, ed. Charles R. Blyth (Kalamazoo, Mich., 1999), ll. 3032–8: 'For whan the kyng this cruel werk had seyn, | The craft of it commendid he ful wel, | But the entente he fully heeld ageyn, | And seide: "Thow that art more cruel | Than I, the maydenhede of this jewel | Shalt preeve anoon; this is my jugement." | And so as blyve he was therin ybrent.'

pitilessness 'riht in the same wise' (7. 3349) simply replicate the pattern of retributive equivalence. These vignettes of Dionysius and Lichaon (7. 3341–69) leave the boundary initially drawn between unrestrained sovereign violence and 'pite' beyond their horizons.

Subsequently, the tale of Spertachus and Thamaris introduces symbolic inflation to the narrative economy of retribution that acts in the name of pity but mirrors tyranny's force. The hard justice and violence of the agency theoretically aligned with pity now exceeds the tyranny it addresses. Duke Spertachus is described as 'A cruel man' whose 'tirannies' amount to the execution of all enemies for 'His lust and al his moste gloire' and without mercy (7. 3420–9). His will to 'do malice' (7. 3439) is said to increase 'A thousendfold' (7. 3438) upon his becoming king of Persia, but only the single killing which prompts Thamaris to enact the 'vengance' which God 'Hath schape' (7. 3440–1) is specifically narrated. Even then no concrete details, and thus no particular horror, are attached to the death of Thamaris's son, whom the king 'dede... slen in his presence' (7. 3453). Indeed, Thamaris's own reaction is represented only in terms of her immediate, practical preparations for vengeance, and remains unelaborated by emotion or speech. Horrific, bloody visual effects are reserved for Thamaris's own merciless justice. Thamaris may not kill most of her prisoners, but for Spertachus and his princely allies a brutally symbolic punishment is devised, against which 'It halp no mercy forto crie | To him which whilom dede non' (7. 3484–5). At Thamaris's bidding, the king's chief counsellors are bled to death over a 'vessel' (7. 3507) and the bloody conqueror is then drowned in the ghoulish brew.

The gruesome fate of Spertachus and his advisers concludes the portion of the pity discussion that has focused on tyranny as pity's negative complement. Remarkably, Genius turns now not to positive elaboration of pity, but to warnings against excess in this virtue, which peak with the tale of Gideon. This transition, or short-circuiting, only intensifies the text's apparent anxiety that pity should not be conceived as a compromising or derogation of regal authority. For, as though the foregoing illustration of the remorseless punishment of tyranny threatened to plant a destabilizing concept of leniency at the root of the kingship ideal, Genius now moves quickly to warn against 'Pusillamite', into which pity decays when it hesitates 'To slen in cause of rihtwisnesse' (7. 3524–7). It is at this point that he figures the ideal wartime king as lion and champion (7. 3532–9).

Having obscured any substantive mediative content of pity by extensively illustrating the arbitrary negating (or overmatching) of its opposite, the lecture in pity has then radically closed down the conceptual
space in which pity can operate. Acts of mercy are not imagined or are
imagined only as excessive pity. Pity seems to own no normalized room
for itself, but to exist as always already an excess.

The Fool and the Courtiers

Gower's treatment of royal pity discloses the tensions and contradictions
of his text's reciprocalist politics, which the *Confessio* is otherwise much
more adept at negotiating and concealing. Even within the particular
theme of kingship, which poses such difficulties for the articulation of a
'total' reciprocalist ideal, Gower can provide relatively secure propositions of obligation. Emerging from the pity section, as a kind of
appendix to it, a discussion of good counsel restores mediative content
to ideal kingship. Something like normal service is resumed. Rule is not
a 'theocratic' recipe of divinely backed virtue and will in this exemplum.
In its strongest formulation, good counsel obliges royal authority to take
the impress of speech and interests outside itself, and one exemplum
works especially hard to implant this reciprocalist ideal into the concept
of kingship. The tale of the Fool and the Courtiers uses the *Confessio's*
familiar image scheme of ordered outwardness and truncated lordship
to describe good counsel as the representation of the common interest
outside the king's personal capability. The tale's king seeks to understand
popular gossip, but ill counsel, as a function of excessively *prive* household relations, erects a barrier between royal authority and publicly
generated signification. Faulty counsel comes from two pre-eminent
household officers—chamberlain and steward—and occurs in an arche-
typal *prive* environment. The king and his intimates meet 'Withinne his
chambre upon a nyht' (7. 3947) where they gather around 'the Chimi-
nee' (7. 3951), the symbol of exclusiveness in Langland's Dame Studie's
complaint about the use of household space.[37] These symptoms of
insularity signal magnificent power's threat to good counsel and the

---

[37] See above, 197–8. Genius has already pessimistically categorized privileged and less
privileged methods of political influence based on a separation between hall and chamber. While office-holding and money suffice for influence at the lower level, flattery—the
more sophisticated tool of the evil counsellor—is required for success 'In chambre' (7.
2321–5). For flattery or verbal facility as the quintessential element of a courtly environment, see Patterson, 'Court Politics', 19–26.

common profit. Both the 'favorable' (7. 3976) steward and the 'soubtil and wys' (7. 3980) chamberlain are vehicles of magnificence not the common interest. They speak the king back to himself, offering counsel purely in order to magnify or at least not to diminish his worship (7. 3971–88).

The fool's explosive vocal irruption into chamber decorum, as he 'to skorne bothe lowh' (7. 3992), pricks the skin of magnificence and leads to the restoration of channels between the king and the people and to the end of oppression. The figure of the fool, it is true, imaginatively dissociates royal restraint from any ordinary political agency because he is penned in the interstices of social structure, in the liminal category of licensed dissenter ('that with his babil pleide'; 7. 3955).[38] Such separation can inter the fool within symbolism of the king's own will, so that good counsel becomes identified with sovereign self-curtailment. Allowing for the fool's marginal status, however, the tale's uncomplicated transition from his emphatic advocacy of truth-telling to the implementation of wise counsel is nevertheless striking when compared with complex and extremely problematic representations of truth-telling and its feasibility at court elsewhere in late medieval English literature. Works such as Clanvowe's *Boke of Cupide*, Chaucer's 'Manciple's Tale', *Sir Gawain and the Green Knight*, and *Mum and the Sothsegger* (?1409) suggest that truth-telling chooses between only alternate forms of impotence, in exclusion from court or absorption and neutralization in the court's own facile language.[39] Gower's narrative, conversely, concludes with the installation of 'the vertuous' (7. 4006), complete social restoration, and a moralization which explains good counsel as effective mediation of the 'clamour' of the 'comun poeple' (7. 4019, 4021). The tale is thus cemented into the poem's reciprocalist, Saturnian vision by the same tiered concept of political exchange employed by the 1388 appeal to constrain King Richard.

---

[38] For Victor Turner's seminal discussions of liminality, see *The Ritual Process: Structure and Anti-Structure* (London, 1969); and *Dramas, Fields, and Metaphors: Symbolic Action in Human Society* (Ithaca, NY, 1974). For fooling as liminal, see Turner, *Ritual Process*, 108–11; Max Gluckman, *Politics, Law and Ritual in Tribal Society* (Oxford, 1965), 97–104.

[39] See Patterson, 'Court Politics', 19–20, 24; Fradenburg, 'Manciple's Servant Tongue'; Helen Barr and Kate Ward-Perkins, '"Spekyng for one's sustenance": The Rhetoric of Counsel in *Mum and the Sothsegger*, Skelton's *Bowge of Court*, and Elyot's *Pasquil the Playne*', in Helen Cooper and Sally Mapstone (eds), *The Long Fifteenth Century: Essays for Douglas Gray* (Oxford, 1997), 249–72.

Pity becomes the flaw which reveals the conflicted core of the reciprocalist ideal pursued throughout Gower's text. Book 7's pity discussion testifies that because reciprocalism seeks to preserve hierarchy it will tend to totalizing pronouncements despite its positing that social capital (and therefore status) is always *mutually* at stake in social relations and exchanges. Gower's inability to accommodate pity to kingship directs a naked light upon negotiations between principles of reciprocity and the treasured keystone of static hierarchy. These negotiations are deeply inscribed in the *Confessio*, but seize up in Gower's absolutist exempla of royal justice. The tale of the Fool and the Courtiers, with its practised narrative denigration of magnificence, its powerful yet liminal agent of correction, and its neat assertion of the possibility of the stable, asymmetric circulation of political capital, negotiates reciprocalism much more successfully. The tales of Tarquin and Brutus, Virginius, and Apollonius to follow, and the earlier tale of Orestes, represent powerful uncentralized aristocratic reciprocalism much more plainly. All of these tales are more typical illustrations of the poem's investment in the great household, its case against magnificence, and its ability to reconcile and suppress reciprocalism's inherent contradictions.

Conclusion

Book 7 of *Confessio Amantis* focuses on kingship as a means to fix a system that depends on internal play. Elsewhere, however, the poem's view of politics is wider and takes in less elevated personal relations. The justice and lordship of monarchs features in tandem with the power of lesser figures in Genius's narrative collection. If Arion's heir is understood to be an uncrowned poet (tentatively even Gower himself), then a king alone cannot achieve the social serenity envisaged at the end of the prologue, and is invisible in its idealized peace of lords and commons, scarcely required when conflict is put aside locally in the first place. In texts of the *Confessio* that retain Gower's Ricardian commission scene, royal power has an improvised quality within the larger reach of history. Unlike more conventional commission and presentation scenes (including frontispiece illuminations), which persuade us that a king is wholly the book's origin and *telos*, when Gower happens upon Richard's barge on the Thames, the ensuing royal commission is hedged by happenstance (with several phrases disclosing narrative's propensity to costume that which 'bifel' by 'chance' as 'thing which scholde...betyde'; prol. 35–45*).[1] The barge-court itself is inconspicuous, even unprepossessing, its introduction so long deferred after mention of the Thames and London in the guise of the New Troy that it is almost lost 'Under' the town (and its aggrandizing historical palimpsest) and in the midst of London's 'flowende' artery.[2] The royal encounter is not the poet's

---

[1] Cf. (on Gower's independence as poet) V. J. Scattergood, 'Literary Culture at the Court of Richard II', in Scattergood and Sherborne (eds), *English Court Culture*, 30–1. On more conventional scenes, see Dhira B. Mahoney, 'Courtly Presentation and Authorial Self-Fashioning', *Mediaevalia*, 21 (1996), 97–160; Elizabeth Salter and Derek Pearsall, 'Pictorial Illustration of Late Medieval Poetic Texts', in Andersen et al. (eds), *Medieval Iconography and Narrative: A Symposium* (Odense, 1980), 111–23. On literary commission and presentation at court, see also Richard Firth Green, *Poets and Princepleasers* (Toronto, 1980), 61–5. On Gower, royal authority, and New Troy, see also Federico, *New Troy*, 1–28, 99–142.

[2] Scanlon argues that Gower's Trojan references here 'diminish Richard's personal importance' as 'only the current player in a much larger scheme of national destiny' (*Narrative, Authority, and Power*, 253).

destination but simply an incident in the ordinary run of events (as he 'be bote cam rowende'; prol. 40*). For the audience that knows of (or knows only) versions of the poem in which the commission scene has been replaced, royal authority is yet further from a central role in Gower's project.[3] In either case, if history's ruin is to be averted, it will be by the poetically inspired reform of individuals throughout the political community and not by royal command.

First and foremost in bearing the effects of such reform would be the household and affinities of the powerful, aristocratic and royal alike. In texts of all kinds, household practice, household space, and material culture are vital to social imagination that serves aristocratic and royal dispositions. *Confessio Amantis* develops its own particular political positions, but in the raw elements of its social imagination it is representative of a vast array of contemporary writings. In late medieval society and its texts, parks, walls, and gateways; halls, chambers, fireplaces, and chimneys; covered chairs, quilted cushions, trestle tables, salt cellars, spices, sauces, game, and rich robes communicate power and are implicated in political exchanges. All of these items, for instance, feature in the second fitt of *Sir Gawain and the Green Knight*, where they make up the character of a castle at once sumptuous and vaguely threatening.[4] Hautdesert imposes its own agenda on Gawain (its luxury nearly stifling its guest's initiative), but this agenda nonetheless objectifies a reciprocalist rule of exchange. By explicit and immediate but inexact reciprocity, the exchange of winnings game at the castle gives regulated, potentially lethal consequence to personal relations in the context of a single visitor's encounter with a single household. Such consequence is implicitly warranted because equivalent relations (of *trouthe*-based reciprocity between lords) underpinned the unofficial economy of power that ordered (or disturbed) aristocratic life in late medieval England. Gawain, of course, falls short on this count and eschews reciprocity, first by holding back the green girdle and then, more conclusively, by refusing Bertilak's invitation to return to Hautdesert at the end of his adventure.[5] When other narratives, like Gower's, drew on the same store

---

[3] For discussions of the relevant versions of the *Confessio*, see above, 57 n. 106.

[4] *Sir Gawain and the Green Knight*, ed. J. R. R. Tolkien, E. V. Gordon, and Norman Davis, 2nd edn (Oxford, 1967), ll. 763–900.

[5] On *Gawain* and exchange, see Heal, 'Reciprocity and Exchange', 187–92; Jill Mann, 'Price and Value in *Sir Gawain and the Green Knight*', *Essays in Criticism*, 36 (1986), 290–318; repr. in Derek Pearsall (ed.), *Chaucer to Spenser: A Critical Reader* (Oxford, 1999), 187–205.

of aristocratic material culture, they too designated a political arena and evoked expectations about good lordship and public consequence. We need go no further than the contemporary controversy over livery to appreciate how heavily household cloth (and its misrecognized exchange) could be freighted with implications for the conduct of politics and public life.

The *Confessio* recognizes the depths of the political economy in a society in which patrimonial memory and worship could overmatch, for example, a legally made contract or will if such a statement were held not to have spoken for atavistic or peripheral (but powerfully connected) interests in a manor. By deftly demeaning Amans and the magnificent politics to which he aspires, the *Confessio* supports a notion of a political community dominated by the mutual interests, aid, and responsibilities of gentry, nobility, and royalty. Other groups are marginalized, to benefit from lordship's steady supervision of public life. The poem voiced this sense of society at a time when lordship was newly embattled by the economic power and political disquiet of social inferiors. Taking up and transforming ideas about the lordship of the most powerful especially, the vocalization provokes consternation at practices that might weaken the importance in public life of carefully constructed personal relationships—that is, histories of obligation—across all levels of landed society. Threats come from commercial exchange, 'prive' power, and unilateral lordship or kingship. Other texts of the 1380s and 1390s use discourse shared by Gower's poem to confront such threats more directly, and I have discussed parliamentary examples in particular in this book.[6] Such texts confirm that there was an influential constituency for the dispositions that the *Confessio* reinforces.

Members of landowning families who encountered *Confessio Amantis*, as well as groups in their households, and the scribes and urban and government professionals amongst whom the poem also circulated (and who often belonged to landed families themselves), were exposed to metaphorical and narrative embodiments of the great household and its affinity-based politics.[7] Gower refashions widespread ideas and a wealth of source material in an enormous expression of the good political economy. This economy is controlled by the resources of the landed household; its unofficial, uncommercial exchanges keep open the busy paths of worship and privileged relationships within local networks and

[6] See above, esp. 43–9, 188–93, 210–19.
[7] For the late medieval ownership and audience of the *Confessio*, see above, 31 n. 12.

between localities and the centre; and it is fixed (contradictorily) by supreme royal authority. Both by means and as part of this economy's idealized expression, Amans's will to serve under Cupid's magnificence is set aside in favour of a vision of less volatile lordship, built up by the work of reciprocalist exchange. This work is the substance of the ideal of 'love' and 'accord' fostered in the new age of Arion. A strong, equivalent disposition for unofficial, household-based solutions to social tensions was evinced in all parts of the country by the political practice of contemporary aristocrats, such as Sir Thomas Fichet of Spaxton, Somerset, whose 'labour' as good lord in a dispute between his lesser local gentry relatives earned him the reversion of the disputed manor.[8] Economic, but misrecognized and ungoverned by central institutions, the actual 'labour' of good lords (and their adherents) and the imagined work behind Gower's ideal of 'love' are both sustained by belief in the same social arrangement of power.

[8] Robert W. Dunning (ed.), *The Hylle Cartulary*, Somerset Record Soc. 68 (Taunton, 1968), no. 156, quoted in Walker, *Lancastrian Affinity*, 259; cf. nos 157–8.

Bibliography

PRIMARY MATERIAL

Manuscripts

London, National Archives: DL 25 (Deeds, ser. L); SC 8 (Ancient Petitions).
Oxford, All Souls' College, MS 98.
Oxford, Bodleian Library, MS Fairfax 3.

Printed primary material

Aeschylus, *Eumenides*, ed. Alan H. Sommerstein (Cambridge: Cambridge University Press, 1989).

Aliscans, ed. Erich Wienbeck, Wilhelm Hartnacke, and Paul Rasch (Halle: Max Niemeyer, 1903).

Aliscans (Rédaction A), ed. Claude Régnier, 2 vols (Paris: Champion, 1990).

Ancrene Wisse: A Corrected Edition of the Text in Cambridge, Corpus Christi College, MS 402, ed. Bella Millett, 2 vols, EETS, os 325–6 (Oxford: Oxford University Press, 2005–7).

Andeli, Henri d', *Le Lai d'Aristote de Henri d'Andeli*, ed. Maurice Delbouille (Paris: University of Liege, 1951).

The Anonimalle Chronicle, 1333–1381, ed. V. H. Galbraith (1927; Manchester: Manchester University Press, 1970).

Aquinas, St Thomas, *Summa theologiæ*, ed. and tr. Dominicans from the English-speaking provinces, 61 vols (London, 1963–76).

Armitage-Smith, Sydney, ed., *John of Gaunt's Register (1371–1375)*, 2 vols, Camden Soc. 3rd ser. 20–1 (London: Camden, 1911).

Augustine, St, *De civitate Dei*, ed. B. Dombart and A. Kalb, 2 vols (Turnholt: Brepols, 1955).

—— *Confessions*, tr. R. S. Pine-Coffin (London: Penguin, 1961).

—— *Confessionum libri XIII*, ed. Lucas Verheijen, Corpus Christianorum, ser. Latina, 27 (Turnholt: Brepols, 1981).

—— *The City of God Against the Pagans*, tr. R. W. Dyson (Cambridge: Cambridge University Press, 1998).

Bailey, Mark, ed., *The English Manor c.1200–c.1500* (Manchester: Manchester University Press, 2002).

Boccaccio, Giovanni, *Teseida*, ed. Salvatore Battaglia (Florence: Sansoni, 1938).

Bracton de legibus et consuetudinibus Angliae, ed. George E. Woodbine, ed. and tr. Samuel E. Thorne, 4 vols (Cambridge, Mass.: Harvard University Press, 1968–77).

Brown, Carleton, ed., *Religious Lyrics of the Fourteenth Century* (Oxford: Clarendon, 1924).

Calendar of Inquisitions Post Mortem and Other Analogous Documents Preserved in the Public Record Office, 20 vols, os (London: HMSO, 1904–95).

Calendar of Letter-Books Preserved among the Archives of the Corporation of the City of London at the Guildhall: Letter-Book H, ed. Reginald R. Sharpe (London: Corporation of London, 1907).

Calendar of the Close Rolls Preserved in the Public Record Office (1381–1402), 6 vols (London: HMSO, 1920–7).

Calendar of the Patent Rolls Preserved in the Public Record Office (1381–1401), 6 vols and suppl. (London: HMSO, 1897–1909 and 1977).

Chandos herald, *La Vie du Prince Noir by Chandos Herald*, ed. Diana B. Tyson, Beihefte zur Zeitschrift für Romanische Philologie, 147 (Tübingen: Max Niemeyer, 1975).

Chaucer, Geoffrey, *The Parlement of Foulys*, ed. D. S. Brewer (1960; Manchester: Manchester University Press, 1972).

—— *The Riverside Chaucer*, ed. Larry D. Benson, 3rd edn (Oxford: Oxford University Press, 1987).

The Chronicle of Walter of Guisborough, ed. H. Rothwell, Camden Soc. 3rd ser. 89 (London: Camden, 1957).

Clanvowe, Sir John, *The Works of Sir John Clanvowe*, ed. V. J. Scattergood (Cambridge: D. S. Brewer, 1975).

Cleanness, in *The Poems of the Pearl Manuscript: Pearl, Cleanness, Patience, Sir Gawain and the Green Knight*, ed. Malcolm Andrew and Ronald Waldron, 5th edn (Exeter: Exeter University Press, 2007), 111–84.

Delle Colonne, Guido, *Historia destructionis Troiae*, ed. and tr. Mary Elizabeth Meek (Bloomington, Ind.: Indiana University Press, 1974).

Deschamps, Eustache, *Œuvres complètes de Eustache Deschamps*, ed. le marquis de Queux de Saint-Hilaire and Gaston Raynaud, 11 vols, SATF (Paris: Didot, 1878–1903).

Dobson, R. B., ed. and tr., *The Peasants' Revolt of 1381*, 2nd edn (London: Macmillan, 1983).

Dunning, Robert W., ed., *The Hylle Cartulary*, Somerset Record Soc. 68 (Taunton: Somerset Record Soc., 1968).

Echard, Siân, and Claire Fanger, *The Latin Verses in the Confessio Amantis: An Annotated Translation* (East Lansing, Mich.: Colleagues, 1991).

Eulogium historiarum sive temporis, ed. Frank Scott Haydon, 3 vols, Rolls Ser. (London, 1858–63).

Euripides, *Orestes*, ed. and tr. M. L. West (Warminster, Wilts.: Aris & Phillips, 1987).

Favent, Thomas, *Historia siue narracio de modo et forma Mirabilis Parliamenti apud Westmonasterium anno domini millesimo ccclxxxvj, regni vero regis Ricardi secundi post conquestum anno decimo, per Thomam Fauent clericum indictata*, ed. May McKisack, Camden Soc. 3rd ser. 37 (London: Camden, 1926); tr.

Andrew Galloway, appendix, in Steiner and Barrington (eds), *Letter of the Law* (2002), 231–52.

The Findern Manuscript: Cambridge University Library MS Ff.I.6, introd. Richard Beadle and A. E. B. Owen (London: Scolar, 1977).

Froissart, Jean, *Œuvres de Froissart: Chroniques*, ed. Baron Kervyn de Lettenhove, 25 vols in 26 pts (Brussels: Devaux, 1867–77).

—— *Œuvres de Froissart: Poésies*, ed. A. Scheler, 3 vols (Brussels: Devaux, 1870–2).

Furnivall, Frederick J., ed., *Hymns to the Virgin and Christ, The Parliament of Devils, and other Religious Poems*, EETS, os 24 (London, 1867).

Giles of Rome, D. *Aegidii Romani archiepiscopi Bituricensis ordinis fratrum eremitarum Sancti Augustini de regimine principum libri III* (Rome, 1556).

Given-Wilson, Chris, ed. and tr., *Chronicles of the Revolution 1397–1400: The Reign of Richard II* (Manchester: Manchester University Press, 1993).

—— Paul Brand, Anne Curry, Rosemary Horrox, Geoffrey Martin, Mark Ormrod, and Seymour Phillips, eds and trs, *The Parliament Rolls of Medieval England 1275–1504*, CD-ROM (Leicester: Scholarly Digital Editions, 2005). Citations refer to *Rotuli parliamentorum* pagination (available in this edn).

Godfrey of Viterbo, *Gotifredi Viterbiensis opera*, ed. George Waitz, Monumenta Germaniae Historica, 22 (Hanover, 1872).

Gower, John, *Complete Works*, ed. G. C. Macaulay, 4 vols (Oxford: Clarendon, 1899–1902); vols ii–iii repr. as *The English Works of John Gower*, 2 vols, EETS, es 81–2 (Oxford: Oxford University Press, 1900–1).

—— *The Major Latin Works of John Gower: The Voice of One Crying and The Tripartite Chronicle*, tr. Eric W. Stockton (Seattle: University of Washington Press, 1962).

—— *Mirour de l'Omme (The Mirror of Mankind)*, tr. William Burton Wilson (East Lansing, Mich.: Colleagues, 1992).

—— *Confessio Amantis*, ed. Russell A. Peck, 3 vols, TEAMS Middle English Texts (Kalamazoo, Mich.: Medieval Institute Publications, 2000–4).

Havely, N. R., ed. and tr., *Chaucer's Boccaccio: Sources of Troilus and the Knight's and Franklin's Tales* (Cambridge: D. S. Brewer, 1980).

'Historia Apollonii regis Tyri', ed. Elizabeth Archibald, in Archibald, *Apollonius of Tyre* (1991), 109–81.

Historia Roffensis, in Rosemary Horrox (ed. and tr.), *The Black Death* (Manchester: Manchester University Press, 1994), 70–3.

Hoccleve, Thomas, *The Regiment of Princes*, ed. Charles R. Blyth, TEAMS Middle English Texts (Kalamazoo, Mich.: Medieval Institute Publications, 1999).

Inquisitions and Assessments Relating to Feudal Aids, with Analogous Documents Preserved in the Public Record Office (A.D. 1284–1431), 6 vols (London: HMSO, 1899–1920).

Jacob's Well: An Englisht Treatise on the Cleansing of Man's Conscience, ed. Arthur Brandeis, EETS, os 115 (London: Kegan Paul, 1900).

Julian of Norwich, *A Book of Showings to the Anchoress Julian of Norwich*, ed. Edmund Colledge and James Walsh, 2 pts (Toronto: Pontifical Institute of Mediaeval Studies, 1978).

Knighton, Henry, *Knighton's Chronicle 1337–1396*, ed. and tr. G. H. Martin (Oxford: Clarendon, 1995).

Langland, William, *The Vision of Piers Plowman: A Critical Edition of the B-Text*, ed. A. V. C. Schmidt, 2nd edn (London: J. M. Dent, 1995).

Latini, Brunetto, *Li Livres dou Tresor*, ed. Spurgeon Baldwin and Paul Barrette (Tempe, Ariz.: Arizona Center for Medieval and Renaissance Studies, 2003).

The Lay Folks' Catechism, or The English and Latin Versions of Archbishop Thoresby's Instruction for the People, ed. Thomas Frederick Simmons and Henry Edward Nolloth, EETS, os 118 (London: Kegan Paul, 1901).

Lille, Alain de, *Liber poenitentialis*, ed. Jean Longère, 2 vols, Analecta Mediaevalia Namurcensia, 17–18 (Louvain: Nauwelaerts, 1965).

—— *De planctu Naturae*, ed. Nikolaus M. Häring, *Studi Medievali*, 3rd ser. 19 (1978), 797–879.

Lodge, Eleanor C., and Robert Somerville, eds, *John of Gaunt's Register, 1379–1383*, 2 pts, Camden Soc. 3rd ser. 56–7 (London: Royal Historical Society, 1937).

Lorris, Guillaume de, and Jean de Meun, *Le Roman de la Rose*, ed. Ernest Langlois, 5 vols, SATF (Paris: Champion, 1914–24).

—— *The Romance of the Rose*, tr. Charles Dahlberg (Princeton: Princeton University Press, 1971).

McNeill, John T., and Helena M. Gamer, eds and trs, *Medieval Handbooks of Penance: A Translation of the Principal Libri Poenitentiales and Selections from Related Documents* (New York: Columbia University Press, 1938).

Mandeville's Travels, ed. P. Hamelius, 2 vols, EETS, os 153–4 (London, 1919–23).

Mannyng, Robert, of Brunne, *Handlyng Synne*, ed. Idelle Sullens (Binghamton, NY: State University of New York, 1983).

Ovid (P. Ovidius Naso), *Metamorphoses*, ed. and tr. Frank Justus Miller, rev. edn, 2 vols, Loeb Classical Library, 42–3 (Cambridge, Mass.: Harvard University Press, 1977).

Ovide moralisé, ed. C. de Boer, 5 vols, Verhandelingen der Koninklijke Nederlandsche Akademie van Wetenschappen, Afdeeling Letterkunde, nieuwe reeks, 15, 21, 30, 37, 43 (Amsterdam: Müller; North-Holland, 1915–38).

Patterson, Frank Allen, ed., *The Middle English Penitential Lyric: A Study and Collection of Early Religious Verse* (New York: Columbia University Press, 1911).

Register of Edward the Black Prince Preserved in the Public Record Office, 4 vols (London: HMSO, 1930–3).

Rotuli parliamentorum, 7 vols (London, 1767–1832).

Russell, John, *The Boke of Nurture*, in Frederick J. Furnivall (ed.), *Manners and Meals in Olden Time*, EETS, os 32 (London, 1868), 115–228.

Rymer, Thomas, *Fœdera, Conventiones, Literæ, et cujuscunque Generis Acta Publica [etc.]*, ed. George Holmes, 3rd edn, 10 vols (1739–45; Farnborough, Hants, 1967).

Sainte-Maure, Benoît de, *Le Roman de Troie*, ed. Léopold Constans, 6 vols, SATF (Paris: Didot, 1904–12).

Schlauch, Margaret, ed., 'The Man of Law's Tale', in W. F. Bryan and Germaine Dempster (eds), *Sources and Analogues of Chaucer's Canterbury Tales* (London: Routledge, 1941), 155–206.

Secretum secretorum cum glossis et notulis, ed. Robert Steele, Opera hactenus inedita Rogeri Baconi, 5 (Oxford: Clarendon, 1920).

Secretum secretorum: Nine English Versions, ed. M. A. Manzalaoui, EETS, os 276 (Oxford: Oxford University Press, 1977).

Select Cases in the Court of King's Bench, ed. G. O. Sayles, vols v–vii, Selden Soc. 76, 82, 88 (London: Quaritch, 1958–71).

Sir Gawain and the Green Knight, ed. J. R. R. Tolkein, E. V. Gordon, and Norman Davis, 2nd edn (Oxford: Clarendon, 1967).

The Statutes of the Realm, ed. A. Luders et al., 11 vols (London: Record Commission, 1810–28).

Sudbury, William, *De primis regalibus ornamentis regni Angliae*, in Richard of Cirencester, *Speculum historiale de gestis regum Angliae*, ed. J. E. B. Mayor, 2 vols, Rolls Ser. (London, 1863–9), ii. 26–39.

Three Prose Versions of the Secreta secretorum, ed. Robert Steele, EETS, es 74 (London, 1898).

Usk, Thomas, *The Testament of Love*, ed. R. Allen Shoaf, TEAMS Middle English Texts (Kalamazoo, Mich.: Medieval Institute Publications, 1998).

Vitalis, Orderic, *The Ecclesiastical History of Orderic Vitalis*, ed. and tr. Marjorie Chibnall, 6 vols (Oxford: Clarendon, 1969–80).

Walsingham, Thomas, *Historia Anglicana*, ed. Henry Thomas Riley, 2 vols, Rolls Ser. (London, 1863–4).

—— *Annales Ricardi Secundi et Henrici Quarti*, in *Johannis de Trokelowe, et Henrici de Blaneforde, monachorum S. Albani, necnon quorundam anonymorum, chronica et annales*, ed. Henry Thomas Riley, Rolls Ser. (London, 1866).

—— *Chronicon Angliæ 1328–1388*, ed. Edward Maunde Thompson, Rolls Ser. (London, 1874).

The Westminster Chronicle 1381–1394, ed. and tr. L. C. Hector and Barbara F. Harvey (Oxford: Clarendon, 1982).

William of Malmesbury, *Vita Wulfstani*, ed. Reginald R. Darlington, Camden Soc. 3rd ser. 40 (London: Camden, 1928).

Wogan-Browne, Jocelyn, Nicholas Watson, Andrew Taylor, and Ruth Evans, eds, *The Idea of the Vernacular: An Anthology of Middle English Literary Theory 1280–1520* (Exeter: University of Exeter Press, 1999).

Woolgar, C. M., ed., *Household Accounts from Medieval England*, 2 pts, Records of Social and Economic History, NS 17–18 (Oxford: Oxford University Press, 1992–3).

SECONDARY MATERIAL

Allen, Elizabeth, 'Chaucer Answers Gower: Constance and the Trouble with Reading', *ELH* 63 (1997), 627–55.

Allen, Judson Boyce, *The Ethical Poetic of the Later Middle Ages: A Decorum of Convenient Distinction* (Toronto: University of Toronto Press, 1982).

Allen, Rosamund, 'Cobham, John, Third Baron Cobham of Cobham (*c.*1320–1408)', *Oxford Dictionary of National Biography* (Oxford: Oxford University Press, 2004), online edn, www.oxforddnb.com/view/article/5744.

Archer, Rowena E., 'Rich Old Ladies: The Problem of Late Medieval Dowagers', in Tony Pollard (ed.), *Property and Politics: Essays in Later Medieval English History* (Gloucester: Alan Sutton, 1984), 15–35.

Archibald, Elizabeth, 'Incest in Medieval Literature and Society', *Forum for Modern Language Studies*, 25 (1989), 1–15.

—— *Apollonius of Tyre: Medieval and Renaissance Themes and Variations* (Cambridge: D. S. Brewer, 1991).

—— *Incest and the Medieval Imagination* (Oxford: Clarendon, 2001).

Aston, Margaret, *Thomas Arundel: A Study of Church Life in the Reign of Richard II* (Oxford: Clarendon, 1967).

Baker, Denise N., 'The Priesthood of Genius: A Study of the Medieval Tradition', *Speculum*, 51 (1976), 277–91; repr. in Nicholson (ed.), *Critical Anthology*, 143–57.

Baker, J. H., *An Introduction to English Legal History*, 4th edn (London: Butterworths, 2002).

Bakhtin, Mikhail, *Problems of Dostoevsky's Poetics*, tr. R. W. Rotsel (Ann Arbor, Mich.: Ardis, 1973).

—— *The Dialogic Imagination: Four Essays*, ed. Michael Holquist, tr. Caryl Emerson and Michael Holquist (Austin, Tex.: University of Texas Press, 1981).

Barker, Juliet R. V., *The Tournament in England 1100–1400* (Woodbridge, Suff.: Boydell, 1986).

Barr, Helen, and Kate Ward-Perkins, ' "Spekyng for one's sustenance": The Rhetoric of Counsel in *Mum and the Sothsegger*, Skelton's *Bowge of Court*, and Elyot's *Pasquil the Playne*', in Helen Cooper and Sally Mapstone (eds), *The Long Fifteenth Century: Essays for Douglas Gray* (Oxford: Clarendon, 1997), 249–72.

Barratt, Alexandra, 'Julian of Norwich and the Holy Spirit, "our good lord" ', *Mystics Quarterly*, 28 (2002), 78–84.

—— 'Lordship, Service, and Worship in Julian of Norwich', in E. A. Jones (ed.), *The Medieval Mystical Tradition in England: Exeter Symposium VII* (Cambridge: D. S. Brewer, 2004), 177–88.

Barron, Caroline M., 'The Tyranny of Richard II', *BIHR* 41 (1968), 1–18.

—— 'The Quarrel of Richard II with London 1392–7', in Du Boulay and Barron (eds), *Reign of Richard II* (1971), 173–201.

—— 'The Deposition of Richard II', in Taylor and Childs (eds), *Politics and Crisis* (1990), 132–49.

—— 'Introduction: The Widow's World in Later Medieval London', in Caroline M. Barron and Anne F. Sutton (eds), *Medieval London Widows 1300–1500* (London: Hambledon, 1994), pp. xiii–xxxiv.

—— 'Centres of Conspicuous Consumption: The Aristocratic Town House in London 1200–1550', *London Journal*, 20 (1995), 1–16.

—— *London in the Later Middle Ages: Government and People 1200–1500* (Oxford: Oxford University Press, 2004).

Barron, W. R. J., 'Luf-Daungere', in F. Whitehead, A. H. Diverres, and F. E. Sutcliffe (eds), *Medieval Miscellany Presented to Eugène Vinaver* (Manchester: Manchester University Press, 1965), 1–18.

—— 'The Penalties for Treason in Medieval Life and Literature', *Journal of Medieval History*, 7 (1981), 187–202.

Bartlett, Robert, *The Making of Europe: Conquest, Colonization and Cultural Change 950–1350* (London: Allen Lane, 1993).

—— *England under the Norman and Angevin Kings 1075–1225*, New Oxford History of England (Oxford: Clarendon, 2000).

Bean, J. M. W., *The Decline of English Feudalism 1215–1540* (Manchester: Manchester University Press, 1968).

—— ' "Bachelor" and Retainer', *Medievalia et Humanistica*, NS 3 (1972), 117–31.

—— *From Lord to Patron: Lordship in Late Medieval England* (Manchester: Manchester University Press, 1989).

Bellamy, J. G., 'Sir John de Annesley and the Chandos Inheritance', *Nottingham Mediaeval Studies*, 10 (1966), 94–105.

—— *The Law of Treason in England in the Later Middle Ages* (Cambridge: Cambridge University Press, 1970).

Bennett, J. A. W., *The Parlement of Foules: An Interpretation* (Oxford: Clarendon, 1957).

—— 'Gower's "Honeste Love" ', in John Lawlor (ed.), *Patterns of Love and Courtesy: Essays in Memory of C. S. Lewis* (London: Edward Arnold, 1966), 107–21; repr. in Nicholson (ed.), *Critical Anthology*, 49–61.

Bennett, Josephine Waters, 'The Mediaeval Loveday', *Speculum*, 33 (1958), 351–70.

Bennett, Michael J., *Community, Class and Careerism: Cheshire and Lancashire Society in the Age of Sir Gawain and the Green Knight* (Cambridge: Cambridge University Press, 1983).

—— 'Richard II and the Wider Realm', in Goodman and Gillespie (eds), *Richard II: The Art of Kingship* (1999), 187–204.

Benson, C. David, 'Incest and Moral Poetry in Gower's *Confessio Amantis*', *Chaucer Review,* 19 (1984–5), 100–9.

Bernheimer, Richard, *Wild Men in the Middle Ages: A Study in Art, Sentiment, and Demonology* (Cambridge, Mass.: Harvard University Press, 1952).

Binski, Paul, *Westminster Abbey and the Plantagenets: Kingship and the Representation of Power 1200–1400* (New Haven, Conn.: Yale University Press, 1995).

Bird, Ruth, *The Turbulent London of Richard II* (London: Longmans, Green, 1949).

Black, Antony, *Political Thought in Europe 1250–1450* (Cambridge: Cambridge University Press, 1992).

Bloomfield, Morton W., *The Seven Deadly Sins: An Introduction to the History of a Religious Concept, with Special Reference to Medieval English Literature* (East Lansing, Mich.: Michigan State College Press, 1952).

Bonfield, Lloyd, 'The Nature of Customary Law in the Manor Courts of Medieval England', *Comparative Studies in Society and History,* 31 (1989), 514–34.

Born, Lester K., 'Ovid and Allegory', *Speculum,* 9 (1934), 362–79.

Bouchard, Constance B., 'Consanguinity and Noble Marriages in the Tenth and Eleventh Centuries', *Speculum,* 56 (1981), 268–87.

Bourdieu, Pierre, *Outline of a Theory of Practice,* tr. Richard Nice (Cambridge: Cambridge University Press, 1977).

—— *The Logic of Practice,* tr. Richard Nice (Cambridge: Polity, 1990).

Brand, Paul, *The Making of the Common Law* (London: Hambledon, 1992).

Braswell, Mary Flowers, *The Medieval Sinner: Characterization and Confession in the Literature of the English Middle Ages* (Rutherford, NJ: Associated University Presses, 1983).

Bray, Alan, *The Friend* (Chicago: University of Chicago Press, 2003).

Brown, A. L., *The Governance of Late Medieval England 1272–1461* (Stanford Calif.: Stanford University Press, 1989).

Brundage, James A., *Law, Sex, and Christian Society in Medieval Europe* (Chicago: University of Chicago Press, 1987).

Bullón-Fernández, María, *Fathers and Daughters in Gower's Confessio Amantis: Authority, Family, State, and Writing* (Cambridge: D. S. Brewer, 2000).

Burger, Glenn, *Chaucer's Queer Nation* (Minneapolis: University of Minnesota Press, 2003).

Burlin, Robert B., *Chaucerian Fiction* (Princeton: Princeton University Press, 1977).

Burrow, J. A., 'The Portrayal of Amans in *Confessio Amantis*', in Minnis (ed.), *Responses and Reassessments* (1983), 5–24.

—— 'The Griffin's Egg: Gower's *Confessio Amantis* I 2545', in Toshiyuki Takamiya and Richard Beadle (eds), *Chaucer to Shakespeare: Essays in Honour of Shinsuke Ando* (Cambridge: D. S. Brewer, 1992), 81–5.

Calin, William, 'John Gower's Continuity in the Tradition of French *Fin' Amor*', *Mediaevalia,* 16 (1993), 91–111.

Camille, Michael, *Mirror in Parchment: The Luttrell Psalter and the Making of Medieval England* (London: Reaktion, 1998).

Canning, Joseph, *A History of Medieval Political Thought 300–1450* (London: Routledge, 1996).

Carlin, Martha, *Medieval Southwark* (London: Hambledon, 1996).

Carpenter, Christine, 'Law, Justice, and Landowners in Late Medieval England', *Law and History Review*, 1 (1983), 205–37.

—— *Locality and Polity: A Study of Warwickshire Landed Society, 1401–1499* (Cambridge: Cambridge University Press, 1992).

—— 'Gentry and Community in Medieval England', *Journal of British Studies*, 33 (1994), 340–80.

Carpenter, D. A., 'The Decline of the Curial Sheriff in England 1194–1258', *EHR* 91 (1976), 1–32; repr. in Carpenter, *Reign of Henry III*, 151–82.

—— 'King, Magnates, and Society: The Personal Rule of King Henry III, 1234–1258', *Speculum*, 60 (1985): 39–70; repr. in Carpenter, *Reign of Henry III*, 75–106.

—— 'An Unknown Obituary of King Henry III from the Year 1263', in Carpenter, *Reign of Henry III* (1996), 253–60.

—— 'The Beginnings of Parliament', in Carpenter, *Reign of Henry III* (1996), 381–408.

—— 'The Burial of King Henry III, the Regalia, and Royal Ideology', in Carpenter, *Reign of Henry III* (1996), 427–61.

—— *The Reign of Henry III* (London: Hambledon, 1996).

—— 'The Second Century of English Feudalism', *Past and Present*, 168 (2000), 30–71.

—— *The Struggle for Mastery: Britain 1066–1284* (London: Allen Lane, 2003).

Carrara, Laura, 'Il processo Areopagitico di Oreste: le *Eumenidi* di Eschilo e la tradizione Attica', *Philologus*, 151 (2007), 3–16.

Castor, Helen, *The King, the Crown, and the Duchy of Lancaster: Public Authority and Private Power 1399–1461* (Oxford: Oxford University Press, 2000).

Cherniss, Michael D., *Boethian Apocalypse: Studies in Middle English Vision Poetry* (Norman, Okla.: Pilgrim, 1987).

Chrimes, S. B., 'Richard II's Questions to the Judges, 1387', *Law Quarterly Review*, 72 (1956), 365–90.

Clanchy, Michael T., 'Did Henry III have a Policy?' *History*, 53 (1968), 207–19.

—— 'Law, Government, and Society in Medieval England', *History*, 59 (1974), 73–8.

—— 'Law and Love in the Middle Ages', in John Bossy (ed.), *Disputes and Settlements: Law and Human Relations in the West* (Cambridge: Cambridge University Press, 1983), 47–67.

—— *From Memory to Written Record: England 1066–1307*, 2nd edn (Oxford: Blackwell, 1993).

—— *England and its Rulers 1066–1272*, 2nd edn (Oxford: Blackwell, 1998).

Clarke, M. V., *Fourteenth Century Studies* (Oxford: Clarendon, 1937).

Clayton, Dorothy J., Richard G. Davies, and Peter McNiven (eds), *Trade, Devotion and Governance: Papers in Later Medieval History* (Stroud, Glos.: Alan Sutton, 1994).

Clogan, Paul M., 'From Complaint to Satire: The Art of the *Confessio Amantis*', *Medievalia et Humanistica*, NS 4 (1973), 217–22.

Coffman, George R., 'John Gower in his Most Significant Role', in *Elizabethan Studies and Other Essays in Honor of George F. Reynolds* (Boulder, Colo.: [no publ.], 1945), 52–61.

Cokayne, G. E., *The Complete Peerage*, ed. Vicary Gibbs et al., rev. edn, 14 vols (London: St Catherine; Stroud, Glos.: Alan Sutton, 1910–98).

Collette, Carolyn P., 'Heeding the Counsel of Prudence: A Context for the *Melibee*', *Chaucer Review*, 29 (1994–5), 416–33.

—— 'Joan of Kent and Noble Women's Roles in Chaucer's World', *Chaucer Review*, 33 (1998–9), 350–62.

Collins, John J., 'Introduction: Towards the Morphology of a Genre', *Semeia*, 14 (1979), 1–20.

Colvin, H. M., ed., *The History of the King's Works*, 6 vols (London: HMSO, 1963–82).

Cooper, Helen, *The English Romance in Time: Transforming Motifs from Geoffrey of Monmouth to the Death of Shakespeare* (Oxford: Oxford University Press, 2004).

Copeland, Rita, *Rhetoric, Hermeneutics, and Translation in the Middle Ages: Academic Traditions and Vernacular Texts* (Cambridge: Cambridge University Press, 1991).

Coss, P. R., 'Bastard Feudalism Revised', *Past and Present*, 125 (1989), 27–64.

—— *The Lady in Medieval England 1000–1500* (Stroud, Glos.: Alan Sutton, 1998).

Crouch, David, D. A. Carpenter, and P. R. Coss, 'Debate: Bastard Feudalism Revised', *Past and Present*, 131 (1991), 165–203.

Dahlberg, Charles, 'First Person and Personification in the *Roman de la Rose*: Amant and Dangier', *Mediaevalia*, 3 (1977), 37–58.

Davies, R. G., and J. H. Denton, eds, *The English Parliament in the Middle Ages* (Manchester: Manchester University Press, 1981).

Davies, R. R., 'Richard II and the Principality of Chester 1397–9', in Du Boulay and Barron (eds), *Reign of Richard II* (1971), 256–79.

Davis, Isabel, *Writing Masculinity in the Later Middle Ages* (Cambridge: Cambridge University Press, 2007).

De Weever, Jacqueline, 'Dangier, the Saracen-Guardian of the *Roman de la Rose*', *Mediaevalia*, 21 (1996–7), 27–45.

Diamond, Arlyn, '*Sir Degrevant*: What Lovers Want', in Nicola McDonald (ed.), *Pulp Fictions of Medieval England: Essays in Popular Romance* (Manchester: Manchester University Press, 2004), 82–101.

Dinshaw, Carolyn, *Chaucer's Sexual Poetics* (Madison, Wisc.: University of Wisconsin Press, 1989).

—— 'Rivalry, Rape, and Manhood: Gower and Chaucer', in R. F. Yeager (ed.), *Chaucer and Gower: Difference, Mutuality, Exchange* (Victoria, BC: University of Victoria, 1991), 130–52.

Donavin, Georgiana, *Incest Narratives and the Structure of Gower's Confessio Amantis* (Victoria, BC: University of Victoria, 1993).

Doyle, A. I., and M. B. Parkes, 'The Production of Copies of *The Canterbury Tales* and the *Confessio Amantis* in the Early Fifteenth Century', in M. B. Parkes and Andrew G. Watson (eds), *Medieval Scribes, Manuscripts, and Libraries: Essays Presented to N. R. Ker* (London: Scolar, 1978), 163–210.

Du Boulay, F. R. H., and Caroline M. Barron, eds, *The Reign of Richard II: Essays in Honour of May McKisack* (London: Athlone, 1971).

Duby, Georges, 'Lineage, Nobility, and Knighthood', in *The Chivalrous Society*, tr. Cynthia Postan (London: Edward Arnold, 1977), 59–80.

—— *Medieval Marriage: Two Models from Twelfth-Century France*, tr. Elborg Forster (Baltimore, Md.: Johns Hopkins University Press, 1978).

—— 'Courtly Love', in *Love and Marriage in the Middle Ages*, tr. Jane Dunnett (Oxford: Polity, 1994), 56–63.

Dyer, Christopher, *Standards of Living in the Later Middle Ages: Social Change in England c.1200–1520*, rev. edn (Cambridge: Cambridge University Press, 1998).

—— *Making a Living in the Middle Ages: The People of Britain 850–1520* (London: Penguin, 2003).

Eales, Richard, 'The Game of Chess: An Aspect of Medieval Knightly Culture', in Christopher Harper-Bill and Ruth Harvey (eds), *The Ideals and Practice of Medieval Knighthood* (Woodbridge, Suff.: Boydell, 1986), 12–34.

Eberle, Patricia J., 'Richard II and the Literary Arts', in Goodman and Gillespie (eds), *Richard II: The Art of Kingship* (1999), 239–40.

Echard, Siân, 'Glossing Gower, in Latin, in English, and *in absentia*: The Case of Bodleian Ashmole 35', in Yeager (ed.), *Re-Visioning Gower* (1998), 237–56.

—— ed., *A Companion to Gower* (Cambridge: D. S. Brewer, 2004).

Economou, George D., 'The Character Genius in Alan de Lille, Jean de Meun, and John Gower', *Chaucer Review*, 4 (1970–1), 203–10; repr. in Nicholson (ed.), *Critical Anthology*, 109–16.

—— *The Goddess Natura in Medieval Literature* (Cambridge, Mass.: Harvard University Press, 1972).

Edwards, A. S. G., 'Gower's Women in the *Confessio*', *Mediaevalia*, 16 (1993), 223–37.

—— 'Selection and Subversion in Gower's *Confessio Amantis*', in Yeager (ed.), *Re-Visioning Gower* (1998), 257–67.

Eiden, Herbert, 'Joint Action against "Bad" Lordship: The Peasants' Revolt in Essex and Norfolk', *History*, 83 (1998), 5–30.

Federico, Sylvia, *New Troy: Fantasies of Empire in the Late Middle Ages* (Minneapolis: University of Minnesota Press, 2003).

Ferster, Judith, *Fictions of Advice: The Literature and Politics of Counsel in Late Medieval England* (Philadelphia: University of Pennsylvania Press, 1996).

Fisher, John H., *John Gower: Moral Philosopher and Friend of Chaucer* (London: Methuen, 1965).

Fisher, Ruth M., ' "Cosyn" and "Cosynage": Complicated Punning in Chaucer's "Shipman's Tale"?', *Notes and Queries*, 12 (1965), 168–70.

Flandrin, Jean-Louis, *Families in Former Times: Kinship, Household, and Sexuality*, tr. Richard Southern (Cambridge: Cambridge University Press, 1979).

Fleming, John V., *The Roman de la Rose: A Study in Allegory and Iconography* (Princeton: Princeton University Press, 1969).

Foucault, Michel, *The History of Sexuality*, tr. Robert Hurley, 3 vols (London: Allen Lane, 1979–88).

Fradenburg, Lousie, 'The Manciple's Servant Tongue: Politics and Poetry in *The Canterbury Tales*', *ELH* 52 (1985), 85–118.

—— *Sacrifice your Love: Psychoanalysis, Historicism, Chaucer* (Minneapolis: University of Minnesota Press, 2002).

Friedman, John Block, *The Monstrous Races in Medieval Art and Thought* (1981; Syracuse, NY: Syracuse University Press, 2000).

Frye, Northrop, *Anatomy of Criticism: Four Essays* (Princeton: Princeton University Press, 1957).

Galbraith, V. H., 'The Death of a Champion (1287)', in R. W. Hunt, W. A. Pantin, and R. W. Southern (eds), *Studies in Medieval History Presented to Frederick Maurice Powicke* (Oxford: Clarendon, 1948), 283–95.

Galloway, Andrew, 'The Making of a Social Ethic in Late-Medieval England: From Gratitudo to "Kyndenesse" ', *Journal of the History of Ideas*, 55 (1994), 365–83.

—— 'The Literature of 1388 and the Politics of Pity in Gower's *Confessio Amantis*', in Steiner and Barrington (eds), *Letter of the Law* (2002), 67–104.

Ganim, John M., 'Chaucer, Boccaccio, Confession, and Subjectivity', in Leonard Michael Koff and Brenda Deen Schildgen (eds), *The Decameron and the Canterbury Tales: New Essays on an Old Question* (London: Associated University Presses, 2000), 128–47.

Gaunt, Simon, *Gender and Genre in Medieval French Literature* (Cambridge: Cambridge University Press, 1995).

—— 'Bel Acueil and the Improper Allegory of the *Romance of the Rose*', *New Medieval Literatures*, 2 (1998), 65–93.

—— and Sarah Kay, eds, *The Troubadours: An Introduction* (Cambridge: Cambridge University Press, 1999).

Giancarlo, Matthew, *Parliament and Literature in Late Medieval England* (Cambridge: Cambridge University Press, 2007).

Gilchrist, Roberta, *Gender and Archaeology: Contesting the Past* (London: Routledge, 1999).

Given-Wilson, Chris, 'Richard II and his Grandfather's Will', *EHR* 93 (1978), 320–37.

—— *The Royal Household and the King's Affinity: Service, Politics, and Finance in England 1360–1413* (New Haven, Conn.: Yale University Press, 1986).

—— *The English Nobility in the Late Middle Ages: The Fourteenth-Century Political Community* (London: Routledge, 1987).

—— 'Service, Serfdom, and English Labour Legislation 1350–1500', in Anne Curry and Elizabeth Matthew (eds), *Concepts and Patterns of Service in the Later Middle Ages*, The Fifteenth Century, 1 (Woodbridge, Suff.: Boydell, 2000), 21–37.

Gluckman, Max, *Politics, Law and Ritual in Tribal Society* (Oxford: Blackwell, 1965).

Goodall, Peter, 'John Gower's *Apollonius of Tyre: Confessio Amantis*, Book VIII', *Southern Review*, 15 (1982), 243–53.

—— '"Unkynde abhomynaciouns" in Chaucer and Gower', *Parergon*, NS 5 (1987), 94–102.

Goodman, Anthony, *The Loyal Conspiracy: The Lords Appellant under Richard II* (London: Routledge, 1971).

—— *John of Gaunt: The Exercise of Princely Power in Fourteenth-Century Europe* (Harlow, Essex: Longman, 1992).

—— introduction, in Goodman and Gillespie (eds), *Richard II: The Art of Kingship* (1999), 1–13.

—— and James L. Gillespie, eds, *Richard II: The Art of Kingship* (Oxford: Clarendon, 1999).

Goody, Jack, *The Development of the Family and Marriage in Europe* (Cambridge: Cambridge University Press, 1983).

Gordon, Dillian, 'The Wilton Diptych: An Introduction', in Gordon et al. (eds), *Regal Image* (1997), 19–26.

—— Lisa Monnas, and Caroline Elam, eds, *The Regal Image of Richard II and the Wilton Diptych* (London: Harvey Miller, 1997).

Green, Judith A., *The Government of England under Henry I* (Cambridge: Cambridge University Press, 1986).

Green, Richard Firth, *Poets and Princepleasers: Literature and the English Court in the Late Middle Ages* (Toronto: University of Toronto Press, 1980).

—— 'Arcite at Court', *English Language Notes*, 18 (1981), 251–7.

—— 'The *Familia Regis* and the *Familia Cupidinis*', in Scattergood and Sherborne (eds), *English Court Culture* (1983), 87–108.

—— *A Crisis of Truth: Literature and Law in Ricardian England* (Philadelphia: University of Pennsylvania Press, 1999).

Hamil, Frederick C., 'The King's Approvers: A Chapter in the History of English Criminal Law', *Speculum*, 11 (1936), 238–58.

Hanawalt, Barbara, 'The Female Felon in Fourteenth-Century England', *Viator*, 5 (1974), 253–68.

Hanna, Ralph, *London Literature, 1300–1380* (Cambridge: Cambridge University Press, 2005).

Hansen, Elaine Tuttle, *Chaucer and the Fictions of Gender* (Berkeley, Calif.: University of California Press, 1992).

Harris, Kate, 'Ownership and Readership: Studies in the Provenance of the Manuscripts of Gower's *Confessio Amantis*', D.Phil. thesis, University of York, 1993.

Harriss, G. L., *King, Parilament, and Public Finance in Medieval England to 1369* (Oxford: Clarendon, 1975).

—— 'The Formation of Parliament, 1272–1377', in Davies and Denton (eds), *English Parliament* (1981), 29–60.

—— introduction, in McFarlane, *England in the Fifteenth Century* (1981), pp. ix–xxvii.

—— 'Political Society and the Growth of Government in Late Medieval England', *Past and Present*, 138 (1993), 28–57.

—— 'The Dimensions of Politics', in R. H. Britnell and A. J. Pollard (eds), *The McFarlane Legacy: Studies in Late Medieval Politics and Society* (Stroud, Glos.: Alan Sutton, 1995), 1–20.

—— *Shaping the Nation: England 1360–1461*, New Oxford History of England (Oxford: Clarendon, 2005).

Haskett, T. S., 'Conscience, Justice, and Authority in the Late Medieval Court of Chancery', in Anthony Musson (ed.), *Expectations of the Law in the Middle Ages* (Woodbridge, Suff.: Boydell, 2001), 151–64.

Heal, Felicity, *Hospitality in Early Modern England* (Oxford: Clarendon, 1990).

—— 'Reciprocity and Exchange in the Late Medieval Household', in Barbara A. Hanawalt and David Wallace (eds), *Bodies and Disciplines: Intersections of Literature and History in Fifteenth-Century England* (Minneapolis: University of Minnesota Press, 1996), 179–98.

Heffernan, Thomas J., 'A Middle English Poem on Lovedays', *Chaucer Review*, 10 (1975–6), 172–85.

Herlihy, David, 'Making Sense of Incest: Women and the Marriage Rules of the Early Middle Ages', in A. Molho (ed.), *Women, Family, and Society in Medieval Europe: Historical Essays 1978–1991* (Providence, RI: Berghahn, 1995), 96–109.

Hilton, Rodney, *Bond Men Made Free: Medieval Peasant Movements and the English Rising of 1381*, 2nd edn (London: Routledge, 2003).

—— and T. H. Aston, eds, *The English Rising of 1381* (Cambridge: Cambridge University Press, 1984).

Hiscoe, David W., 'The Ovidian Comic Strategy of Gower's *Confessio Amantis*', *Philological Quarterly*, 64 (1985), 367–85.

Holmes, G. A., *The Estates of the Higher Nobility in Fourteenth-Century England* (Cambridge: Cambridge University Press, 1957).

—— *The Good Parliament* (Oxford: Clarendon, 1975).

Holt, J. C., 'The Prehistory of Parliament', in Davies and Denton (eds), *English Parliament* (1981), 1–28.

Jameson, Fredric, *The Political Unconscious: Narrative as a Socially Symbolic Act* (Ithaca, NY: Cornell University Press, 1981).

Johnson, Matthew, *Behind the Castle Gate: From Medieval to Renaissance* (London: Routledge, 2002).

Jones, Richard H., *The Royal Policy of Richard II: Absolutism in the Later Middle Ages* (Oxford: Blackwell, 1968).

Jong, Mayke de, 'To the Limits of Kinship: Anti-Incest Legislation in the Early Medieval West (500–900)', in Jan Bremmer (ed.), *From Sappho to De Sade: Moments in the History of Sexuality* (London: Routledge, 1989), 36–59.

Justice, Steven, *Writing and Rebellion: England in 1381* (Berkeley, Calif.: University of California Press, 1994).

Kaeuper, Richard W., 'Law and Order in Fourteenth-Century England: The Evidence of Special Commissions of Oyer and Terminer', *Speculum*, 54 (1979), 734–84.

—— *War, Justice, and Public Order: England and France in the Later Middle Ages* (Oxford: Clarendon, 1988).

Kantorowicz, Ernst H., *The King's Two Bodies: A Study in Mediaeval Political Theology* (Princeton: Princeton University Press, 1957).

Kay, Sarah, *Subjectivity in Troubadour Poetry* (Cambridge: Cambridge University Press, 1990).

—— *The Romance of the Rose*, Critical Guides to French Texts, 110 (London: Grant & Cutler, 1995).

—— 'The Contradictions of Courtly Love and the Origins of Courtly Poetry: The Evidence of the *Lauzengiers*', *Journal of Medieval and Early Modern Studies*, 26 (1996), 209–53.

Keen, Maurice, 'The Wilton Diptych: The Case for a Crusading Context', in Gordon et al. (eds), *Regal Image* (1997), 189–96.

Kendall, Elliot, 'The Great Household in the City: The *Shipman's Tale*', in Ardis Butterfield (ed.), *Chaucer and the City* (Cambridge: D. S. Brewer, 2006), 145–61.

Kerby-Fulton, Kathryn, *Books under Suspicion: Censorship and Tolerance of Revelatory Writing in Late Medieval England* (Notre Dame, Ind.: University of Notre Dame Press, 2006).

—— and Steven Justice, 'Scribe D and the Marketing of Ricardian Literature', in Kathryn Kerby-Fulton and Maidie Hilmo (eds), *The Medieval Professional Reader at Work: Evidence from Manuscripts of Chaucer, Langland, Kempe, and Gower* (Victoria, BC: University of Victoria, 2001), 217–37.

Kiefer, Lauren, 'My Family First: Draft-Dodging Parents in the *Confessio Amantis*', *Essays in Medieval Studies*, 12 (1995), www.luc.edu/publications/medieval/vol12/kiefer.html.

Kinneavy, Gerald, 'Gower's *Confessio Amantis* and the Penitentials', *Chaucer Review*, 19 (1984–5), 144–61.

Knight, Stephen, 'The Social Function of the Middle English Romances', in David Aers (ed.), *Medieval Literature: Criticism, Ideology and History* (Brighton: Harvester, 1986), 99–122.

Lachaud, Frédérique, 'Liveries of Robes in England *c.*1200–*c.*1330', *EHR* 111 (1996), 279–98.

Lander, J. R., *The Limitations of English Monarchy in the Later Middle Ages* (Toronto: University of Toronto Press, 1989).

Le Goff, Jacques, *The Medieval Imagination*, tr. Arthur Goldhammer (Chicago: University of Chicago Press, 1988).

Lea, Henry Charles, *A History of Auricular Confession and Indulgences in the Latin Church*, 3 vols (London: Swan Sonnenschein, 1896).

Leland, John L., 'Burley, Sir Simon (1336?–1388)', *Oxford Dictionary of National Biography* (Oxford: Oxford University Press, 2004), online edn, May 2006, www.oxforddnb.com/view/article/4036.

Lévi-Strauss, Claude, *The Elementary Structures of Kinship*, tr. James Harle Bell, John Richard von Sturmer, and Rodney Needham, rev. edn (London: Eyre & Spottiswoode, 1969).

Lewis, C. S., *The Allegory of Love: A Study in Medieval Tradition* (Oxford: Oxford University Press, 1936).

Lindenbaum, Sheila, 'The Smithfield Tournament of 1390', *JMRS* 20 (1990), 1–20.

Lynch, Joseph, *Godparents and Kinship in Early Medieval Europe* (Princeton: Princeton University Press, 1986).

McFarlane, K. B., ' "Bastard Feudalism" ', *BIHR* 20 (1943–5), 161–80; repr. in McFarlane, *England in the Fifteenth Century*, 23–43.

—— 'Parliament and "Bastard Feudalism" ', *TRHS* 4th ser. 26 (1944), 53–79; repr. in McFarlane, *England in the Fifteenth Century*, 1–21, 262–7.

—— *Lancastrian Kings and Lollard Knights* (Oxford: Clarendon, 1972).

—— *The Nobility of Later Medieval England: The Ford Lectures for 1953 and Related Studies* (Oxford: Clarendon, 1973).

—— *England in the Fifteenth Century: Collected Essays* (London: Hambledon, 1981).

McGinn, Bernard, 'Early Apocalypticism: the Ongoing Debate', in C. A. Patrides and Joseph Wittreich (eds), *The Apocalypse in English Renaissance Thought and Literature: Patterns, Antecedents and Repercussions* (Manchester: Manchester University Press, 1984), 2–39.

McHardy, A. K., 'Haxey's Case, 1397: The Petition and its Presenter Reconsidered', in James L. Gillespie (ed.), *The Age of Richard II* (Stroud, Glos.: Alan Sutton, 1997), 93–114.

Macherey, Pierre, *A Theory of Literary Production*, tr. Geoffrey Wall (London: Routledge, 1978).

McIntosh, Angus, M. L. Samuels, and Michael Benskin, eds, *A Linguistic Atlas of Late Mediaeval English*, 4 vols (Aberdeen: Aberdeen University Press, 1986).

McKenna, John W., 'How God Became an Englishman', in Delloyd J. Guth and John W. McKenna (eds), *Tudor Rule and Revolution: Essays for G. R. Elton* (Cambridge: Cambridge University Press, 1982), 25–43.

Maddicott, J. R., 'Edward I and the Lessons of Baronial Reform: Local Government 1258–80', in P. R. Coss and S. D. Lloyd (eds), *Thirteenth Century England I* (Woodbridge, Suff.: Boydell, 1986), 1–30.

—— *Simon de Montfort* (Cambridge: Cambridge University Press, 1994).

Mahoney, Dhira B., 'Courtly Presentation and Authorial Self-Fashioning: Frontispiece Miniatures in Late Medieval French and English Manuscripts', *Mediaevalia*, 21 (1996), 97–160.

—— 'Gower's Two Prologues to *Confessio Amantis*', in Yeager (ed.), *Re-Visioning Gower* (1998), 17–37.

Mainzer, H. C., 'A Study of the Sources of the *Confessio Amantis* of John Gower', D.Phil. thesis, University of Oxford, 1967.

—— 'John Gower's Use of the "Mediæval Ovid" in the *Confessio Amantis*', *Medium Ævum*, 41 (1972), 215–29.

Mann, Jill, 'Price and Value in *Sir Gawain and the Green Knight*', *Essays in Criticism*, 36 (1986), 290–318; repr. in Derek Pearsall (ed.), *Chaucer to Spenser: A Critical Reader* (Oxford: Blackwell, 1999), 187–205.

Manzalaoui, M. A., '"Noght in the Registre of Venus": Gower's English Mirror for Princes', in P. L. Heyworth (ed.), *Medieval Studies for J. A. W. Bennett* (Oxford: Clarendon, 1981), 159–83.

Marx, Karl, *Economic and Philosophic Manuscripts of 1844*, ed. Dirk J. Struik, tr. Martin Milligan (London: Lawrence & Wishart, 1970).

Mathew, Gervase, *The Court of Richard II* (London: John Murray, 1968).

Mauss, Marcel, *The Gift: The Form and Reason For Exchange in Archaic Societies*, tr. W. D. Halls (London: Routledge, 1990).

May, Teresa, 'The Cobham Family in the Administration of England 1200–1400', *Arch. Cant.* 82 (1967), 1–31.

Mertes, Kate, *The English Noble Household 1250–1600* (Oxford: Blackwell, 1988).

Middle English Dictionary (Ann Arbor, Mich.: University of Michigan Press, 1952–2001), http://quod.lib.umich.edu/m/med/

Middleton, Anne, 'The Idea of Public Poetry in the Reign of Richard II', *Speculum*, 53 (1978), 94–114.

—— 'The Audience and Public of *Piers Plowman*', in David Lawton (ed.), *Middle English Alliterative Poetry and its Literary Background: Seven Essays* (Cambridge: D. S. Brewer, 1982), 101–23.

Minnis, A. J., 'John Gower, *Sapiens* in Ethics and Politics', *Medium Ævum*, 49 (1980), 207–29; repr. in Nicholson (ed.), *Critical Anthology*, 158–80.

—— 'Langland's Ymaginatif and Late-Medieval Theories of Imagination', *Comparative Criticism*, 3 (1981), 71–103.

—— '"Moral Gower" and Medieval Literary Theory', in Minnis (ed.), *Responses and Reassessments* (1983), 50–78.

—— *Medieval Theory of Authorship: Scholastic Literary Attitudes in the Later Middle Ages*, 2nd edn (Aldershot, Hants: Wildwood, 1988).

—— *Oxford Guides to Chaucer: The Shorter Poems* (Oxford: Clarendon, 1995).

—— ed., *Gower's Confessio Amantis: Responses and Reassessments* (Cambridge: D. S. Brewer, 1983).

Mitchell, Shelagh, 'Richard II: Kingship and the Cult of Saints', in Gordon et al. (eds), *Regal Image* (1997), 115–24.

Monnas, Lisa, 'Fit for a King: Figured Silks Shown in the Wilton Diptych', in Gordon et al. (eds), *Regal Image* (1997), 165–77.

Morgan, Nigel, 'The Signification of the Banner in the Wilton Diptych', in Gordon et al. (eds), *Regal Image* (1997), 179–88.

Muscatine, Charles, 'The Emergence of Psychological Allegory in Old French Romance', *PMLA* 68 (1953), 1160–82.

Musson, Anthony, 'Legal Landmarks: The Architecture of Justice in Late Medieval England', *Australia and New Zealand Law and History E-Journal*, 2 (2006), paper 15, 1–9, www.anzlhsejournal.auckland.ac.nz.

—— 'Court Venues and the Politics of Justice', in Nigel Saul (ed.), *Fourteenth Century England V* (Woodbridge, Suff.: Boydell, 2008).

—— and W. M. Ormrod, *The Evolution of English Justice: Law, Politics, and Society in the Fourteenth Century* (Basingstoke: Macmillan, 1999).

Nicholson, Peter, 'Gower's Revisions in the *Confessio Amantis*', *Chaucer Review*, 19 (1984–5), 123–43.

—— 'Poet and Scribe in the Manuscripts of Gower's *Confessio Amantis*', in Derek Pearsall (ed.), *Manuscripts and Texts: Editorial Problems in Later Middle English Literature* (Cambridge: D. S. Brewer, 1987), 130–42.

—— 'The Dedications of Gower's *Confessio Amantis*', *Mediaevalia*, 10 (1988 [for 1984]), 159–80.

—— *Love and Ethics in Gower's Confessio Amantis* (Ann Arbor, Mich.: University of Michigan Press, 2005).

—— ed., *Gower's Confessio Amantis: A Critical Anthology* (Cambridge: D. S. Brewer, 1991).

Nightingale, Pamela, 'Knights and Merchants: Trade, Politics, and the Gentry in Late Medieval England', *Past and Present*, 169 (2000), 36–62.

O'Connor, Stephen, 'Adam Frounceys and John Pyel: Perceptions of Status among Merchants in Fourteenth-Century London', in Clayton et al. (eds), *Trade, Devotion, and Governance* (1994), 17–35.

Olsson, Kurt, 'Natural Law and John Gower's *Confessio Amantis*', *Medievalia et Humanistica*, NS 11 (1982), 229–61; repr. in Nicholson (ed.), *Critical Anthology*, 181–213.

Olsson, Kurt, *John Gower and the Structures of Conversion: A Reading of the Confessio Amantis* (Cambridge: D. S. Brewer, 1992).

Orme, Nicholas, 'The Education of the Courtier', in Scattergood and Sherborne (eds), *English Court Culture* (1983), 63–85.

—— *From Childhood to Chivalry: The Education of the English Kings and Aristocracy 1066–1530* (London: Routledge, 1984).

Ormrod, W. M., 'In Bed with Joan of Kent: The King's Mother and the Peasants' Revolt', in Jocelyn Wogan-Browne, Rosalynn Voaden, Arlyn Diamond, Ann Hutchison, Carole Meale, and Lesley Johnson (eds), *Medieval Women: Texts and Contexts in Late Medieval Britain* (Turnhout: Brepols, 2000), 277–92.

Palmer, J. J. N., 'The Parliament of 1385 and the Constitutional Crisis of 1386', *Speculum*, 46 (1971), 477–90.

Parkes, M. B., 'Patterns of Scribal Activity and Revisions of the Text in Early Copies of Works by John Gower', in Richard Beadle and A. J. Piper (eds), *New Science Out of Old Books: Studies in Manuscripts and Early Printed Books in Honour of A. I. Doyle* (Aldershot, Hants: Scolar, 1995), 81–121.

Parsons, John Carmi, 'Ritual and Symbol in the English Medieval Queenship to 1500', *Cosmos*, 7 (1992), 60–77.

Patterson, Lee, 'The "Parson's Tale" and the Quitting of *The Canterbury Tales*', *Traditio*, 34 (1978), 331–80.

—— *Chaucer and the Subject of History* (London: Routledge, 1991).

—— 'Court Politics and the Invention of Literature: The Case of Sir John Clanvowe', in David Aers (ed.), *Culture and History 1350–1600: Essays on English Communities, Identities, and Writing* (New York: Harvester, 1992), 7–41.

Payling, Simon J., 'Law and Arbitration in Nottinghamshire 1399–1461', in Joel Rosenthal and Colin Richmond (eds), *People, Politics, and Community in the Later Middle Ages* (Gloucester: Alan Sutton, 1987), 140–60.

—— 'The Ampthill Dispute: A Study in Aristocratic Lawlessness and the Breakdown of Lancastrian Government', *EHR* 104 (1989), 881–907.

—— *Political Society in Lancastrian England: The Greater Gentry of Nottinghamshire* (Oxford: Clarendon, 1991).

—— 'Social Mobility, Demographic Change, and Landed Society in Late Medieval England', *EconHR* 45 (1992), 51–73.

—— 'Murder, Motive and Punishment in Fifteenth-Century England: Two Gentry Case-Studies', *EHR* 113 (1998), 1–17.

—— 'The Economics of Marriage in Late Medieval England: The Marriage of Heiresses', *EconHR* 54 (2001), 413–29.

Pearsall, Derek, 'Gower's Narrative Art', *PMLA* 81 (1966): 475–84; repr. in Nicholson (ed.), *Critical Anthology*, 62–80.

—— 'Gower's Latin in the *Confessio Amantis*', in A. J. Minnis (ed.), *Latin and Vernacular: Studies in Late-Medieval Texts and Manuscripts* (Cambridge: D. S. Brewer, 1989), 13–25.

—— 'The Manuscripts and Illustrations of Gower's Works', in Echard (ed.), *Companion to Gower* (2004), 73–97.

Peck, Russell A., *Kingship and Common Profit in Gower's Confessio Amantis* (Carbondale, Ill.: Southern Illinois University Press, 1978).

—— 'The Politics and Psychology of Governance in Gower: Ideas of Kingship and Real Kings', in Echard (ed.), *Companion to Gower* (2004), 215–38.

Pfander, H. G., 'Some Medieval Manuals of Religious Instruction in England and Observations on Chaucer's Parson's Tale', *JEGP* 35 (1936), 243–58.

Phillips, Susan E., 'Gossip and (Un)official Writing', in Strohm (ed.), *Middle English* (2007), 476–90.

—— *Transforming Talk: The Problem with Gossip in Late Medieval England* (University Park, Pa: Pennsylvania State University Press, 2007).

Pocock, J. G. A., 'Languages and their Implications: The Transformation of the Study of Political Thought', in *Politics, Language, and Time: Essays on Political Thought and History* (London: Methuen, 1972), 3–41.

—— 'Texts as Events: Reflections on the History of Political Thought', in Kevin Sharpe and Steven N. Zwicker (eds), *Politics of Discourse: The Literature and History of Seventeenth-Century England* (Berkeley, Calif.: University of California Press, 1987), 21–34.

Poos, Larry, 'The Social Context of Statute of Labourers Enforcement', *Law and History Review*, 1 (1983), 27–52.

Porter, Elizabeth, 'Gower's Ethical Microcosm and Political Macrocosm', in Minnis (ed.), *Responses and Reassessments* (1983), 135–62.

Powell, Edward, 'Arbitration and the Law in England in the Late Middle Ages', *TRHS* 5th ser. 33 (1983), 49–67.

—— 'Settlement of Disputes by Arbitration in Fifteenth-Century England', *Law and History Review*, 2 (1984), 21–43.

—— 'After "After McFarlane": The Poverty of Patronage and the Case for Constitutional History', in Clayton et al. (eds), *Trade, Devotion and Governance* (1994), 1–16.

Prestwich, Michael, 'Parliament and the Community of the Realm in Fourteenth-Century England', in Art Cosgrove and J. I. McGuire (eds), *Parliament and Community* (Belfast: Appletree, 1983), 5–24.

—— *Plantagenet England 1225–1360*, New Oxford History of England (Oxford: Clarendon, 2005).

Putter, Ad, 'Gifts and Commodities in *Sir Amadace*', *Review of English Studies*, NS 51 (2000), 371–94.

Quilligan, Maureen, *The Language of Allegory: Defining the Genre* (Ithaca, NY: Cornell University Press, 1979).

Rawcliffe, Carole, 'The Great Lord as Peacekeeper: Arbitration by English Noblemen and their Councils in the Later Middle Ages', in J. A. Guy and H. G. Beale (eds), *Law and Social Change in British History* (London: Royal Historical Society, 1984), 34–54.

Rawcliffe, Carole, 'Parliament and the Settlement of Disputes by Arbitration in the Later Middle Ages', *Parliamentary History,* 9 (1990), 316–42.

Reynolds, Susan, *Fiefs and Vassals: The Medieval Evidence Reinterpreted* (Oxford: Oxford University Press, 1994).

Richardson, H. G., 'The Commons and Medieval Politics', *TRHS* 4th ser. 28 (1946), 21–45.

—— 'The English Coronation Oath', *Speculum,* 24 (1949), 44–75.

Rigby, S. H., *English Society in the Later Middle Ages: Class, Status, and Gender* (Basingstoke: Macmillan, 1995).

Robbins, Rossell Hope, 'The Findern Anthology', *PMLA* 69 (1954), 610–42.

Robertson, D. W., 'The Cultural Tradition of *Handlyng Synne*', *Speculum,* 22 (1947), 162–85.

Robertson, Kellie, *The Laborer's Two Bodies: Literary and Legal Productions in Britain, 1350–1500* (New York: Macmillan, 2006).

Rogers, Alan, 'Parliamentary Appeals of Treason in the Reign of Richard II', *American Journal of Legal History,* 8 (1964), 95–124.

Roskell, J. S., 'Sir Arnald Savage of Bobbing: Speaker for the Commons in 1401 and 1404', *Arch. Cant.* 70 (1956), 68–83.

Rowney, Ian, 'Arbitration in Gentry Disputes of the Later Middle Ages', *History,* 67 (1982), 367–76.

Rubin, Gayle, 'The Traffic in Women: Notes on the "Political Economy" of Sex', in Rayna R. Reiter (ed.), *Toward an Anthropology of Women* (New York: Monthly Review, 1975), 157–210.

Runacres, Charles, 'Art and Ethics in the "Exempla" of *Confessio Amantis*', in Minnis (ed.), *Responses and Reassessments* (1983), 106–34.

Russell, M. J., 'Accoutrements of Battle', *Law Quarterly Review,* 99 (1983), 432–42.

—— 'Trial by Battle Procedure in Writs of Right and Criminal Appeals', *Tijdschrift voor Rechtsgeschiedenis,* 51 (1983), 123–34.

St John, Michael, *Chaucer's Dream Visions: Courtliness and Individual Identity* (Aldershot, Hants: Ashgate, 2000).

Salter, Elizabeth, *Fourteenth-Century English Poetry: Contexts and Readings* (Oxford: Clarendon, 1983).

—— and Derek Pearsall, 'Pictorial Illustration of Late Medieval Poetic Texts: The Role of the Frontispiece or Prefatory Picture', in Flemming G. Andersen, Esther Nyholm, Marianne Powell, and Flemming Talbo Stubjær (eds), *Medieval Iconography and Narrative: A Symposium* (Odense: Odense University Press, 1980), 100–23.

Samuels, M. L., and J. J. Smith, 'The Language of Gower', in Smith (ed.), *English of Chaucer* (1988), 13–22; orig. publ. in *Neuphilologische Mitteilungen,* 82 (1981), 295–304.

Sandquist, T. A., 'The Holy Oil of St Thomas of Canterbury', in T. A. Sandquist and M. R. Powicke (eds), *Essays in Medieval History Presented to Bertie Wilkinson* (Toronto: University of Toronto Press, 1969), 330–44.

Saul, Nigel, *Knights and Esquires: The Gloucestershire Gentry in the Fourteenth Century* (Oxford: Clarendon, 1981).

—— 'The Commons and the Abolition of Badges', *Parliamentary History*, 9 (1990), 302–15.

—— 'Conflict and Consensus in English Local Society', in Taylor and Childs (eds), *Politics and Crisis* (1990), 38–58.

—— 'Richard II and the Vocabulary of Kingship', *EHR* 110 (1995), 854–77.

—— *Richard II* (New Haven, Conn.: Yale University Press, 1997).

—— 'Richard II's Ideas of Kingship', in Gordon et al. (eds), *Regal Image* (1997), 27–32.

—— 'The Kingship of Richard II', in Goodman and Gillespie (eds), *Richard II: The Art of Kingship* (1999), 37–57.

Scala, Elizabeth, 'Canacee and the Chaucer Canon: Incest and Other Unnarratables', *Chaucer Review*, 30 (1995–6), 15–39.

Scanlon, Larry, *Narrative, Authority, and Power: The Medieval Exemplum and the Chaucerian Tradition* (Cambridge: Cambridge University Press, 1994).

—— 'The Riddle of Incest: John Gower and the Problem of Medieval Sexuality', in Yeager (ed.), *Re-Visioning Gower* (1998), 93–127.

Scattergood, V. J., 'The Authorship of "The Boke of Cupide"', *Anglia*, 82 (1964), 137–49.

—— 'Literary Culture at the Court of Richard II', in Scattergood and Sherborne (eds), *English Court Culture* (1983), 29–43.

—— and J. W. Sherborne, eds, *English Court Culture in the Later Middle Ages* (London: Duckworth, 1983).

Scheifele, Eleanor, 'Richard II and the Visual Arts', in Goodman and Gillespie (eds), *Richard II: The Art of Kingship* (1999), 255–71.

Schlauch, Margaret, *Chaucer's Constance and Accused Queens* (New York: New York University Press, 1927).

Schmitz, Götz, 'Rhetoric and Fiction: Gower's Comments on Eloquence and Courtly Poetry', in Nicholson (ed.), *Critical Anthology* (1991), 117–42.

Schueler, Donald, 'The Age of the Lover in Gower's *Confessio Amantis*', *Medium Ævum*, 36 (1967), 152–8.

Sedgwick, Eve Kosofsky, *Between Men: English Literature and Male Homosocial Desire* (New York: Columbia University Press, 1985).

Shoaf, R. A., ' "Unwemmed Custance": Circulation, Property, and Incest in the *Man of Law's Tale*', *Exemplaria*, 2 (1990), 287–302.

Simpson, James, *Sciences and the Self in Medieval Poetry: Alan of Lille's Anticlaudianus and John Gower's Confessio Amantis* (Cambridge: Cambridge University Press, 1995).

—— *Reform and Cultural Revolution*, The Oxford English Literary History, 2 (Oxford: Oxford University Press, 2002).

Skinner, Quentin, 'The Principles and Practice of Opposition: The Case of Bolingbroke versus Walpole', in Neil McKendrick (ed.), *Historical Perspec-*

tives: Studies in English Thought and Society in Honour of J. H. Plumb (London: Europa, 1974), 93–128.

Skinner, Quentin, 'Some Problems in the Analysis of Political Thought and Action', in James Tully (ed.), *Meaning and Context: Quentin Skinner and his Critics* (Cambridge: Polity, 1988), 97–118.

Smith, D. Vance, *Arts of Possession: The Middle English Household Imaginary* (Minneapolis: University of Minnesota Press, 2003).

Smith, Jeremy J., 'Linguistic Features of Some Fifteenth-Century Middle English Manuscripts', in Derek Pearsall (ed.), *Manuscripts and Readers in Fifteenth-Century England: The Literary Implications of Manuscript Study* (Cambridge: D. S. Brewer, 1983), 104–12.

—— 'Spelling and Tradition in Fifteenth-Century Copies of Gower's *Confessio Amantis*', in Smith (ed.), *English of Chaucer* (1988), 96–113.

—— ed., *The English of Chaucer and his Contemporaries: Essays by M. L. Samuels and J. J. Smith* (Aberdeen: Aberdeen University Press, 1988).

Spacks, Patricia Meyer, *Gossip* (New York: Knopf, 1985).

Staley, Lynn, 'Gower, Richard II, Henry of Derby, and the Business of Making Culture', *Speculum*, 75 (2000), 68–96.

—— *Languages of Power in the Age of Richard II* (University Park, Pa: Pennsylvania State University Press, 2005).

Staniland, Kay, 'Extravagance or Regal Necessity? The Clothing of Richard II', Gordon et al. (eds), *Regal Image* (1997), 85–114.

Starkey, David, 'The Age of the Household: Politics, Society and the Arts *c*.1350–*c*.1550', in Stephen Medcalf (ed.), *The Context of English Literature: The Later Middle Ages* (London: Methuen, 1981), 225–90.

Steiner, Emily, and Candace Barrington, eds, *The Letter of the Law: Legal Practice and Literary Production in Medieval England* (Ithaca, NY: Cornell University Press, 2002).

Storey, R. L., 'Liveries and Commissions of the Peace 1388–90', in Du Boulay and Barron (eds), *Reign of Richard II* (1971), 131–52.

Stow, George B., 'Richard II in John Gower's *Confessio Amantis*: Some Historical Perspectives', *Mediaevalia*, 16 (1993), 3–31.

Strohm, Paul, 'Form and Social Statement in *Confessio Amantis* and *The Canterbury Tales*', *SAC* 1 (1979): 17–40.

—— 'A Note on Gower's Persona', in Mary J. Carruthers and Elizabeth D. Kirk (eds), *Acts of Interpretation: The Text in its Contexts 700–1600; Essays on Medieval and Renaissance Literature in Honor of E. Talbot Donaldson* (Norman, Okla.: Pilgrim, 1982), 293–8.

—— *Social Chaucer* (Cambridge, Mass.: Harvard University Press, 1989).

—— 'Politics and Poetics: Usk and Chaucer in the 1380s', in Lee Patterson (ed.), *Literary Practice and Social Change in Britain 1380–1530* (Berkeley, Calif.: University of California Press, 1990), 83–112.

—— *Hochon's Arrow: The Social Imagination of Fourteenth-Century Texts* (Princeton: Princeton University Press, 1992).

—— *Theory and the Premodern Text* (Minneapolis: University of Minnesota Press, 2000).

—— ed., *Middle English*, Oxford Twenty-First Century Approaches to Literature (Oxford: Oxford University Press, 2007).

Sutherland, Donald W., 'Legal Reasoning in the Fourteenth Century: The Invention of "Color" in Pleading', in Morris S. Arnold, Thomas A. Green, Sally A. Scully, and Stephen D. White (eds), *On the Laws and Customs of England: Essays in Honor of Samuel E. Thorne* (Chapel Hill, NC: University of North Carolina Press, 1981), 182–94.

Swanson, R. N., 'The Origins of the *Lay Folks' Catechism*', *Medium Ævum*, 60 (1991), 92–100.

Taylor, John, and Wendy Childs, eds, *Politics and Crisis in Fourteenth-Century England* (Gloucester: Alan Sutton, 1990).

Taylor, P. B., 'Chaucer's *Cosyn to the Dede*', *Speculum*, 57 (1982), 315–27.

Thrupp, Sylvia L., *The Merchant Class of Medieval London* (Chicago: University of Chicago Press, 1948).

Tierney, Brian, 'Bracton on Government', *Speculum*, 38 (1963), 295–317.

Tilsley, David, 'Arbitration in Gentry Disputes: The Case of Bucklow Hundred in Cheshire 1400–1465', in Diana E. S. Dunn (ed.), *Courts, Counties, and the Capital in the Later Middle Ages* (Stroud, Glos.: Alan Sutton, 1996), 53–70.

Todd, Henry J., *Illustrations of the Lives and Writings of Gower and Chaucer* (London: Rivington, Payne, Caddell & Davies, Evans, 1810).

Tout, T. F., *Chapters in the Administrative History of Mediaeval England: The Wardrobe, the Chamber and the Small Seals*, 6 vols (Manchester: Manchester University Press, 1920–33).

—— *The Place of the Reign of Edward II in English History*, 2nd edn (Manchester: Manchester University Press, 1936).

Travis, Peter W., 'Chaucer's Trivial Fox Chase and the Peasants' Revolt of 1381', *JMRS* 18 (1988), 195–220.

Tuck, J. A., 'The Cambridge Parliament, 1388', *EHR* 84 (1969), 225–43.

—— *Richard II and the English Nobility* (London: Edward Arnold, 1973).

Turner, Marion, *Chaucerian Conflict: Languages of Antagonism in Late Fourteenth-Century London* (Oxford: Oxford University Press, 2007).

—— 'Conflict', in Strohm (ed.), *Middle English* (2007), 258–73.

Turner, Victor, *The Ritual Process: Structure and Anti-Structure* (London: Routledge, 1969).

—— *Dramas, Fields, and Metaphors: Symbolic Action in Human Society* (Ithaca, NY: Cornell University Press, 1974).

Ullmann, Walter, *The Individual and Society in the Middle Ages* (London: Methuen, 1967).

Vale, Malcolm, *The Princely Court: Medieval Courts and Culture in North-West Europe 1270–1380* (Oxford: Oxford University Press, 2001).

Verduyn, Anthony, 'The Commons and the Early Justices of the Peace under Edward III', in Peter Fleming, Anthony Gross, and J. R. Lander (eds), *Regionalism and Revision: The Crown and its Provinces in England 1200–1650* (London: Hambledon, 1998), 87–106.

Vincent, Nicholas, *The Holy Blood: King Henry III and the Westminster Blood Relic* (Cambridge: Cambridge University Press, 2001).

Walker, Simon, *The Lancastrian Affinity 1361–1399* (Oxford: Clarendon, 1990).

—— 'Letters to the Dukes of Lancaster in 1381 and 1399', *EHR* 106 (1991), 68–79.

—— 'Yorkshire Justices of the Peace 1389–1413', *EHR* 108 (1993), 281–311.

Wallace, David, *Chaucerian Polity: Absolutist Lineages and Associational Forms in England and Italy* (Stanford Calif.: Stanford University Press, 1997).

Waller, J. G., 'The Lords of Cobham, their Monuments, and the Church', *Arch. Cant.* 11 (1877), 49–112.

Watson, Nicholas, 'Censorship and Cultural Change in Late-Medieval England: Vernacular Theology, the Oxford Translation Debate, and Arundel's Constitutions of 1409', *Speculum*, 70 (1995), 822–64.

Watt, Diane, *Amoral Gower: Language, Sex, and Politics* (Minneapolis: University of Minnesota Press, 2003).

Watts, John, *Henry VI and the Politics of Kingship* (Cambridge: Cambridge University Press, 1996).

—— 'Looking for the State in Later Medieval England', in Peter Coss and Maurice Keen (eds), *Heraldry, Pageantry, and Social Display in Medieval England* (Woodbridge, Suff.: Boydell, 2002), 243–67.

—— 'The Pressure of the Public on Later Medieval Politics', in Linda Clark and Christine Carpenter (eds), *Political Culture in Late Medieval Britain*, The Fifteenth Century, 4 (Woodbridge, Suff.: Boydell, 2004), 159–80.

Waugh, Scott L., 'Tenure to Contract: Lordship and Clientage in Thirteenth-Century England', *EHR* 101 (1986), 811–39.

—— *The Lordship of England: Royal Wardships and Marriages in English Society and Politics 1217–1327* (Princeton: Princeton University Press, 1988).

Waugh, W. T., 'The Lollard Knights', *Scottish Historical Review*, 11 (1913–14), 55–92.

Weber, Max, *The Theory of Social and Economic Organization*, ed. and tr. A. M. Henderson and Talcott Parsons (London: William Hodge, 1947).

Webster, Bruce, 'The Community of Kent in the Reign of Richard II', *Arch. Cant.* 100 (1984), 217–29.

Wetherbee, Winthrop, 'The Theme of Imagination in Medieval Poetry and the Allegorical Figure "Genius" ', *Medievalia et Humanistica*, ns 7 (1976), 45–64.

—— 'Constance and the World in Chaucer and Gower', in Yeager (ed.), *Recent Readings* (1989), 65–93.

—— 'Classical and Boethian Tradition in the *Confessio Amantis*', in Echard (ed.), *Companion to Gower* (2004), 181–96.

Wilkins, Eithne, *The Rose-Garden Game: The Symbolic Background to the European Prayer-Beads* (London: Victor Gollancz, 1969).

Williamson, Janet, 'Dispute Settlement in the Manorial Court: Early Four-teenth-Century Lakenheath', *Reading Medieval Studies*, 11 (1985), 133–41.

Winston, Anne, 'Tracing the Origins of the Rosary: German Vernacular Texts', *Speculum*, 68 (1993), 619–36.

Wood-Legh, K. L., 'Sheriffs, Lawyers, and Belted Knights in the Parliaments of Edward III', *EHR* 46 (1931), 372–88.

—— 'The Knights' Attendance in the Parliaments of Edward III', *EHR* 47 (1932), 398–413.

Woolgar, C. M., *The Great Household in Late Medieval England* (New Haven, Conn.: Yale University Press, 1999).

Yeager, R. F., '*Pax Poetica*: On the Pacifism of Chaucer and Gower', *SAC* 9 (1987), 97–121.

—— *John Gower's Poetic: The Search for a New Arion* (Cambridge: D. S. Brewer, 1990).

—— ed., *John Gower: Recent Readings* (Kalamazoo, Mich.: Western Michigan University, 1989).

—— ed., *Re-Visioning Gower* (Asheville, NC: Pegasus, 1998).

Index